Contents   ix

The Theatre of Martin McDonagh

A World of Savage Stories

The Theatre of Martin McDonagh

A World of Savage Stories

Edited by Lilian Chambers and Eamonn Jordan

Carysfort Press Ltd

A Carysfort Press Book

The Theatre of Martin McDonagh: A World of Savage Stories
Edited by Lilian Chambers and Eamonn Jordan

First published in Ireland in 2006 as a paperback original by
Carysfort Press, 58 Woodfield, Scholarstown Road
Dublin 16, Ireland
©2006 Copyright remains with the authors

Typeset by Carysfort Press
Cover design by Alan Bennis

Printed and bound by eprint limited
Unit 35, Coolmine Industrial Estate, Dublin 16, Ireland

This book is published with the financial assistance of
The Arts Council (An Chomhairle Ealaíon), Dublin, Ireland

Table of Contents

Section Two: Critical Frameworks

Acknowledgments

We would like to thank Bernadette Reynolds who worked as editorial assistant on this project. Thanks to Barbara Brown for her expert advice and skilled proofing of the document, and to Sunali Munshi for her work on production research. Thanks to Patrick Lonergan for his invaluable advice and support on this book. Thanks also to Michelle Corcoran and Garry Hynes at Druid Theatre Company for their help. We wish to acknowledge the following journals for permission to republish work: *Irish University Review, Modern Drama, New Theatre Quarterly, Irish Studies Review, Working Papers Irish Studies, Yearbook in English Studies, Contemporary Theatre Review, Hungarian Journal of English and American Studies*. Thanks to *The Guardian, Observer, The Irish Times, New York Times, irish theatre magazine*, and *Variety* for permission to reprint reviews and comments. To Methuen and Faber & Faber for permission to quote from the published texts. Thanks to Martin McDonagh and to the Rod Hall Agency for permission to use the cover photo. Most of all, we would like to thank Dan Farrelly for his unstinting work as General Editor of Carysfort Press.

Introduction: The Critical Debate

Like anything that is novel, different, challenging, irreverent, apparently prejudicial, uncompromising, or difficult to place, the theatre work of Martin McDonagh has come in for very diverse responses. Sometimes the criticism is overwhelming, appreciative and respectful, almost awe. Such respondents regard the work as adventurous, and as a celebratory and dialogical fusion of old and new. For them, there is a conscious reminder and reiteration of forms, characters, language, locations, and realities that are nebulously and indefinably familiar, onto which something strange, uncanny and atypical is superimposed. This feat appears to unsettle the gaze of the spectator and to make easy emotion, sentiment, and analysis somewhat problematic.

For those commentators venting negative views on McDonagh's work, they operate from an almost similar base line, only to find little or nothing novel or exciting in the process. In this vein, the texts are seen as merely the vague and thoughtless recycling of old-fashioned and stale dramatic structures, which are marinated with gore, and spliced with a notional pop/postmodern sensibility. Further, the plays are brought down by caricature and unjust stereotypes, infiltrated by depthlessness, and numbly polluted by endlessly rehashing threadbare sensibilities and situational dynamics. These less than positive responses range from mild resistance to blatant, unsubtle and savage criticism of McDonagh's work. However, it is above all else the violence, brutality and mayhem in the plays which prove to be most controversial and divisive. Perversely perhaps, many of McDonagh's characters that carry out acts of murder remain at large and are not held accountable for their crimes.

In a sense, Garry Hynes, the Artistic Director of Druid Theatre in Galway, 'discovered' McDonagh. And it was *The Beauty Queen of Leenane* which kick-started his career in 1996. He had then a series of successes with *The Cripple of Inishmaan* (1997), *The Lonesome West* (1997), and *A Skull in Connemara* (1997). At one point in that year he had four plays running in London, a major achievement for a relatively new playwright. Apart from *The Pillowman* (2003) the West of Ireland is the locale for all of the work performed to date: Leenane for *The Beauty Queen of Leenane, The Lonesome West* and *A Skull in Connemara* and the Aran Islands, Inishmaan and Inishmore for *The Cripple of Inishmaan* (1997) and *The Lieutenant of Inishmore* (2001) respectively. The Oscar-winning live action short film *Six Shooter* (2005) is set in Ireland, but has no named locale. ┼ ⱶ Bⱦ

Partly because the early plays were set in Ireland, and produced(₂₀₀₃) mainly with Irish actors, designed with distinctly Irish stage environments in mind, and conceived of through the mobile lens of Irishness, whatever that happens to mean, McDonagh is cate- gorized by many as an Irish playwright. (See the Methuen website for instance.) However, he was born in London on 26 March 1970 and was reared initially in Elephant and Castle, amongst a sig- nificant Irish immigrant community, and later in Camberwell. His parents were from Ireland originally, his father from Lettermullan, in county Galway and his mother hailed from Killeenduff, Easkey, in county Sligo. During his childhood, McDonagh regularly took holidays in Connemara and in Sligo. Having left school early, McDonagh started to write short stories, radio plays and to take up pretty menial jobs, having spent some time on the dole. He had a series of rejections,[1] apart from two radio plays broadcast by an Australian radio station, and he turned to theatre almost as a last resort, or so the mythology goes.[2]

Many other critics have highlighted McDonagh's obvious Anglo-Irish heritage, and many have been quick to point towards other figures caught in a similar sensibility, those constituting second generation Irish, who were reared, educated, and socialized in Britain, but also exist with strong, complex, and ambivalent connections with Ireland. Within the specifics of that Irish community operating within a London environment, McDonagh absorbed and rehearsed notions and conventions of Irishness and much more besides. (The Northern Irish troubles and the bombing campaigns by paramilitaries in the United Kingdom often led to hostile and stereotypical responses to the Irish communities.) When asked by Sean O'Hagan as to how he responds to 'the inevitable accusations of cultural stereotyping', McDonagh responded by saying, 'I don't even enter into it. I mean, I don't feel I have to defend myself for being English or for being Irish, because, in a way, I don't feel either. And, in another way, of course, I'm both'.[3]

Critics, productions and audiences can get hung up in particular on the perceived nationality of McDonagh, and by so doing make great and inopportune claims as to the convoluted motivations and inflated intentionalities of the writer – in an era when authorial intentionality has lost a great deal of currency. There is of course another tendency, namely, to filter the violence in the plays through the notion of McDonagh's perceived Irishness, in a way that aligns, discretely or otherwise, Irishness and violence in most unproblematic and unchallenging ways.

All writing has conscious and unconscious motivations, stimuli, biases, suppositions, imperatives, and precedents. To discuss and demarcate influences usually means that critics can establish connections and find it easier to place work and to elaborate on its potential meanings. Concepts of McDonagh as imitator, copyist, intertextualist and parodist, are frequently raised. The playwright clearly writes within and against traditions, like any other writer. Many see the Irish tradition as the one within which he primarily operates. As examples, in this collection of essays McDonagh is considered in relation to Lady Augusta Gregory, John Millington Synge, Sean O'Casey, Samuel Beckett, Conor McPherson, and Marina Carr. Others also see McDonagh in relation to the British theatre movement and playwrights such as Joe Orton, Harold Pinter, Sarah Kane, and Mark Ravenhill are mentioned. Others link the work to a whole range of cultural forms from the writings of Vladimir Nabokov and Jorge Luis Borges to American detective shows such as *Tom and Jerry* cartoons, *I Love Lucy* and *Beavis and Butt-head* to *Steptoe and Son*, *Father Ted*, and Australian soap operas,

Brookside, slasher/horror movies and puppet theatre. Many point out the specific influences of cinema and film makers, like Martin Scorsese, David Lynch, Sam Peckinpah, Terence Malick, John Woo, and Quentin Tarantino. The Pogues, the Clash, the Sex Pistols, and Nirvana are bands mentioned as having inspired the playwright. Clearly, McDonagh appears to have a great deal of influences, some of which he absorbed by reading and viewing, and some by osmosis. A contemporary susceptibility is allowed to run amuck amongst traditional forms, values, and sensibilities.

Over the past few years McDonagh has refused almost all requests for public interviews, and previous comments that he has made about either the Irish tradition or his own exposure to theatre writing generally can be taken almost with a grain of salt. Too much trust has been placed in his statements, and too much opportunistic exploitation has ensued. Reliable or not, his own general comments, on what plays he had read/seen before he began to write, and on who are his influences, seem to feed a certain distrust of his motives. We can add to this his general unwillingness to mouth platitudes about those playwrights who have gone before him, which does not seem to be abiding by the usual rules of the game; instead he calls them ugly and second rate. Most upcoming playwrights pay due deference to their traditions at least in public; McDonagh's reported disrespect seems more to be schooled by the Gallagher brothers, Liam and Noel, of *Oasis* fame, who gained significant PR thanks to their notorious antics and vocalised disrespect. By generating sensation, infamy, and good copy, McDonagh feeds the celebrity mill. His reported altercation with the actor, Sean Connery, at the *Evening Standard Awards* gained certain notoriety in the tabloid press. At times, one gets the feeling that all McDonagh needs to do is to appear on some reality television show – *I'm A Celebrity Get me Out of Here!* or *Celebrity Love Island* – for many of the biases about him to be absolutely confirmed in some peoples' minds.

It is merely ten years since McDonagh's first success as a writer, but it seems that he has written very little for the theatre since 1994, the year he accredits to the writing/drafting of all of his plays.[4] And while it is obvious that McDonagh is no short-term wonder, the true measurement of the body of work is its ability to be revised and reconsidered through performance and interpretations over time. Yet, it would be an error to postpone evaluation or contextualization on the basis of such a short period of time. Fundamentally, we need to see clear distinctions between the author and the work that emerges through the testing ground of production and reception, while at the same time not eliminating the writer from the writing process and as the initial facilitator of the text. At that stage, how much conscious control a writer has over creativity and meaning is debatable. What happens between the writer's draft presented to a company for consideration, the process of rehearsal and production and the script that eventually emerges after the initial production, is anybody's guess. What ends up as the published text can have a complicated relationship to the production that is presented on opening night.

In this volume we have not only gathered some of the best criticism already published on McDonagh, but we have also sought new work from a variety of individuals, which engages with some, but not all of the previously published analysis. Far too often, volumes of critical analysis all sing more or less off the same hymn sheet. Unlike the writings on much of contemporary theatre practices, these writers seem to be full-bodied and full-blooded in their approaches, less wary and less circumspect than is the norm. Still, despite the open intent, as in theatrical dialogue, what is said often masks the unsaid, thus subtextual readings and systematic consideration of structures of belief and ideology of both plays and criticism is well founded. Hopefully the insistent dialogue between these articles opens up the debate, and gives consideration to multiple, often conflicting, and self-contradictory points of view. As theatre performances require cultural, dramaturgical, translation, production, and audience reception contexts, both the theatre and the academic critic offer not only evaluative frameworks and contextualizations, but they also function as gatekeepers. Yet in the strident efforts to praise and claim, damn and rebuff, there is the persistent drive for myth-making that has long haunted theatre practices. And it is not only writers who are out to mould their own myths.

For the collection, we have also decided to re-publish a series of reviews of plays in performance and articles that deal with the productions and reception of McDonagh's work in Hungary, Australia, Flanders/Holland, and Turkey. They are not offered as some complete overview, but to provide some snapshot or insight into how the plays are considered, produced and received internationally. It is vital to see not only the potential of scripts to operate in different contexts, but also to be produced in a variety of different ways, especially those that jeopardize the staging and sensibilities of the original productions.

Playwrights cannot control meaning and cannot control production choices, apart from agents granting licenses to perform. Fundamentally, despite intentionalities, the reception of the work is always up for grabs globally. It is important to recognize the impact of globalization itself and the piggybacking that McDonagh's plays seem to do on the back of this phenomenon. Many productions of McDonagh's work will invariably misconstrue things, make unwarranted assumptions, and will project values, aspirations and identities that may not be apposite reflections of space, language, character and action. Yet, the sense of getting it 'wrong' is problematic in its own right. Every act of translation is one of mistranslation, and every production is a supplement and unfaithful in many ways to the published text. Yet, in finding a new context, scripts can be liberated from other types of constraints. So the vaunted Irish dimension is far more complex in reality. Yet it is necessary to be reminded constantly that McDonagh's plays are performed and regarded internationally, not just as representative of the Irish tradition, but as indicative of new British or European trends. Funding of the arts and commerical and subsidised realities are the ultimate contexts through which we must view the work.

It is necessary to ask what makes the West of Ireland the draw for a young man raised in London. McDonagh is on record with numerous comments on this fact. *Lieutenant* has an Aran island location, according to him, simply because it is far enough from Belfast to delay the return of Padraic. He states that he also wrote about the West of Ireland simply because he wanted to get away from the influence of writers like Harold Pinter, David Mamet, and Joe Orton. This fleeing has obvious cultural, social, and political ramifications, as does the notion of creative liberation, sanctuary, and pastoral regeneration in Ireland's western seaboard.

On first viewing/reading, the characters in the plays speak in what could be regarded as a hybrid Hiberno-English. Many critics in this volume investigate McDonagh's use of language from many different perspectives. As with language, critics are divided on the characterizations that McDonagh presents across the body of the work. The characters are regularly regarded as caricatures, puppet-like, adult children without depth. McDonagh is frequently accused of pandering to old colonial stereotypes of Irishness. Often there is a casual homophobia and naturalized racism in what the characters express. Most of it is grounded in fear and not in the experience of contact between those of different sexual orientations, genders, or races. McDonagh's characters are not rampantly sexual, but operate from a celibate reality or a childlike dysfunctional take on sexual relationships. The world of McDonagh's dramas is almost always where intimacy and empathy are in abeyance. Relative poverty is a significant marker.

As with most contemporary plays, questions about gender and agency are raised. McDonagh's plays are open to that scrutiny. Across genders, agency is a complex notion. Obviously, one can test the dramatic action of play to see if the women characters have access to similar types of behaviour, thoughts, and feelings as those of their male counterparts, or if not, analogous access to a wide array of simple, complex, and comparable emotions, whether there are isolations, immobility, exclusions, or the absence of restraints on agency. Clearly, there are gender expectations in the work of McDonagh. The actions of the characters seem to be motivated without real depth, desire or longing. That way, it is the incidental which paves the way for the catastrophic. In the main, they are characters that are invoking the games of children into their adult lives; murder is just child's play, the violence of the fairy tale or nursery rhyme given licence in the world of the characters. What complicates characterization is that there is irreverence, simultaneity, and ambivalence as to motive. The plays are a motive monger's nightmare.

Destructiveness proves to be the most difficult thing to place or countenance. Violence, which can be appalling at times, is shared across all gender characterizations and is the social bind, not bonding, not family blood lines. People get uneasy with such a representation, especially if there is no moral structure acutely activated to counterbalance such destructiveness. Whatever moral voice is harnessed in the plays, it often appears to be as perverse as it is absurd. Violence is that which must not be condoned but also which challenges perceptions of authenticity. In relation to *Lieutenant*, McDonagh believes that the violence has a purpose:

> Having grown up Catholic and, to a certain degree, Republican, I thought I should tackle the problems on my own side, so to speak. I chose the INLA because they seemed so extreme and, to be honest, because I thought I'd be less at risk. I'm not being heroic or anything – it was just something I felt I had to write about. The play came from a position of what you might call pacifist rage. I mean, it's a violent play that is wholeheartedly anti-violence. The bottom line, I suppose, is that I believe that if a piece of work is well written, you can tackle anything.[5]

When McDonagh does deal with political violence he is accused of air-brushing the depth of political complexity in favour of sensationalism. Anthony Roche, having seen *Lieutenant* in London, left the theatre thinking that the play would never get an Irish production.[6] It can be argued that McDonagh uses Gothic or carnivalesque frames to destabilize violence. In other words, by re-contextualizing, different types of questions and responses can be available to an audience. Many critics in this volume point out that justice has no place in the work – eased out or never there to begin with. When asked about identity McDonagh had the following to say:

> Well, we're all cruel, aren't we? We're all extreme in one way or another at times, and that's what drama, since the Greeks, has dealt with. I hope the overall view isn't just that, though, or I've failed in my writing. There have to be moments when you glimpse some-thing decent, something life-affirming even in the most twisted character. That's where the real art lies. See, I always suspect characters who are painted as lovely, decent human beings. I would always question where the darkness lies.[7]

The West of Ireland offers the potentialities of pastoral, exilic consciousness, and the exhilaration sanctuary, redemptive senti-ment and nostalgia for bonds, rurality and orality.[8] However,

McDonagh generates a reality that cannot be bound up with old pastoral images of the West of Ireland.[9] The frugality, simplicity, community, and scale of pastoral are there, but something else is also accommodated; community morphs into perverse dis-connection, sympathy twists into rivalry and petty vindictiveness, and sharing transforms into crude individuality and ownership. The traditional Irish kitchen, instead of smelling of bacon and sausages, smells of urine in *Beauty Queen.*.

Into that western world McDonagh grounds the work notion-ally with allusions to real incidents, atrocities, people and football championships. References abound to Complan, Kimberley bis-cuits, Swingball, Tayto Crisps, women's magazines – *Take a Break* and *Bella*, for instance, which sounds almost ironically like product placement. Despite surrounding the environment with real locations and the props of authenticity, there are temporal and factual anomalies that may perhaps be intentional or casual carelessness. Fintan O'Toole argues that:

> As descriptions of sociological reality, these [the plays] are, of course, dramatic exaggerations. But they are not pure inventions. McDonagh makes sure that the action is continually brushing up against verifiable actuality.[10]

O'Toole pushes very hard for a connection between the world on stage and the real; however, all of the plays put that relationship under considerable strain. The idea of realism seems to come under enormous pressure, especially when the relationship between cause and effect breaks down, when time is elastic, or where props, symbols, characters, myths and metaphors are be manipulated, amplified or foregrounded through staging or dramatic structure. By implication, McDonagh is accused, knowingly or otherwise, of disfiguring the notion of a mimetic reality within which these texts socio-politically and superficially operate. For many, the reality must be served in a particular way, carrying obligations and responsibilities. To do otherwise, is somehow to distort, falsify, perjure, and to deny truth. To that consciousness, the capturing of power dynamics, gender im-balances, implausibility, and social injustices matter a great deal. The tensions then are between sociology and fiction, fabrication and verisimilitude, between complexity and slighted representations. It is often within these sensitivities and sensibilities that the texts are adjudicated. Whether we conceive of the play as 'real' or not has huge implications as to how we respond to the play itself. Garry Hynes argues:

> There's this issue about Martin and authenticity – the response that his is not Irish life now and it's not Connemara life. Of course it isn't. It's an artifice. It's not authentic. It's not meant to be. It's a complete creation, and in that sense it's fascinating.[11]

Inauthenticity can be seen as the fault line or fatal flaw, but it may also be its opposite, the great strength of the work. It creates an alienated reality, but not true alienation in the Brechtian sense, because, unlike Bertolt Brecht, McDonagh does not necessarily want his audiences to get back to the real. In this way, there is a fundamental dissociation from the real. Ultimately, the median between utopia and dystopia is not simply fecktopia.

With much of post-colonial theory there is an anxiety around national self-criticism, disparaging imaginings, and anything that remotely looks like the perpetuation of degrading stereotypes. There is a need to contend with both positive and negative imaginings and with a more expansive meaning of Irishness to include the indigenous Irish, the diasporic, second and third generation Irish, and non-Irish nationals. There is also the notion of an international, globalized Irishness being fostered, some of which is creative, dynamic, confident and assured, but much of it is just commodification. Defining a writer by nationality is just as problematic as establishing a single reality, sensibility, frame or tradition for the work.

It is a challenge but not impossible to explain how the same work can be read as mercenary, simplistically conservative, spitefully reactionary, and regurgative by some and as artifice, comedic, challenging, positively controversial, innately intelligent, and radically postmodern by others. Far too much of this debate rests on the writer and the plays and little is said of companies who produce the work, or the directors, actors, and designers who shape the performance text or on the openness of texts to be interpreted and construed in different ways.

McDonagh is the man from nowhere,[12] elsewhere, anywhere and everywhere, displaced without the longing for a place or a position either within a single nationality or canon. Ultimately the plays are constituted as much by what they lack, truncate, or exaggerate, as by what they present, represent or by what they are made to mean. It is necessary to understand and to negotiate the permissive and prejudicial frames through which audiences and critics respond to the work. His work bears all the hallmarks of internationalization, multiple influences, dialectical sensibilities, and incongruities. As such, McDonagh's work is much more than a debate about originality, justice, violence, authenticity, and representation.

If, as Katurian passionately believes, in *The Pillowman*, 'The only duty of a storyteller is to tell a story', then Martin McDonagh has told us a variety of 'savage stories' which have a life of their own.

---

[1] It has been claimed that the BBC rejected twenty-two or twenty-four depending on the source of his radio plays. His radio play *The Tale of Wolf and the Woodcutter* was chosen as one of the five winners of the London Radio Playwrights' Festival during late 1994/early 1995.

[2] He wrote '200 short stories that he planned to incorporate in a feature film called *57 Tales of Sex and Violence* .... only one was actually about sex: 'Anarcho-Feminists' Sex Machines in Outer Space', the remainder about violence. Cited in 'The 'greatest playwright looks forward to Oscar night', (no journalist acknowledged) *Sunday Times* 5 Feburary 2006, p.19.

[3] Quoted in Sean O'Hagan, 'The Wild West', *The Guardian* 24 March 2001, p.32.

[4] Fintan O'Toole, 'A Mind in Connemara: The Savage World of Martin McDonagh', *New Yorker* 6 March 2006, p.44. In this article McDonagh claims that he has only one piece of work *The Banshees of Inisheer* that remains unperformed, but the Rod Hall Agency listed a number of other plays on their website, until very recently, namely, *The Retard is Out in the Cold* and *Dead Day at Coney*, while some previous articles on McDonagh mention a play titled *The Maamturk Rifleman*. See http://www.rodhallagency.com/index.php?art_id=000075

[5] Quoted. in Sean O'Hagan, p.32. His account of the same creative impulse is rather different in the O'Toole *New Yorker* piece, where McDonagh claims, 'I was trying to write a play that would get me killed. I had no real fear that I would be, because paramilitaries never bothered with playwrights anyway, but if they were going to start I wanted to write something that would put me top of the list'. Ibid., p.45.

[6] Anthony Roche, 'The "Irish" Play on the London Stage: 1990-2004' in *Players and the Painted Stage, Aspects of Twentieth-Century Drama in Ireland,* ed. Christopher Fitz-Simon (Dublin: New Island, 2004), pp.128-142.

[7] Quoted in Sean O'Hagan, p.32.

[8] See Terry Gifford, *Pastoral* (London: Routledge, 1999).

[9] Nicholas Grene has coined the phrase 'Black Pastoral'. See 'Black Pastoral: 1990s Images of Ireland.' *Litteraria Pragensia* 20.10. 23 October 2004. <http://komparatistika.ff.cuni.cz/litteraria/no20-10/grene.htm>

[10] Fintan O'Toole, 'Introduction' to *Plays: 1* (London, Methuen, 1999), p.xv.

[11] Garry Hynes in an interview with Cathy Leeney, *Theatre Talk: Voices of Irish Theatre Practitioners*, eds Lilian Chambers et al. (Dublin: Carysfort Press, 2001), p.204.

[12] Fintan O'Toole, 'Nowhere Man' *The Irish Times* 26 April 1997.

1 | The Early Plays: Shooting Star and Hard Man from South London[1]

Werner Huber

In the late 1990s Martin McDonagh was heralded as the shooting star of the contemporary theatre scene on the strength of four published plays alone.[2] Any amount of praise has been heaped on McDonagh ever since he made his stage debut with *The Beauty Queen of Leenane* in Galway on 1 February 1996. Within a year McDonagh won a number of prestigious prizes – among them the George Devine Award for Most Promising Playwright, the Evening Standard Award for Most Promising Newcomer, and the Writers' Guild Award for Best Fringe Play. This is only a small indication of what theatre critics in London (and Dublin, for that matter) perceived in McDonagh's work: a new voice, a new quality in Irish drama, which could be described as action-centred, grotesque, manipulative, postmodern even, as regards its ironic potential for deconstruction. The comparison has frequently been made that McDonagh is doing to contemporary playwriting what The Pogues did to traditional Irish music in the 1980s.

Without a doubt, part of McDonagh's success can be attributed to the lucky circumstance that from the start productions of his plays have been associated with the most distinguished names and institutions of the contemporary theatre scene in the British Isles. The Galway production of *The Beauty Queen of Leenane,* a co-production by the Druid Theatre Company and the Royal Court Theatre, was directed by former Abbey director Garry Hynes and immediately transferred from Galway's Druid Theatre to London's Royal Court Upstairs. McDonagh's association with the Royal National Theatre, London, as a writer-in-residence during the 1996/97 season resulted in his second play, *The Cripple of Inishmaan*, being produced at the National Theatre under no less a director than Nicholas Hytner (the play opened on 7 January 1997). In the summer of 1997 two further plays, *A Skull in Connemara* and *The Lonesome West,* were produced under the continuing aegis of the Druid Theatre/Royal Court co-operation. Together with *The Beauty Queen of Leenane* these plays form the Leenane Trilogy, and in a unique move all three plays were offered as combined matinee and evening performances opening in Galway (Town Hall Theatre) and London (Royal Court Downstairs) on June 21 and July 26, respectively, before transferring to the Dublin Theatre Festival in October of 1997. In June 1998, Garry Hynes's production of *The Beauty Queen of Leenane* won no less than four Tony Awards, including one for Best Director. Apart from enjoying sensationally successful runs on New York's Broadway, McDonagh's plays have been and are being produced in places as far afield as Australia, Austria, the Czech Republic, Finland, France, Germany, Italy, Poland, Sweden, and Switzerland.

McDonagh's experience of Ireland is very much a limited and mediated one. Born in 1970 in South London his father and mother (from Connemara and Sligo respectively) left him and his elder brother John, a novelist and screen-writer, to fend for themselves, when they returned to Ireland. In a series of interviews and public appearances – in 1996 he appeared drunk at the Evening Standard Award ceremony and insulted Sean Connery as a 'one good film' man – McDonagh fashioned for himself the image of a loud mouth, genius, and punk artist.[3] If we take his word for it, then McDonagh would have left school at the age of 16 and spent the next ten years as a recluse living on dole money and odd jobs, watching films and TV soaps, and doing his own writing in between. Over the years McDonagh graduated from the writing of film scripts, short stories, and radio plays to the writing of plays which he perceives as the easiest art form of all: '[...] Just get the dialect, a bit of a story and a couple of nice characters, and you're away'.[4] In much the same way as McDonagh came to the writing of plays as a way of avoiding permanent failure and rejection his experience of Ireland, of his Irish ancestry, is anything but systematic or methodical. His contacts with, and impressions of, Irish culture were largely shaped during his visits with relatives on the west coast of Ireland or through the pervasive influence of London Irish neighbourhoods. As will become clear below, his image of Ireland is a highly anti-traditional one, an outsider's view characterized by satire, black humour, cartoon-like reductions, and grotesque and 'Gothic' distortions.

Just as his choice of genre has something of the accidental about it, so does McDonagh explain his choice of dramatic language and (by implication) subject as a way of avoiding anxiety of influence. McDonagh, who apparently speaks with a strong South London accent himself, has always been fascinated by the speech of his Irish relatives (especially in cases where English is not their native language). He perceives their idiosyncratic linguistic patterns as a 'stylized way of talking', which he appreciated for its inherent potential for originality and dramatic effect: 'And that seemed an interesting way to go, to try, to do something with that language that wouldn't be English or American.'[5] In more concrete terms, this signifies a way of avoiding the influence of Harold Pinter and David Mamet, respectively.[6] That McDonagh's dramatic language, a hybrid of contemporary street-talk and rural Irish speech, is also a distancing device which opens up an enormous incongruity between the world of his plays and traditional images of Ireland is another matter.

Martin McDonagh has variously been described as a cross between Joe Orton, Brendan Behan, Orson Welles, and Muhammad Ali or as the Paul Gascoigne of contemporary theatre. This image of the *enfant terrible* should make us wary of any statements he chooses to make concerning his literary models and his personal poetics in general. McDonagh is reported to have boasted that he had never seen more than twenty plays in his life. He also claimed at one time that he had no previous knowledge of the Irish literary tradition.[7] His preferences clearly lie elsewhere:

> I'm coming to the theatre with a disrespect for it. I'm coming from a film fan's perspective on theatre. [...] Theatre bored the socks off me. I only ever went to see film stars, Martin Sheen or Tim Roth.

The best was probably David Mamet's *American Buffalo* with Al
Pacino.[8]

On the positive side, McDonagh acknowledges the influence of
such writers as Jorge Luis Borges (on his prose), Harold Pinter,
David Mamet, and filmmakers Martin Scorsese and Terence
Malick. As regards films, the following receive significant
mentions: the *Star Wars* Trilogy, *Taxi Driver*, *Night of the Hunter*,
Reservoir Dogs.

In general, McDonagh's plays seem to confirm the influence of
a line of tradition which, to use McDonagh's own words apropos
of Tracy Letts's play *Killer Joe,* is characterized by a combination of
'its blackness, the Jacobean themes, the wit'.[9]

McDonagh's Dramatic Art

It may well be worth our while to isolate a number of themes and
motifs as well as aesthetic and dramatic structures that can be seen
as contributing to the unique character of the corpus of
McDonagh's four early plays. In structural(ist) terms the common
denominator to be derived from these features might be described
analytically in terms of polarized structures, positions, and movements, e.g., centrifugal vs. centripetal, diastole vs. systole, exile vs.
home, or synthetically as unresolved juxtapositions, clashes, jarring
sounds and emotions, dramatic twists of fate, and the overturning
of expectations.

'I have lived in important places' (Patrick Kavanagh)

The fact that the plays in McDonagh's Trilogy are all set in the
township of Leenane (in the 1990s) has several advantages. Not
only does it provide a great degree of thematic coherence in the
sense that a microcosm is created by the life-stories of three
different families living in contact, however tenuous, with each
other. It is also a felicitous dramatic device facilitating exposition
and the introduction of characters. By the end of *The Beauty Queen
of Leenane* almost all the *dramatis personae* of the Trilogy have been
mentioned or prefigured in some story-context or other, and in
each play there are allusions and cross-references to characters
which figure only in one or the other of the two remaining plays.
Thus, the confusion over the pronunciation of the priest's name

(Walsh/Welsh) is a running gag which already by itself makes for some kind of coherence in this circumscribed microcosm. Likewise, short but effective reminders of past and imminent events such as Mag Folan's funeral (*SC* 11),[10] Tom Hanlon's suicide (*LIW* 19), Pato Dooley's wedding (*SC* 53) establish a chronological order by building on an irreversible sequence of events.

As a quasi sociological picture Leenane is portrayed as a tight-knit community with a 'common human pattern' that is greatly exaggerated and outright bizarre. As Pato says, 'You can't kick a cow in Leenane without some bastard holding a grudge twenty year' (*BQ* 22). This comes from the same Pato who experiences the other extreme, abstract society and the anonymity of urban life, as he describes it to Maureen in his letter from London: 'I do go out for a pint of a Saturday or a Friday but I don't know nobody and don't speak to anyone. There is no one to speak to' (*BQ* 34). In the typical McDonagh locale, everything is put into a 'parochial' perspective. Thus, in *The Cripple of Inishmaan*, set in 1934, Johnny-pateenmike juxtaposes the latest local scandal of a cat bitten by a goose and news of sheep deformities with news of 'a fella here, riz to power in Germany, has an awful funny moustache on him' (*CI* 35-6). This device of relating local events to world history is in direct imitation of Patrick Kavanagh, whose portrayal of rural Ireland equally evokes a world of petty-mindedness, greed, raw emotions, and self-importance. Compare these lines from Kavanagh's poem 'Epic':

> I have lived in important places, times
> When great events were decided, who owned
> That half a rood of rock, a no-man's land
> Surrounded by our pitchfork-armed claims.
> I heard the Duffy's shouting 'Damn your soul'
> And old McCabe stripped to the waist, seen
> Step the plot defying blue cast-steel –
> 'Here is the march along these iron stones'
> That was the year of the Munich bother. Which
> Was more important? [...] [11]

Such concentration on the life of the parish as a microcosm is counteracted by a centrifugal tendency which is made obvious not only by the subject of exile, as experienced or desired by many of McDonagh's characters, but also by simple markers in the plays whether these be passing references to international soccer events or to icons of popular culture. It is largely through the media (television in the Trilogy, Hollywood as a complex metaphor in *The Cripple of Inishmaan*) that McDonagh's characters keep a window open onto the wider world. Detective series and Australian soaps are the moral points of reference in the world of the Trilogy and begin to take the place of traditional systems of popular or religious mythology. Thus, we have a clear dichotomy between the extreme inward-looking tendencies of the communities portrayed and their participation in a media-dominated global culture. This tension remains unresolved, and as a structure it is mirrored on the level of the characters' psychological set-up.

Nec tecum, nec sine te

In all of McDonagh's plays we find that the main characters are tied to their partners in complicated relationships. They may strive to break away from this situation, but they eventually come to realize that they are highly dependent on their opposite numbers, that they cannot live without the other – even if the other has been reduced to symbolic representations. Most obviously, Coleman and Valene in *The Lonesome West* need each other as sparring partners in their aggressive 'games' of treachery and abuse. Maureen and Mag depend on each other superficially for reasons of household economy and habit; beyond that, they are paradoxically united in their hatred of each other. Yet even after killing her mother all that is left for Maureen to do is to sit in her mother's rocking-chair and ask Ray to pass on to Pato the message of 'The beauty queen says "goodbye"' (*BQ* 59); Maureen has become, in Ray's words, 'the exact fecking image of your mother' (*BQ* 60).[12]

Billy's attitude towards his aunts and the island community of Inishmaan as a whole is equally ambivalent, as his double movement of exile and return makes clear. We find this relationship pattern extending to the most macabre of situations. Even if we assume that he intentionally killed his wife, Mick, 'the wife-butcherer' (*SC* 36), is deeply upset by the desecration of her grave; his fondling of her skull[13] is a symbolic act of reunion and reconciliation with jarring undertones. On a historical note, the motto of *nec tecum, nec sine te* (Juvenal) could be cited as a summary description of mutual interdependence linking McDonagh's characters to Beckett's prototypical pairings of Pozzo-Lucky, Didi-Gogo, and Hamm-Clov.[14]

'Ireland can't be such a bad place ...'

The world of McDonagh's plays has summarily been described as 'a colourful surreal Wild West of Ireland, populated by outlaw hill-billies doomed to family murder or desolate suicide. Yet all pitched at a perception-altering satiric level'.[15] It is probably on account of the excessive vulgarity of action and language as well as the moral chaos apparent in the McDonagh universe that the image of Ireland conveyed in his plays is pushed to the limits of veri-similitude and credibility. The plays certainly satirize cliché-ridden representations of Ireland and the Irish, and project an image of the hard life in Ireland that runs counter to a pastoral view of the Emerald Isle as entertained by outsiders, e.g., tourists. The theme of exile is raised again and again, especially in *The Beauty Queen of Leenane*, where Maureen makes mention of what might be dubbed her double exile: to have been hospitalized in a mental asylum in England (*BQ* 31). Maureen's epigrammatic definition of Irishness, 'That's Ireland, anyways. There is always someone leaving' (*BQ* 21), is then ironically counteracted in *The Cripple of Inishmaan*, when the characters keep assuring themselves by the modified catch-phrases of 'Ireland can't be such a bad place if French/German/cripple fellas/Yanks want to come to it' (*CI* 14).

This ironic undercutting of pathetic images and stereotypes imposed from the outside is most effectively and, as it were, meta-cinematically presented in Scene Eight of *The Cripple of Inishmaan*, during the public and, one might add, strangely self-reflexive screening of Flaherty's *Man of Aran* to an island audience in a makeshift cinema. Not only does the film ('some oul shite about thick fellas fecking fishing' (*CI* 51)) fail to impress the islanders, let alone hold their attention, but it also provokes violent reactions from people like Helen, who keeps throwing eggs at the screen: 'What's to fecking see anyways but more wet fellas with awful jumpers on them' (*CI* 60).

The 'demythologization of the West'[16] as conducted in McDonagh's plays reaches a point where it becomes facile and gratuitous, especially so as a moral centre or standard of reference for McDonagh's satire does not become apparent. If one were to take Billy's patently obvious words ('well, there are plenty round here just as crippled as me, only it isn't on the outside it shows' (*CI* 66)) to cover most, if not all of McDonagh's characters, then one would have to concede that McDonagh is engaging in a Joycean diagnosis of paralysis. (Maureen Folan and Eveline from *Dubliners* would make an interesting comparison in this context.) However, as in the case of Synge and his portrayal of Mayo peasants in *The Playboy of the Western World*, there is greater ambivalence and controversy involved as regards the terms of reference (subject, theme) and audience reactions. The plays seem to suggest throughout that McDonagh is aiming beyond the writing of a 'chapter of the moral history' of Ireland. This extra dimension has then to be discovered in some of his characteristic dramatic techniques.

'The Quentin Tarantino of the Emerald Isle'

The general mode of McDonagh's plays might perhaps best be described as 'grotesque'. The grotesque has been defined as 'the unresolved clash of incompatibles in work and response'[17] and, from what we have seen, would thus serve as a supreme principle for the categorization of McDonagh's drama.

McDonagh's 'black humour' works on exactly such a principle which juxtaposes elements of zaniness and paddywhackery with elements of horror and the macabre. The latter elements point to the bewildering aspect of the excesses of physical violence in McDonagh's plays – not only reported violence (especially cruelty to animals), but more directly violence as it is openly acted out on stage bringing injury and death to other characters. Following Mikhail Bakhtin such an emphasis on the body and bodily realism would also link this aspect of violence back to definitions of the grotesque.[18]

Critics of McDonagh's plays have named the godfathers of this line of affinities: Synge, O'Casey, Martin Scorsese, and Quentin Tarantino,[19] or – perhaps even closer still to McDonagh's idiosyncratic media preferences – 'the endlessly unravelling murder mysteries of *Twin Peaks*, tinged with the relentless serial iconoclasm of *Father Ted*'.[20]

'Conversing me arse. Do you have something to say to me?' (*SC* 34)

The qualities of the grotesque and the surreal also inform the language of McDonagh's plays, which one critic described as 'a hybrid of the Irish-English that Synge invented for his own Aran Island characters, and a street-wise Dublin-London 1990s argot'.[21] Bringing Synge up to date and also overcoming 'Synge-song' in that sense means that one is struck first of all by the accumulation of swear words and the generally restricted code of McDonagh's characters. Without a doubt, 'feck' and its derivatives would rank highest in a word count. (All this, of course, is in line with the characters' deliberate and playful offences against political correctness of any kind.)

What McDonagh shares with Synge, however, is an insight into the defamiliarization effect of English as spoken in Ireland. As McDonagh clearly recognizes, 'in Connemara and Galway, the natural dialogue style is to invert sentences and use strange inflections. Of course, my stuff is a heightening of that, but there is a core of strangeness of speech, especially in Galway'.[22] While Synge appreciated the fierce poetic temperament of the inhabitants of the Western World and dedicated himself to its artistic recreation in the language of his characters, Joyce's Stephen Dedalus in the 'funnel/tundish' episode of *A Portrait of the Artist as a Young Man* experienced 'strangeness of speech' quite explicitly as a (post-) colonial trauma.

As mentioned above, the stylization of Irish English has been of crucial importance to McDonagh in his efforts to find his own dramatic voice. But as if stylization was not enough to draw attention to the grotesque qualities of the language of his characters, McDonagh also introduces playful elements of meta-communication. His characters regularly, and sometimes even at the most crucial moments, leave the ordinary level of conversation in order to redirect the line of argumentation, comment on faulty pronunciation and stylistic peculiarities or regulate the opening and closing of a subject for discussion (e.g. *SC* 39, 56; *CI* 25, 50, 58). Together with the intentionally tedious exchanges of small talk (especially between Mick and Mary in *A Skull in Connemara* and between Valene and Coleman in *The Lonesome West*), this adds up to the impression that the linguistic behaviour of his characters amounts to some kind of play-acting within the play thereby distancing itself from the dimension of the play's realism. On the level of pragmatics, a similar phenomenon can be observed. Apart from the various strategies of irony employed, further confusion is created through contradictory versions of the same event: whose story can we ultimately trust? Not all of these contradictions are finally resolved, some, it seems, are deliberately left in abeyance. The characters' verbal behaviour in all its 'strangeness' thus becomes the principal vehicle to convey the unresolved tensions inherent in the plays' aesthetic and thematic structures.

The Art of 'Codding'

The value system of the McDonagh universe appears in constant flux and in a state of destabilization. This has the corollary effect that the satire loses sight of its targets. Perhaps with the exception of the deconstruction of Irish stereotypes sociopolitical themes and issues (e.g. exile) are not really foregrounded. Due to their special aesthetic qualities (regarding questions of both dramaturgy and reception) McDonagh's plays seem to forestall any probing for easy 'messages' or themes even. Their emphasis on action and pure physicality is clearly their most prominent feature and puts them in a different class from, for example, the moral assertiveness of John B. Keane or the static wordiness of the later Brian Friel or, for that matter, McDonagh's exact contemporary Conor McPherson in *The Weir*.[23]

What is perhaps most telling is the structural similarity between all four plays. All begin with cleverly crafted expositions which uphold the traditional conventions of confidence-building and the gradual taking in of the spectators. In each case, there comes a point (about half-way into the play) when the 'codding' starts, when the 'booby traps'[24] are set for *dramatis personae* and spectators alike.[25]

In *The Beauty Queen of Leenane* Maureen appears not so strong and in an altogether different light after we have heard of her breakdown (in Scene Four). Her story of the night with her 'lover' (during which nothing apparently happened) deceives not only her mother, and her version of her farewell scene with Pato as well as her other grand illusions are deflated and cancelled out in the end by other versions and other news.

In *A Skull in Connemara* Mick's confession does not concern the death of his wife, as one would expect, but Mairtin, who (Mahon *redivivus*) in turn re-appears against all expectations. Further twists are provided by the burning of Mick's confession and the revelation that it was Thomas the Policeman himself who perpetrated the grave-robbery.

Coleman and Valene's secret in *The Lonesome West*, i.e., the shooting of their father, is revealed only half-way into the play undeceiving a third character, the priest, and the audience at the same time. Coleman's bluffing game with the gun (loaded or not) explicitly implicates the audience and is only part of a vicious circle that lets 'play' develop into serious violence (and back again, as it seems).

In *The Cripple of Inishmaan* the deceiving and undeceiving of audience and characters alike is even more elaborate. Billy's forged letter tricks Bobby into pitying and helping him, but ironically Billy's forecast concerning his own health becomes sadly true in the end. In the course of the play, Bobby changes from a positive, engaging character to a cruel and negative one (much to Billy's painful cost), while Johnny is revealed as the exact opposite from what he appeared to be at first. The most extended and therefore the most bewildering 'cod' is Billy's deathbed scene, when he breaks into his stage-Irish lament interspersed with snatches of the ballad of 'The Croppy Boy'. However realistic Billy's dying may appear, it is only from the following scene that the audience is made fully aware that he has only been rehearsing a part, possibly for an 'Oirish' movie made in Hollywood.

One might argue that McDonagh finds in such dramatic devices his 'objective correlatives' for the depiction of a world of postmodern instability, loss of values and general relativity.[26] This might then be considered as a distant reflex, at most, but by no means as a realistic depiction, of the pluralist Ireland of the 1990s. However, considering the action-orientation and the plethora of dramatic development in McDonagh (as the plot synopses would show), one is tempted to suggest that McDonagh is restoring an original dimension to the meaning of drama as 'action'. For once, it seems we can trust McDonagh when he puts the principles of his dramatic art in a nutshell:

> People should leave a theatre with the same feeling that you get after a really good rock concert. You don't want to talk about it, you just let it buzz into you. I can't stand people analysing things. A play should be a thrill like a fantastic rollercoaster.[27]

[1] A version of this was originally published in: *Twentieth-Century Theatre and Drama in English: Festschrift for Heinz Kosok on the Occasion of His 65th Birthday*, ed. Jürgen Kamm (Trier: WVT Wissenschaftlicher Verlag Trier, 1999), pp.555-571.

[2] The most comprehensive source for bio-bibliographical information on McDonagh is found in Joseph Feeney, 'Martin McDonagh: Dramatist of the West,' *Studies* 87, 1998, p.25. For a sample of reviews of the London productions of McDonagh's plays, see *London Theatre Record* 16, 1996, pp.288-291, 1551-1554; 17, 1997, pp.17-25, 921-928.

[3] See Kate Bassett, 'The Beauty of Staying Power,' *Daily Telegraph* 30 November 1996 (= *Electronic Telegraph* # 556); Rupert Christiansen, 'If you're the greatest you must prove it', *Daily Telegraph* 7 January 1997 (= *Electronic Telegraph* # 592); Michael Raab, 'Der Dichter als Großmaul,' *Die Deutsche Bühne* 1, 1997, pp.37-38; and Richard Zoglin, 'When O'Casey Met Scorsese,' *Time Magazine* 13 April 1998.

[4] Martin McDonagh quoted in Joseph Feeney, p.25.

[5] Ibid., p.28.

[6] See Fintan O'Toole, 'Nowhere Man', *The Irish Times* 26 April 1997; and Michael Raab, 'Die Muhammad Ali-Methode: Der englische Dramatiker Martin McDonagh,' Programmheft: *Die Schönheitskönigin von Leenane* von Martin McDonagh, Münchner Kammerspiele/Werkraum [programme note, Munich 1998], p.6.

[7] Feeney, p.28.

[8] Ibid., p.28.

[9] Ibid., p.29.

[10] For quotations from McDonagh's plays these sigla are indicated throughout referring to the following editions: *The Beauty Queen of Leenane*, The Royal Court Writers Series (London: Methuen, 1996) [*BQ*]; *A Skull in Connemara*, The Royal Court Writers Series (London: Methuen, 1997) [*SC*]; *The Lonesome West* (London: Methuen, 1997) [*LW*]; *The*

Cripple of Inishmaan (London: Methuen, 1997)[*CI*].

[11] Patrick Kavanagh, *Collected Poems* (London: Martin Brian and O'Keeffe, 1977), p.136.

[12] The parallels with Samuel Beckett's short plays *Footfalls* (1976) and *Rockaby* (1981), especially with regard to the motifs of the rocking-chair and the mother-daughter relationship, are more than obvious. McDonagh, however, has been known to shrug at the mention of Beckett (See Christiansen, 1997).

[13] The second play in the Leenane Trilogy, *A Skull in Connemara*, takes its title from a phrase in Lucky's 'Think' tirade in Act I of Beckett's *Waiting for Godot*.

[14] Martin Esslin, *The Theatre of the Absurd*, rev. ed. (Harmondsworth: Penguin, 1976), p.66.

[15] Mic Moroney, rev. of *The Leenane Trilogy*, by Martin McDonagh, *Independent* 25 June 1997 [rpt. in *London Theatre Record* 17, 1997, p.921].

[16] Fintan O'Toole sees the McDonagh Trilogy as the culminating point of the elaboration of this theme in Garry Hynes's long-standing association with the Druid Theatre ('Murderous Laughter,' rev. of *The Leenane Trilogy*, by Martin McDonagh, *Irish Times* 24 June 1997).

[17] Philip Thomson, *The Grotesque, The Critical Idiom*, 24 (London: Methuen, 1972), p.27.

[18] See Toni O'Brien Johnson, *Synge: The Medieval and the Grotesque, Irish Literary Studies* 11 (Gerrards Cross: Colin Smythe, 1982), p.18.

[19] Feeney, p.29; and Zoglin.

[20] Moroney, p.921.

[21] C.L. Dallat, 'From the Outside,' rev. of *The Cripple of Inishmaan*, by Martin McDonagh, *TLS* 17 January 1997, p.14.

[22] Feeney, p.28.

[23] For an interesting parallel to the 'graveyard shenanigans' (*SC* 11) in *A Skull in Connemara*, compare Jim's ghostly graveyard story (and it is merely a story told in the play) in Conor McPherson's *The Weir* (London: Methuen 1997), pp.76-78.

[24] Penelope Dening, 'The Wordsmith of Camberwell,' *The Irish Times* 8 July 1997.

[25] Again, the model for this appears to be Synge's *Playboy*, when one thinks of the reappearance of Old Mahon and the upstaging of Christy.

[26] Maria Tymoczko, 'A Theatre of Complicity,' rev. of *The Beauty Queen of Leenane*, by Martin McDonagh, *Irish Literary Supplement* 16.2, 1997, p.16; and Feeney, p.30.

[27] Alannah Weston, 'Starlife,' *Daily Telegraph* 12 July 1997, p.74, quoted in Feeney, p.28.

2 | Macabre Merriment in *The Beauty Queen of Leenane*[1]

Rebecca Wilson

In the common perception of melodrama as sensational, emotionally hyperbolic theatre, the comic dimension is often neglected. Yet the comic element is as integral to the basic formula as are the villain, the hero and the heroine. Initially, in traditional melodrama, comedy was located in a benevolent clown figure, virtue in the hero and heroine, and evil in the villain. As this mutable form developed, characterization became less rigid and character traits merged and/or overlapped, giving rise to 'villains who were more to be pitied than censured',[2] flawed heroes and heroines, and comedy that no longer centred in a benevolent clown. John McCormick notes that:

> As a greater psychological element crept in, and as the clear distinctions between good and evil, which has been so much a hallmark of the genre, were increasingly eroded…audiences were expected to 'understand' the villain rather than conspue [sic] him.[3]

In Martin McDonagh's *Beauty Queen of Leenane*, first performed at the Town Hall Theatre Galway on 1 February 1996, we have victim-villains as protagonists, and comedy, rather than residing in a comic characterization, is the woof in the warp of McDonagh's melodramatic dramaturgy; it is this comic weft that this paper is concerned with. In the words of Charles Spencer, this play is 'wildly funny, deeply affecting and generally macabre, all at the same time',[4] and these other moods must also be touched upon in order to contextualize the comic element, particularly since the comedy here does not at all offer comic relief, but rather intensifies the pain; it is the lightning flash that illuminates and etches the tragic moment.

McDonagh both upholds and inverts the tenets of traditional melodrama in this play which, in its Irish localization, is redolent of a Syngean aesthetic, and is universal in its depiction of human pain, loss and absurdity. Here is a landscape painted by Francis Bacon. This is rustic Ireland, but the poetic, bitterly romantic terrain of Synge and the idyllic picturesque pastoral land of Boucicault have been flayed away to expose a bleak 'big ould hill', steep, muddy and rocky that, without a car, can only be reached by 'wading through all that skitter'. Here, incidentally, we see an inversion of a fairy-tale trope in melodrama: in a tower on top of a mountain, incarcerated by an ogress-cum-wicked witch, the virgin heroine, albeit a forty-year-old resentful, frustrated and repressed virgin, waits for a lover-saviour. The lover-saviour, after braving 'all that skitter' rather than an enchanted forest, proves impotent to deliver her from the ogress. But then what can the heroine be but an ogress herself, since one ogress can only beget another?

Mother, Mag, and daughter, Maureen, live in mutually destructive symbiosis in a dreary village in the West of Ireland. Mag is dependent, selfish, demanding, manipulative; Maureen is mentally fragile, frustrated, trapped. At a neighbour's party, Maureen renews her acquaintance with Pato, a man near her own age who works in England, leading to mutual attraction and an unconsummated one-night stand. Mag attempts to destroy the budding relationship. Pato returns to England but writes to Maureen, asking her to go to America with him. Mag intercepts and burns the letter, but when Maureen later taunts her with the sexual exploit that in fact never happened, Mag inadvertently lets slip comments that arouse Maureen's suspicions. Under torture by Maureen scalding her with boiling oil, Mag confesses to the knowledge of the letter and reveals its contents. This precipitates Maureen's murder of Mag and descent into madness. In the final scene we learn that Pato went off to America believing that Maureen did not want to see him. Pato's brother, Ray, tells her that

Pato is engaged to a girl in America and Maureen, the 'beauty queen of Leenane', succumbs to the madness that was always hovering around her.

Mag and Maureen do not represent an idealized, sentimentalized mother-and-child relationship; they are two unhappy, malignant harpies tearing and empoisoning each other. Into this nest of vipers comes the stranger, Pato, neither romanticized man of mystery nor villain, but a normal, ordinary man who, unwittingly, is the catalyst that will ignite the catastrophe. Here is an astringent inversion of a formulaic melodramatic structure: instead of the villain despoiling the place of innocence and activating the plot, the potential hero enters a vile place and activates the plot. There is also the reverse, absolute adherence to the moral principles (the 'moral occult') of melodrama: because she has tortured and killed, Maureen cannot be saved. The ordinary, normal, innocent man offers Maureen escape and a normal, ordinary life which the ethics of the 'moral occult' must perforce deny her. And throughout this baleful tale, comedy glitters wickedly.

McDonagh has intermeshed a double-edged, interlocked retention and inversion of much ideology, iconography, and topography of 'classic' melodrama; thematics of Gothic melodrama flavoured with elements of Grand Guignol; a macabre 'gallows humour' and streaks of lasciviousness recalling those lode veins of the Irish comic tradition delineated by Vivian Mercier in *The Irish Comic Tradition*; comedy carried by the protagonists (or rather antagonists) rather than clown figures; and damaged victim-villains, 'injured scoundrels', rather than a villain figure serving as a cipher of evil. Thus, instead of a fleshly embodiment of evil, there is 'a disembodied presence of evil', here allegorized by the foul-smelling kitchen – a hell's kitchen indeed.

The set of the *Beauty Queen* is the typical country-cottage kitchen of much Irish melodrama (or Eamon de Valera's bucolic fantasy) but this kitchen is no fragrant hearthstone of nurture and nourishment, nor is it the impersonal space of, for example, John McGahern's *The Power of Darkness* (1991), where evil is plotted, nor Louis D'Alton's *Lovers' Meeting* (1941), where old sins fester, nor John B. Keane's *Sive* (1959), where greed sacrifices innocence.

These are neutral rooms, innocent in themselves of the human malevolence and/or mischance breeding in them. Disease and evil are palpable in the *Beauty Queen's* kitchen, which stinks of the diseased urine that Mag, suffering from a urine infection, pours down the sink. This kitchen is a fetid miasma of unwholesomeness, as warped as the symbiotically empoisoned mother and daughter who inhabit it; it signifies 'evil as a real, irreducible force'.[5] Yet it is also a fount of humour, a powerful, dicephalous dramatic device engendering both comedy and revulsion. The revulsion caused by the stench (effectively projected in performance by a grimace or a shudder) of diseased urine is comically leavened by Mag pouring a potty of 'wee' down the sink and 'wee' down the kitchen sink gives rise to several episodes of comedy, verbal and visual. The following exchange is one of the funniest episodes in the play:

> **Ray:** This house does smell of pee, this house does.
> **Mag:** (*Pause. Embarrassed*) Em, cats do get in.
> **Ray:** Do cats get in?
> **Mag:** They do. (*Pause*) They do go to the sink.
> **Ray:** (*Pause*) What do they go to the sink for?
> **Mag:** To wee.
> **Ray:** To wee? They go to the sink to wee? (*Piss-taking*)
> [McDonagh seems to be enjoying a pun here] Sure, that's mighty good of them. You do get a very considerate breed of cat up this way so.
> **Mag:** (*Pause*) I don't know what breed they are (*BQ*, 40-41).

The verbal comedy is self-explanatory and, punctuated by the pauses accentuating the contrasting moods of preposterous dissembling, discomfiture, mild bewilderment, and sarcasm, give ample room for expressive visual performance comedy.

The putrid sink gives rise to somewhat more uncomfortable comedy in the scene in which Maureen, after offering Pato a mug of tea, drags him over to 'smell that sink', upon which *Pato leans into the sink, sniffs it, then pulls his head away in disgust (BQ* 28). This is a facial gesture which is bound to raise a laugh, albeit a squeamish one, which is rather in keeping with Pato *'sipping'* his tea *'squeamishly'* (*BQ* 29), another facial gesture which often arouses laughter in an audience. The entire vista is a horrid and hilarious melee of Mag demanding attention for her 'scoulded hand' and deploring all mention of 'wee', Maureen complaining that she has to wash her 'praities' in an unhygienic sink while serving Pato tea, and Pato trapped in embarrassment and too polite to refuse the tea. Indeed, the incompatible juxtaposition of disgust and gustatory hospitality – 'And doesn't even rinse it either. Now is that hygienic? And she does have urine infection too, is even less hygienic. I wash me praities in there. Here's your tea now, Pato' – is an ingeniously funny and disturbing construct. The incongruity of the situation supplies the comedy, provoking an effect somewhat akin to the Freudian theory of 'humorous displacement … a means of withdrawing energy from the means of unpleasure that is already in preparation and transforming it by discharge into pleasure'. This scene borders on farce. The scene hurtles toward psychic violence and culminates in bitter bathos. Like all intensely narcissistic creatures, Mag is oblivious to anyone else. Treachery is a staple of melodrama. McDonagh interweaves both these factors in this astonishing scene of terrible pathos and cruel comedy, which builds to Mag, viciously and exultingly, telling Pato of Maureen's stay in a mental hospital. Mother and daughter shout at each other with mounting, venomous aggression, Pato steps between them, Mag exits to get Maureen's hospitalization papers, Maureen sadly confesses her mental instability, and Pato tries to comfort her, Mag returns triumphantly brandishing the papers, Pato leaves, promising to write, and Maureen, crouching on the floor, hugging her new dress that Mag has thrown in a corner, is as shattered as if Mag has taken a club to her. After the medley of frenetic stage business Maureen exits, an image of heart-rending despair. Nothing is funny any more. Then Mag, utterly indifferent to the devastation she has caused, sticks her finger in her porridge and, horrifically and comically, complains, twice, that her 'porridge is gone cold now' *(BQ* 34). The effect on an audience must be to produce a laugh, a Beckettian 'dianoetic laugh' that laughs at that which is not happy.[6]

Porridge – Complan – cod-in-butter-sauce – shortbread fingers – Mag's world revolves around food. Typical of the infant personality craving constant feeding, Mag is obsessed with being fed. Food is a recognized signifier of need and comfort, the primary demand of the infant for its survival, the centre of its world, and of Mag's. A rare excursion into town is looked forward to less for the outing than for the possibility of getting shortbread fingers. Food provides the axle for a scene that, ingeniously and comically, expresses a complex psychological nexus of narcissistic self-absorption and infantile demands for nurturing. Ray, waiting to give Pato's letter to the absent Maureen, is getting more and more impatient. Mag wants him to go before Maureen can get the letter, urging him, 'Be off and give your letter to me … I'll make sure she gets it' *(BQ* 38) and insinuating that Maureen may not be back until morning. Yet her need for nurturing pulls her the other way as, totally oblivious to Ray's irritation, she asks him to make her 'a mug of tea … Or a mug of Complan … Or a Cup-a-Soup do me' (*BQ* 41). The incongruity of conflicting moods and desires, in-cluding the pitted stubbornness of fixated age versus restless youth, furnishes an acerbic comedy.

Prophetic violence lurks in the comedy of Ray's yearning for the women's 'great oul poker', with which he could 'take out a half a dozen coppers … just for the fun of seeing the blood running out of them' *(BQ* 39). There is a sinister dramatic prolepsis in Ray's comic fantasy of battering coppers with the poker and seeing bloody gouts, since Mag is later in fact bloodily battered with the selfsame poker. Ironically Mag, by refusing to sell Ray the poker, is retaining the instrument of her murder. In terms of performance, Ray's *'wielding the poker'* (*BQ* 39) suggests a comic orgy of mimed violence reminiscent of the frenetic film clown, Jimmy Finlayson, of the old Hal Roach comedies. Aggression is common to comedy and staged violence is often, though by no means always, risible; the motives for our laughter are complex and seem to be partly impelled by context and degrees of identification. For example, we laugh as Punch clobbers Judy and the policeman and throws his baby out of a window, although domestic and civic violence and infanticide are not laughing matters. (Our glee as he hangs the hangman and cheats the devil is straightforward, self-explanatory recoiling from mortality.) We do not at all laugh at the Carney brothers' violence in Tom Murphy's *A Whistle in the Dark*, but can barely stop laughing as brothers Valene and Coleman consistently batter each other in McDonagh's *The Lonesome West*. Laughter provoked by theatrical violence seems to be contingent on context, treatment, and style rather than content.

To return briefly to the poker: in the last scene Ray, unaware that Maureen has murdered Mag with the poker, still covets it. As Vivian Mercier has so diligently traced, 'gallows humour' has long featured in Irish culture and the poker provides a conduit for this when Ray's bargaining ('A fiver I'll give you … G'wan. Six!' (*BQ* 58-9)), for that 'awful good poker' is refused by Maureen's, 'No. It does have sentimental value for me' *(BQ* 59). From a performance viewpoint, Ray unknowningly handling the poker while countering Maureen's assertion that drugs are dangerous with, 'Maybe they are, maybe they are. But there are plenty of other things just as dangerous, would kill you just as easy. Maybe even easier' *(BQ* 54) would certainly present grimly comic dramatic irony.

Comedy and suspense, both staple ingredients of melodrama, revolve around that archetypal generic device, the letter. The letter or document is a standard, crucial iconic device of melodrama, sometimes to detonate the catastrophe, at other times as a sort of *deus ex machina* to resolve it. McDonagh uses Pato's letter to pre- cipitate disaster, but with an ironic bitter twist that accentuates the pain. Had Pato's letter reached Maureen, she could have escaped; that chance was stolen from her by Mag stealing the letter, by archetypal melodramatic treacherous villainy. This sets in motion the chain of events that ultimately entraps Maureen; thus, ironi- cally, the potential key to her liberation is the key that locks her finally in her prison, as McDonagh offers us four iconic in- gredients of traditional melodrama: secretive treachery, the letter, the oath, and the thwarted escape, as well as comic instances laced throughout the scene. The spectators may ultimately be left with the bitter aftertaste of John Greenleaf Whittier's couplet:

> For of all sad words of tongue or pen
> The saddest are these: it might have been!

But they may well giggle – or guffaw – while holding their breath in suspense when Ray, breaking his word to Pato, leaves the letter with Mag, making her swear not to open it: 'And may God strike you dead if you do open it?' She responds with, 'And may God strike me dead if I do open it, only he'll have no need to strike me dead because I won't be opening it' (*BQ* 41). The ludicrousness of the childish oath, recalling playground oaths of 'swear to God and hope to die' and Mag's barefaced lies supply a verbal comedy which suitable gesture and vocal tone may reinforce; Ray's indecisive stage business with the letter, repeatedly putting it down and picking it up, and Mag's stealthy moves towards the letter, to be unwittingly truncated, with the meticulous timing of farce by Ray, present a well-worn but nonetheless always effective visual motif of comic suspense. Also in keeping with patterns of time-tested comic exits, Ray goes out the door but does not leave. Mag starts out of the rocking chair then, remembering she hasn't heard Ray's footsteps, she '*sits back serenely*' (*BQ* 42). The door bursts open, Ray sticks his head in, Mag '*smiles at him innocently*' and Ray exits. It might be a cliché but it works. Then all comedy stops as Mag reads the letter and burns it.

As is typical of this play, the comedy is not presented in set pieces but is interleaved within the melodramatic plot and process. Consider, for example, the comic oath and Mag's murderous end. Gothic poetic justice and the 'moral occult' of 'classic' melodrama, Peter Brooks's theories of a morally based ideological apparatus that supplanted notions of divinely ordained justice, can be perceived in Mag's nemesis. Mag has broken a vow, one of melodrama's sacrosanct icons. (Ray did not do as Pato asked, but Ray never promised anything, let alone take an oath.) Not only has she sworn dishonestly, she has dishonestly invoked the Sacred. She does open the letter and she is struck dead, not by God but by Maureen. Thus Mag's retribution is not numinous, it can be rationally explained by Maureen's rage, yet a Gothic reverberation is unmistakable in the manner of her death. However, the instrument of her nemesis is not some metaphysical phenomenon but a corporeal fury. All this accords with Brooks's stance (in reference to the 'moral occult') that, 'in the absence of a true Sacred … what is most important in a man's life is his ethical drama and the ethical implications of his psychic drama'.[7] Thus McDonagh, within a melodramatic frame, has interwoven elements of the serious and the merry play.

Licentious humour, like macabre and gallows humour, with roots in Irish myth and legend, introduces episodes which tumble into pain and dismay. In the already mentioned scene 4, the morning after Pato has stayed overnight, Maureen comes out in bra and slip, flaunting sexuality and, much to Pato's embarrassment, sits across his lap (her state of undress and exhibitionism recalling a lap-dancer), kissing him and taunting Mag with licentious remarks. Her, 'We was careful, weren't we, Pato? Careful enough, cos we don't need any babies coming, do we? We do have enough babies in this house to be going on with', *(BQ* 27) uses sexual innuendo, always sure to raise a titter, to torment Mag with both the notion of active sexuality and the reversed situation of child-as-carer and mother as child-cum-tyrant, the situation which imprisons and embitters Maureen. The innuendo accelerates into blunt licentiousness – rude, crude, and sure to bring the house down with laughter:

> **Maureen:** *(To Pato)*: You'll have to be putting that thing of yours in me again before too long is past, Pato. I do have a taste for it now, I do …
> **Pato:** Maureen …
> **Maureen:** A mighty oul taste. Uh-huh.
> *Pato gets up and idles around in embarrassment (BQ 28).*

Mercier suggests laughter at licentiousness could be prompted by the 'excessive and absurd',[8] here typified by Maureen's behaviour, and also by its function as a release of sexual repression. Mercier's observations could well apply to this scene.

Maureen's narcissistic need to irritate Mag totally ignores Pato's discomfiture; the poisonous relationship with Mag of hate and spite overrides any constructive feeling for Pato. Her self-destructive goading of Mag provokes Mag's vicious, treacherous retaliation: the insistent divulging of Maureen's stay in a mental hospital. Then the scene tilts: Maureen's state of undress, at first intentionally sexually provocative, now exposes her helplessness; what had begun as a brazen sexual ploy transmutes into naked vulnerability. She descends into a slough of self-pity as she relays her status as victim, victim of racism in England, victim of mental instability, victim of her mother in Ireland. Her abysmal lack of self-esteem misconstrues Pato's suggestion that she put some clothes on as revulsion and rejection.

Shamed by her 'doolally' *(BQ* 30) breakdown, shamed by her assumption of Pato's rejection, and, in line with the melodramatic process through the centuries, this pathetic, broken figure is very likely to arouse pity in the spectator, a pity intensified by contrast with the earlier 'excessive and absurd' brazen hussy, as lewd comedy transmutes into naked despair.

A similar schema can be seen in Scene Seven. The scene opens with a sexually charged duel, fraught with mother-daughter sexual antagonism: Maureen licentiously bragging about her fictitious sexual experience and taunting Mag as being 'past it', and Mag smugly sneering with her knowledge that there was no sexual adventure – Pato was too drunk to perform sexually and Maureen is as virginal as ever. Maureen's lewd braggadocio gives the hostility a comic dimension; witness Maureen playing on Mag's obsessive craving for food as food for lascivious language and gesture:

> **Maureen:** Do you want a shortbread finger?
> **Mag:** I do want a shortbread finger.
> **Maureen:** Please.
> **Mag:** Please.
> *Maureen gives Mag shortbread finger, after waving it phallically in the air a moment.*
> **Maureen:** Remind me of something, shortbread fingers do.
> **Mag:** I suppose they do now.
> **Maureen:** I suppose it's so long since you've seen what they remind me of, you do forget what they look like *(BQ* 45-6).

Again lewd and crude, plangent with gesturement and certain to raise convulsive laughter. (In a local performance in Westport the actress stroked, sucked, and nibbled another shortbread finger and the hall shook with laughter; vulgar comedy, absolutely, but so, reportedly, was *komos,* although the *Beauty Queen* ends not with marriage but living entombment.) Then the scene tilts as Maureen suspects that Mag is withholding information about Pato, and an episode that started with sexual braggadocio transmogrifies into sadism with the torture of Mag; again an episode that started with lascivious comedy ends in brutal despair, this time Mag's as, tortured and abandoned, she quietly intones, 'But who'll look after me, so?' *(BQ* 49)

Maureen's torture of Mag, a harrowing scene steeped in the horror of Grand Guignol, is a cardinal scene in the play, and thus,

I feel, merits further comment. This may seem a digression from the main thrust of this article, but since agony, horror, and humour are as symbiotically inextricable in this play as the protagonists, further commentary seems called for, especially as the torture seems to have a sexual motivation and so is linked to the earlier comic lascivious bravado (which in itself carries a bitter irony, since it pretends to celebrate a non-event). Maureen's scalding of Mag's previously scalded hand with boiling oil seems to be motivated by her desire to extract information about Pato. But the ritualistic procedure, the donning of the rubber gloves, the turning up of the radio to drown Mag's screams, the patient waiting for the oil to boil and the excruciating, intense brutality of the act, '*Maureen slowly and deliberately takes her mother's shrivelled hand, holds it down on the burning range, and. starts slowly pouring some of the hot oil over it*' *(BQ* 47), suggests a sadism that has little to do with pressuring for information. Also, Mag's terror at the ritualistic preparations before the oil has been near her suggests a repeat performance, something which Mag claims has indeed happened. The preparations are enough to make Mag confess to having intercepted Pato's letter and read it; it is after that confession that Maureen actually starts to pour the hot oil over Mag's hand. After Mag admits to having burnt the letter and reveals its contents, (Pato's apology for being too drunk to perform sexually and his offer to take Maureen to America), Maureen throws '*the considerable remainder of the oil*' *(BQ* 48) over her, an act of pure sadistic hate, since she now has the information. Given Maureen's sexual repression, which is such a fundamental feature of the play, and the sexually loaded context of the scene, it can only be assumed that, along with the hatred fanned by vengeance, that last splurge of hot oil is a sadistic act charged with sadism's inherent sexuality. Also, a cruel parallelism can be discerned in the burning of the letter and the burning of the hand.

Macabre humour opens and closes this play; in the first scene it hinges on a grimly amusing fantasy, 'excessive and absurd'; in the last it is funny and harrowing, a comedy that highlights misery, a reification of the comic instant that illuminates the tragic moment. The earlier comic episode opens with Mag's Agony Aunt-like advice not to speak to strangers, accelerates into the macabre-grotesque with Maureen's gleeful (and proleptic) fantasy of clobbering Mag and is abruptly – and comically – terminated by Mag's narcissistic demands for feeding:

> **Mag:** … Although some people it would better not to say hello to. The fella up and murdered the poor oul woman in Dublin and he didn't even know her. The news that story was on, did you hear of it? Strangled, and didn't even know her. That's a fella it would be better not to talk to. That's a fella it would be better to avoid outright. [Ironically, Mag is talking to her murderer]
> (**Maureen** brings **Mag** *her tea, then sits at the table.*)
> **Maureen:** Sure, that sounds exactly the type of fella I would like to meet, and then bring him home to meet you, if he likes murdering oul women.
> **Mag:** That's not a nice thing to say, Maureen.
> **Maureen**: Is it not, now?
> **Mag:** (*Pause*) Sure why would he be coming all this way out from Dublin? He'd just be going out of his way.
> **Maureen:** For the pleasure of me company he'd come. Killing you, it'd just be a bonus for him.
> **Mag:** *Killing you* I bet he first would be.
> **Maureen:** I could live with that so long as I was sure he'd be clobbering you soon after. If he clobbered you with a big axe or something and took your oul head off and spat in your neck, I wouldn't mind at all, going first. Oh no, I'd enjoy it, I would. No more oul Complan to get, and no more oul porridge to get, and no more …
> **Mag:** (*Interrupting, holding her tea out*) No sugar in this, Maureen, you forgot, go and get me some (*BQ* 67).

Maureen's oxymoronic reply heightens the comedy in this scene, a darkly comical scene which establishes the grotesque bitterness of their relationship. The last scene abounds in terrible pathos and hilarity, the one providing a bizarre, absurd context for the other. The previous scene, eerily set by Mag, motionless in her chair which rocks of its own volition, and Maureen idling about holding the poker, continues with Maureen's hallucinatory delusion of having seen Pato off at the train station with the promise of shortly joining him in America and ends with the Grand Guignol image of Mag toppling forward from her chair: '*A red chunk of skull hangs from a string of skin at the side of her head*' (*BQ* 51). In the next scene Maureen brings in a suitcase and we assume she is preparing to go to America until Ray, that benighted messenger, arrives and disabuses her with, 'What station? Be taxicab Pato left' *(BQ* 56). Thence the comedy, already set earlier by Ray's comparing the relative merits of Kimberley biscuits, Jaffa Cakes, and Wagon Wheels, percolates alongside disaster. Ray, after telling Maureen that Pato was sad not to have seen her again, announces that Pato has become engaged to a girl in America. Maureen '*is dumbstruck*', descending further into madness as Ray chatters on breezily about Pato's fiancée's brown eyes, the priorities of European Championships football over weddings, and the problems of matrimonial name changing:

> It won't be much of a change for her anyways, from Hooley to Dooley. Only one letter. The 'h'. That'll be a good thing. (*Pause*) Unless it's Healey that she is. I can't remember. (*Pause*) If it's Healey, it'll be three letters. The 'h', the 'e' and the 'a' (57).

Maureen, stunned and confused, can only intone, 'Dolores Hooley'. The juxtaposition of the trivial and the tragic heighten them both and also suggest a Pirandellian concept of humour as a conflation of the ridiculous (Ray's inane chatter) and the sad (Maureen). This intermesh of the trivial and the tragic – and sinister – is repeated when Maureen, enraged by Ray's scoffing at 'loons', advances on him with the poker and is distracted by his disproportionate, childish tantrum at finding a swingball confiscated by Maureen years ago. '*Maureen lets the poker fall to the floor with a clatter*' *(BQ* 58), paving the way for another round of gallows humour with Ray's advice not to bang the poker against anything hard and Maureen promising that she won't. Finally, the comic dimension exits with Ray, leaving Maureen sitting in Mag's rocking chair, in Gothic nemesis, 'the exact fecking image' of her mother *(BQ* 60). The play's inextricable admixture of the hilarious, the sad, and the terrible haunts us with the caution that, 'What is funny had better not be laughed at'.[9]

In the *Beauty Queen* McDonagh ingeniously upholds and inverts basic components of the Irish dramatic canon and generic melodrama generally. He retains the comic ingredient, mainly using licentious and macabre facets of humour, highlighting 'the tragic side of gaiety', dispersed throughout the dramatis personae rather than concentrated in a clown figure. This structure parallels the locus of evil as a presence inflecting sad victim-villains rather than as a singular, unmitigated personification of evil. Having said that, Ray with his addiction to Australian soaps and 'clobbering coppers' and debating the status of Kimberley biscuits versus Wagon Wheels could well be a modern-day clown figure.

In the wake of melodramatic precedent, the *Beauty Queen* articulates aspects of cultural transition in the Ireland of the 1990s. Notably, there is the demythologizing, indeed deconstruction, of the ideal family unit enshrined by much traditional melodrama and promulgated in a rustic utopia by Eamon de Valera. Not that earlier families were perfect, but miscreants (apart from the villain) almost always saw the error of their ways, and redemption and forgiveness, reconciliation of a sort or at least guilty regret, usually followed. This paradigm has been eroded over time, but in the *Beauty Queen* it is positively shattered in the morbidly dysfunctional relationship between Mag and Maureen, wherein mother-child bonding has twisted into venomous bondage. Here also, in keeping with the tenor of the play, can be assumed a double edge, on the one side dissecting familial tensions, which were always there but not often (before the advent of psychodynamic therapy) admitted; on the other side possibly relating to the wider context of contemporary family breakdown. Either way, de Valera's fantasy of 'cosy homesteads' and 'comely maidens' is harshly, and hilariously, demolished. Still in the realm of family matters lurks the quandary of the place of the old within the disintegration of the extended family, the burden on the carer, the problems of responsibility in a shifting value system. Emigration is lightly touched on, possibly because, with the recent expanding Irish economy, emigration is no longer the economic exigency it once was but still retains a vestigial place; perhaps because of the tentacles of history; perhaps because it offers escape from rural boredom, be it as insubstantial as Ray's fascination with drugs in Manchester and Australian soaps or as substantial as Pato's sense of 'psychic displacement',[10] not wanting be either here or there – the plight of many an emigrant, Irish or not. A factor that seems particularly to mark this play as belonging to the Ireland of the 1990s (or the 1980s) is the crude language and blatant sexuality, taboo areas in the 1960s and not really visible in the 1970s either.

This seems to be contingent on a number of factors: the major social revolution of the 1960s, the confluence of different cultures due to increased travel, the weakening hold of the Catholic Church, to name three. In the *Beauty Queen* McDonagh has demythologized the West of Ireland, assuredly, and echoes of the Irish dramatic canon reverberate throughout the play, yet a much broader context is unmistakable; as John Peter comments, McDonagh's drama is 'universal but could be set nowhere except in Ireland'.[11]

---

[1] A version of this essay was previously published in *The Power of Laughter: Comedy and Contemporary Irish Theatre*, ed. Eric Weitz (Carysfort Press, Dublin, 2004).

[2] Frank Rahill, *The World of Melodrama* (Pennsylvania State: University Press, 1967), p.xv.

[3] John McCormick, 'Origins of Melodrama' in *Prompts 6. Irish Theatre Archives* (September 1983), p.12.

[4] Charles Spencer reviewing '*The Beauty Queen of Leenane*' in *The Daily Telegraph* 8 March 1996.

[5] Peter Brooks, *The Melodramatic Imagination* (Yale: University Press, 1995), p.13.

[6] See Vivian Mercier, *The Irish Comic Tradition* (London: Souvenir, 1991).

[7] Brooks, p.52.

[8] Mercier, p.49.

[9] Walter Kerr, *Tragedy and Comedy* (New York: Simon and Schuster, 1967), p.15.

[10] Christopher Murray, *Twentieth-Century Irish Drama* (Manchester: Manchester University Press, 1997), pp.170-175.

[11] John Peter in Karen Vandevelde's 'The Gothic Soap of Martin McDonagh' in *Theatre Stuff*, ed. Eamonn Jordan (Dublin: Carysfort Press, 2000), p.299.

3 | Ireland in Two Minds: Martin McDonagh and Conor McPherson[1]

Nicholas Grene

It's been an extraordinary double phenomenon, the nearly simultaneous rise and rise of Martin McDonagh and Conor McPherson. McDonagh's first play, *The Beauty Queen of Leenane*, was produced by Druid Theatre Company in association with the Royal Court in 1996 when the author was 25. It swept up a string of London prizes – Evening Standard Award for Most Promising Newcomer, Writers' Guild Award for Best Fringe Theatre Play, George Devine Award for Most Promising Playwright – before eventually going on to do equally well with Tony Awards when it transferred to New York. McPherson was born in 1971, a year after McDonagh, but by the time *The Weir* followed *The Beauty Queen of Leenane* into the Royal Court in 1997, it was already his fifth professionally produced play. *The Weir* was very nearly as successful as *Beauty Queen*, with its share of prizes (including a couple that McDonagh had won the year before), a long run in London and an international tour. In the event, neither playwright has proved to be a one-hit wonder. *Beauty Queen* was followed by two more plays making up the *Leenane Trilogy* – *A Skull in Connemara* and *The Lonesome West*, both produced in 1997 – and with the production of *The Cripple of Inishmaan* by the National Theatre in the same year, McDonagh is said to have been the first playwright since Shakespeare to have four plays running in London at the same time.[2]

Though there was a hiatus before the staging of the second of his Aran trilogy, *The Lieutenant of Inishmore* by the RSC in 2001, due to the very controversial nature of its subject, it too transferred successfully to the West End. McDonagh's work has been staged all over the world in English and in translation; it has been claimed that by 2000 he was more produced in the United States than any other dramatist but Shakespeare.[3] Neither of McPherson's two full-length plays since *The Weir*, *Dublin Carol* (2000), and *Port Authority* (2001), though critically warmly received, has had the scale of commercial success of *The Weir*. But McPherson has made himself an additional double career as theatre director and film-maker, directing his own and other playwrights' plays, making three feature films: *I Went Down* (1997) as screenwriter, the prizewinning *Saltwater* (2001) (adapted from his own stage play *This Lime Tree Bower*), and *The Actors* (2003), both as screenwriter and director. And McPherson, like McDonagh, continues to have his plays regularly revived.

The twinned successes of the two young Irish playwrights, so utterly different in style, temperament, and attitude, has been the subject of endless media stories. Theatre critics have tended to pre-fer one or the other, some regarding McDonagh as brash and heartless, some accusing McPherson of lacking dramatic edge. Both have been quickly assimilated into the heritage of Irish theatre stretching back to Synge and O'Casey, in spite of McDonagh's claims that he had never read Synge before he wrote *Beauty Queen*, McPherson's uneasiness at being labelled an 'Irish' playwright.[4] What is most interesting in McDonagh and Mc-Pherson's work is the contrasting versions of Ireland the plays dramatize and the varieties of the Irish imaginary reflected in their reception. The special category of the Irish play conditions the context in which their plays are staged, however little the dramatists themselves may like it. They speak to already formed Irelands of the mind. The aim of this essay is to explore *Beauty Queen* and *The Weir*, as late twentieth-century interventions in the history of Irish self-representation.

Views from the city

Romantic pastoral was a formative part of the Literary Revival from the beginning: urban writers rejecting metropolitan life – 'Give up Paris', Yeats told Synge – 'Go to the Aran Islands' – renewing themselves 'Antaeus-like' by contact with the soil, by escape into the otherness of the West. Even Joyce, most defiantly city-oriented, could at least toy with the idea in 'The Dead' that it was time to set out on the journey westward. McDonagh and McPherson belong to a much later period, and the different configuration of city and country in their lives produce different versions of pastoral. McDonagh is London Irish, typical of any number of children of rural Irish immigrants to the big cities of Britain or North America. His mother and father came to South London from Sligo and Galway respectively, and it was to these two counties that Martin was brought on regular family holidays as a child. He remained in London with his brother when his parents moved back to Ireland to settle permanently in Lettermullan. McPherson is one generation further removed from western origins, having grown up in north Dublin, the child of urban parents but with a grandfather in Leitrim. In this he fits the demographic trend that has transformed Ireland in the last half of the twentieth century from a rural into a predominantly city-dwelling society, with a constant flow of people into the Dublin area. The vacation visits of McDonagh to Sligo and Connemara, of McPherson to Leitrim, resulted in the sharply different views from the city that constitute *Beauty Queen* and *The Weir*:

> **Mag:** Wet, Maureen?
> **Maureen:** Of course wet.[5]

The opening laconic exchange between mother and daughter sets the keynote. What else would it be but wet in Leenane? One suspects that the adolescent Ray Dooley speaks for his creator when he wonders 'Who wants to see Ireland on telly?': All you have to do is look out your window to see Ireland. And it's soon bored you'd be. 'There goes a calf.' (*Pause*) I be bored anyway. I be continually bored (*Plays 1*, 53).

Revenge for the ennui of protracted summers in small-town Connemara where it rained continually seems to animate *Beauty Queen*. Connemara may be all the tourist brochures claim it to be scenically, but that hardly compensates for the sheer pettiness of its life. Returning emigrant worker Pato, Ray's brother, in spite of the discomforts of navvying in London, is not sure he would ever want to live in Leenane, even if there were work for him there:

> Of course it's beautiful here, a fool can see. The mountains and the green, and people speak. But when everybody knows every-body else's business … I don't know. (*Pause.*) You can't kick a cow in Leenane without some bastard holding a grudge twenty year (*Plays 1*, 22).

Dystopic views of the small Irish town have been common-place at least as far back as Brinsley McNamara's vicious satire *The Valley of the Squinting Windows* (1918) but *Beauty Queen* has the peculiar animus of the mutinous adolescent in revolt against the mythology of an earlier generation.

Part of the comic appeal of the play is the short shrift given to the pieties of Irish kitsch. 'The Spinning Wheel' by Delia Murphy is played on the radio in Scene Three during the uneasy courtship of Pato and Maureen with Mag asleep next door, exactly re-producing the situation of the song where the girl tries to steal to her lover without her grandmother knowing:

> **Maureen:** [...] Me mother does love this oul song. Oul Delia Murphy.
> **Pato:** This is a creepy oul song.
> **Maureen:** It *is* a creepy oul song. […]
> **Pato:** […] They don't write songs like that any more. Thank Christ (*Plays 1* 23).

The laugh-line detonates under the expected sentimental response. It is of course to an ironic reprise of the 'Spinning Wheel', played specially on the radio in the long-promised dedi-cation for the now murdered Mag from her two absent daughters, that the play ends. The cult of Connemara, the culture of weepy Irish nostalgia, is treated to a savagely sardonic iconoclasm.

The violently dysfunctional relationship of Mag and Maureen is central to this strategy of demythologizing Ireland. Once again negative figurations of mother Ireland and her children are nothing

new from Joyce's 'old sow that eats her farrow' down to Tom
Murphy's brilliantly resonant *Bailegangaire* (1985) with the senile
grandmother Mommo repeating endlessly her unfinished story.
What is new in *Beauty Queen* is the explicitness of the aggression
and a sort of comic exhilaration in its expression. Here, for instance, is Maureen early on in the play, fantasizing about the arrival
in Leenane of 'the fella up and murdered the poor oul woman in
Dublin'. She wouldn't care about being one of his victims herself,
if he took out her mother as well:

> If he clobbered you with a big axe or something and took your oul
> head off and spat in your neck, I wouldn't mind at all, going first.
> Oh no, I'd enjoy it, I would (*Plays* 1, 6).

There is a cartoon-like gleefulness in this, a grotesque excess in
the language that actually reduces its shock value by taking it out of
the realm of the real. For much of the play, the snarling combat of
Mag and Maureen is the stuff of sitcom, a sort latter-day Irish
Steptoe and Son, the crafty mother using her weakness as strength
against the impotently raging daughter.

But of course the threat of real violence is always there from
the beginning of the play, with the poker as theatrically highlighted
future murder weapon and Mag's burned hand as evidence of
Maureen's past physical abuse of her mother. Maureen's torture of
her mother with the boiling oil later on is a moment of genuine
horror in the theatre. And yet, for all the thrillerish psychological
play with Maureen's past history of mental illness, the emotional
thrust of the action builds behind her urge towards matricide. The
character of Mag, ignorant, cunning, and predatory – a splendid
comic part splendidly created in the original production by Anna
Manahan – has no redeeming features. Audience sympathy, in so
far as a play cauterized by irony allows sympathy, is all directed
towards the situation of Maureen, frustrated, entrapped in her role
as domestic carer, above all, denied the chance of escaping from
the incestuous awfulness of Leenane.

This is the vista of possibility offered in Pato's letter home to
Maureen, love and a future in America which (in this play) is not as
stigmatized as Britain. It is when she discovers that her mother has
destroyed the letter and the glimpse of happiness beyond Leenane,
that Maureen is driven to murder. There is a *grand guignol* frisson in

the moment of revelation at the end of Scene Eight where the dead Mag topples out of her rocking-chair; the futility of the murder is pointed in the last scene where Maureen, like the woman in Beckett's *Rockaby*, has already taken her mother's place in that same rocking-chair. Yet *Beauty Queen* encourages a kind of comic collusion in the need to destroy the mother as it figures the recoil against the motherland with all its mythology of the rural west as primal place of origin. With a mother like Mag, with a home like Leenane, matricide is all but justified.

The scene of *The Weir* may not be exactly a rural idyll but its atmosphere stands in marked contrast to the boredom and brutality of Leenane. We can see some clues why the tone should be so different from McPherson's own account of the source of the play in visits to his grandfather in Jamestown, Co. Leitrim.

> He lived on his own on a country road in a small house beside the Shannon. I remember him telling me once that it was very important to have the radio on because it gave him the illusion of company. We'd have a drink and sit by the fire. And he'd tell me stories. And then when you're lying in bed in the pitch black silence of the Irish countryside it's easy for the imagination to run riot.[6]

The connection back to family country roots, the stories told by the fire, the imaginative liberation of the young writer by rural space and quiet, all these features relate McPherson's vignette of his Leitrim time with his grandfather to traditional romantic pastoral. McPherson's perspective on the rural west, however much less jaundiced than McDonagh's, is equally a view from the city. In fact, McPherson is essentially an urban writer; *The Weir* is his only play with a country setting. All of his other work has been based in or near his home territory of North Dublin, with one excursus to London for *St Nicholas*. His imagination of the rural pub in *The Weir* is a construction of those occasional city boy's visits to his Leitrim grandfather, as McDonagh's Leenane may be assumed to be the product of enforced family holidays in Connemara.

The micro-community that we meet in *The Weir* is a kindly and beneficent one. The very opening piece of business – Jack entering the empty bar, helping himself to a bottle of Guinness in default of a pint due to the broken tap, and punctiliously paying for it – conjures up a homely familiarity breaking down the normal boundaries of the barroom. Even the meaningless exchanges about the weather between Jack and the publican Brendan when he does appear are positive by comparison with the sour opening words of *Beauty Queen*. Though the wind may be strong, Jack comments 'it's mild enough though', and Brendan agrees 'Ah yeah. It's balmy enough'.[7] The threesome of bar regulars, Brendan the publican, Jack the garage owner, and his side-kick and part-time helper Jim, are mutually supportive. Brendan more or less keeps pace with the other two in their drinks, only putting in a purely ritual demurrer:

> **Jack:** Are you having one yourself?
> **Brendan:** I'm debating whether to have one (*The Weir*, 11).

Jack puts bits of work in the way of the less well-off Jim; there is a tacit agreement not to force Jim to pay for full rounds of drinks, and Brendan refuses payment for a small bottle of whiskey from Jim when he is leaving. Jack benefits from Jim's study of racing-form for the occasional tip when he bets in the nearby town of Carrick-on-Shannon.

Somewhat apart from this core group is the other male character, Finbar. A prosperously married auctioneer and hotel-owner, from the locality but having moved to the town, he belongs to the genus of the gombeen-man, the preferred villain of Irish fiction and drama from the nineteenth century on. His characteric vaunting of his material success, his twitting of the backward lads in the country bar with their celibacy, make him an object of suspicion for all of them, downright hostility from Jack, all the more so when he arrives with the young and attractive Valerie in tow. But by gombeen-man standards, Finbar is relatively innocuous. Though the sniping between himself and Jack does flare up into real bad temper at one point, it is followed almost immediately by a reconciliation. We are apparently intended to take at face value his protests against the men's insinuations that he has designs on Valerie:

> That's not fair. The woman's moved out here on her own. There's something obviously going on … in her life. I'm just trying to make it easier for her. Give her a welcome, for fuck's sake. So don't … be implying anything else. I don't like it (*The Weir*, 35).

If Finbar is somewhat apart from the others, he is easily assimilated back into the homosocial bonding of the pub.

Brendan behind the bar, who listens to all the others' stories but never tells one of his own, is the theatrical binding force of the play, and the central representative of its values. He is resistant to the demands of his offstage sisters who want him to realise more of the assets of the pub and farm that are their joint property. He is specially evasive on the subject of the 'top field'. When Jack raises the possibility of making it into a campsite for the German tourists who come each summer, he has his objection ready: 'Ah there wouldn't be a lot of shelter up there, Jack. There's be a wind up there that'd cut you' (*The Weir*, p.10); when Jack suggests a reversal of the plan, with the cattle going up to the top field and the campsite taking their place in a lower field, he is equally non-committal. It is only later, indirectly, that Brendan's real reason for not making any use of the top field comes out, when Finbar introduces the subject of the fairies:

> **Finbar:** […] There was stories all, the fairies be up there in that
> field. Isn't there a fort up there?
> **Brendan:** There's a kind of a one.
> **Valerie:** A fairy fort? […]
> **Brendan:** Well there's a … ring of trees, you know (*The Weir*, p.9).

Brendan will not quite admit his piety towards the local folklore of the fairy rath, but in the light of the story that follows immediately of the consequences of building a house across a fairy road, we are encouraged to respect his traditionalism.

Brendan's pub is imagined close to the Shannon, a popular tourist destination for foreign tourists who holiday on river barges, and the implied time of the action is late spring, shortly before the arrival of the 'Germans'. Even though his livelihood must largely depend on this influx of summer visitors, Brendan does not look forward to their arrival. Jack and Jim, deprived of their familiar habitat will be off to a small pub in town, deserting Brendan as he points out indignantly:

> The two of yous leaving me standing behind that bar with my arms
> folded, picking my hole and not knowing what the hell is going on.
> And them playing all old sixties songs on their guitars. And they
> don't even know the words (*The Weir*, 49).

The 'Germans' are a running subject of conversation through-out the play until, right at the end, Jack raises the question of whether they are in fact German at all: 'Where are they from. Is it Denmark, or Norway?' The play closes on Brendan's muttered throwaway as he prepares to exit – 'Ah I don't know where the fuck they're from' (*The Weir*, 50).

Comic complicity with this mild xenophobia is encouraged in the audience as part of the play's underlying resistance to moder-nity. Remote and desolate as the pub may be, its homely atmosphere and relaxed story-telling represent an alternative life to that of the town or the city. The barroom stands at the edge of the modern world, a last dying vestige of an older community. With its inheritance of oral folklore, it thus represents a late descendant of the Celtic Twilight, and McPherson's *Weir* is a version of Synge's *Aran Islands* pastoral. In this it stands as polar opposite to *Beauty Queen*, where the deadly ennui of Leenane, Ray Dooley's addiction to Australian soaps are taken as normative. Round the Folan fireside no one tells enthralling ghost stories. The best that could befall Maureen or Ray or Pato would be to escape from the intolerable claustrophobia of Leenane. If there is little prospect of them thriving in London or Birmingham or even Boston, if they are likely to return from emigration mentally damaged as Maureen has from Leeds, it is because they carry the stigma of their back-ward provincial Irishness with them. McDonagh's treatment of the modern world is hardly celebratory; but the full force of his satiric scorn is turned on the pastoral trope that privileges the rural over the urban, the trope that *The Weir* works to reinstate.

Archaism and modernity

Both *Beauty Queen* and *The Weir* are set in the contemporary period of their composition and production. *The Weir* announces itself quite simply in the text as 'Present day' (*The Weir*, 2), that is presumably 1997, the date of its première. *Beauty Queen* contains 1990s allusions that specify its period. Mag remarks that 'There was a priest the news Wednesday had a babby with a Yank!', a reference to the Bishop Casey affair. But for Ray Dooley, this is no longer any kind of sensation: 'That's no news at all. That's every-day. It'd be hard to find a priest hasn't had a babby with a Yank'

(*Plays: 1*, 10). The huge disenchantment with the Church in Ireland, initiated by the Bishop Casey scandal and enormously accelerated by the revelation of hushed-up sex abuse cases by priests in the mid-1990s, has already taken hold. Shaun Richards goes so far as to maintain that the 'whole *Trilogy* is set across a matter of months from the summer of 1995 to that of 1996'.[8] But the more you look at the plays, the more this security of period setting unravels.

Ray remembers indignantly Maureen's confiscation of the ball from his swingball-set: 'that was ten years ago and I still haven't forgotten it'; later in the play he gives the exact date as 1979 (*Plays 1*, 38, 58). The picture of the Kennedy brothers on the wall of the Folan cottage is a vignette from the 1960s. The supposedly 1990s Leenane is underwritten by a palimpsest of earlier periods. There is a comparable chronological slippage in *The Weir*. Valerie and her husband both work at DCU, Dublin's most recently created university, upgraded from the NIHE in the 1980s. Their daughter has her swimming lessons in the pool of the CRC, the Central Remedial Clinic. The Dublin milieu she sketches in as the background to her story is perfectly ordinary and contemporary. But even in Leitrim by the mid-1990s how many pubs would there have been where the only wine available was a Christmas present to the publican from several years before: '1990. Now. Vintage, eh?' (*The Weir*, 14) One of the most distinctive features of the modernization of Irish drinking habits in recent years has been the large increase in the consumption of wine. And pubs that cater to summer tourists, even in the depths of the country, have not been slow to stock the range of drinks their customers require.

Both plays show us backward places that are archaic in the context of the modernity of their ostensible setting in time. The difficulty is to pinpoint to what actual socio-cultural period those backward places can be related or to what traditions of literary or theatrical representation. A popular sociological study such as Hugh Brody's *Inishkillane: Change and Decline in the West of Ireland* highlighted the miseries of depopulated rural communities with high rates of celibacy and mental illness.[9] But Brody's research was completed in 1971, the year of McPherson's birth and a year after McDonagh's. Brian Friel, Tom Murphy, and John B. Keane in the 1960s dramatized the moral and social stagnation of the small

town Ireland of the previous decade. Before them there was
Kavanagh's fierce 1940s indictment of land-bound, Church-
oppressed sexual starvation in *The Great Hunger*. And further back
still, a key dimension to the controversy over *The Playboy* was the
erotic charge generated by the supposed father-killer in a parish so
deprived that 'you'd be ashamed this place, going up winter and
summer with nothing worth while to confess at all'.[10] An archaic
West of Ireland, sexually unfulfilled, depleted, and demoralized,
has remained imaginatively live and theatrically viable well past its
period sell-by date. But the uses to which this archaic Ireland is put
by McDonagh and McPherson in its updated modern time-frame
is significantly different.

Some interpreters of McDonagh see the very anomalousness of
the period setting as reflective of the realities of the Irish socio-
cultural situation. Michael Billington, for instance, places Mc-
Donagh's characters as all victims 'of history, of climate and of
rural Ireland's peculiar tension between a suffocating, mythical past
and the banalities of the global village where American soaps hold
sway'.[11] Shaun Richards equally stresses the social actualities that lie
behind McDonagh's grotesque stage images as they do, Richards
argues, behind Synge's. Both playwrights are 'just as alert to the
condition of those idealized on stage but marginalized in reality'.[12]
Alternatively McDonagh can be seen as a postmodernist emptying
out any construction of historical actuality. Fintan O'Toole puts
the paradox of the *Beauty Queen*'s ontological status acutely in his
Introduction to McDonagh's plays:

> The country in which McDonagh's play is set is pre-modern and
> postmodern at the same time. The 1950s is laid over the 1990s,
> giving the play's apparent realism the ghostly, dizzying feel of a
> superimposed photograph. All the elements that make up the
> picture are real, but their combined effect is one that questions the
> very idea of reality (*Plays 1*, xi).

In another context, O'Toole has placed McDonagh's *Trilogy* as
'the culmination of a long demythologization of the West', 'a final
reversal of Romanticism'.[13] What is extraordinary is just how long
that demythologization has gone on, how much of Irish literature
since the time of the Revival has been devoted to this enterprise.
Archaic Ireland is dead but it won't lie down: the fierceness of

McDonagh's iconoclasm feels like an effort to kill it at last. This may also help to explain the peculiar nature of his relationship to Synge as precursor. McDonagh has repeatedly disavowed any knowledge of Synge before starting to write the *Leenane Trilogy*, but the two are always and inevitably compared by theatre reviewers and academic interpeters alike. There are certainly obvious re-semblances between the play in which the son thinks he has murdered his father and that in which the daughter succeeds in murdering the mother. It is as though McDonagh has to take up where Synge left off, outdo him in violence, destroy the parent that Christy so repeatedly failed to kill. At the same time, there is strong sense of parody in his adoption of the Syngean manner, particularly noticeable in the language. McDonagh claims, like Synge, to have based his style on the forms of Irish-English heard in the West:

> In Connemara and Galway, the natural dialogue style is to invert sentences and use strange inflections. Of course, my stuff is a heightening of that, but there is a core strangeness of speech, especially in Galway.[14]

But where Synge put this Hiberno-English strangeness to defamiliarizing poetic effect, in McDonagh it characteristically comes across as uncouth, ungainly and deflationary:

> If it was getting rid of oul lumps I was to be, it wouldn't be with Complan I'd be starting'. 'Be taxicab Pato left, and sad that he never got your goodbye, although why he wanted your goodbye I don't know (*Plays:* 1, 41, 56).

Some critics accuse McDonagh of simply not knowing the dialect well enough to reproduce it correctly, but it may be more de-liberate than that: a caricature of the lyricism of Synge-song, sardonically consigning it to an antiquated stageland of which Leenane is the knowing latter-day travesty.

McPherson's language is in some ways also a challenge to the tradition of Irish fluency and eloquence. His characters speak a convincingly broken demotic, the pauses and silences, the non-signifying noises of 'ahs', 'mms', and 'yeahs' as important as the actual dialogue. Where McDonagh uses the euphemistic obscenity 'feck' throughout, 'fucks' bespatter every other line of

McPherson's male talk. Even when the stories are told, it is with no specially spell-binding *seanchaí* style but in the men's normal colloquial manner.

They arise as it were naturally out of the to and fro of the conversation about the locality to the newcomer Valerie. What the old-fashioned pub offers in fact is a place that naturalizes such story-telling. Valerie does not time-travel back to a community where the tradition of the *seanchas* is still preserved. The men constantly belittle the tales they tell – 'these are only old stories, Valerie', 'You hear all old shit around here, it doesn't mean anything' (*The Weir*, 20). But the recovery of these half-disbelieved folk-stories in the almost derelict pub allows for a progression that brings the uncanny lore of the past forward into the contemporary present.

The stories, in the sequence of their telling, become steadily closer, more personal, and more sinister. Jack's original tale of Maura Nealon's haunted house, though it has the immediacy of being the house Valerie now lives in, is recalled as an incident of 1910 or 1911, coming down at second hand from an old woman who remembered it from childhood. Finbar's story is of something that happened to himself just eighteen years ago and, for all his loud scoffing at the ghostly apparition seen by his neighbour Niamh Walsh, it was enough to change his life by sending him to live in the town. Jim's story of the paedophile, who appears at the digging of his own grave and wants to be buried with his victim, is the more shocking not only because of its subject but because of the unlikeliness of the teller: Jim, by contrast with Finbar and Jack, is no sort of fantasist, nor yet a show-off trying to impress Valerie. He tells it as he remembers it happening to him, desperate to disbelieve it, and it carries the more credibility as a result.

This trajectory supports Valerie's story when it comes. Though hers is directly personal, her experience of bereavement in the death of her young daughter and the haunting comes in the modern technological form of ghost telephone calls it actually re-capitulates the signs and images of the men's stories. Her daughter's name is Niamh, like the girl in Finbar's tale. Niamh suffered from night fears, Valerie tells her listeners:

there were people at the window, there were people in the attic, there was someone coming up the stairs. There were children knocking, in the wall. And there was always a man standing across the road who she'd see (*The Weir*, 38).

This is a reprise of the motifs from the earlier stories: the fairies came knocking at Maura Nealon's doors and at her windows; the little girl's namesake Niamh Walsh was convinced that there was 'something on the stairs'. Even the feared man standing across the road could be seen a reproduction of the child-abuser of Jim's tale.

The strategy of *The Weir* is in fact to collapse the distinction between the world of the archaic country pub and the modern city milieu from which Valerie comes. Loneliness, desolation, sexual perversion, mortality are human experiences common to rural and urban life, the past and the present. What the remote pub setting makes possible is the expression of these experiences in the code of the uncanny which still retains some degree of authority. An implicitly modern urban audience is drawn with Valerie into the atmosphere of the pub and encouraged to believe in a scene that is simultaneously quaintly different and familiarly recognizable. The naturalizing of the men's traditional style storytelling then facilitates a return to Valerie's ordinary modern tragedy. It is a system of double bridging back to the past and forward to the present again that supports a universal humanism common to both. By contrast, *Beauty Queen* denies reality as much to the modern Leenane fed on re-run imported TV as to the antiquated idea of the rural west that it so mercilessly parodies.

Conclusion: conflict and consolation

In a 1992 essay looking back on traditions of Irish drama, Thomas Kilroy concluded:

A place apart, a place retaining some of the innocence of the pre-modern, a kind of literary environmentalism, a version of greenery, some Irish writing has always answered this appeal, sometimes shamelessly, from readers and audiences outside Ireland. Certain stereotypes of Irish writing and the Irish writer have thereby become entrenched, the Irish writer as roaring boyo, for example, or as untutored, natural genius and Irish writing as a pure, natural flow of words, untouched by a contaminating intelligence. As traditional Ireland fades into the past these stereotypes become even more absurd and are best consigned to pulp fiction. And as it does, nostalgia may no longer be enough, indeed it may not even be necessary as Irish drama begins to locate itself more in the present.[15]

José Lanters, who quotes this passage, comments on how ironic it is coming five years before the spectacular success of Martin McDonagh. Certainly McDonagh has been cast by the media in the role of Irish 'roaring boyo': the much-publicized incident when he told Sean Connery to 'fuck off' is the exact equivalent of Brendan Behan's drunken appearance on British television just forty years earlier.[16] McPherson's *The Weir* equally answers to other parts of Kilroy's taxonomy of Irish dramatic stereotyping: 'a place apart, a place retaining some of the innocence of the pre-modern'. The poster advertising the play in its two-month summer season run at the Gate Theatre in Dublin in 1998 showed that most traditional of Irish pastoral images, a little grey cottage beside a mountain stream. Kilroy could not foresee the new variations played upon these standard tropes of Irishness by McDonagh and McPherson, nor yet their remarkable popularity, even when traditional Ireland in the late 1990s was fading into the past more rapidly than at any other time in its history.

What the two plays analysed in this essay illustrate are the very different Ireland of the mind that remain current and available. One enthusiastic reviewer of *The Weir* hailed it for its difference: 'McPherson's play is not, like every other Irish play, about betrayal and conflict – more about the powers of consolation and community'.[17] *Beauty Queen*, and even more McDonagh's plays that have succeeded it, represent some sort of culmination of the tradition of the Irish play about betrayal and conflict. Synge's *Playboy* may be said to have started that tradition, outraging its audiences by the portrayal of a violent crime-loving Mayo community at a time when nationalists felt the urgent need to combat British misrepresentations of the Irish as irredeemably lawless. The latter-day audiences of the late twentieth century, Irish or non-Irish, were coolly unshockable, conditioned by the films of McDonagh's much-admired Quentin Tarantino among others. Ireland, though, provided a satisfyingly appropriate setting for unending, grotesque, and unresolvable conflict. There was not only the precedent of Synge, the tragicomic tradition of O'Casey and Behan, to sponsor a staged Ireland of violent absurdity; there were the bloody, continuing 'Troubles' in the North. It is only in *The Lieutenant of Inishmore* that McDonagh has taken a politically related subject, the central figure Padraic being an INLA dissident, too bloodthirsty even for the INLA. But its representation of the futile, meaningless, and mindless violence of the fringe para-militaries may cast light back on the reception of the *Leenane Trilogy*, non-political as the subject there may have appeared to be. McDonagh's hyperviolent Ireland is of one piece and chimes satis-factorily with a composite Irish imaginary matching of rural depression with irrational fanaticism. Whether daughter murdering mother or one political faction torturing another, this is a scene of primal, internecine feuding: what can you do but laugh?

If in *Beauty Queen* the sheer empty eventlessness of the characters' lives builds inexorably to a climax of violent action, the pub talk of *The Weir* goes nowhere in particular, issues in no denouement or catastrophe. The play is nothing but the language of which it is made up. It may not constitute the 'pure, natural flow of words' Kilroy sees as typical of the received notion of Irish writing. Rather it is a dramatic manifestation of Coleridge's line used as part of the epigraph to one of McPherson's earlier plays: 'No sound is dissonant which tells of life'.[18] But if McPherson's dialogue is halting and colloquial, without the obvious fluent lyri-cism of a Synge or O'Casey, or indeed of Sebastian Barry nearer McPherson's own time, it depends for its success with audiences on the accumulated credibility of language in the Irish dramatic tradition. To Irish playwrights it is permitted to trust the voice in the theatre, to depend, as McPherson does, on language alone without the support of spectacle and action. Hence his preference for the monologue form used in almost all his plays; in *The Weir* the monologues are only masked by the device of the pub story-telling.

'Consolation and community' are the distinctive features of the play so highly valued by Robert Gore Langton. The community spirit of the little group of bar regulars is certainly one of the at-tractive features of *The Weir*, seen as a necessary solidarity in people living in this remote, out-of-the-way place. But the reason they need communal consolation is the desolate separateness of their lives. The monologue itself is expressive of the loneliness that is McPherson's master theme in all his work. The consolations afforded to the men by sharing the stories in the pub, to Valerie in being able to tell hers, are passing alleviations of an isolated condition for which nothing ultimately can be done. However, the theatrical structure of the play allows the audience to share in such consolations, to be incorporated in this temporary community by becoming listeners to the stories. This simple space, conjured up in talk, in which we can feel at one with the characters in their transient togetherness, is another version of an imagined Ireland and its otherness. For those who appreciate McDonagh's harder-edged satire, McPherson may seem soft-centred and sentimental; McPherson partisans may find McDonagh heartless and meretricious. But neither playwright could have made the impact he has done without the alternate fields of Irishness in which *Beauty Queen* and *The Weir* are theatrically located.

---

[1] This essay was originally published in *Yearbook of English Studies* 35 (2005), 298-311.

[2] Sean O'Hagan, 'The Wild West', *The Guardian* 24 March 2001.

[3] See Ian Kilroy, 'The One-trick Pony of Connemara', *Magill* January 2000.

[4] Conor McPherson, 'If you're a young Irish playwright come to London. If you can put up with being defined by your nationality, the opportunities are huge', *New Statesman* 20 February 1998.

[5] Martin McDonagh, *Plays: 1* (London: Methuen, 1999), p.1. Further quotations from the play from this edition will be cited parenthetically in the text.

[6] Conor McPherson, Preface, *St Nicholas and The Weir: Two Plays* (Dublin: New Island Books; London: Nick Hern Books, 1997), p.viii.

[7] Conor McPherson, *The Weir* (London: Nick Hern Books, 1998), p.4. This revised edition is used for all further quotations from the play, cited parenthetically in the text.

[8] Shaun Richards, '"The Outpouring of a Morbid, Unhealthy Mind": The Critical Condition of Synge and McDonagh', *Irish University Review* 33 (Spring/Summer 2003), p.203.

[9] Hugh Brody, *Inishkillane: Change and Decline in the West of Ireland*

(Harmondsworth: Penguin, 1974).

[10] J.M. Synge, *Collected Works* Vol. IV: *Plays*, Book 2, ed. Ann Saddlemyer (London: Oxford University Press, 1968), p.97.

[11] Quoted in José Lanters, 'Playwrights of the Western World: Synge, Murphy, McDonagh' in *A Century of Irish Drama: Widening the Stage*, eds Stephen Watt, Eileen Morgan, and Shakir Mustafa (Bloomington and Indianapolis: Indiana University Press, 2000), p.220.

[12] Richards, p.207.

[13] Quoted by Lanters, p.221.

[14] Quoted in Joseph Feeney S.J., 'Martin McDonagh: Dramatist of the West', *Studies* 87, 1998, p.28.

[15] Thomas Kilroy, 'A Generation of Playwrights', *Irish University Review* 22 (Spring-Summer 1992), p.141.

[16] See Sean O'Hagan, 'The Wild West' for an account of the Connery incident.

[17] Robert Gore Langton, *The Express* 19 October 1998.

[18] Conor McPherson, *Four Plays* (London: Nick Hern Books, 1999), p.85. The play is *This Lime Tree Bower*; both the title and the epigraph are taken from Coleridge's poem 'This Lime Tree Bower My Prison'.

4 | The Stage Irish Are Dead, Long Live the Stage Irish: *The Lonesome West* and *A Skull in Connemara*

Paul Murphy

When the brothers Valene and Coleman Connor learn of Father Welsh's suicide from Girleen Kelleher in Martin McDonagh's play *The Lonesome West*, their initial response is one of nervous amusement until the enormity of the situation hits them:

> **Coleman**: *(pause)* Did you see 'Roderick' his name is?
> **Valene**: *(snorts)* I did.
> **Coleman**: *(pause. Seriously)* We shouldn't laugh.
> **Valene** *nods. Both pull serious faces. Blackout.*[1]

In this brief exchange we witness the incursion of a traumatic event; the knee-jerk reaction to that event with nervous amusement; then the guilty recognition that such a reaction is ethically dubious. The first two stages of this exchange are typical of McDonagh's theatrical formula in the deployment of a common human response to traumatic events, and could go some way to explaining his popular success in the UK, Ireland, and the USA. The third stage of this exchange however is untypical as it involves somber reflection on the ethics of laughing away the traumatic effects of another person's demise, the reflective quality of which is made more profound because the exchange ends the scene, thus allowing the audience time to reflect. Such moments are rare in a fast and furious style based largely on proven devices from the theatrical traditions of farce and melodrama. The problem which this chapter focuses on is McDonagh's reliance upon the first two stages of this device, which involves the comic mediation of traumatic events in *The Lonesome West* and is the hallmark of his style in the related plays in the Leenane trilogy, *The Beauty Queen of Leenane* and *A Skull in Connemara*. To analyse this problem I will combine a traditional text-based reading of *The Lonesome West* with a performance analysis of the An Grianán Theatre/Lyric Theatre co-production of the play at the Lyric Theatre from 16 September to 15 October, during its tour in Autumn 2005. I will relate the comic mediation of trauma to the notion of Stage Irishry allegedly inherent to McDonagh's dramaturgy, and conclude that the popular acclaim which McDonagh's plays have received involves a degree of complicity with and even endorsement of the comic mediation of pain and suffering.

Much of the debate around McDonagh's work has engaged with his London-Irish provenance; his insistence that he is an Irish playwright; and the veracity of his representation of Irish rural communities. Anthony Roche notes that:

> the charge of stage Irishry, and in particular of racial stereotyping and mis-representation of the Irish peasant as prone to violence, has been levelled at McDonagh, as it was before him at Synge. These writers, it is claimed, do not know these people and sub-stitute for their lack of understanding a wilful and calculated stage effect.[2]

For Roche, the question 'whether negatively or positively put, has to do with distance' and he cites Thomas Kilroy's observation that plays by Anglo-Irish dramatists involve "a characteristic distancing effect, a cool remove of the playwright from his subject matter"'.[3] Later in the article Roche questions Kilroy's implication that 'a native Catholic playwright could achieve an almost unmediated intimacy with his or her audience', and engages with the 'generally accepted humour in McDonagh's plays and their infliction of pain', concluding that 'there is relish of the sadism and punishment for its own sake'.[4]

What is interesting here is Roche's adroit shift from the debate on national identity and its link to representational authenticity which has formed the superstructure of many debates in Irish theatre studies, to a focus on the ethics of McDonagh's autotelic representation of pain and suffering. Aleks Sierz situates McDonagh's plays in the 'in-yer-face' genre of 1990s British New Brutalist theatre, arguing that

> [h]owever hilarious, they seemed to be repeating the same postmodern trick[…] they do lack compassion. If this does not matter too much in one play, its absence in a trilogy leads to a sense of depressing futility.[5]

Sierz suggests that the 'widest definition of in-yer-face theatre is any drama that takes the audience by the scruff of the neck and shakes it until it gets the message.'[6] With in-yer-face

> the language is usually filthy, characters talk about unmentionable subjects, take their clothes off, have sex, humiliate each other, experience unpleasant emotions, become suddenly violent.[7]

Many of these elements are part and parcel of McDonagh's theatrical formula, but the message that is supposed to underlie and ultimately justify the vulgarity and brutality is obscured to the point of nullity.

The grab-the-audience-by-the-scruff-of-the-neck approach is evident in the opening scene of *The Lonesome West*. Coleman remarks under his breath what a 'dumb fecking question' it is to ask the alcoholic priest Father Welsh for a drink, after they have just buried Coleman and Valene's father. When Welsh remarks that 'Valene does be a biteen tight with his money,' Coleman retorts:

> A biteen? He'd steal the shite out of a burning pig, and this is his poteen too, so if he comes in shouting the odds tell him you asked me outright for it. Say you sure enough demanded. That won't be hard to believe.[8]

As far as Coleman is concerned, the mourners at the funeral are a 'pack of vultures only coming nosing' with 'Maryjohnny' singled-out for particular scorn:

> *Vol-au-vents*, feck. The white-haired oul ghoulish fecking whore. She's owed me the price of a pint since nineteen-seventy-fecking-seven. It's always tomorrow with that bitch. I don't care if she does have Alzheimer's. If I had a *vol-au-vent* I'd shove it up her arse.[9]

When Valene returns with more of his beloved figurines of Catholic saints, the dysfunctional relationship between the siblings is made abundantly clear:

> **Valene**: Fibreglass.
> **Coleman**: *(pause)* Feck fibre-glass.
> **Valene**: No, feck you instead of feck fibreglass.
> **Coleman**: No, feck you two times instead of feck fibreglass.[10]

The response which I witnessed to this opening gambit from Lyric audiences across the run from the first night through several performances up to the closing night, was regularly one which began with nervous giggling at the start of the scene, developing to muted sniggering and then raucous laughter as the remorseless rhythm of sarcasm kept pounding on.

The vulgar tone continues unabated in the rest of the scene when the seventeen-year-old Girleen (capably performed by Charlene McKenna) enters intent on selling poteen to Valene, and responds with indifference to news of the funeral as she delivers a letter from the postman she met on the way in:

> **Girleen:** That postman fancies me, d'you know? I think he'd like to be getting into me knickers, in fact I'm sure of it.
> **Coleman:** Him and the rest of Galway, Girleen.
> *Welsh puts his head in his hands at this talk.*
> **Girleen:** Galway minimum. The EC more like. Well, a fella won't be getting into my knickers on a postman's wages. I'll tell you that, now.[11]

When Valene tries to swindle her out of a pound her response is as ferocious as it is irreverent:

> **Girleen**: You're the king of stink-scum fecking filth-bastards you, ya bitch-feck, Valene.
> **Welsh**: Don't be swearing like that now, Girleen.
> **Girleen**: Ah me hairy arse, Father.[12]

A Skull in Connemara similarly opens with smutty references to teenage sexuality conjoined with sacrilegious banter. When the septuagenarian Maryjohnny catches the local school children kissing she calls them 'a pack o' whores' and complains about them to the quinquagenarian Mick Dowd:

> No harm to anybody, is it, Mick? And the three I caught weeing in
> the churchyard and when I told them I'd tell Father Cafferty, what
> did they call me? A fat oul biddy![13]

Maryjohnny's vinegary attitude is paralleled in the same scene in
the interaction between Mick and the young Mairtin Hanlon
whose conversation is more diatribe than dialogue. Mairtin's constant begging for poteen irritates Mick into a display of malice:

> **Mick:** *pours a small amount of poteen out onto his fingers and tosses it at*
> ***Mairtin** as if it's holy water. It hits **Mairtin** in the eyes.* Bless yourself,
> now, Mairtin.[14]

Spiteful provocation is also the order of the day in *The Lonesome
West* as Coleman and Valene seize every opportunity to savage
each other. When the letter Girleen delivers is revealed to be
Valene's inheritance cheque which he rubs under the disinherited
Coleman's nose, a fight breaks out between the brothers and the
beleaguered Welsh gets a kick in the shin for trying to break them
up:

> **Welsh:** What kind of a town is this at all? Brothers fighting and
> lasses peddling booze and two fecking murderers on the loose?
> **Girleen:** And me pregnant on top of it. *(Pause.)* I'm not really.
> **Welsh** *looks at her and them sadly, moving somewhat drunkenly to the
> door.*[15]

The answer to Welsh's question is of course that the 'town' is a
conglomeration of social problems which are hyperbolized
through slapstick routines that serve to render the characters as
clowns and thus desensitize the audience to the trauma underlying
the representation of those problems in theatrical form. Judging
from their jovial reaction the Lyric audiences consistently received
the play as a broad farce, and while the roles of Valene and
Coleman were exquisitely played respectively by Frank McCusker
and Lalor Roddy, and skilfully directed by Mikel Murfi, the
traumatic effects of the social problems which are alluded to in the
play are subdued by its farcical nature.

McDonagh's plays are often discussed in relation to those of
J.M. Synge and debate usually centers on their representation
and/or perceived misrepresentation of rural communities. While
the comparisons are understandable insofar as McDonagh offers a

postmodern debunking of truisms about the West of Ireland that have accumulated over the years, in contradistinction to Synge's modernist fetishization of peasant life on the western seaboard and derogation of bourgeois aspiration,[16] a more useful comparison would be with Sean O'Casey's Dublin trilogy. In *Twentieth Century Irish Drama* Christopher Murray argues that

> [f]rom the perspective of the 1990s O'Casey stands out as Ireland's greatest playwright of the century. He it was who most passionately, most powerfully and most memorably dramatized the traumatic birth of a nation[…] He was the first English-speaking dramatist to make the poor, the undereducated and the dispossessed the subjects of modern tragi-comedy.[17]

In contrast Declan Kiberd states that

> O'Casey's code scarcely moved beyond a sentimentalization of victims, and this in turn led him to a profound distrust of anyone who makes an idea the basis for an action.[18]

Kiberd suggests that *The Plough and the Stars* is indicative of O'Casey's uneven account of the birth of a nation insofar as

> the nationalist case is never put, merely mocked.[…] not for even twenty minutes of a two-and-a-half hour play are the rebels allowed to state their case. The extracts used from Pearse's speeches are highly selective, focusing on his blood-rhetoric at the grave of O'Donovan Rossa, but giving no indication of his support for Dublin workers during the Lock Out of 1913.[19]

Sentimentalization of victims is the key issue in O'Casey's representation of socially subordinate characters, especially in the deployment of comedy as a dramaturgical strategy which mediates class disparity. Comic mediation is indicated in Aristotle's definition of comedy as

> an imitation of inferior people – not, however, with respect to every kind of defect: the laughable is a species of what is disgraceful. The laughable is an error or disgrace that does not involve pain or destruction; for example, a comic mask is ugly and distorted, but does not involve pain.[20]

In this sense one can see how comedy can be used as a way of mediating the trauma of class disparity, to render socially 'inferior' people as ridiculous and 'disgraceful' in a way that 'is ugly and distorted, but does not involve [the] pain' of absorbing the opprobrium intrinsic to that social inferiority. Kiberd notes O'Casey's 'delight in the comic male pair', highlighting the influence upon his dramaturgy of Victorian melodrama, especially the work of Dion Boucicault which goes some way to explain O'Casey's popular appeal which 'saved the Abbey from financial ruin by wooing large numbers of the Queen's audience to his plays'.[21]

While O'Casey registers the social symptoms inherent to bourgeois hierarchies, he does so in a way which mediates the ant-agonistic nature of those hierarchies, turning the Dublin proletariat into a spectacle to be viewed from a safe symbolic distance. O'Casey's reliance on comedy to soften the edge of his dramatic representation can be explained somewhat in this extract from Joseph Holloway's journal:

> I was speaking to Sean O'Casey who doesn't like [T.C.] Murray's plays because they take too much out of him. Both *Birthright* and *Maurice Harte* distressed him very much in witnessing. He likes his plays with brightness intermingled with sadness. The comedy of life appeals to him most. [...] O'Casey loves Shaw's work because in the very kernel of tragedy he can introduce something to make one laugh its sting away. Murray never does this his tragedy is ever unrelieved.[22]

Where O'Casey uses comic mediation to over-sentimentalize his characters, McDonagh uses the same device to radically de-sentimentalize his characters – in both cases comic mediation serves to neutralize or at the very least diminish rather than enhance a traumatic effect on the audience. The effect to be achieved is of course a matter of interpretation of the play for the stage and direction of the play on the stage, and while the performance accretions since the first productions of O'Casey's plays have resulted in a legacy of increasingly broad, comic renditions, Garry Hynes's 1991 production of *The Plough and the Stars* at the Abbey Theatre served to heighten the traumatic potential of the play.[23] Whether McDonagh's plays will have to wait a similar period of time before the traumatic potential is realized remains to be seen, as the performance accretions since their first productions in the 1990s have resulted in a legacy not dissimilar to O'Casey's, specifically where UK and USA receptions of McDonagh's work are concerned, which will be discussed in the conclusion to this chapter.

The poet F.R. Higgins's reaction to the first production of *The Plough and the Stars* and the concomitant protests at the production, constitutes an acerbic analysis of O'Casey's portrayal of Dublin life:

> One is eager to have the opinions of our dramatic critics on a technique largely based upon the revue structure, in the quintessence of an all-Abbey burlesque, intensified by 'divarsions' and Handy Andy incidents, with the more original settings offered by Sean O'Casey. That aspect of comedy so gushly over-portrayed from Dublin artisan life, as seen only by this playwright, merely affords laborious bowing on one-string fiddle – and 'Fluther' Good's is just the successor of Captain Boyle's more lively ragtime. […] If, as a sincere artist, Mr O'Casey interpreted the raw life he is supposed to know, the sure strokes of a great dramatist would have painted such a picture of the Dublin underworld that instead of driving some to demolish the theatre, they would be driven out in horror to abolish the slum.[24]

The spirit of Higgins's critique and its relationship to comic mediation can be brought to bear upon McDonagh's portrayal of Galway life specifically in terms of the theatricalization of social problems including: domestic violence; religious disillusionment; sibling rivalry; emotional and intellectual under-development.

The plot structure of *The Lonesome West* is in many ways driven by the traumatic consequences of domestic violence inasmuch as most of the play deals with the fallout subsequent to Coleman's act of patricide and its effect on the two brothers, which Valene explains here to Welsh:

> Didn't dad make a jibe about Coleman's hairstyle, and didn't Coleman dash out, pull him back be the hair and blow the poor skulleen out his head, the same as he'd been promising to do since the age of eight and da trod on his Scalectrix, broke it in two.[25]

The implications of years of patriarchal abuse stretching back to early childhood is evident here, but the farcical way in which the consequences of that abuse are presented serves to trivialize what was and still is a problem in Irish society. Prior to Valene's explanation to Welsh of Coleman's patricide, Coleman had melted all Valene's figurines in a bowl in Valene's new oven in a childish act of vengeance. Valene's reaction is one of melodramatic anguish and his cartoon fury against Coleman is falteringly negotiated by an exasperated Welsh:

> **Welsh:** Tell me you didn't shoot your dad on purpose, Coleman. Please, now.
> **Valene:** This isn't about our fecking dad! This is about me fecking figurines!
> **Coleman:** Do you see this fella's priorities?[26]

Sandwiched as it is between Coleman's childish destruction of Valene's figurines and Valene's hysterical reaction to his brother's juvenile prank, the factum brutum of patricide is enveloped by tomfoolery and the cycle of domestic violence keeps on turning.

The melodrama escalates to the point where Valene threatens to shoot Coleman with the same shotgun used to kill their father. During the brothers' tooing-and-froing to grab hold of the 'bullets', Welsh intervenes with perhaps the most viscerally shocking act in the entire play as he immerses his hands in the bowl containing the burning liquid until he can bear it no longer and then emits a '*horrifying high-pitched wail lasting about ten seconds, during which **Valene** and **Coleman** stop fighting, stand, and try to help him.*'[27] The use of boiling liquid in a similarly horrific manner occurs earlier in the trilogy in *The Beauty Queen of Leenane* in the particularly grizzly scene seven, where Maureen tortures her elderly mother Mag because she has witheld important information regarding a potentially life-changing liaison between Maureen and her paramour Pato Dooley. Maureen's demeanour during the torture is perhaps the most chilling aspect as her cold, matter-of-fact pragmatism contrasts with the searing pain her mother endures:

> **Maureen** *slowly and deliberately takes her mother's shrivelled hand, holds it down on the burning range, and starts slowly pouring some of the hot oil over it, as* **Mag** *screams in pain and terror.*[28]

The torture continues through the scene as Maureen ruthlessly interrogates Mag until she gets the information she wants and prepares to leave her mother presumably to die on the floor as

Maureen sets out on what she thinks will be a new life in America with Pato:

> **Mag:** (*quietly*) But who'll look after me, so?
> **Mag**, *still shaking, looks down at her scalded hand. Blackout.*[29]

At no point during the scene is the trauma neutralized with re-assuring comic relief; Maureen behaves like an archetypal psycho-path as she calmly brutalizes her mother with the easy familiarity of someone who has (judging by the shrivelled state of Mag's hand before the oil is poured on) done this before.

In sharp contrast to Mag's ordeal, Father Welsh's torment is juxtaposed with the brothers' buffoonery through scene three in *The Lonesome West*. When the brothers try to calm the priest down, the mispronunciation of Welsh's name by characters throughout the Leenane trilogy reaches its farcical apogee:

> **Valene:** Father Walsh, now …
> **Coleman:** Father Walsh, Father Walsh …
> **Welsh** *pulls his fists out of the bowl, red raw, stifles his screams again, looks over the shocked* **Valene** *and* **Coleman** *in despair and torment, smashes the bowl off the table and dashes out through the front door, his fists clutched to his chest in pain.*
> **Welsh:** (*exiting, screaming*) Me name's Welsh!!!
> **Valene** *and* **Coleman** *stare after him a moment or two.*
> **Coleman:** Sure that fella's pure mad.
> **Valene:** He's outright mad.[30]

While this act is physically shocking on the page, the reaction to it on the stage was much less so at least in terms of the Lyric production, where the effects of Welsh's self-immolation were sidelined by the brothers' antics. The waves of laughter rippling through the audiences at every performance I attended, both before and during the event, served to wash away the traumatic effects of the horrifying spectacle. Indeed the audiences continued laughing as Welsh dashed off the stage screaming in agony, and a fresh wave of laughter greeted the brothers' dim-witted reaction to Welsh's masochism.

The 1990s witnessed a plethora of scandals each of which successively rocked the Catholic Church in Ireland: in 1992 Eamon Casey, the Bishop of Galway, was revealed as the father of a teenage boy; in 1994 a Dublin priest died in a gay sauna, while in the same year Father Brendan Smyth's litany of paedophilia came to the fore. In 1995

> the hypocrisy of the country's best-known priest, Fr Michael Cleary, was exposed after his death. He had used his own radio show and newspaper column to espouse his extreme conservatism in relation to celibacy and matters of sexual morality, and was now revealed to have had a child with his live-in house-keeper.[31]

In this context, McDonagh's 1997 portrayal of Father Welsh is all the more resonant, but the exaggerated portrayal of Welsh is typical of the media representation of the priesthood at the time. As Diarmaid Ferriter explains,

> the media occasionally went overboard, to the extent that one newspaper in reviewing the year 1997 referred to it as the 'the year of the paedophile priest,' narrowing the scope of a discussion and reflection that needed to go much further than that.[32]

Such 'narrowing' is manifest in the play in terms of the two-dimensional approach to the traumatic issue of paedophilia in the Irish Catholic Church and is typified in this instance:

> **Welsh:** I'm a terrible priest, so I am. I can never be defending God when people go saying things agin him, and, sure, isn't that the main qualification for being a priest?
> **Coleman:** Ah there be a lot worse priests than you, Father, I'm sure. The only thing with you is you're a bit too weedy and you're a terror for the drink and you have doubts about Catholicism. Apart from that you're a fine priest. Number one you don't go abusing five-year-olds so, sure, doesn't that give you a head-start over half the priests in Ireland?[33]

The Lyric audience response at each performance I saw was a cacophony of 'oohs' and 'aahs' and uncertain laughter at the severity and irreverence, which turned into general jollity when Welsh responds:

> That's no comfort at all, and them figures are overexaggerated anyways. I'm a terrible priest, and I run a terrible parish, and that's the end of the matter. Two murderers I have on me books, and I can't get either of the beggars to confess to it. About betting on the horses and impure thoughts is all them bastards ever confess.[34]

The quick undermining of such a serious and complex issue as paedophilia with the mundane naughtiness of Welsh's flock is typical of McDonagh's bathetic style in which anything and anyone are fair game.

The problem with such radical iconoclasm in the classical sense of the term is that in the final analysis we are left, like Valene at the end of the play when Coleman has destroyed his replacement figurines in another childish act of vengeance, standing in the wreckage of broken icons, with nothing and no one left to believe in. The precedent for sacrilegious destruction is established in McDonagh's earlier play *A Skull in Connemara* in scene seven where Mick Dowd has been driven to the brink of despair in the discovery that his dead wife's remains have been violated by the corrupt Garda officer Thomas Hanlon. In a surreal parody of the existential crisis of the graveyard scene in *Hamlet*, the drunken grave-digger Mick retrieves the relics peculiar to his profession and '*brings the mallet crashing down on the skull nearest to him, shattering it, spraying pieces of it all over the room*'.[35] What starts out as a moment of surrealism tinged with more than a tint of alcohol fuelled anguish, quickly descends into farcical clowning as Mick and young Mairtin start smashing skulls and bones with wild abandon as:

> **Mairtin** *takes a little run-up and starts smashing another of the skulls and its bones to pieces. The smashing continues more or less unabated by at least one of the men throughout most of the rest of the scene.*[36]

Such desecration recurs in *The Lonesome West* when Coleman experiences a momentary lapse of reason in his fury at Valene and

> *holding the shotgun by the barrel, starts smashing it violently into the figurines, shattering them to pieces and sending them flying around the room until not a single one remains standing.* **Valene** *screams throughout. After* **Coleman** *has finished he sits again, the gun across his lap.* **Valene** *is still kneeling.*[37]

While the trauma felt by the various protagonists in both plays is quite palpable, it is simultaneously rendered farcical by the slapstick quality inherent to such grotesque antics. While the moral vacuity in this scene may be symptomatic of the late postmodern condition, its bleakness is untenable and for Welsh it is unlivable as he decides to take his own life in order to shock the two brothers into an act of profound self-reflection. Welsh's dictation of his suicide letter received a round of applause at all the performances that I attended, and it is indeed the only redeeming feature in a play where the characters are at various stages on the road to perdition. However the applause seemed more in admiration of Enda Kilroy's sustained delivery of Welsh's monologue, with excellent diction at a whip-cracking pace, than for the sincerity of the speech's emotional content and the brute fact of Welsh's supreme sacrifice in his effort to redeem the wayward brothers.

When the brothers engage in a short-lived process of reconciliation inspired by Welsh's suicide note, the years of accumulated spite born of sibling rivalry explodes in a highly theatricalized chain reaction of cathartic exchanges. A typical exchange involves this evocation of childhood malice:

> **Valene:** Half me childhood you spent stepping on me head, and for no reason. And d'you remember when you pinned me down and sat across me on me birthday and let the stringy spit dribble out your gob and let down and down it dribble 'til it landed in me eye then?
>
> **Coleman:** I remember it well, Valene, and I'll tell you this. I did mean to suck that spit back up just before it got to your eye, but what happened I lost control o'er it.[38]

The manner in which these lines were delivered in the Lyric production served to enhance the childish quality of the language, insofar as the brothers' posture was sufficiently juvenile and their tone of voice manifested the whiny consistency of pre-pubescent school boys. When combined with the repellent image of dripping saliva, which made many in the audience moan and squirm with muted disgust before laughing uncomfortably, the overall effect served to nullify the distressing content of the exchange by conflating fraternal abuse with boyish silliness.

The cathartic exchange designed to purge the bitterness of sibling rivalry quickly descends into a heartless game of attrition:

> **Valene:** This is a great oul game, this is, apologizing. Father Welsh wasn't too far wrong.
>
> **Coleman:** I hope Father Welsh isn't in hell at all. I hope he's in heaven.[39]

Matters escalate in the penultimate exchange when Valene describes how he thwarted a potential liaison between Coleman and his childhood sweetheart:

> **Valene:** D'you remember when Alison O'Hoolihan went sucking that pencil in the playground that time, and ye were to go dancing the next day, but somebody nudged that pencil and it got stuck in her tonsils on her, and be the time she got out of hospital she was engaged to the doctor who wrenched it out for her and wouldn't be giving you a fecking sniffeen. Do you remember, now?
> **Coleman:** I do remember.
> **Valene:** That was me nudged that pencil, and it wasn't an accident at all. Pure jealous I was.
> *Pause.* **Coleman** *throws his sausage rolls in* **Valene's** *face and dives over the table for his neck.* **Valene** *dodges the attack.*[40]

When Coleman manages to control his rage, then his sorrow and palpable sense of loss become abundantly clear: 'I did fecking love Alison O'Hoolihan! We may've been married today if it hadn't been for that fecking pencil!'[41] Valene's heartless dismissal of his brother's feelings and inability to show remorse or any real sense of guilt is rendered in such a facile way that it makes a mockery of his brother's pain: 'That pencil is water under a bridge and I've apologized whole-hearted for that pencil. (*Sits down.*) And she had boss-eyes anyways.'[42] The quick-fire rate of delivery served to heighten the comedy for the Lyric audiences, insofar as Coleman's rage seemed like melodramatic histrionics and Valene's remorse-lessness rendered the exchange as a childish squabble instead of an adult discussion about emotional scarification.

The sibling rivalry and fraternal abuse are themselves related to the brothers' emotional and intellectual underdevelopment. A par-ticularly problematic instance of this is their description of Africans and Asians respectively as 'Darkies' and 'Paki-men', terms that are childishly racist and serve to render the brothers as ignorant brutes who are unaware of the shift in language con-sequent to the civil rights movements which led to political correctness. It is interesting that the childish language which the brothers use seemed to mediate the inherent racism of the terms, insofar as the audiences laughed off the effects as easily as they laughed at Girleen's bawdy language or Welsh's self-immolation. The way in which Valene describes 'Paki-men, same as whistle at the snakes'[43] evokes the sentiments of a bygone age, before the new phenomenon of immigration presented challenges to how

Irish people perceived different races within their own national borders. As Ferriter notes:

> The writer John Ardagh, who compiled his book *Ireland and the Irish* in the early 1990s, remarked: 'if Asiatics or Africans were ever to arrive in some numbers, would the Irish remain so tolerant?' Judging by the racism evident in Ireland by the end of the 1990s, the answer was a resounding no.[44]

In this context McDonagh's use of such childish racism is ethically spurious as it serves to render the brothers as backward buffoons in a theatrical formula overstuffed with swaggering, postmodern mischief. Another example of this kind of overblown pastiche is the discussion of the Bosnian amputee:

> **Valene:** There's a lad here in Bosnia and not only has he no arms but his mammy's just died. (*Mumbles as he reads, then:*) Ah they're only after fecking money, the same as ever.
> **Coleman:** And no fear of you sending that poor no-armed boy any money, ah no.
> **Valene:** They've probably only got him to put his arms behind his back, just to cod ya.
> **Coleman:** It's any excuse for you.
> **Valene:** And I bet his mammy's fine.[45]

The effect of Valene's cynicism on the Lyric audiences was variously: bemusement; sniggering; nervous amusement; and guilty yet fairly raucous laughter. The sheer nihilism of this exchange in terms of any underlying message which might justify Valene's heartlessness stands in stark contrast to the impact that the Bosnian civil war had on McDonagh's contemporary Sarah Kane, whose play *Blasted*[46] deliberately attempted to drive the horror of civil war into the minds of theatregoers in Britain. Kane clearly states that:

> I think with *Blasted* that it was a direct response to material as it began to happen [...] I switched on the news one night while I was having a break from writing, and there was a very old woman's face in Srebrenica just weeping and looking into the camera and saying – 'please, please, somebody help us, because we need the UN to come here and help us.' I thought this is absolutely terrible [...][47]

It is this political commitment which ultimately justifies all the brutality and shock tactics that are used in *Blasted* to get Kane's message across that 'the seeds of full-scale war can always be found in peace-time civilization'.[48] In McDonagh's *The Lonesome West* there is no such justification for the brutality, viciousness and cynicism. While one could argue that in postmodern aesthetics there does not have to be a justification, that the 'message' is a matter of interpretation, what we are left with in this case is the autotelic use of brutality for no reason other than audience titillation through the comic mediation of pain and destruction.

This raises difficult ethical questions about not only the production but also the reception of McDonagh's plays. Regarding the UK reception, *Time* magazine reported that in 1997 McDonagh was 'the only writer this season, apart from Shakespeare, to have four plays running concurrently in London'.[49] In terms of the USA reception, the 1998 Broadway production of *The Beauty Queen of Leenane* won four Tony Awards. Apropos the Northern Ireland reception, the 2005 Lyric/An Grianán production of *The Lonesome West* enjoyed both popular success and critical acclaim. The problem then is not only the ethical dimension of the plays in and of themselves, but also the ethical dimension of the audience response. The plays in the Leenane trilogy, particularly *The Lonesome West*, are in the final analysis based on the manipulation of the dark side of emotional arousal and the farcical representation of fundamentally traumatic events. The reception of McDonagh's plays is thrown into relief by the fact that the 2001 Broadway production of Mel Brooks's *The Producers*, which won a record breaking twelve Tony Awards, featured a play-within-a-play called 'Spring-time for Hitler' that had at its centre-piece Nazi showgirls dancing in the formation of a swastika which could be seen reflected in a mirror situated directly above the stage. The problem with both McDonagh's *The Lonesome West* and Brooks's *The Producers* is the overblown, postmodern playfulness where irony folds back on itself to ultimately sustain the very ideology it is supposed to subvert.

The counter-argument that the creator of *The Producers* is Jewish and is quite obviously being blatantly, extravagantly tongue-in-cheek in his portrayal of Nazi Germany would surely make Theodor Adorno turn in his grave. It seems we live in a time where Adorno's statement 'that to write lyric poetry after

Auschwitz is barbaric'[50] has been so warped by the cultural logic of late capitalism, that postmodern irony has become a hall of mirrors where ethical value is more a matter of clever refraction than critical reflection. As Adorno said of Schoenberg's *Survivor of Warsaw*: 'The so-called aristic representation of the sheer physical pain of people beaten to the ground by rifle-butts contains, however remotely, the power to elicit enjoyment out of it.'[51] It follows that McDonagh's postmodern Stage Irishry with its comic mediation of pain and suffering, its titillation of spiteful, cynical emotions not only sells but must, judging by the popular success of his Leenane trilogy, 'elicit enjoyment' for the majority of audience members who saw it. The Stage Irishry that made Dion Boucicault several fortunes and sealed Sean O'Casey's place in the world theatrical canon has, with a bit of cleverness and a lot of cynicism, done both for McDonagh. The message, if there is one, seems to be: the Stage Irish are dead, long live the Stage Irish.

---

[1] Martin McDonagh, *The Lonesome West* in *Plays: 1* (London: Methuen, 1999), p.178.

[2] Anthony Roche, '"Close to Home but Distant": Irish Drama in the 1990s', *Colby Quarterly*, 34. 4 (December 1998), p.287.

[3] Ibid., p.287.

[4] Ibid., p.288.

[5] Aleks Sierz, *In-Yer-Face Theatre: British Drama Today* (London: Faber and Faber, 2000), p.223.

[6] Ibid., p.4.

[7] Ibid., p.5.

[8] *The Lonesome West*, p.130.

[9] Ibid., p.130.

[10] Ibid., p.131.

[11] Ibid., p.137.

[12] Ibid., p.138.

[13] Martin McDonagh, *A Skull in Connemara*, in *Plays: 1* (London: Methuen, 1999), p.65.

[14] *A Skull in Connemara*, p.76.

[15] *The Lonesome West*, p.140.

[16] See Paul Murphy, 'J.M. Synge and the Pitfalls of National Consciousness', in *Theatre Research International*, ed. Brian Singleton, 28.2 (Summer 2003), pp.125-142.

[17] Christopher Murray, *Twentieth Century Irish Drama: Mirror up to Nation* (Manchester: Manchester University Press, 1997), p.88.

[18] Declan Kiberd, *Inventing Ireland* (London: Vintage, 1996), p.223.

[19] Ibid., p.228.

[20] Aristotle, *Poetics*, trans.Malcolm Heath (London: Penguin 1996), p.9.

[21] Declan Kiberd, p.220.

[22] Robert Hogan and M.J. O'Neil, *Joseph Holloway's Abbey Theatre* (Carbondale and Edwardsville: Southern Illinois University Press, 1967), p.220.

[23] For a thoroughgoing analysis of Hynes's production see Brian Singleton, 'The Revival Revised', in *The Cambridge Companion to Irish Drama*, ed. Shaun Richards (Cambridge: Cambridge University Press, 2004), pp.258-270. It is interesting to note here that Hynes won a Tony award for Best Director in the 1998 Broadway production of *The Beauty Queen of Leenane*; indeed Hynes's direction of McDonagh's plays helped to establish his reputation.

[24] F.R. Higgins, 'The Plough and the Stars,' *Irish Statesman* 6 March 1926, pp.797-98, quoted in Robert Hogan and Richard Burnham, *The Modern Irish Drama*, Vol. 6, *The Years of O'Casey, 1921-1926* (Newark: University of Delaware Press; Gerrards Cross, Buckinghamshire: Colin Smythe, 1992), p.325.

[25] *The Lonesome West*, p.157.

[26] Ibid., p.157.

[27] Ibid., p.159.

[28] Martin McDonagh, *The Beauty Queen of Leenane* in *Plays 1* (London: Methuen, 1999), p.47.

[29] Ibid., p.49.

[30] *The Lonesome West*, p.159.

[31] Diarmaid Ferriter, *The Transformation of Ireland, 1900-2000* (London: Profile Books, 2004), p.736.

[32] Ibid., p.665.

[33] *The Lonesome West*, p.135.

[34] Ibid., p.135.

[35] *A Skull in Connemara*, p.103.

[36] Ibid., p.104.

[37] *The Lonesome West*, p.193.

[38] Ibid., p.180.

[39] Ibid., p.181.

[40] Ibid., p.187.

[41] Ibid., p.188.

[42] Ibid., p.188.

[43] *The Lonesome West,* p.142.

[44] Diarmaid Ferriter, p.664.

[45] *The Lonesome West*, pp.173-74.

[46] Sarah Kane, *Blasted*: first performed at the Royal Court Theatre Upstairs, London, 12 January 1995; first published in *Frontline Intelligence 2* (London: Methuen, 1995).

[47] Sarah Kane cited in Graham Saunders *'Love me or kill me': Sarah Kane and the theatre of extremes* (Manchester: Manchester University Press, 2002), p.38.

[48] Ibid., p.39.

[49] Mimi Kramer, 'Three for the Show', *Time* 4 August 1997, p.71.

[50] Theodor Adorno, 'Commitment' in *Aesthetics and Politics* ed. and trans. Ronald Taylor (London: New Left Books, 1977), p.188.

[51] Ibid., p.189.

5 | The Cripple of Inishmaan Meets Lady Gregory

Christopher Murray

1

Much discussion on Martin McDonagh's work is judgmental before it is analytical. McDonagh's phenomenal international success and the celebrity status such success inevitably brings in the media nowadays pose considerable obstacles to adequate critical approaches to the work. As the darling of the post-modernists he is available as contemporary icon, stylistically diverse, conspicuously playful, the very Autolycus of our time, a snapper-up of unconsidered trifles from bricolage to brickbats. He needs a context, or else the conclusions reached in discussions of his plays can be as unsatisfactory as the inflated views they are often so impatiently constructed to deflate.

For the purposes of this essay I am rather quixotically putting forward the comedies of Lady Gregory as a useful framework for the reconsideration of McDonagh's plays. In the first instance I think comedy is the niche in which he belongs, specifically modern tragicomedy. In the second, I think we have probably heard enough about Synge for the present; quite recently a reviewer of DruidSynge in Edinburgh gave the usual list of modern play-wrights indebted, including McDonagh, 'whose scabrous work is an extended argument with Synge'.[1] Whatever about the loaded term 'scabrous' we can accept this common view as valid, though it tends to close down rather than open up debate. I suggest that Lady Gregory may now provide a fresher context. I am not suggesting influence: not only is the idea particularly laughable in this case but I cannot think of a single modern playwright who was in fact influenced by her work. Rather, what I have in mind is a bringing together of these two writers who are never thought of in contiguity with a view to clarifying McDonagh's comic procedures and tragicomic vision. The justification for this manoeuvre is to be found in Gregory's *Spreading the News* (1904), *Hyacinth Halvey* (1906), *The Image* (1909), and other such comedies which explore identity and representation in ways less obvious than Synge and more capable of offering useful (because less emotive) contrasts with McDonagh's plays. Specifically, I want here to look at *Spreading the News* in relation to *The Cripple of Inishmaan* (1996).

2

Augusta Gregory began to write plays in 1902 not in a vacuum but in order to help on the struggling Irish dramatic movement. She was sharing in an ideological as well as an artistic endeavour. As nationalist what she wrote was always to be understood as sym-pathetic to the liberationist cause while at the same time she remained detached from her material in quizzical amusement. She wrote farces and comedies mainly as filler material for the man-datory double or triple bill at the time. *Spreading the News* was thus inserted into the three-play programme for the opening of the Abbey on 27 December 1904 alongside Yeats's *On Baile's Strand* (also a premiere) and his and Gregory's *Cathleen Ni Houlihan* (1902). Synge's *In the Shadow of the Glen* (1903) alternated with the latter on succeeding nights. As Lennox Robinson saw it, with *Spreading the News* 'in one stride [Lady Gregory] had achieved a small masterpiece'.[2] On 27 December 2004 the Abbey revived the four above-mentioned plays in a centenary gesture, allowing ama-teur companies to stage them in commemoration of the amateur status of the early Abbey. *Spreading the News*, as interpreted by St Patrick's Dramatic Society, Dalkey, showed that Robinson was right: this now neglected play is a little masterpiece.

Sharing Yeats's insistence on the personal as key to artistic vision, Lady Gregory felt free to offer her ironic portraits of rural character in absurd situations that stopped just short of outright mockery. She had a theory of comedy rooted above all in Ben Jonson and Molière (four of whose comedies she translated for production by the Abbey),[3] satirical, ironic and exuberant with a strong emphasis on neoclassical tightness of plot. These are features to be found also in McDonagh's plays, always constructed along classical lines. *Spreading the News* is a farce, which Gregory called 'comedy with character left out',[4] and this, too, applies to McDonagh's work where the characters are two-dimensional servants of a farcical plot. *Spreading the News* is set in a village or small town in the West of Ireland, based on Gort, Co. Galway, beside which she lived in Coole. The play concerns the way in which a simple inoffensive man, Bartley Fallon, ends up accused of murder for adultery through a series of stories told which arise in the first place from a remark misheard and spread in the community. Since the setting is a fair, with stalls in the foreground, one thinks of the much larger canvas of Jonson's *Bartholomew Fair* (1614), with its gallery of pickpockets, rogues and conmen. Gregory avoids these types and focuses instead on the hidden vindictiveness of the community frequenting the fair in search of bargains and gossip in equal measure. The plot is like an unleashed spring, laughably and yet unsettlingly speeding towards what is by no means a happy ending. The theme is the fragility of reputation and what Gregory called the 'incorrigible genius for myth-making' in the Irish character.[5] She first conceived the situation as tragic,[6] and the mood of the farce darkens as rumour seizes control. We sense this mood as Bartley's wife confronts one of the women she sees as slandering Bartley's good name to the point of calling for his hanging:

> Is that what you are saying, Bridget Tully, and is it what you think? I tell you it's too much talk you have, making yourself out to be such a great one, and to be running down every respectable person! A rope is it? It isn't much of a rope was needed to tie up your own furniture the day you came into Martin Tully's house [. . .]. It is too much talk the whole of you have. A rope is it? I tell you the whole of this town is full of liars and schemers that would hang you up for half a glass of whiskey.[7]

The sting in 'half' indicates how cheap the community is. Even the speaker herself falls victim to the rumour mongering, however, as after this speech the evidence seems to accumulate pointing to a love affair between the hapless Bartley and the wife of the supposed dead man. The play ends with both Bartley and the supposed dead man in handcuffs, the frenzy having built up crazily to the point where the law announces: 'I see it all now. A case of false impersonation, a conspiracy to defeat the ends of justice' (p.29). In this case the law is colonialist and represented as hostile to the people. Gregory balances the farcical against the real implications of this political background. Without reference to this background, this colonialist context, the play can easily be diluted into farcical nonsense. Eric Weitz, for instance, having quoted the opening dialogue of the play, comments:

> The two characters in this introductory passage convey something of a generalized city/ country opposition: a policeman responds with provincial simplicity to each of a visiting Magistrate's string of disapproving questions.[8]

This is to ignore the imperialist attitude of the Magistrate, who constantly refers to his experience in the Andaman Islands as a way of justifying his suspicions of the Irish natives. The policeman, in this regard, is clearly depicted as an RIC man totally on the side of the colonialist regime. That Gregory was interested in such a character is borne out by her exploration of his repressed patriotism in *The Rising of the Moon* (1907).

Gossip or 'spreading the news' is also a prime motif in MacDonagh's *The Cripple of Inishmaan*, this time in a post-colonialist atmosphere. The political contrast is significant. McDonagh's nihilism emerges the more sharply when his farce is contrasted with Gregory's. In *Spreading the News*, set carnival-like at a fair, justice is mocked far more than at the end of Jonson's *Bartholomew Fair* where, after all, order is restored. In Gregory's play the crazy situation is not resolved at the curtain because she wanted the Abbey audience of 1904 to recognize the Magistrate and the Policeman for the twin dangers they were. Justice is something to be postponed. In McDonagh's work in general justice has no place. As a second-generation Irishman in Britain his confusion is such that post-colonial Ireland, with its shreds of republicanism and veneer of globalization in a many-coloured coat, is a site where farce is followed logically by suicide. In *The Cripple* in particular he presents a society without leadership. Johnnypateenmike (hereafter referred to as Johnny) does not simply spread the news; he creates it and is accountable to nobody for its effects.

The Cripple is set in the year 1934 and imagines a community starved of news and dependent accordingly on stories passed around by word of mouth in a debased form of oral tradition. To enliven the conversation of neighbours Johnny has created a role for himself analogous to the minstrel or *file* of old, a figure probably last seen in Irish drama in M.J. Molloy's *The King of Friday's Men* (1948). Johnny is presented as both malicious and mercenary, since he looks for the worst in any emerging news of local misfortune and expects reward for passing this news on. He is many things, including a version of the playwright himself. Where Lady Gregory did not target a specific agent of mischief in a community but saw a force for mischief in the community acting in consort, McDonagh likes to target. Johnny is a version not just of the story-teller in a rural, pastoral setting but also of the informer. He carries vestiges of the old landlord's agent as represented by Boucicault in his Irish melodramas. He is ill-natured and vicious, as in his treatment of his aged mother (more melodrama?). In scene 1 he hopes there will be a feud over the stealing of the cat and the goose from two solitaries (and here we can see the shape of *The Lieutenant of Inishmore* (2001) emerging). By scene 5 he reports: 'A feud is starting and won't be stopped 'til the one or the two of them finish up slaughtered. Good.'[9] Johnny has no sense of loyalty. At a key moment he spitefully lets out the secret Bobby had confided in him that Billy, the eponymous cripple of Inishmaan, left the island because he had tuberculosis, 'preferring to take his TB to Hollywood for his dying than bear be in the company of her [his Aunt Kate]' (59). The news leaves Billy's other aunt, Eileen, as '*stunned*' as it does its source Bobby, who demands of Johnny, 'Can't you keep anything to yourself?' And the reply is: 'Johnnypateenmike was never a man for secrets' (59). In Lady Gregory's work the secret is a precious thing, a 'heart-secret' as she calls it, a belief not to be destroyed.[10]

But Johnny is not just a careless promulgator of gossip. He is also a trickster in the traditional sense, a *cleasaí*, a liar, and disturber of the peace.[11] He manipulates truth for effect, telling the Doctor, who like Eileen is '*stunned*' (71) at the news, lies about his latest acts of cruelty to his mother. He tells Billy the supposed truth about his parents' suicide, a sentimental tale of a sacrifice for Billy's sake, which concludes:

> **Billy:** (*Pause*) It was for me they killed themselves?
> **Johnny:** The insurance paid up a week after, and you were given the all-clear afore a month was out.
> **Billy:** So they *did* love me, in spite of everything.
> **Eileen:**They did love you *because* of everything, Billy.
> **Johnny:** Isn't that news?
> **Billy:** That is news. I needed good news this day (74).

Though Johnny's story is later revealed to be a lie it covers an act of heroic intervention by Johnny himself, if we can believe this. 'We should tell Billy the true story some day, Kate,' Eileen remarks (80). The whole point in McDonagh is that there is *no* true story. He is the unreliable author par excellence.

In general, McDonagh's characterization is unreliable. The characters are comic-book representations of an adult world from a child's perspective. This makes them two-dimensional, a frequently remarked point in discussion of his plays, but it also makes them inordinately cruel. This I take to be a form of defensiveness on McDonagh's part, a reluctance to declare 'heart' in relation to any secrets his characters might trade in. This coldness contrasts with Lady Gregory's humanism even though, according to Yeats, she 'has written comedies where the wickedest people seem but bold children. She does not know why she has created that world where no one is ever judged, a high celebration of indulgence.'[12] At the same time, her perspective, in contrast to McDonagh's, was 'ironically loving'.[13] In *The Cripple of Inishmaan* the characterization of Helen is conspicuously hostile to the point of parody: anti-romantic, cruel, and streetwise (in sub-pastoral Inis Meán) this Helen will never launch a thousand ships. She has her excuse for being a termagant: 'I do have to be so violent, or if I'm not to be taken advantage of anyways I have to be so violent' (76). She is like McDonagh in this respect.

The theme of *The Cripple* is the debunking of sentimental representation in favour of hard-nosed realism. Setting the play in 1934 allows McDonagh to distance his characters but it also allows him a metatheatrical device to reinforce his theme. This is Robert Flaherty's film *Man of Aran* (1935), made on location on the neighbouring island of Inis Mór. Often regarded as a magnificent slice of Aran life this famous documentary is actually highly romanticized. It lacks a plot and goes for the picturesque and the moment stylized in spectacle. Every activity in the film is heroicized. The fight with the shark is well done but irrational since even if the fishermen won the contest (which they do not) they do not appear to have calculated the economic value of the prize, in sharp contrast to Lady Gregory's *The Image*, where the arrival of two whales on shore is greeted with ecstasy because of the riches the fish oil will bring. That McDonagh's characterization in *The Cripple* deconstructs Flaherty's is obvious, for the latter deals with a family who might have sat for a series of portraits by Seán Keating: they are types invariably caught in heroic poses battling the elements. Flaherty himself confessed that he selected 'a group of the most attractive and appealing characters we can find, to represent a family, and through them tell our story'.[14] In Lance Pettitt's account of the film, Flaherty as

> Irish-American adventurer […] unconsciously deployed a colonial discourse in representing native Irish people, undifferentiated from Inuits and Polynesians.[15]

McDonagh gleefully responds. In the play mother and father are conspicuously dead (plot material here, it emerges), while the boy who matches their courage and enterprise in the film (even though he does rather foolishly desert his valuable fishing line at the top of a cliff (!) in order to raise the alarm over the sharks) is transformed into Billy and is always, with deliberate political incorrectness, referred to as 'Cripple Billy'. Frailty and disease replace the myth of heroic endurance. Ugliness, insult, and obscenity take the place of Flaherty's representation of an idealized world. *Man of Aran* is seen by McDonagh's characters in Scene Eight of *The Cripple*, where it is dis-missed as 'A pile of fecking shite' (61). It means nothing to the viewers. They have never seen a shark off the shores of Aran.

3

Use of language is an important feature of both Lady Gregory's and McDonagh's plays. It is a commonplace to remark that

McDonagh at once exploits and parodies stage-Irish speech. This double purpose, I would maintain, is part of his general ambivalence and it is shared with Gregory. First, let us distinguish between speech and dramatic language, which, however close to the real thing it may be, is always in some measure transformed as stage speech. P.W. Joyce's *English As We Speak It in Ireland* (1910) made quite clear what the dialectal and philological features are.[16] They include syntax and tenses borrowed from Gaelic usage. Lady Gregory preceded Synge in using these features for her stage dialogue, beginning with *Cathleen Ní Houlihan* (1902), and learning much from Douglas Hyde's attempts, *Casadh an tSúgáin* (1901) and *An Pósadh* (1902), she incorporated many Gaelicisms into her Abbey plays.

Examples of syntax from *Spreading the News* would be: '*Showing off he was* to the new magistrate', *Ag teaspáint é fein a bhí sé*, and 'there was hurry on them', *bhí brostú ortha*, where the order in each example is taken from the Irish. Being more flexible, Irish allows inversions for emphasis disallowed in Standard English. An example of an Irish tense in *Spreading* would be: '*To be going about* with this fork *and to find* no one to take it'. This is the famous Kiltartan infinitive which Lady Gregory used extensively in imitation of the Irish usage, *ag dul thart … is gan duine a aimsigh*. Since she had learned Irish and lived among people who were bilingual it was no surprise that Gregory was attracted to Hiberno-English. Synge followed in her footsteps, making Aran usages the staple of his stage dialogue. But Synge was more interested in elaborating the speech rhythms poetically and in incorporating words and phrases he regarded as exotic whereas they were either straight from the Irish or archaic forms of English surviving from the seventeenth and eighteenth centuries.[17] The colonized had learned to adapt as well as adopt the language of the colonizer. Between them, Gregory and Synge established a new stage language at the Abbey modelled on this hybrid style. It became a somewhat standardized dialect for what was termed peasant drama up to the end of the 1950s at least. It was revived to great effect and without the least embarrassment by Tom Murphy in *Bailegangaire* (1985), and has since with a rather different emphasis but still with the purpose of authenticity been deployed by Marina Carr.

The question is, how far is McDonagh following the Abbey tradition and how far is he parodying it? It seems to me there is a certain amount of confusion on this issue, a confusion possibly shared by McDonagh himself. On the one hand, McDonagh is quoted as declaring that he came to write plays without prior knowledge even of *The Playboy of the Western World* and apparently with no interest in the great tradition.[18] On the other hand there is no disputing his use of Hiberno-English for effect. *The Beauty Queen of Leenane* is arguably his best play to date and this is as linguistically traditional as John B. Keane's *Sive* (1959), which it sometimes calls to mind. Having seen on stage Micheál Ó Conghaile's translation into Irish of *The Beauty Queen*, I am convinced of this point. A striking aspect of the audience response to *Banríon Álainn an Líonáin* was its seriousness in contrast to the Druid production in English: the production was seen far less as comedy than as melodrama bordering on tragedy.[19] *The Cripple of Inishmaan*, lying as it does outside the trilogy, is less serious and, quite obviously, stylistically compromised by its parodic relation to *Man of Aran*. At the same time the language is rooted in Hiberno-English. McDonagh often makes use of the Irish consuetudinal or continuous tense with the addition of 'do' or 'did' as auxiliary. For example: 'I *do worry* awful about Billy' (2), which is not the emphatic 'do' of standard English but the compound or continuous present tense of Gaelic, *bíonn mé* followed by the infinitive. Again: 'I suppose your Aunt Mary *did send* you some' (11), or 'In America they *do have* Mintios' (10) and 'What's this, now, that the French fella *does do*, Helen?' (13), or best of all in these early pages, 'Johnnypateenmike *does have* three pieces of news *to be telling ye* this day' (4), where the last phrase also replaces the straightforward standard English ('to tell') with the continuous Irish (*le rá libh*). Other usages crop up: 'there was nothing *on* me chest at all but a bit of a wheeze' (6), a translation of *ar* (compare the once-common Galway expression, 'what's *on* you?' for 'what's wrong with you'). The inversions Gregory and Synge were so fond of are scarce enough in McDonagh, showing that he is not out to mock the usage, but one could cite: 'Trying to get to America be the mainland *they were* (15), or 'Hurt me ribs that punch *did*' (16). Then there is the Irish usage *ag dul* ('going') to create a compound tense, '*To go making* a moving picture film [they're coming]' (7), and 'Is it another oul book you're *going reading*?' (11) In his preface to *The Playboy* Synge said, 'I have used one or two words only, that I have not heard among the country people of Ireland, or *spoken in my own nursery* before I could read the newspapers.'[20] Until the biography appears we cannot say for sure about McDonagh's nursery, but I think we can take it that he picked up these Gaelicisms within the family (father from Connemara, mother from Sligo) and from his uncles in Galway. 'My father's first language was Gaelic', he has said, 'and there is something about that stylized way of talking that appeals to me.'[21] In that regard he might still agree with Synge that in Ireland still 'we have a popular imagination that is fiery and magnificent', if no longer 'tender', 'so that those of us who wish to write start with a chance that is not given to writers in places where the springtime of the local life has been forgotten.' All of this has been McDonagh's heritage directly or indirectly.

Leaving aside the question of dialect, I want to draw attention to McDonagh's use of repetition involving stichomythia or rapid exchange as part of a pursuit of logic in argument. For example, as *The Cripple* begins Eileen complains to her sister Kate of an accident:

> **Kate:** Was it your bad arm?
> **Eileen:** No, it was me other arm.
> **Kate:** It would have been worse if you'd banged your bad arm.
> **Eileen:** It would have been worse, although it still hurt.
> **Kate:** Now you have two bad arms.
> **Eileen:** Well, I have one bad arm and one arm with a knock (1).

Repetitious dialogue symptomatic of a community built on boredom (compare Tom MacIntyre's dramatization of Kavanagh's *The Great Hunger*) must have been a source of some amusement to the young McDonagh during his assumed sojourns among his relatives in the West of Ireland. He catches the trick of it again and again, sometimes too self-consciously, as at the opening of Scene Five where Kate, anxious for the return of Billy, who has disappeared, says, 'Not a word [from him]' nine times successively. When her sister objects, Kate asks if she is not 'allowed' to say

'Not a word', 'and me terrified o'er Billy's travellings?' She is assured she is indeed allowed to say 'Not a word', 'but one or two times and not ten times' (37-8). Most of the dialogue is comprised of one-liners, and the argument on which they are based always takes a logical turn. I am in some doubt how true this usage is to Irish speech; I think not as a habitual mode, as in McDonagh. But it appears in Lady Gregory's plays and commentators have sometimes linked it to her love for Molière, four of whose comedies she translated into her distinctive Kiltartanese for production at the Abbey to provide fruitful parallels with Irish experience.

Even in her farces Gregory upholds a certain logical strain in the dialogue, which Ann Saddlemyer has called 'a quick series of successive encounters between different pairs of characters'.[22] A good example is provided by the exchange between the two old men at the end of *The Workhouse Ward* after the sister of one of them has failed in her attempt to seduce her brother Mike McInerney to go home and live with her by conjuring up an idyllic life of spaciousness and plenty, including such exotica as 'a handful of periwinkles … or cockles maybe'. McInerney tries to get her to accept his mate Miskell also; he fails; she goes. The two men fall into silence. Then Miskell consoles:

> **Miskell:** Maybe the house is not so wide as what she says.
> **McInerney:** Why wouldn't it be wide?
> **Miskell:** Ah, there does be a good deal of middling poor houses down by the sea.
> **McInerney:** What would you know about wide houses? Whatever sort of a house you had yourself it was too wide for the provision you had into it.
> **Miskell:** Whatever provision I had in my house it was wholesome provision and natural provision. Herself and her periwinkles! Periwinkles is a hungry sort of food.
> **McInerney:** Stop your impudence and your chat or it will be the worse for you. I'd bear with my own father and mother as long as any man would, but if they'd vex me I would give them the length of a rope as soon as another!
> **Miskell:** I would never ask at all to go eating periwinkles.[23]

The final line in the marvellous sequence could have been written by McDonagh, though as a rule Gregory writes longer speeches. If she is recording here from reality – and in passages such as Mrs Tully's speech already quoted from *Spreading the News*, her delight in the lively cut and thrust of the people in daily conversation or argument is abundant – it is possible that McDonagh had a similar response in Connemara and on Aran. In making a comparison between *The Workhouse Ward* and McDonagh's *The Lonesome West*, Anthony Roche stresses the similarity in the use of two men locked in verbal combat, with violence always simmering as subtext. Roche agrees, however, that 'the main activity is verbal, with an element in one statement seized on and developed as the key animating principle in the second, as the basis of the retort'.[24] An exploration of *The Image* would yield similar results, for it too is rich in neighbourly argument.

In general, the difference in this area between the two playwrights lies in MacDonagh's self-consciousness and self-reflexiveness. He is fond of a running gag, such as the one about Ireland not being a bad place to live. It begins with the line, 'Ireland musn't be such a bad place so if the Yanks want to come to Ireland to do their filming' (8). It's not a great line, with the awkward repetition of 'Ireland'. But it is recycled with variations five times, referring to the presence in the locality of French, 'coloured fellas', German, sharks, and 'cripple fellas' (13, 25, 37, 55, 63). The climax comes during a discussion on the shark sequence in *Man of Aran*, when Bartley, perhaps named for Synge's character in *Riders to the Sea*, remarks: 'It's rare that off Ireland you get sharks. This is the first shark I've ever seen off Ireland', and Johnny then delivers the punch line: 'Ireland musn't be such a bad place so if sharks want to come to Ireland' (55). Behind the joke lies an age-old, colonialist shame and lack of self-esteem which McDonagh mocks and defuses. In the final use of the gag, in scene 8, when Billy appears melodramatically from behind the sheet used to screen the film, it falls to Bartley to exclaim: 'Ireland *can't be* such a bad place, so, if cripple fellas turn down Hollywood to come to Ireland' (63, emphasis added). The returned exile assuages the native uncertainty. Or not.

McDonagh's style in *The Cripple* as elsewhere is mainly aggressive in tone with little room for sentiment. Characters – such as Slippy Helen – reduce any such space by filling it with expressions of violence. When Billy feels the need towards the end of the play to explain to Bobby why he deceived him and went to Hollywood, McDonagh gives him a long speech which becomes emotional in its summation of life on Inishmaan (*recte* Inis Meán):

> I had to get away from this place, Babbybobby, be any means
> […]. Going drowning meself I'd often think of when I was here,
> just to … just to end the laughing at me, and the sniping at me, and
> the life of nothing but shuffling to the doctor's and shuffling back
> from the doctor's and pawing over the same oul books and finding
> any other way to piss another day away. Another day of sniggering
> […] (66)

It is a touching speech. In case we fall for it Bobby beats Billy up with a lead pipe. When Helen visits the injured Billy he declares his love for her and she pokes his wounds in reply before walking out. When in a double take she returns and agrees to walk out with Billy, or 'shuffle' as she puts it, she interrupts his plan to drown himself. All seems set fair for a happy ending until Billy, alone, coughs up blood and realizes that the lie he told about tuberculosis has ironically backfired. Hence the final stage direction, '*Fade to black*' (82). Alienation is the name of McDonagh's game.

4

What may be concluded from the juxtaposition of *Spreading the News* and *The Cripple of Inishmaan* is that McDonagh is at once within and without the Irish dramatic tradition. No doubt that is where he wants to be, on the periphery. Yeats, in the description of Lady Gregory's comedies quoted above, said they reflected 'a high celebration of indulgence'; perhaps the same criticism can be made of McDonagh's. They have that in common, as well as Hiberno-English. On the other hand, in current commentaries on McDonagh's plays much space is given to intertextuality, as if this were an accolade. It is so only in a postmodern context. Moreover, in drama, as opposed to the novel, intertextuality can sometimes be the mark of an immature or ill-defined style. The weakest parts of *The Cripple* occur where bits of Beckett obtrude, as when Billy rebukes Bartley for laughing at others' 'misfortunes', even though Bartley thinks them 'awful funny' (64) as in *Endgame*; or as when we get the Hamm-like self-awareness of Johnny's line, '"Bigness" isn't a word, I know, but I can't be bothered to think of a better one for the likes of ye' (8).

The violence in McDonagh's plays, including *The Cripple of Inishmaan*, is another common concern. In *Spreading the News* an image is conjured up of a mountainy man gone wild through the fair brandishing a hay fork which he intends to drive into another man's heart. That it is all fabrication does not abolish the fact that the people believe this and see reason for it. Lady Gregory lived to see the day when wild men roamed the countryside around Coole in 1922 raging for vengeance; her family home at Roxborough was burned out, her daughter-in-law ambushed on the roads; she herself was lucky to be allowed stay on at Coole for her lifetime. Her *Journals* for the 1920s record the violence of the times. For McDonagh writing in post-colonial times it is altogether a different matter. He can do the 'murder in jest' stuff as well as any play-within-the-play merchant going, but does he see 'any offence in't?' *The Beauty Queen* is exempt: violence that seems gratuitous here is dramatically justifiable; it is shocking but it tells the awful truth. The violence in the other plays is more cartoon-like, verging towards the infantile and toppling completely into it in *The Lieutenant of Inishmore*. This seems a pity, since McDonagh under-stands the depair which underlies affluent Ireland today. There is a lot of anger in the work, and interestingly it is voiced by women, as in Lady Gregory's plays.

Politically, the two writers are far apart. Lady Gregory was committed to cultural nationalism. Even in such an art-conscious play as *The Image*, Gregory can see beneath the natural order to the heroic endurance of a people living independently of government interference or hegemony, including standard designs for public statues. For her, history was part of that natural order and available to mobilize change (as in her homely Irish history plays and in *The Deliverer* (1911), an allegory of Parnell). There are always the makings of a revolution in Gregory which are depressingly absent in McDonagh. Thus it is hard to agree with John Waters that McDonagh's plays are 'acts of revolution rather than acquies-cence'.[25] The best McDonagh can do in this regard is belatedly to slag off the IRA in *The Lieutenant of Inishmore* in a style reminiscent of Behan's *The Hostage* (1958); at least Behan had through his activism earned the right to turn politics into theatre of the absurd. McDonagh responds in fury to the natural order, in which he sees no heroic endurance to provide meaning as in Gregory's plays. For him, child of the postmodern, globalized world, heroism is dead; so also are politics. He has nothing to replace Gregory's nationalism except cynicism. He himself is the cripple as author, his cries of reconciliation invariably smothered by the hollow laugh and the sadistic infliction of pain disguised as slapstick. His idea of theatre is 'some kind of punk destruction of what's gone on before'; it is less easy to believe that this idea also includes 'hav[ing] respect for the decent things that have gone before'.[26]

McDonagh's love-hate relationship with the West of Ireland remains unresolved. The question of identity, which Gregory constantly recognized as problematic not only in *Spreading the News* and *The Image* but in virtually all of her work right up to her play on Don Quixote, *Sancho's Master* (1927), is literally foreign to McDonagh. By contrast, he is maddeningly complacent. If she is the matriarch of a national theatre, McDonagh remains its seriously mixed-up kid. But at least she provides the context for the kid to show off.

---

[1] Susannah Clapp, 'Playwright of the Western World: The Genius of J.M. Synge', *Observer* 'Review', 4 September 2005, p.11. For a very useful summary of this relationship see Shaun Richards, '"The Outpouring of a Morbid, Unhealthy Mind": The Critical Condition of Synge and McDonagh', *Irish University Review* 33 (2003), pp.201-14.

[2] Lennox Robinson, *Ireland's Abbey Theatre: A History 1899-1951* (London: Sidgwick and Jackson, 1951), p.46.

[3] See Mary FitzGerald, 'Four French Comedies: Lady Gregory's Translations of Molière', in *Lady Gregory Fifty Years After*, eds Ann Saddlemyer and Colin Smythe (Gerrards Cross: Colin Smythe, 1987), pp.277-90.

[4] Cited by Ann Saddlemyer, *In Defence of Lady Gregory, Playwright* (Dublin: Dolmen Press, 1966), p.32. This remains the best introduction to Gregory's dramaturgy.

[5] *Collected Plays of Lady Gregory*, ed. Ann Saddlemyer, Vol. 1: *Comedies* (Gerrards Cross: Colin Smythe, 1971), p.260.

[6] Ibid., p.253.

[7] Ibid., p.22.

[8] Eric Weitz, 'Lady Gregory's Humour of Character: A *Commedia* Approach to *Spreading the News*,' *Irish University Review, Special Issue: Lady Gregory*, 34 (2004), p.147.

[9] Martin McDonagh, *The Cripple of Inishmaan* (London: Methuen, 1997), p.41.

[10] *Collected Plays of Lady Gregory*, Vol. 2: *The Tragedies and Tragic-Comedies* (New York: Oxford UP, 1970), p.296.

[11] For a definitive account of the *cleasaí* figure see Alan Harrison, *The Irish Trickster* (Sheffield: Sheffield Academic Press, 1989).

[12] W.B. Yeats, *Mythologies* (London: Macmillan, 1959), p.326.

[13] Hazard Adams, *Lady Gregory* (Lewisburg: Bucknell UP, 1973), p.75.

[14] Cited by Lance Pettitt, *Screening Ireland: Film and Television Representation* (Manchester: Manchester UP, 2000), p.78.

[15] Ibid., p.80.

[16] See T.P. Dolan's edition of Joyce's book (Dublin: Wolfhound Press, 1979, rev. 1988). The introduction, pp.vi-xxxiv, is very useful. See also T.P. Dolan, ed., *The English of the Irish: Special Issue, Irish University Review* 20 (1990), and the introduction to his *Dictionary of Hiberno-English: The Irish Use of English* (Dublin: Gill & Macmillan, 1998), pp.xix-xxix.

[17] See Alan Bliss, 'The Language of Synge', in *J.M. Synge Centenary Papers 1971*, ed. Maurice Harmon (Dublin: Dolmen Press,1972), pp.35-62.

[18] McDonagh told Fintan O'Toole in an interview in the *The Irish Times* in 1997: 'I'm coming to theatre with a disrespect for it. I'm coming from a film fan's perspective on theatre.' Cited by Anthony Roche, 'Re-Working *The Workhouse Ward*: McDonagh, Beckett, and Gregory', *Irish University Review: Special Issue: Lady Gregory*, 34 (2004), p.172. In the same interview McDonagh said he hadn't know Synge's *Playboy* 'at all' when writing the *Leenane Trilogy*. See Shaun Richards, 'The Outpouring of a Morbid, Unhealthy Mind', p.202.

[19] See Micheál Ó Conghaile, trans., *Banríon Álainn an Líonáin* (Indreabhán, Galway: Chló Iar-Chonnachta, 1999). See also Declan Kiberd, 'For Galway's upcoming Irish-language arts festival, Féile 2000, Micheál Ó Conghaile has translated Martin McDonagh's *The Beauty Queen of Leenane* into the Irish language', *The Irish Times* 12 October 1999.

[20] J.M. Synge, *Collected Works*, Vol. 4, *Plays 2*, ed. Ann Saddlemyer (London: Oxford UP, 1968), pp.53-4.

[21] Cited by Joseph Feeney S.J., 'Martin McDonagh: Dramatist of the West',

Studies 87, 1998, p.28.

[22] Ann Saddlemyer, *In Defence of Lady Gregory*, p.96.

[23] Lady Gregory, *Collected Plays*, 1, 104.

[24] Anthony Roche, p.173.

[25] John Waters, 'The Irish Mummy: The Plays and Purpose of Martin McDonagh', in *Druids, Dudes and Beauty Queens: The Changing Face of Irish Theatre*, ed. Dermot Bolger (Dublin: New Island, 2001), p.39.

[26] Cited by Feeney, p.28.

6 | Gender, Sexuality and Violence in the Work of Martin McDonagh

Mária Kurdi

The London-based young playwright of Irish descent Martin McDonagh's work, with its defiance of clear categorization on many fronts, has been provoking critics to write commentaries and analyses which alternate between extremes. One thing virtually all of them share, however, is that they ambitiously identify the predecessors McDonagh draws from to add to his dramatic pastiche, or ventures to parody, or at least shows traceable parallels with. This eagerness to look for points of reference is urged, of course, by the substance itself, the enigma that unfolds in front of whoever touches it with the intention to produce a new interpretation. The usually long and detailed lists of both earlier authors and contemporaries that critics come up with are impressive and, arguably, at times reveal more about the direction of the approaches than the McDonagh plays themselves. On the one hand, several of the inquiries conclude on the note that the young author's achievement is very much part of the Irish dramatic tradition, primarily for its blending tragedy with comedy, tears with laughter, a sense of disaster with the triumph of survival. Because of its particular setting and themes, on the other hand, McDonagh's work invites being looked at more closely in relation to the 'Western' plays of J.M. Synge and Tom Murphy, which is done in a fine article by José Lanters most extensively.[1] Far less reference is made in critical literature, however, to McDonagh's affinities and connections with the tendencies prominent in the English theatre, past and present. Writing about In-Yer-Face Theatre, a revolutionary new British phenomenon, Aleks Sierz is among those few to mention the name of McDonagh together with authors like Sarah Kane, David Harrower, Patrick Marber, and Mark Ravenhill, as a representative of the trend in his own right.[2] Reinforcing this view and highlighting the main feature of the notorious theatre phenomenon mentioned, an American critic deploys the label 'New Brutalism' as most appropriate for describing the Irish-English playwright's affiliation.[3]

Interestingly, it is in a couple of Irish commentaries that the reader encounters the name of an English dramatist to serve as parallel, even a definitely close parallel to McDonagh. In his review of the 1996 Town Hall Theatre, Galway, production of *The Beauty Queen of Leenane* Fintan O'Toole sets the tone of his further discussion by the sentence: '[i]n it, Harold Pinter, and Joe Orton blend seamlessly with Tom Murphy and John B. Keane to create a vibrantly original mixture of absurd comedy and cruel melodrama'.[4] More specifically, in his introduction to the essay collection *Theatre Stuff* Eamonn Jordan considers Joe Orton (and his *Loot* first of all) as a significant point of reference for *The Lonesome West*.[5] A fellow Irish playwright's description may provoke further thinking in relation to the Orton parallel. When a couple of years ago I interviewed Declan Hughes about his own work, its cultural context, and the perspective he himself takes on the contemporary theatre, he surprised me by the following:

> I think Martin [McDonagh] can be compared to Joe Orton; he has subverted the traditional Irish country kitchen play, mixing it with elements of Hitchcock, with elements of the Coen Brothers, with elements of surreal humour, in very much the way Orton subverted the conventions of English drawing-room comedy. […] I see him as a Connemara Orton.[6]

'Connemara Orton' – read Ortonesque techniques applied to plays set in the West of Ireland by McDonagh. This summarizing phrase welds together an example of the English comic tradition as artistic precedent (perhaps inspiration?) and the world of rural Ireland, which is likely to evoke the subject of national ideals as well as their widely polarized treatment in Irish cultural discourse throughout the twentieth century.

Both playwrights, Joe Orton (1933-1967) and Martin Mc-Donagh (1970-) earned reputation very early in their respective careers and at an exceptionally young age for that. Surface similarities aside, it is hard not to notice that the kind of intertextuality which verges on the parasitical by exploiting the style and motifs of other authors and popular entertainment quite shamelessly, is an important feature linking the two. Oscar Wilde's farcical absurdities and artificiality of phrase are haunting Orton, suffice it to refer to Prentice's Lady Bracknell-like cross-questioning of Geraldine at the onset, and the revelation of Geraldine and Nick's parentage at end of *What the Butler Saw*. On his part, McDonagh has been found feeding on Syngean themes and strategies, turning the master's satire inside out through parody and multiplying his grotesqueries ad absurdum. In view of the moral (or, rather, immoral) climate of their respective plays, what a critic says of Orton is strikingly true of McDonagh: they offer a 'deeply disturbing vision of man's animality', that is of his 'selfishness, lust, and greed' without the perception of any counter-balancing value for comparison.[7] Restructuring the dramaturgy of the comic and farcical to create an effect of unredeemed horror, complete moral disorder and mad chaos, both authors transgress boundaries, shatter social taboos, and undermine traditional pieties. Christopher Innes contends that in Orton, if beside the several unscrupulous villains there is an innocent-looking character who shows belief in moral principles the others deny, he is sure to become victimized or receive some kind of severe punishment. A most conspicuous example is, Innes continues, the husband figure in *Loot*.[8] Likewise, McDonagh constructs the odd conscientious or at least not too aggressive character who is then ridiculed, beaten up or driven to suicide: Billy in *The Cripple of Inishmaan*, father Welsh/Walsh in *The Lonesome West*, and the childlike Mairtin in *A Skull in Connemara*, whom both of the two older male characters hit on the head, qualify as such scapegoats. McDonagh replicates Orton's shaping the policeman, the representative of law in *Loot* to become even more corrupt than the rest: Thomas, the guard in *A Skull* carves a hole in the long-dead Oona's skull in the course of investigating a case of supposedly domestic violence. Thus he himself applies violence to fabricate evidence in the hope of gaining promotion and approaching or even eclipsing the status of his idol, Petrocelli.

A most pervasive subject of the two playwrights proves to be sex, more often than not anomalous and perverse, the range of its manifestations being conjoined with various forms of violence, verbal and physical, including fight, torture, and homicide. Orton's comedy, Susan Rusinko argues in the chapter on *Loot* of her monographic study, attacks middle-class pretensions of respectability and unmasks the hypocrisy they generate and maintain in the society.[9] However, the achievement of the English playwright is normally not seen by critics in terms of interrogating and undermining something distinctively national, and this is the point where McDonagh's dramaturgy demonstrates a notable difference from Orton's by exploiting Irish stereotypes, although in a non-naturalistic and rather disconcerting way. Aware of the breadth and depth of critical attention paid to the subversive use of these in McDonagh so far, the present paper focuses on the playwright's manipulative linking of the traditional comic themes of sex and violence in a West of Ireland setting, a culturally distinct area because it was once regarded as the source and basis of genuine Irishness. McDonagh shapes his protagonists by recycling certain gender stereotypes that emerged and became notoriously characteristic of the national culture and made their way into the literature as well. It is important to stress, however, that the playwright's is an Ireland reconstructed in the postmodern fashion, enmeshing the local in the global and relativizing the truth value of what is portrayed. Karen Vandevelde rightly observes that '*The Leenane Trilogy* is an imaginary, exaggerated picture of the West of Ireland, including plenty of elements which simultaneously underline and undermine its authenticity'.[10]

By what means does the McDonagh drama localize notions and manifestations of the connection between sex and violence, and which aspects and shades of these make up the target of its subversion and irony? Focusing on such questions my analysis departs from the assumption that they are relevant pertaining to the earlier plays, the pieces of the *Leenane Trilogy* and *The Cripple of Inishmaan* first of all. Allegedly, the discourse and practices of sexuality in post-colonial Ireland form a huge area of study, considering their historical, socio-political as well as cultural contexts and ramifications through which they have influenced communal strategies and individual life styles. In the chapter titled *Sexuality, 1685-2001* of *The Field Day Anthology of Irish Writing*, Vol. IV, the subject receives an appropriately detailed, acutely critical and conscientiously up-to-date treatment by experts, relying on the latest findings of both national and international scholarship. The subchapter *Public Discourse, Private Reflection, 1916-70* is introduced by an inquiry into particular social and discursive aspects and functions of sexuality examined against the developments of Irish post-colonial history, where the author makes the point that:

> Since independence sexuality has been an important, if somewhat confusing, marker of Irish national difference [...] The hierarchy had always policed the sexual morality of the faithful, but now their pronouncements were intertwined with the post-revolutionary quest for national self-definition. They often cast sexual immorality as English or, more generally, foreign, and sexual purity as naturally and genuinely Irish [...] One thing most observers of Irish sexual culture, liberal and conservative, shared during this period was an acute sense of Irish sexual uniqueness. Over time, the meaning of that uniqueness became increasingly unclear and worrisome, but the sense that the Irish were sexually isolated persisted.[11]

Looking at the early work of McDonagh, Patrick Lonergan claims that each piece of the trilogy

> represents one of the authorities in Irish life – *The Beauty Queen* deals with the family, *A Skull in Connemara* with the law, and *The Lonesome West* with the church – at a time when the power of those authorities in Ireland was being eroded by revelations about political corruption, child abuse, and institutional incompetence.[12]

The list can be extended by including the ideal labelled 'sexual uniqueness' or isolation in the above quotation from *The Field Day Anthology*, which has also proven itself a kind of ideological authority governing beliefs and attitudes. Like the others mentioned by Lonergan, it has come under scrutiny since the 1980s in the context of the increasingly heated public controversies about divorce, contraception, alternative sexual identities, women's place in the society, teenage pregnancy and abortion.

The plays of McDonagh contain allusions to ingrained patterns of behaviour and culturally determined habits as the recognizable contextual forces underpinning the gender stereotypes and the sexual tensions occuring in their plot and action. In an exaggerated form, they frequently evoke difficulties which have been present and had a bearing on the fate and fulfilling potential of male-female relations in the post-colonial Irish society. As part of her psychological analysis of the powerful and diehard heritage of mistrust and divisiveness among Irish people, Geraldine Moane spots its effects, among others, in the joint fields of gender and generation. The pitfalls of social communication rendered un-healthy by colonialist discourses and imperial politics, she implies, have had a long-lasting, damaging influence on interpersonal and gender exchanges, and also on the process of individual sexual maturation well into modern Ireland.[13] McDonagh rehashes and recycles certain aspects of this burdened legacy as postmodern farce in his drama. He creates grotesque versions of well-known Irish gender stereotypes, suggesting the destructive underside of or the possibility of a perverted alternative to surface realities, which are none the less real and threatening. In this way he ruthlessly de-constructs and caricatures traditionally inviolable notions and norms of chastity, sexual purity, and idealized gender relations in the trilogy and *The Cripple*, as well as highlighting how emotional immaturity and sexual frustration may easily become the source of violent acts.

In *The Beauty Queen* the parent-child relationship of Mag, the mother, and Maureen, the daughter minding her, is rife with mutual suspicion and hatred, and the plot concludes with Maureen's matricide. The obtrusive dysfunction of this family setup, the play demonstrates, differs from the staple of genera-tional conflict in Irish literature in that it can be traced back to the effects of sexual repression and the aggressivity that they are likely to generate in frustrated individuals. Mag, the mother, is presented as an ugly old hag of dirty habits, who is vicious and destructive like the Joycean parody of the Mother Ireland figure as an 'old sow', with the addition that she not only exploits her child but also bars her from growing up sexually. While preoccupied with satisfying the claims of her body in terms of food and drink to be served up by the daughter at her order, she eagerly repeats the ultra-conservative moral demand that the bodily needs of younger people should be regulated and severely policed. For her, the forty-year old spinster Maureen's having kissed two men so far counts as 'plenty', and the daughter's wish to be kissed again and not live forever 'being stuck up here' is reason enough to call her a 'Whore!', which she does with great relish.[14] However, the claim that asceticism and resistance to desire are absolute values to govern an unmarried person's self-conduct and life style finds no justification in deep-rooted religiousness in the case of Mag. Far more important a motive for her is the fear that once the daughter finds a lover she herself remains alone, without the care and support she needs but also selfishly abuses when regarding only her own interest: 'But how could you go with him? You do still have me to look after' – she keeps on whining (48). Eventually, Hag-Mag's both infantile and tyrannical self-centeredness and hypocrisy invest her with enough shrewdness and power of manipulation to deprive Maureen of her probably last chance of securing partnership and leaving with a man, Pato, who asks her to join him in exile.

The stereotype of the Irish maiden waiting for a lover to rescue her from bondage is as widely known from Irish cultural history as the Hag appearing in a variety of guises. A late twentieth-century representation, middle-aged Maureen embodies a thoroughly re-shaped or even ill-fitting version of this maiden figure in *The Beauty Queen*. Ironically, she is shown as suffering not from the yoke of an outside hostile power but from the moral restrictions the present oppressive family scenario involves for her. The fantasy world she cultivates about having a lover is associated with violence, given that her ardently craved freedom seems to be possible only after the enforced death of her mother. In accordance, the background to a romantic encounter she envisages for herself is Mag's wake and funeral:

> I have a dream sometimes there of you, dressed all nice and white, in your coffin there, and me all in black looking in on you, and a fella beside me there, comforting me, the smell of aftershave off

him, his arm round me waist. And the fella asks me then if I'll be going for a drink with him at his place after (16).

When Maureen goes out and then spends the whole night with Pato, she wears a black dress to charm him, marking a symbolic victory over Mag, the obstacle to her sexual gratification. In fact, Maureen's matricide is the realization of her dream, the dream-like quality reinforced by the deed not being enacted on stage but merely suggested to have happened through displaying the outcome in a mode which verges on the surreal. Emphasizing the intersection of sexuality and violence, the horrifying outcome is introduced by the woman's wildest fantasies about herself and Pato at the station, where they never met, as she sees him off and they exchange long farewell kisses like lovers in romantic films.

The pressure of increasing sexual frustration is known to be capable of propelling people to transgress boundaries of right and wrong, and resort to different levels and degrees of violence. Since the night spent with Pato fails to bring about her long overdue defloration, Maureen is but supplied 'with ammunition in her never-ending war of attrition with her senile mother', Peter James Harris writes in his article about sex and violence in the play.[15] In the morning after the sexual fiasco Maureen comes down to the kitchen wearing only a bra and a slip to show off her newly achieved liberation. Invoking the century-old, stereotypical Irish response to failure, she seeks a way of compensation at least in words, the eloquent force of speech acts, which substitute for the lacking result of the actual deed. To shock her mother by demonstrating her denial of the morals Mag represents and had imposed on her during her upbringing, Maureen addresses what follows to the man, though intends it much rather for the ears of the old woman: 'You'll have to be putting that thing of yours in me again before too long is past, Pato' (28). When she gets to know that Mag destroyed Pato's love letter to her before she could have read it, she takes revenge by spilling hot oil on her mother's hand, a method she uses not for the first time during their troubled relationship as it is made clear. The huge and heavy iron poker with which she strikes Mag dead is an object loaded with phallic significance, and as such is ostentatiously made on display in the setting throughout the drama to call attention to the source and nature of Maureen's rage and motivation to murder.

Despite using a small cast, the playwright manages to extend the idea that in Leenane self-serving brutality is not at all exceptional. Maureen is depicted as just one of a world where sex and violence are suggested to prevail as ubiquitous and interlinked ingredients of the people's experience, ambitions and interests. The nineteen year-old character, Ray evokes the stereotype of the 'disoriented juvenile', being refashioned as a figure who complains of boredom and is incapable of any kind of attachment whatsoever on his part to anything and anybody in the 'frozen, locked-in society' of Leenane.[16] Ray is an emotional casualty of the seduction of the worst products of popularized global culture. At the expense of cultivating local values and relationships he watches TV, his favourite show being, as he describes it zealouly, a foreign one, in which 'Everybody's always killing each other and a lot of the girls do have swimsuits' (37). The roots of middle-aged Maureen and young Ray's aggressive thoughts and behaviour are shown as comparable in the last scene of The Beauty Queen, where the boy voices an irresistible wish to take possession of the 'awful good poker' (58) he catches sight of and becomes fascinated with while scrutinizing the woman's household. Deploying the power of the visual for psychological effects, the interlude dramatizes Ray's secret dream to grab such a weapon-like, phallic-shaped instrument as an extension of his own masculinity and realize, by using it, his movie-inspired fantasies, the dealing of blows and the spilling of blood 'just for the fun' (39).

McDonagh continues to be intrigued by inverting the stereotype of the country youth, and endows him with an 'education' which involves the loss of direction amidst corruption and antagonisms – in the next piece of the Leenane trilogy, A Skull in Connemara, Mairtin is another revised version of the figure. The central occupation of the male characters in the play, the digging up of old bones in the cemetery is the context to the rise of violent acts, inspired by their misdirected physical energy and the pursuit of selfish causes. Being in his late teens or early twenties, Mairtin's concern with sexuality and the body is not at all surprising, yet the morbid and grotesque forms of its direction and expression certainly are. He is curious to know whether the bodies he and Mick turn out of the earth still have their 'thing' attached to them (26), which little boyish obsession with the male genitals has a shade of the Freudian castration complex about it. Another sign of his sexual immaturity is that he cultivates fantasies about women in adolescent fashion: he is longing to kiss the singer Dana and has naïve suppositions about the looks and sexual habits of 'lesbos' (63). His desires remaining wild and unfulfilled, it is in physically violent acts that he can find satisfaction. Even with his own skull smashed after both Mick and Thomas took revenge on him for interfering with their goings-on, the boy remembers 'that oul battering them skulls to skitter [as] the best part of the whole day' (64), a kind of climactic point in the drama where gravediggers Mick and Mairtin, both fairly soaking with drink, are unmistakably enjoying the smashing of skulls and bones to smithereens. Rage and frustration underlie their desperate aggressivity, exercising it being the way the two are able to counterbalance their respectively unsuccessful commerce with other people, since '[t]his is the only lesson skulls be understanding'.[17]

With Mick the figure of the forlorn widower is introduced, who lost a wife prematurely under dubious circumstances and mourns her recollecting details of their married life. However, the details add up to a rather contradictory picture, not unlike what socio-logists' analyses reveal about the fate of the Irish rural marriage, a largely economy-driven phenomenon until recent times. On the one hand, Oona 'didn't have big faults really' as a housewife: she would just 'never wrap up cheese properly' and 'never wrap up bread properly' either, and 'was terrible at scrambled eggs' (54), according to her husband. On the other hand, Mick misses 'the talk of her' (54), the way she stood up for him against people and would defend him even now, he maintains, if she were alive. The obvious contrast between these accounts suggests that the mar-riage may well have had its dissatisfactions multiplying throughout time, presumably in the domain of sexuality that the references to Oona's not being good at certain basic duties of their marital life disguise in Mick's talk. At the end of the play, only Mick is on stage as he is looking '*at the rose locket then picks up the skull and stares at it a while, feeling the forehead crack. He rubs the skull against his cheek, trying to remember'* (66). The moment carries sentimentality which balances the savagery of the action including Oona's one-time mysterious death as well as the secret exhumation of her corpse by Thomas, the bachelor policeman, who is overwhelmed with the memory of the dead body of a fat man found 'stark naked' (30) in his armchair. Thus Mick's caressing of the skull provides an adequately grotesque closure to the black comedy of *A Skull* replete with violence, past and present, and a perverse interest in sex and bodily functions.

Another side of adults' sexual inexperience and its possible links with self-centered indifference and even mindless brutality toward others is examined in *The Lonesome West*, the closing piece of the trilogy. Protagonists Coleman and Valene embody the stereo-type of the bachelor farmers who live 'with no women to enter the picture for either of ye to calm ye down, or anyways not many women or the wrong sort of women' as Father Welsh quite precisely words it in his farewell letter to them.[18] In her book on cultural identity in contemporary Irish drama, Welsh critic Margaret Llewellyn-Jones draws an insightful comparison between the portrayal of rural brothers by Sebastian Barry's *Boss Grady's Boys* and the dramatic conception of such figures in McDonagh. She contends that whereas the former play

> celebrates the caring and loving potential of men, even within the confines of a narrow rural existence, the blackly comic *The Lonesome West* explores masculine violence in such frustrating circumstances.

Investigating the parallels of the two plays is well justified on account of theme and setting, but Llewellyn-Jones seems to judge McDonagh's strategy of representation inferior insofar as it does not 'provide a consistent critique of the negative quality of masculine violence'.[19] To argue on the grounds of such an expectation betrays subscription to the dogmatic view that literature in general and drama in particular are obliged to fulfill the task of exposing and criticizing social wrongs and thus re-establish the moral balance in the created world to satisfy the audience. One could hardly deny that McDonagh's brothers are vastly different from Barry's. The former are introduced through the medium of a style which hovers between the real and surreal to unmask secrets about the potentially brutal underside of human behaviour, whereas the Grady pair is drawn with lyricism, understanding, and compassion. Essentially, the two kinds of approach and choice of emphasis have called for divergent ways of dramatic construction and the shaping of character as well as context in the two plays.

The lack of sexual maturity in *Lonesome* is signified by a whole spectrum of characteristic gestures and remarks. Like adolescents, Coleman and Valene, the middle-aged celibate brothers indulge in bragging about their sexual adventures: Coleman about his sex appeal which, as he says, aroused poitín-seller Girleen to offer a bottle to him if he lets her touch him 'below' (17). Valene, in his turn, mentions having kissed '[n]earer two million' proper women (44) as opposed to his brother, whom nobody kisses according to him. The stories are never about consummation or actual love-making, and the apparent exaggeration involved but confirms how little they have to do with reality and much rather with the need to outdo the other brother. Girleen, in fact, makes fun of Coleman and Valene as incompetent males who never get any use of condoms 'unless they want using them on a hen', and it 'need[s] to be a blind hen' (39) on top of it, her mockery reflecting the nature of conventional assumptions about the private life of aging bachelors. The sexually charged bragging and self-flatteries of the brothers are usually combined with a variety of verbal insults that they throw at each other. These tend to carry a paradoxical if not entirely nonsensical mixture of hetero and homosexual reference, the more fantastic, obscene, and perverse the better, for instance the abusive label 'virgin fecking gayboy' (19, 20, 23, 45) or 'sissy-arse' (64), which prevail like ordinary catch-phrases in their vocabulary. Since homosexuality had been criminalized and stig-matized as a form of contemptible deviance in traditional Irish socio-cultural discourse, the above phrases in the brothers' language are serving to debase and abject the other. To the same effect, the argument of the two about the identity of immigrant Paki-men culminates in Coleman declaring Valene, who shows more understanding toward them, suspect of 'falling in love with Paki-men' (14). As a rule, Valene is quick to retort. Coleman interprets his having put the letter 'V' on all objects in the house to indicate his ownership as meaning 'Virgin' (21), and taunts Valene with his reading a women's magazine in his pastime. When

Coleman takes the magazine in hand, Valene snatches it away as his property from him, and strikes home with: 'Have these fingers you (*V-sign*) and take them to bed with you' (45).

Joan FitzPatrick Dean observes that in *The Lonesome West*, similarly to the rest of the trilogy, sex is pervasive, yet the consummation of desire 'remains the rarest of occurrences',[20] if it ever takes place at all. Even what begins as a budding relationship becomes soon aborted and buried in misplaced and incompetent gestures. In scene four Father Welsh and Girleen disclose their Christian names to each other and do as much as hug, almost finding intimacy and understanding. Yet the vague signs of love and tenderness are stifled by the strength of mutual fears to believe that the expression of genuine emotions and sexual attraction are normal and human:

> **Girleen:** I do only tease you now and again, and only to camouflage the mad passion I have deep within me for ya …
> (**Welsh** *gives her a dirty look. She smiles.*)
> **Girleen:** No, I'm only joking now, Father.
> **Welsh:** Do ya see?! (33)

After Father Welsh's suicide Girleen gives vent to her rage over the thwarting of her amorous hopes and plans by the violent act of cutting into two the chain with a heart pendant on it, which she had ordered from 'me mam's Freeman's catalogue' (48) to give the priest as a token of love. Concurrently, the language of her mock-keening reveals that what she is actually mourning is not so much the death of Welsh but the sudden collapse of her own dreams and ambitions, love being shown as a sentimental and selfish absorption:

> All my poteen money gone. I should've skittered it away on the boys in Carraroe, and not go pinning me hopes on a feck I knew full well I'd never have (48).

Being stigmatized as feminine and childlike in the colonialist discourse had sent the Irish male on a long-term fight to reclaim his masculinity, nationalist ideology itself linking the values of manhood with violence and positing sexual prowess as the opposite of weakness. McDonagh magnifies how, against the background of this legacy of the national experience, frustration stemming from the pitfalls of gender and family relations provokes a man to engage in extreme action. The play begins with the return of the brothers from their father's funeral, who had been shot dead by Coleman in revenge for the old man's criticism, inflated into an inexcusable insult, of the messiness of his hair when saying that it was like 'a drunken child's' (30). What particularly sensitizes Coleman to remarks that refer to something being wrong with his body is not so much the feeling of actual loss (he used to be in love with a girl who married another man), but the self-indulging memory of the blow his masculinity once suffered, evoking the stereotypical Irish preference for imagined wrongs. Moreover, grotesque analogies with the contradictory turns of twentieth-century Irish history and their consequences are presented here on the level of family squabble. Intended to solve a conflict between generations, the act of killing the interfering father has its Oedipal side: to get rid of patriarchal dominance in the house, and breathe 'free and easy' (3) as Father Welsh words it. Ironically, the deed but leads to the further disempowerment of Coleman, who has to buy his brother's silence about the patricide by allowing Valene to become the new boss over him and have all the property to himself. The gun, an object now belonging to Valene, is a counterpart of the poker in *The Beauty Queen* as a phallic symbol of power. Coleman grabs it to fight back and destroy whatever he can to parade his damaged manhood. His first onstage violent act, the putting of Valene's plastic saint-figurines inside the oven is fuelled by a further insult to his masculinity: his brother calls him a 'virgin fecking gayboy' (23), who is hardly able to accomplish the manly job of dragging the drowned policeman's body out of the water.

'[A] good fight' (67), the traditional test of manhood is set up before the protagonists decide to go out for a drink to refuel themselves at the end of the play. They nearly kill each other with knife and gun, yet in the Beckettian fashion all will probably begin again, since the brothers need to prove their masculinity constantly in some physically forceful way, so as not to look an 'oul sissy' (67), their label for Father Welsh, who begged them in his farewell letter not to fight any more. The scene is introduced by a game of apologizing, 'a great oul game'(53) in that it is an exercise to prepare for battle, similar to the ritual-like course of the sexualized games the older couple play in *Who's Afraid of Virginia Woolf?* The whole is taking a really dangerous turn when the apologies run for offences that involve violation of the other's emotional life and experiences concerned with sex. Valene confesses to Coleman that it was he who nudged a pencil down the throat of the girl the other was in love with at school out of pure jealousy, to prevent that she and Coleman go dancing together the following day as planned. In addition to its brutality, the act of shoving a pointed object into a female body obviously gains a sexual overtone by functioning as a coital substitute. Coleman, in turn, apologizes to his brother for having snipped off the ears of Lassie, a bitch that must have held the place of a lass in the heart of her owner, Valene.

Parallelling the enlarged vision of the stereotypically inextricable ties between the need to prove masculinity and fight in *Lonesome*, *The Cripple of Inishmaan* offers a parody of the entangled issues of femininity and violence in modern Ireland. For the present analysis Helen is the most strategic character of the play, her combative spirit anticipated by Girleen in *Lonesome* keeping a butcher's knife in her drawers to take it out whenever needed. A pretty girl called Helen naturally evokes the image of the heroine of the same name from Greek mythology, and the war and destruction her beauty caused and has remained associated with. Also, in the Irish context, the name brings to mind Yeats's perception of his beloved, the revolutionary spirited Maud Gonne as a modern-time Helen whose beauty is 'like a tightened bow' and who has 'taught to ignorant men most violent ways'.[21] Elizabeth Butler Cullingford contends that

> figuring her Helen, Yeats radically modifies the archetype: Homer's passive queen, the sex object over whom men fight their battles, becomes a warrior, identified by the simile of the bow as an Amazon [...] instead of causing Troy to be destroyed, she burns it herself.[22]

Through her senselessly aggressive deeds, McDonagh's Helen of Inishmaan looks much like a caricature of the revolutionary spirited, independent-minded and determined Irishwoman engaged in anticolonial struggle. Equally to her predecessors she is beautiful and full of energy but both her attractive sexuality and her ferocity find expression in ways which entirely lack any sign of heroic nobility and dignity.

The stereotype of the kind-hearted, bashful while vigourous, yet certainly virginal Irish country colleen is known from nineteenth-century oral tradition and sentimental literature like Dion Boucicault's melodrama. In seventeen-year-old Helen with a rural background this figure receives a subversive refashioning as well. On the one hand, she kisses men to earn favours, for instance the male members of the crew involved in the shooting of the film *Man of Aran*, as she seeks to win their assistance to be selected for getting a role in the next American film. On the other hand, she routinely assaults men and is in the habit of pegging eggs, which she sells and usually has a couple with her, at whomever and whatever she happens to dislike or find some kind of fault with. The film the characters from Inishmaan are actually watching in the play (and do not recognize for a story about themselves) is no exception: 'Oh they still haven't caught this fecking Shark! How hard is it? […] *throws an egg at the screen*'.[23] Nevertheless, the gesture hardly expresses a genuine criticism of the representational short-comings of the film, it is more like Ray's ambition in *The Beauty Queen* to have fun by dealing blows at whatever the target. Helen's treatment of Cripple Billy, the only inhabitant of Inishmaan who has genuine feelings and love for her, and her 'winks and nudges' attitude to the idea of intimacy with a boyfriend duly signal her emotional immaturity. She looks at Billy with a mixture of infantile intolerance toward bodily imperfection and the mindless curiosity of a child who does not yet know when it inflicts pain, poking the boy '*hard in the bandaged face*' (82) once she has agreed to walk with him like lovers.

Political analogies involving gender occur in *The Cripple* lowered to the level of the petty and mundane. Introducing her analysis of Yeats's *The Herne's Egg* in her book on gender in modern Irish drama, Susan Canon Harris dwells on the significance of eggs in the socio-political discourse of 1930s Ireland when the play she deals with was written and when McDonagh's takes place. The critic lists examples for the contemporary comic representations of Eamon De Valera breaking bucketfuls of eggs while failing to make a proper omelette, that is to revitalize the home economy as he envisaged it in one of his speeches using the metaphor of the egg. Another aspect of the metaphorical role of eggs in the early post-colonial period was that the Irish woman, Harris continues, was expected 'to protect her eggs' and 'allow the state to use them', in other words her reproductive abilities had to serve higher interests than just her own.[24] Helen's pegging of eggs in *The Cripple* seems to offer a grotesque echo of the phenomena that Harris discusses. Eggs are symbolic of fertility, therefore a young female's de-struction of them in 1930s Ireland could qualify as a symbolic feminist protest against the conservative ideology of gender exploitation. Helen, however, does not employ the gesture as a form of meaningful resistance: her serial pegging of eggs expresses merely her barren rage against the whole world without distinction. In reply to Billy's question about why she needs to be so violent Helen gives a rather peculiar explanation for her behaviour to-wards men: 'I do have to be so violent, or if I'm not to be taken advantage of anyways I have to be so violent' (76). With its chaotic and tautological wording her nonsensical claim sounds like an empty mockery of the principles of feminism formulated on behalf of and in defence of women who have to cope in a male-dominated society. The latter principles have frequently been couched in terms connected with battle, but for a well-defined goal, suffice it to quote from the charter of Irish Women United, completed in 1975: 'At this time, the women of Ireland are beginning to see the need for, and are fighting for liberation'.[25] Likewise, the girl's fierce demand that the film *Man of Aran* about the life and culture of her home community should have 'The Lass of Aran' as its title is a perversion of the idea that a reversal of the conventional gender hierarchy and the reallocation of privileges will be an appropriate solution to the century-old oppression of and discrimination against women.

In the four early McDonagh plays under scrutiny above there is endless talk, all too often indulging in obscenities about sex and related bodily activities, but the more than obvious importance of these for the characters comes down to be a sure sign that they have no healthy and satisfactory sex life. 'Matching the violence and madness of the plays is the pervasive sense of bodily functions, [and] sexual desire', Shaun Richards contends,

reminding us, at the same time, that McDonagh is on already
known territory, that of Synge, but 'McDonagh's work is even
more tragic', without a playboy to emerge and transform at least
himself.[26] While the emotionally and sexually immature
protagonists of the trilogy and *The Cripple* attack and torture each
other in words as well as deeds, they show no control of and
respect for the body, confirming Cheryl Herr's analysis of the
relative lack of a 'comfortable sense of the body' in Ireland and the
historically evolved, long-lasting troubled relationship between the
Irish mind and the Irish body.[27] Inhibited and incapacitated to join
their body with that of another human being or allow it to happen
in the case of other people to achieve mutual sexual fulfillment,
McDonagh's characters trans-gress the borders between bodies in
ways which deny under-standing and intimacy. Instead of love they
make war and tend to resort to various forms and degrees of
violence including the extremity of homicide.

It is evident, however, that McDonagh's mirror up to the
deficiencies of Irish morals is a grossly distorting one, given that
the intensity and relentlessness of evil and the manifestations of
contempt for and murderous hatred of the fellow individual are
assuming strikingly (and suspiciously) unrealistic proportions.
Responsible for the overall effect, the writer's comic and tragicomic dramaturgical arsenal is by all means complex, relying on the
subtle interplay of grotesque exaggeration, subversive irony,
parody, and caricature. The latter collaborate in creating such a
negative and unsettling picture that it calls for an adjusting comparison with lived experience and/or the awareness of authentic
cultural images. Conversely, believers in the myth of Irish 'sexual
uniqueness' or its remnants along with those who still hope 'to
preserve the vision of a morally pure Ireland'[28] are challenged,
provoked, even forced to reconsider and question their too
positive convictions and complacencies, as well as measure them
against contemporary socio-cultural realities. Through its shrewdly
calculated strategies the McDonagh drama manages to drive the
audience to responses that range between laughter, disturbed or
bitter as it may be, and a keen sense of confronting fundamentally
and disconcertingly shocking material on both page and stage. Not
at all unlike what Orton's farces achieved and inspired some

decades before, displaying uncomfortable truths by telling them at a slant, which method is complicated by the postmodern in McDonagh hallmarking his work as a kind of 'Irish psycho'.

---

[1] José Lanters, 'Playwrights of the Western World: Synge, Murphy, McDonagh'., *A Century of Irish Drama: Widening the Stage* , eds Stephen Watt, Eileen Morgan, and Shakir Mustafa (Bloomington and Indianapolis: Indiana University Press, 2000),pp.204-222.

[2] Aleks Sierz, 'In-Yer-Face Theatre. Mark Ravenhill and 1990s Drama', in *British Drama of the 1990s*, eds Annelie Knapp, Otto Erwin, Gerd Stratmann, Merle Tönnies (Heidelberg: Universitätsverlag C. Winter, 2002), p.108.

[3] Joan FitzPatrick Dean, 'Tales Told by Martin McDonagh', *Nua: Studies in Contemporary Irish Writing*, 3.1 & 2, 2002, p.64.

[4] Julia Furay and Redmond O'Hanlon, eds., *Critical Moments: Fintan O'Toole on Modern Irish Theatre* (Dublin: Carysfort Press, 2003), p.160.

[5] Eamonn Jordan, ed., Introduction to *Theatre Stuff: Critical Essays on Contemporary Irish Theatre* (Dublin: Carysfort Press, 2000), p.xlii.

[6] Mária Kurdi, 'American and Other International Impulses on the Contemporary Irish Stage: A Talk with Playwright Declan Hughes', *Hungarian Journal of English and American* Studies, 8.2, 2002, pp.76-7.

[7] Joan Fitzpatrick Dean, 'Joe Orton and the Redefinition of Farce'. *Theatre Journal* 34.4, 1982, pp.483-5.

[8] Christopher Innes, *Modern British Drama 1890-1990* (Cambridge: Cambridge University Press, 1992), p.272.

[9] Susan Rusinko, *Joe Orton* (New York: Twayne Publishers, 1995), p.90.

[10] Karen Vandevelde, 'The Gothic Soap of Martin McDonagh', Eamonn Jordan, ed., *Theatre Stuff*, p.299.

[11] Marjorie Howes, Introduction to 'Public Discourse, Private Reflection, 1916-70', *The Field Day Anthology of Irish Writing* Vol. IV, eds Angela Bourke et al. (Cork: Cork University Press in association with Field Day, 2002), pp.923-7.

[12] Patrick Lonergan,'"The Laughter Will Come of Itself. The Tears Are Inevitable": Martin McDonagh, Globalization, and Irish Theatre Criticism', *Modern Drama* 47. 4 (Winter 2004), p.637.

[13] Geraldine Moane, 'A psychological analysis of colonialism in an Irish context'. *The Irish Journal of Psychology*, 15. 2&3, 1994, pp.259-260.

[14] Martin McDonagh, *The Beauty Queen of Leenane* (London: Methuen, 1996), p.15. (All further references are to this edition.)

[15] Peter James Harris, 'Sex and Violence: The Shift from Synge to McDonagh', *Hungarian Journal of English and American Studies* 10. 1-2 (Spring/Fall 2004), p.56.

[16] Peter Lenz, '"Anything new in the feckin' west?": Martin McDonagh's *Leenane Trilogy* and the Juggling with Irish Literary Stereotypes', in *(Dis)Continuities: Trends and Tradition in Contemporary Theatre and Drama in English*, eds. Margarete Rubik and Elke Mettinger-Schartmann (Trier: Wissenschaftlicher Verlag, 2002), p.29.

[17] Martin McDonagh, *A Skull in Connemara* (London: Methuen, 1997), p.43. All further references are to this edition.

[18] Martin McDonagh, *The Lonesome West* (London: Methuen, 1997), pp.41-42. All further references are to this edition.

[19] Margaret Llewellyn-Jones, *Contemporary Irish Drama and Cultural Identity* (Bristol, UK: Intellect, 2002), pp.96-7.

[20] Joan FitzPatrick Dean, p.63, 'Tales Told by Martin McDonagh', p.63

[21] W.B. Yeats, *The Collected Poems* (London: Macmillan, 1965), p.101.

[22] Elizabeth Butler Cullingford, *Gender and History in Yeats's Love Poetry* (Cambridge: Cambridge University Press, 1993), p.81.

[23] Martin McDonagh, *The Cripple of Inishmaan* (London: Methuen, 1997), p.7. All further references are to this edition.

[24] Susan Cannon Harris, *Gender and Modern Irish Drama* (Bloomington and Indianapolis: Indiana University Press, 2002), p.247.

[25] From *Banshee* (1975), in *The Field Day Anthology of Irish Writing*, Volume V, eds Angela Bourke et al. (Cork: Cork University Press in association with Field Day, 2002), p.213.

[26] Shaun Richards '"The Ourpouring of a Morbid, Unhealthy Mind": The Critical Condition of Synge and McDonagh', *Irish University Review* 33.1, (2003), pp.204-6.

[27] Cheryl Herr, 'The Erotics of Irishness', *Critical Inquiry* (Autumn 1990), p.6.

[28] Siobhán Kilfeather, 'Irish Feminism', *The Cambridge Companion to Modern Irish Culture*, eds Joe Cleary and Claire Connolly (Cambridge: Cambridge University Press, 2005), p.111.

7 | *Lieutenant of Inishmore*: Selling (-Out) to the English[1]

Mary Luckhurst

Much has been made of Martin McDonagh in the last few years and Martin McDonagh has never been at a loss to make much of himself; as one critic recently put it 'like Wilde, he seems to have nothing to declare but his own genius'.[2] As notorious for his 'offstage brio' as he is for his brand of rural brutishness,[3] he originally found fame with the *Leenane Trilogy* (1996-97),[4] and all his plays up until the latest – *The Pillowman* (National Theatre, 2003) – have been set in the West of Ireland. Though it is not surprising that McDonagh wanted to move away from Irish settings (even some of his advocates had wearied of their predictability).[5] *The Pillowman* is a re-write of a play penned in the 1990s at a time before he had hit on his successful Irish formulae.[6] This article concentrates on *The Lieutenant of Inishmore*, which was premièred by the Royal Shakespeare Company in April 2001.[7]

McDonagh relished the gratifying fact that *The Lieutenant* had originally been turned down by the National Theatre and the Royal Court in England, and by Druid Theatre Company in Ireland. His pronouncements to the press were manifold and strident, insisting that the refusals were 'completely ludicrous' and 'gutless' and claiming that the reason for its rejection lay in managements' fears about how damaging the play would be to the Northern Irish peace process.[8] He had completed *The Lieutenant* in 1996 by the time *The Cripple of Inishmaan* opened at the National Theatre; thus it circulated for four years (during which time the playwright rejected the offer of a New York première) before the Royal Shakespeare Company's then literary manager, Simon Reade, declared it to be 'a genre-bursting and taboo-breaking play'.[9] McDonagh hoped that his play would 'cause a stink' and positioned himself as an *enfant terrible*, seeing himself as liberating English and Irish theatre from a deadening complacency. 'I want to shake it up,' he said, 'I want to push it in interesting directions.'[10] He also wanted to earn lots more money, a subject that he refers to in most interviews, and about which he is nothing if not frank. He has always claimed that he began playwriting when all else failed: 'It was a way of avoiding work and earning a bit of money.'[11]

At the opening of *The Lieutenant* McDonagh was undecided about which was more exciting: theatre for its own sake or the large sums of money. 'When I started writing plays, I was going to just get in, get out and take the money, but now I'm going to stick with it because it excites me.'[12] On *The Leenane Trilogy* he was much clearer: asked about the international popularity of the plays, especially in the States, in Scandinavia and in Germany, he replied: 'I just count the money'.[13] Of course, such blatancy about art and consumerism borrows from 1990s fine art marketing strategies in Britain, namely the packaging of temperament and tactics by the so-called Young British Artists, explored so tellingly by Stallybrass in *High Art Lite*.[14] What the Young British Artists 'discovered' was that causing offence and manufacturing sensation guaranteed them coverage by the mass media, especially if 'the courting of publicity was cloaked with an all-knowing irony'.[15]

Whatever one may think either of his plays or his concerted attempts to play it cool, McDonagh has a fine appreciation of the pecuniary rewards of giving audiences what they want – particularly English audiences – a fact which Dominic Dromgoole, the former Artistic Director of the Bush Theatre in London, recognized early and which led him to 'pass' on his plays.[16] Here I argue that McDonagh is a thoroughly establishment figure who relies on monolithic, prejudicial constructs of rural Ireland to generate himself an income. I wish to counter the disturbingly widespread notion amongst English commentators that McDonagh's excess is of itself radical, and to challenge arguments that his use of stereotypes undermines received ideas of 'Ireland'. Stereotyping is as much a feature of McDonagh's person as it is of his plays: a typical example of the dominant construction of him by the English press is an article by Liz Hoggard in which he is presented as 'One of London's Angriest Young Men', a 'punk playwright', and a man with a 'rock'n'roll reputation'.[17] All are constructions that McDonagh consciously seeks to sustain as the same article demonstrates.

The plot of *The Lieutenant* is composed as black farce. It centres on Padraic, a Lieutenant in the INLA (the Irish National Liberation Army) whose dissidence is a cause of concern to other INLA members. Padraic is first depicted plucking the toe-nails of a dope-pusher in Northern Ireland, a task he perceives as a necessary step in the nationalist cause. News that his cat, Wee Thomas, is ailing is enough to reduce him to tears and send him rushing home to Inishmore, one of the Aran islands. Wee Thomas is thought dead and has been killed by members of the INLA, intent on punishing Padraic for his supposed disloyalty. To cut a long story short, the confusion surrounding the exact circumstances of the cat's death led to the deaths of four members of the INLA and Padraic himself (shot by his would-be lover when she realizes he has killed *her* cat). At the end Padraic's father and his neighbour Davey are left with the corpses which they dutifully begin hacking up in what critics referred to as the 'splatter-fest' ending.[18] The best of the comic moments are splendidly audacious, for example when Donny and Davey are given instructions to cut up the corpses:

> **Donny:** Sure, you can't be asking me to go chopping up me own son, now!
> **Davey:** Well, *I'm* not doing all the work! I'll tell you that!
> **Mairead:** One of ye's chop up Padraic, the other be chopping the fella there with the cross in his gob. And don't be countermanding me orders, cos it's a fecking lieutenant ye're talking to now.
> **Davey:** (*to* **Donny**) That sounds fairer, splitting the workload.
> **Donny:** I suppose.[19]

And some of the one-liners and extended jokes are undoubtedly funny. When Padraic is dragged off by INLA gun-men who intend to execute him, his father says: 'It's incidents like this does put tourists off Ireland.'[20] Broadly, the play depicts an orgy of random violence, and individuals fuelled by a mixture of puritanism, sentimentality, and mindless fanaticism, whose political aims have long been subsumed by a desire to terrorize for its own sake.

This is all very well, but McDonagh's characters are also *all* psychopathic morons and it is this that troubles me. All the characters in *The Lieutenant* have the same profile and the only competition is between who can say the stupidest thing and who can commit the stupidest act. Their two favourite insults for one another are 'feck' and 'thick', which are clearly interchangeable and by insisting on the pig ignorance of every character McDonagh makes any serious debate impossible. Even a single intelligent person, able to challenge, or comment on proceedings in order to expose contrary views and set up an interrogative dynamic would have allowed space for some interesting reflection, but McDonagh is intent on avoiding the possibility of allowing informed politics into the play. Some may think that I need to work on my sense of humour, but the choice of farce as a form does not, as is widely known, presuppose a refusal of serious political debate (often precisely the reverse is true as Dario Fo has proved). Nor does farce inevitably contain characters who are hopelessly dumb, out-and-out psychopaths.

It is the sheer stupidity of McDonagh's characters that English audiences revel in; 'laughter is actually the only proper response to these brain-dead goons' wrote Charles Spencer of the West End transfer in June 2002.[21] Elsewhere they are referred to as 'eejits'[22] and 'clowns';[23] and like Spencer, Jane Edwards thinks 'hysterical laughter is the only appropriate response'.[24] We have no sense of McDonagh's characters interacting as family members or as people who need to earn a living, no sense of their geographical ties or social community, no sense of how they have become what they are. What do McDonagh's characters actually do other than brutalize one another (or animals)? They certainly do not show signs of an intellectual or emotional life, and never engage in meaningful political discussion – indeed they appear bankrupt of historical knowledge. None of this would matter but for the fact that many English critics, while arguing that *The Lieutenant* can be laughed off as a clever joke, also claim that it is a play of political gravitas.

Their reasoning for this conviction is invariably vague and more than imbued with a guilty compulsion to speak in its defence. McDonagh is a 'ferociously moral writer', proclaims John Peter in an extraordinarily elegiac review:

> The violence is neither gratuitous nor self-admiring: it pays its way as drama because it is soaked in moral anger and lit up by the comedy of humane reason.[25]

Given the singular lack of the playwright's interest in either his characters' reason or humanity, this is a peculiarly dislocated panegyric. Indeed, a persistent criticism of McDonagh is that he fails to show compassion for any of the characters in his plays.[26] 'The violence has an undoubted point'[27] asserts John Gross, but fails to explain what it might be. Michael Billington ends his column with the statement that 'this is not simply a splatter play but a fierce attack on the double standards of terrorist splinter groups',[28] though he has not striven to reach this point through argument and this seems a somewhat cavalier description of the INLA.[29] Billington, like other critics, states that the 'serious point' is 'that there's a maudlin core to murderous killers symbolized by the disproportionate grief over a dead cat'.[30] The problem with taking this line is that Padraic and his comrades are portrayed first and foremost as incompetent idiots not 'murderous killers', and there is nothing to persuade spectators that anyone who dies was (a) intelligent enough to understand anything about themselves or about politics; and (b) worth keeping alive anyway. 'Padraic's as thick as a mongo fecking halfwit'[31] says one of the characters in the play, but little distinguishes him from the others. Dominic Cavendish reluctantly admits that 'scaled against the horrors perpetuated over the last thirty years, the net result of the characters' trivial obsessions is to make *Lieutenant* feel like a small play about a big subject'.[32]

The dominant underlying reason for so many English critics' insistence on the political weight of *The Lieutenant* seems to originate in the construction of McDonagh as 'brave' for writing it. 'Brave' is a favourite word in the reviews and if the word is not directly used, the tone of the majority is admiration for what McDonagh apparently 'dares' to do.[33] *The Lieutenant* is overwhelmingly received as 'taboo-breaking' (to borrow Reade's hype) for its 'determination to take the piss out of Irish terrorists'.[34] This is a depressing state of affairs: even cheap laughs require skill and McDonagh certainly knows how to structure comedy, but political substance is all but air-brushed away. *The Lieutenant* is 'alco-pop' drama, as Nicolas de Jongh put it – one of the few critics to express dismay at 'a triumph of bad taste'. De Jongh finds the brutality gratuitous and the humour cheap, nor is he persuaded by the portrayal of the INLA as 'a haven for emotionally retarded, puritanical psychopaths, tainted by sentimentality, ignorant of history, and addicted to murderous violence that proves futile and self-destructive'.[35] As a 'dissection of the Troubles' (that billing again) the play is an offensive failure',[36] wrote Patrick Carnegy. It is a play, however, that lets the English off the hook because it reinforces familiar stereotypes about 'Irishness' and 'Ireland' that were originally invented to brutalize a nation and justify colonization. *The Lieutenant* feeds spectacularly well into a propaganda machine that has been so horribly effective that most English-born people are ignorant of the politics of Ireland's history and still believe that The Troubles have little to do with England.[37] Though recent books such as Brian Graham's *In Search of Ireland* have begun to 'deconstruct the monolithics of exclusive identity in Ireland' and stress the plurality of identities and narrative in existence, it will take a long time to break down culturally ingrained constructions of the 'Irish' as backward and inferior.[38] In fact, in the last decade, the stage is the one place on the English Arts scene where a range of serious, politically engaged voices about the Conflict have been heard. Irish voices are fashionable in England and theatre is particularly susceptible to fashion. *The Lieutenant* has been elevated to commercial status only because it does *not* challenge the Little Englander's view of himself as benevolently superior. Vic Merriman is scathing about the insidiousness of McDonagh's plays, which he likens to Marina Carr's:

> By representing their own countrymen as 'others', and scorching them in the heat of their derision, McDonagh and Carr offer bourgeois audiences course after course of reassurance [...] McDonagh's plays and Carr's substitute for human vitality a set of monsters frozen in the stony gaze of the triumphant bourgeoisie.[39]

McDonagh predictably speaks with a forked tongue: on the one hand, he insists the play is about 'The Troubles', and is an attack on Catholic republicanism, a product of what he calls his 'pacifist rage'; on the other hand, he is adamant that his plays are not rooted in realities: 'none of my plays are especially accurate pictures … they're all just stories'.[40] Yet he states that *The Lieutenant* was the only play with political muscle in 2001 and denounces every other 'stupid empty fucking play' the Royal Shakespeare Company did, while at the same time saying that his main objective with the play was sensationalism, 'was to get as much John Woo and Sam Peckinpah into theatre as possible.'[41] It is clear that McDonagh recognized the flavour of the theatrical times after Sarah Kane's *Blasted*, and *The Lieutenant* does seem a rather obvious attempt to outdo her for blood and guts. But whereas Kane's aesthetic agenda was serious and uncompromising in terms of her refusal to accept limits on naturalistic representation, McDonagh has responded with comic strip violence and a set of characters who merge into a single cod stereotype of 'Oirishness'. McDonagh was certainly shrewd in his recognition that Irish credentials currently count for a lot on the London theatre scene. He has worked hard at forging speech patterns and representations that build on prejudicial constructs of the Irish as little more than bone-headed buffoons. His characters are not quite peasants but they rely on the worst aspects of rural stereotyping. He has been very successful in finding the 'right' formula; of his earliest plays Dromgoole notes: 'There was nothing remotely Irish about them, nor was there anything particular to say. There was just talent.'[42] Troubled also by the recent work Dromgoole elucidates further:

> Martin's work is drenched in the plays of other Irish authors, of Tom Murphy, Billy Roche, Beckett, Synge, O'Casey, even Wilde. Since his greatest talent is as a pasticheur, he is able to produce perfect forgeries of any of these writers at will […] This remains the flaw for me in Beauty Queen of Leenane and the subsequent trilogy. There is too much quotation, it is too directly from other fiction. The rub and resistance of life is absent here. The slow comedy of the world is not reflected in its manic hysteria, nor is the deep pain reflected in its titillating sadomasochistic narrative structures. As pot-boilers they are masterful, but they are not yet a lot more […] It's a pastiche soup, a blend of Irish greats, with a

pinch of sick punk humour thrown in. Its greatest achievement is
that it is entertaining. Martin gives audiences what they want.[43]

Perhaps I would not react so strongly if I could find a single
intelligent Irish character in any of McDonagh's plays, but they are
all apparently victims of their own stupidity, ignorance, and futility.
I question the English critics' representation of McDonagh as
authentically 'Irish'. Though a defender of McDonagh, Karen
Vandevelde asserts that the supposed representativeness of his
Irish plays extends far further than England. Abroad, McDonagh's
drama is often in danger of becoming 'an authentic, re-presentative
picture, made attractive with funny, hilarious incidents'.[44]

McDonagh, born and brought up in London, who holidayed in
Galway as a child, and who identifies himself as 'a Londoner',[45]
more 'authentic' than other playwrights who focus on Ireland? To
promote *The Lieutenant* as a serious political play simply perpetuates
colonially derived propaganda that Ireland is a quaint backwater
full of mentally deficient boors. Pastiche can only go so far, and
even McDonagh recognizes that he has spun himself a trap and is
anxious to get away from Irish themes in future projects.[46] The
English like particular commercial packages where Irish playwrights are concerned: playwrights such as Gary Mitchell and
Frank McGuinness present a world view that is less palatable to
them. It is no accident that Brian Friel's *Dancing At Lughnasa* was
elected for West End and film projects, rather than the more
politically painful *Translations* which is confined to smaller enter-
prises.[47] Sebastian Barry's latest play, *Hinterland* (2002), certainly
showed a continuing thirst for self-examination with Irish audiences; in England the play was met with politeness and political
apathy; in Ireland Barry was castigated for failing to go far enough
in indicting the protagonist, based on Charles Haughey. Nicholas
Grene strains even at the mention of McDonagh in his book *The
Politics of Irish Drama*:

> The phenomenon of Irish drama as a commodity of inter-national
> currency has produced mixed results. It has allowed early success
> to very talented writers such as McGuinness, Barry, McPherson; it
> has enabled McDonagh, a playwright of much more dubious
> originality, to achieve quite astonishing success by manipulating the
> formulae of the Irish play.[48]

Brian Friel would argue that McDonagh is following what used to be a traditional route: 'apart from Synge, all our dramatists have pitched their voices for English acceptance and recognition ... However I think that for the first time this is stopping.'[49] Merriman goes further and condemns Irish audiences too: such plays, he argues, contain

> gross caricatures with no purchase on the experience of today's audiences, their appeal to the new consumer-Irish consensus lies in their appearance as ludicrous Manichaean opposites – the colonial simian reborn.[50]

McDonagh, it seems to me, is in the thoroughly respectable tradition of playwrights who like offending middle-class tastes. His primary concern is with aesthetics – and his so-called politics are less than skin deep. 'If your play is angry at stupid violence it's going to be timeless', said McDonagh in an interview for the *Independent*.[51] If the play also upholds a received ideology in which many English people invest, it is no guarantee of timelessness but unfortunately it will tap into a rich vein of appreciation. At the Barbican I was chilled by the raucous laughter of the audience, who were baying for blood. 'How typically Irish!' was not an uncommon exclamation in the interval and it was not attached to specific condemnation of the INLA but a judgment about the madcap antics of the characters. Similarly, Padraic's madness, described by one character in the play as too mad for consideration by the IRA[52] is treated as a metaphor by one English critic not of the madness of certain INLA terrorists, but of madness 'in the true Irish fashion'.[53] Once again it is McDonagh's ability to conjure monolithic English notions of Irishness that win the day; as Alistair Macauley says 'Oirishness is his domain'.[54] 'Martin McDonagh's bloody Irish farce is the ultimate Irish joke' wrote Robert Hewison – 'Manic terrorism'.[55] Robert Gore-Langton sums up: 'the play's message is simple', he tells us: 'Irish terrorist equals eejit'. He concludes that 'The result is the slickest, sickest, most appallingly bad taste comedy in years. You can only admire the author.'[56] Time and time again English critics conflate McDonagh's character either with all Irish terrorists, or with the Irish *per se*. Exactly why is *The Lieutenant* 'just what the West End needed', as Marlowe claims?[57] He is only right if he thinks the West

End needs a 'gross-out' comedy that relies on a deep-seated English antipathy of the Irish, but can also be interpreted fondly by Americans as a manifestation of a supposedly innate Irish sensibility for high jinx. West End audiences also like to be charmed, or so the critics would have us believe, and 'charm' is another word that is regularly used of McDonagh's plays. By this critics seem to mean that they find McDonagh's ear for language enchantingly accurate, despite the fact that many of his idioms for the Aran Islands are incorrect.[58] Other critics such as Benedict Nightingale become expansively indulgent as they read reality into fiction, expatiating on 'these charming islands', without giving the impression that they even know where they are.[59] Grene has argued about the importance in Ireland of linguistic accuracy on stage,[60] which may be another reason why McDonagh is regarded with uneasy distaste by the majority of Irish critics and academics – even Fintan O'Toole's romanticism of him sounds strangely extreme, and Christopher Morash's argument lacks the author's usual conviction.[61]

My point is that the relentless comic elements in *Lieutenant* are precisely what makes it *safe* for English theatres and audiences alike. We all saw how the press responded to Kane's absence of humour in *Blasted*. Mark Lawson, may write that *The Lieutenant* 'makes *Blasted* look like Teletubbies'[62] (though I think he may have got it the wrong way round), but predictably Lawson is thinking only in terms of comparative gore and schlock. Lawson finds it more of a 'sick bag piece' than *Blasted* and he explores how he reaches this profound judgement in graphic detail. Of course there is an implicit politics in the selection of INLA members for comic demolition, but McDonagh chooses not to pursue it in any depth. English critics generally exaggerate its supposed political import, overlook the political pointers in favour of the comedy (as Lynne Truss puts it: 'what marks it out is not the alarming subject matter but the comedic skill),[63] try to argue it both ways, or decide it is about Irish terrorists, and after 11 September 2001 one writer has decided that it is really 'a complex metaphor for violent sectarianism'.[64]

As for McDonagh's politics, who is he to pour contempt on the peace process? In the mid-1990s peace negotiations were entering a critical new phase and the Conservatives revealed that the Government had conducted extensive secret talks with the Irish Republican Army for years.[65] There was a real but fragile hope. If as McDonagh claims, the National Theatre and the Royal Court were concerned that the play might have a detrimental effect on the peace process, are their decisions not to be lauded? In fact, Graham Whybrow, the Royal Court's Literary Manager is on public record as saying that the play was rejected on grounds of quality.[66] McDonagh's political statements about *The Lieutenant* are few and shallow. It seems to me that it is McDonagh who is getting away with murder – and it suits the English just fine. Perhaps McDonagh does not know the 'Manifesto for the Irish Literary Theatre', written over a century ago, in which the founders pledged to right a wrong:

> We believe [. . .] that our desire to bring upon the stage the deeper thoughts and emotions of Ireland will ensure for us a tolerant welcome, and that freedom to experiment which is not found in theatres in England, and without which no new movement in art or literature can succeed. We will show that Ireland is not the home of buffoonery and of easy sentiment, as it has been represented ....[67]

but I would like to invite him to read it.

---

[1] This essay has been previously published in *Contemporary Theatre Review*, Vol. 14:4 (November 2004), pp.34-41. See journal website http://www.tandf.co.uk

[2] Charles Spencer, *Daily Telegraph* 14 November 2003.

[3] See Matt Wolf, 'Martin McDonagh on a Tear', in *American Theater*, 15:1, (2000), pp.48-50.

[4] Comprising *The Beauty Queen of Leenane* (1996); *A Skull in Connemara* (1997); and *The Lonesome West* (1997). All were Druid Theatre Company/Royal Court co-productions.

[5] See, for example, Peter Lenz, 'Anything New in the Feckin' West? Martin McDonagh's *Leenane Trilogy* and the Juggling with Irish Literary Stereotypes', in *(Dis)continuities: Trends and Traditions in Contemporary Theatre and Drama in English*, eds Margarete Rubik and Elke Mettinger-Schartmann (Trier: Wissenschaftlicher Verlag, 2002), p.35.

[6] It is too early to say whether *The Pillowman* marks an alternative territory

for McDonagh. Reviews were enthusiastic but it was treated as a comic piece, enjoyable in its own right but without much substance. There was a distinct problem with its form: the horror of the protagonist's stories became predictable, and the stories themselves were derivative in style and needed cutting.

7 It opened at The Other Place, Stratford-upon-Avon, 11 April 2001.

8 *Independent* 11 April 2001.

9 Ibid.

10 Ibid.

11 Aleks Sierz, *In-Yer-Face Theatre: British Drama Today* (London: Faber and Faber, 2000), p.222.

12 *Independent* 11 April 2001.

13 Ibid.

14 Julian Stallybrass, *High Art Lite* (London: Verso, 1999).

15 Ibid., p.20.

16 Dominic Dromgoole, *The Full Room: An A-Z of Contemporary Playwriting* (London: Methuen, 2000), p.199.

17 *Independent (Magazine)* 15 June 2002.

18 Paul Taylor, *Independent* 16 January 2001.

19 Martin McDonagh, *The Lieutenant of Inishmore* (London: Methuen, 2001), p.66.

20 Ibid., p.50.

21 *The Daily Telegraph* 28 June 2002. It transferred to the Garrick Theatre.

22 Robert Gore-Langton, *Express*, 18 May 2001.

23 John Peter, *Sunday Times* 20 May 2001.

24 *Time Out* 16 May 2001.

25 *Sunday Times* 20 May 2001.

26 *In-Yer-Face Theatre*, p.242. Sierz, who is otherwise an ebullient enthusiast of 1990s British drama, finds McDonagh's plays of limited appeal: 'the writer disposes of people and their aspirations with a carelessness that eventually irritates'.

27 *Sunday Telegraph* 20 May 2001.

28 *The Guardian* 12 May 2001.

29 'INLA: Established 1975 by breakaway elements from the then Official IRA (Irish Republican Army) who had also founded the Irish Republican Socialist Party in 1974.' See Tim Pat Coogan, *The Troubles: Ireland's Ordeal 1966-1996 and the Search for Peace* (London: Arrow Books, 1996), p.544.

30 *The Guardian* 12 May 2001. Susannah Clapp agrees that the 'important perception' is the highlighting of 'the sentimentality which often

accompanies thuggishness'. *Observer* 20 May 2001.

[31] *Lieutenant*, p.19.

[32] *The Daily Telegraph*, 12 May 2001.

[33] See Lawson, *The Guardian* 28 April 2001; Keith Bruce, *Herald* 14 May 2001; Billington begins his review: 'McDonagh is a brave man', *The Guardian* 20 May 2001; Benedict Nightingale describes it as 'dangerously brave' in *The Times* 14 May 2001; Edwardes finds it 'courageous', *Time Out* 16 May 2001.

[34] Edwardes, *Time Out* 16 May 2001.

[35] *Evening Standard* 14 May 2001.

[36] *Spectator* 19 May 2001.

[37] Irish history is generally a glaring omission in English school curriculae.

[38] Brian Graham (ed.), *In Search of Ireland* (London: Routledge, 1997), p.xii. See also Luke Gibbons, *Transformations in Irish Culture* (Cork: Cork University Press, 1996) and Declan Kiberd, *Inventing Ireland* (London: Jonathan Cape, 1995).

[39] Vic Merriman, 'Heartsickness and Hopes Deferred', in *Twentieth Century Irish Drama*, ed. Shaun Richards (Cambridge: Cambridge University Press, 2004), pp.255-56.

[40] See *Independent* 11 April 2001 and *Independent* (*Magazine*) 15 June 2002. This seems a more accurate description of *The Pillowman*.

[41] *Independent* 11 April 2001. Woo's and Pekinpah's films specialise in violence, McDonagh's debt to the latter, known as 'Bloody Sam' in the trade, is especially manifest.

[42] *The Full Room*, p.199.

[43] Ibid., pp.199-200.

[44] See Eamonn Jordan, ed., *Theatre Stuff: Critical Essays on Contemporary Irish Theatre* (Dublin: Carysfort Press, 2000), pp.299-300.

[45] *Independent* (*Magazine*) 15 June 2002. McDonagh's parents are from the West of Ireland.

[46] Ibid.

[47] Though it is increasingly taught at A Level in the UK school system.

[48] Nicholas Grene, *The Politics of Irish Drama* (Cambridge: Cambridge University Press, 1999), p.262.

[49] See Marilynn J. Richtarik, *Acting Between the Lines: The Field Day Theatre Company and Irish Cultural Politics 1980-1984* (Oxford: Clarendon Press, 1994), p.12.

[50] Merriman, 'Heartsickness and Hopes Deferred', p.253.

[51] *Independent* 11 April 2001.

[52] *The Lieutenant of Inishmore*, p.7.

[53] Lynne Truss, *Daily Mail* 28 June 2002.

[54] Alastair Macauley, *Financial Times*, 28 June 2002.

[55] Robert Hewison, *Sunday Times* 7 July 2002.

[56] *Express* 18 May 2001.

[57] Sam Marlowe, *What's On* 3 July 2002.

[58] Verified for me by Patricia Palmer at the University of York, a specialist in Irish dialects.

[59] *The Times* 14 May 2001.

[60] *The Politics of Irish Drama*, p.263.

[61] See the introduction to Martin McDonagh, *Plays: 1* (London: Methuen, 1999), pp.ix-xvii; and Christopher Morash, *A History of Irish Theatre 1601-2000* (Cambridge: Cambridge University Press, 2002), pp.268-9.

[62] *The Guardian* 28 April 2001. *Teletubbies* is a children's programme for the under-fives, its very inanity causing controversy when it was released.

[63] Coogan, *The Troubles*, pp.385-481.

[64] Liz Hoggard, *Independent (Magazine)* 15 June 2002.

[65] Coogan, *The Troubles*, pp.385-481.

[66] *Independent* 11 April 2001.

[67] See Lady Gregory, *Our Irish Theatre*, 3rd ed. (Gerrards Cross: Colin Smythe, 1972), p.20.

8 | The Politics of Morality:
The Lieutenant of Inishmore

Catherine Rees[1]

Irish Drama is, it would appear, unable to escape from the politics either of its writing or its subject. Martin McDonagh, a playwright who has set all but one of his plays in the rural landscape of the West of Ireland, has been attacked and praised in equal measure for both responding to and refusing to be restrained by the accepted trajectory of Irish theatre. Born in London of Irish parentage, McDonagh is in the perfect position to interrogate the mythology of Irish drama, while simultaneously able to claim this heritage as his own. As Graham Whybrow, literary manager at the Royal Court, puts it, 'McDonagh writes both within a tradition and against a mythology'.[2]

Critics have attacked McDonagh's theatrical technique, and especially his recent Olivier Award-winning play, *The Lieutenant of Inishmore* (2001), arguing that he provides English audiences with stereotypical images of the Irish, existing purely to be laughed at. It is this claim which I will be contesting here. Mary Luckhurst, who finds that its characters are 'all psychopathic morons' and so 'make … any serious debate impossible'. Her argument is that *The Lieutenant* fails in that it provides no overt political commentary. She finds the lack of seriousness in the characters to be an in-dication of a lack of clear political angle, challenging the absence of 'a single intelligent Irish character in any of McDonagh's plays' as proof of 'a set of characters who merge into a single cod stereo-type of "Oirishness".[3]

Luckhurst and other critics clearly feel let down by *The Lieutenant of Inishmore*. Because McDonagh has written a violent play about the violence of terrorism within the INLA, he is seen as not being responsible enough to provide his audiences with adequate moral coordinates to negotiate and respond to his play. The concern is that English audiences are merely laughing at the farcical elements and forgetting to think about the political message that Irish playwrights are traditionally supposed to deliver.

The weakness of this argument is the mistake of aligning Irish drama with political drama *per se*. As Nicholas Grene points out, 'As long as there has been a distinct Irish drama it has been so closely bound up with national politics that the one has often been considered more or less a reflection of the other'.[4] While McDonagh's play is, I would argue, a clear and absolute political satire, there is no reason why Luckhurst should seek a defining politics in his play. The mere fact of his writing an Irish drama on an Irish subject does not dictate a resolute didactic purpose, and to wish for such a moral outlook in the work of a playwright such as McDonagh is, arguably, to miss the point of his drama.

The political impetus behind the writing of *The Lieutenant of Inishmore*, as claimed by McDonagh himself, is, however, clear. What 'spurred him to write [the play] was the IRA atrocity in Warrington, in which two boys were killed', writes theatre critic Charles Spencer in the *Daily Telegraph* (28 June 2002), quoting McDonagh as saying: 'I thought, hang on, this is being done in my name and I just feel like exploding in rage.' Indeed, McDonagh seems to answer Luckhurst's criticism directly when he remarks:

> The violence has a purpose … otherwise there's nothing par-ticularly interesting about shooting people on stage. If people who've had violence inflicted on them on either side of the Troubles see this play, I hope they'll see it as anti-violence.[5]

Comedy and Cruelty

The violence in *The Lieutenant of Inishmore* is one of the aspects of the play that critics object to. Luckhurst speaks of 'an orgy of ran-dom violence' and of 'a rather obvious attempt to outdo her [Sarah

Kane's *Blasted*] for blood and guts'. It is undeniably a violent and horrific play, whose plot involves a *Reservoir Dogs*-style torture scene in which a drug dealer is hung upside down on stage at the mercy of 'Mad Padraic', a terrorist refused membership to the IRA because he was '*too* mad'.[6]

What makes the violence harder to stomach is the comedy which accompanies it, and it is this irreverence to the violence of the Northern Irish political situation which so unnerves critics. The sinister torture scene is cut short by a telephone call from Padraic's father and includes moments of black comedy such as 'I'm torturing one of them fellas pushes drugs on wee kids, but I can't say too much over the phone, like', and Padraic politely apologizing to his victim for the delay: 'I'll be with you in a minute now, James.' The on-going joke in the play is established as it emerges that Padraic cares more for his sick cat than for the human victims of his crimes, finally allowing James to go after he feigns a love of cats himself and Padraic '*gives the confused James some change*' for the bus to the hospital, 'because you want to get them toes looked at. The last thing you want now is septic toes.'[7]

The brutality in the play certainly resembles that of farce. The bodies which pile up by its end recall the carnage of Alfred Jarry's infamous *Père Ubu*, 'in which crowds of victims are gleefully tortured and murdered before our eyes'.[8] But, like Jarry's play, which sought to challenge the accepted conventions of the French theatre, McDonagh uses cruelty not to titillate middle-class audiences and create an *enfant terrible* reputation, but to expose the cruelty and pointlessness of the terrorism he is criticizing. As Charles Spencer puts it, 'The more gory and outrageous the action becomes … the more forcefully he makes his point about mindless barbarity.'[9] And McDonagh himself tells us:

> I walk that line between comedy and cruelty … because I think one illuminates the other. And, yeah, I tend to push things as far as I can because I think you can see things more clearly through exaggeration than through reality … There is a humour in there that is straight-ahead funny and uncomfortable. It makes you laugh and think.[10]

Deflating Mythology

David Ian Rabey argues (paraphrasing Marx) that 'by intensifying a situation it becomes a revolutionary one'.[11] Arguably, when Luckhurst finds the characters of McDonagh's plays one-dimensional and stereotypical, she is reacting against McDonagh's use of caricature to deflate the Irish mythology of previous drama and to make a very specific point about the sentimentality of both Irish rural drama and of the approaches to radical terrorism.

W.A. Armstrong writes of J.M. Synge's *The Playboy of the Western World*, a play that is often seen as having influenced McDonagh's *Lonesome West* and *A Skull in Connemara*, 'Synge had a great affection for the peasant communities that he knew, but in his plays he satirizes their credulity, violence, and parochialism'.[12] This is, I'd suggest, exactly what McDonagh is doing – writing within this classical Irish tradition of the idyllic, pastoral countryside, while savagely attacking the sentimentality of the terrorist movement as a noble response to 'the love of one's land' by employing the overt and dramatic tactics of the London playwrights of the late 1990s, the so-called 'in yer face' British drama.[13] It is this combination of dramatic styles which makes *The Lieutenant* so hard for critics.

Aleks Sierz characterizes this trend in British drama by stressing 'its intensity, its deliberate relentlessness, and its ruthless commitment to extremes'. He also argues for the need for violence and provocative images on stage as they undermine traditional stage constraints,

> affronting the ruling ideas of what can or should be shown on stage [and] also tap[ping] into more primitive feelings, smashing taboos, mentioning the forbidden, creating discomfort.[14]

A good example of a play that employed some of these techniques in an earlier era is Edward Bond's controversial *Saved* (1965), in which a baby is stoned to death in its pram. Sarah Kane, a leading figure of 'In-yer-face' drama, was influenced by it, remarking, 'When I read *Saved*, I was shocked by the baby being stoned. But then I thought, there isn't anything you can't represent on stage.'[15]

This attitude leads to a refusal to ignore the sometimes sordid and violent aspects of life, and a determination to represent them in the theatre. The justification for the explicit violence in these plays is that in the 'jagged and violent decade' of the 'nineties, plays sometimes need shocking images which are 'impossible to ignore'. Similarly, comedy is a valid device for tapping into the audience's psyche: Sierz argues that 'a common reaction to terror is either to ignore it or to laugh at it'.[16] We cannot ignore the terror in McDonagh's play because we are laughing at it, but on a deeper level the audience is also implicated in the violence because we are vicariously enjoying it. This is exactly the uncomfortable position McDonagh wishes to put us in.

Squeam Tactics

When Luckhurst argues that McDonagh is pandering to his English audiences, she seems to overlook the complex trap he is setting for them. Mark Lawson argues that McDonagh intends to confound audiences' expectations by 'mak[ing] us worry more about the cats than the humans involved', while Susannah Clapp says that McDonagh

> uses the squeamishness of his audience – who are more accustomed to seeing a stage littered with human corpses than witnessing the death of one pet puss – to highlight the sentimentality which often accompanies thuggishness.[17]

By increasing our attachment to the cats of the play, McDonagh is cleverly trapping the very audience that Luckhurst argues he is courting into an alignment with Padraic. In doing so, McDonagh is subverting the theatrical convention – notably that of the Jacobean revenge tragedy, which accepts the loss of human life as part of the theatrical occasion – and is instead focusing our attention on the absurd sentimentality which worries and fusses over the death of a terrorist's cat. The irony of animal rights campaigners protesting at the use of live cats in a Dutch performance of the play would surely not be lost on McDonagh.[18]

In exposing the inconsistencies in both the audience and in the creation of Padraic's character, McDonagh is not only 'razor sharp on the terrorists who quite happily torture and murder human beings, but are desperately concerned about the welfare of cats', but he is also mounting a scathing attack on 'a band of men … whose murderous activities are motivated by adolescent absolutes and maudlin sentimentality'.[19]

When Luckhurst states that she finds 'political substance all but air-brushed away'[20] in *The Lieutenant of Inishmore*, she is clearly overlooking the subtle inversion of political idealism and Irish political history. Not only is McDonagh confronting the audience with a sentimentality which forces them to question their own moral system, he is simultaneously challenging them to condemn the utopian ideals that are becoming meaningless and forgotten.

Against Political Sentimentality

The Irish history presented in the play is based on particularly shaky knowledge, not due to McDonagh's personal dismissal of its significance but because the characters are operating in a world which no longer understands it. For instance, the INLA understand they should be antagonistic towards Oliver Cromwell, but can no longer remember why. Christy's remark, 'Do you know how many cats Oliver Cromwell killed in his time?' (30) exposes the absurd reduction of Irish history into the image of a maltreated cat, thus condemning the terrorist movement which still fights in its name. Mairead's choice of name for her own cat, Sir Roger Casement, similarly reduces Irish history to the laughably absurd. More recent history does not escape McDonagh's scorn, either, when Joey tries to liken the battering of a cat to the Bloody Sunday massacre (28).

McDonagh's criticism of the misuse of Irish political history doesn't end with *The Lieutenant of Inishmore*. Ray Dooley in *The Beauty Queen of Leenane* equates his drunken escapade of kicking a cell door in just his socks with the injustice of the Birmingham Six case. Similarly, Padraic completely misses the point when he remarks, 'Ah feck the Guildford Four. Even if they didn't do it, they should've taken the blame and been proud.' When Mick Dowd in *A Skull in Connemara* remarks, 'That's the trouble with young people today, they don't know the first thing about Irish history', McDonagh is clearly challenging the validity of this past as a basis for terrorism.[21]

In challenging the sentimentality and also absurdity of the Irish terrorist movement, McDonagh also exposes the pointlessness of the terrorists' fight. By setting the plays in southern rather than northern Ireland, he instantly retracts the immediacy of the situation and exposes the farce of extreme terrorist violence in a *'cottage on Inishmore'* in which there is a *'framed piece of embroidery reading "Home Sweet Home"'* (3) – an environment which says very little to the audience in terms of justifying terrorism.

Likewise, McDonagh takes care to undermine the utopian ideals of his characters by showing them as lacking in vital respects. Padraic's advice to Mairead, to 'be staying at home, now, and marry some nice fella. Let your hair grow out a tadeen and some fella's bound to be looking twice at you some day, and if you learn to cook and sew too, sure, that'd double your chances. Maybe treble' (36), along with his insistence that 'We don't be letting girls in the INLA. No. Unless pretty girls' (35), demonstrates that his ideals are based on a foundation which is hypocritical and opportunistic.

The direct link McDonagh makes between the drugs trade and the funding of terrorism again undermines Padraic's ideal. Christy points out to Padraic that the drug dealers he is so fond of tortur-ing, because they sell to Catholics as well as Protestants, are 'fella[s] without whom there'd be no financing for your ferry crossings and chip-shop manoeuvres' (45). The constant reference in the play to 'freeing Ireland' is shown to be, in the hands of terrorists, a worthless ideal. Brian Logan writes, 'There's no room for ambi-guity … no one could think of these terrorists as freedom fighters. They're sexist, emotionally stunted, and con-cerned with the implications for tourism … McDonagh's scorn of pig-headed Utopianism and false history has a wide application.'[22] In this con-text, the use of stock characters, whom Luckhurst condemns as '[not] worth keeping alive anyway', become political tools, larger-than-life cartoons who have lost any sense of what they are fighting for.[23]

Challenging the Idyllic

McDonagh's view of Ireland, like his presentation of history and character, is not accidental. Nicholas Grene traces the presentation of pastoral Ireland, citing the film *The Quiet Man* as an archetypal 'classic use of Ireland', employing the 'idyllic landscape' and creating an Ireland which is 'archaic [and] traditional'.[24] McDonagh takes this rural myth and challenges it, deliberately using *The Quiet Man* to destroy the mythology it creates.

In *A Skull in Connemara*, Mick berates Mary for pandering to the tourist 'Yanks', 'telling them your Liam's place was where *The Quiet Man* was filmed, when wasn't it a hundred miles away?' (67). Tourism is an issue McDonagh chooses to confront, acknowledging Ireland's need for it but laughing at 'them eejit Yanks' (67) at the same time. During the violence at the ending of *The Lieutenant of Inishmore*, Donny dryly remarks, 'It's incidents like this does put tourists off Ireland' (50).

The play thus articulates the widening and hybridizing of Ireland into the 'global village', and is punctuated by references to media influence.[25] The characters understand and articulate their experiences through television programmes, for instance, the local policeman glamorizing his job as 'just like *Hill Street Blues*', while Catholic doctrine is reduced to, 'So that fella from *Alias Smith and Jones*, he'd be in hell?', and Padraic's view of women is limited to idealizing 'Evie off *The House of Elliott*'.[26]

Critics of McDonagh would have it that the idiocies of the characters in *The Lieutenant* make 'serious debate impossible'.[27] In the light of the above discussion, perhaps one could further respond by pointing out that this is McDonagh's point. His characters are deliberately extreme and consciously controversial. The very real brutality of the play not only locates it in the tradition of 'in-yer-face' drama, it deliberately forces the audience not to laugh at the stupidities of the Irish but to confront their own approaches to the sentimentality of the Irish political movement and to interrogate the causes of Padraic's dislocation and isolation in a world which no longer remembers the history it is fighting for.

To question the intelligence of McDonagh's characters is also to overlook the fact that he does not want us to find them intelligent and eloquent spokespeople for a political cause, such as John Osborne's Jimmy Porter in *Look Back in Anger* (1956) or David Hare's Susan Traherne in *Plenty* (1978); rather he would prefer we saw them as the gang from Edward Bond's *Saved*, brutal

and thuggish without offering any justification for or comprehension of their actions.

The characters in *Lieutenant* cannot be judged within a naturalistic, believable, and realistic context. As Sierz remarks, 'The
problem with judging 'nineties new writing in terms of naturalism
or social realism is that this tries to impose the conventions of a
previous era onto the present.' Sierz also argues that: 'Of course,
'in-yer-face' drama is not strong on either plot or characterization
– but its power lies in the directness of its shock tactics, the
immediacy of its language, the relevance of its themes, and the
stark aptness of its stage pictures.'[28] Failure to appreciate this often
lies at the heart of criticism of McDonagh and can be expressed as
the dichotomy laid out at the beginning of this paper: the use of
1990s shock tactics on the one hand, and the exploration and
interrogation of traditional political drama and Irish dramatic
tradition on the other.

Conclusion

I would argue that it is impossible to appreciate *The Lieutenant of
Inishmore* without an understanding of its context. The violence and
shock-potential of this play not only align it with a 1990s trend
which is seeking to test the limits of theatricality and to push the
boundaries of what can be shown on stage, it is also reminiscent of
Jacobean tragedies, ending as they do in bloodshed and the piling
up of corpses on stage.

The Lieutenant of Inishmore recalls this classic technique, with its
'blood-soaked living room strewn with body parts' (55), but it also sits well
in the tradition of farce and surrealism. The politics of the play are
made clear in the absurdity of the ending, when the real 'Wee
Thomas' nonchalantly wanders across the stage, unaware of the
carnage which has taken place in his name. When Davey remarks,
'So all this terror has been for absolutely nothing?' (68), we would
be foolish to ignore the political seriousness in this line, as we
would be to overlook the warmth of the ending in which neither
Davey nor Donny can bring themselves to shoot the cat, instead
feeding it, in an image not unlike Len's mending of the chair at the
close of *Saved*: a clear suggestion of hope among futility. If audiences choose to ignore this message, and the constant ridiculing of

the political extremists which runs throughout the play, it is because of an inability to see past the physical staging and the black humour, which not only give the play its form, but also contribute to its message.

———————————————

[1] This essay was originally published in *New Theatre Quarterly* 21.1 (February 2005).

[2] Graham Whybrow, Introduction to *The Methuen Book of Modern Drama* (London: Methuen, 2001), p.x.

[3] Mary Luckhurst, 'Martin McDonagh's *Lieutenant of Inishmore*: Selling (-Out) to the English', *Contemporary Theatre Review* 24. 4 (November 2004), pp.34–41.

[4] Nicholas Grene, *The Politics of Irish Drama: Plays in Context from Boucicault to Friel* (Cambridge: Cambridge University Press, 1999), p.1.

[5] Daniel Rosenthal, 'How to Slay 'Em in the Isles', *The Independent* 11 April 2001; Charles Spencer, 'Devastating Masterpiece of Black Comedy', *Daily Telegraph* 28 June 2002.

[6] Ibid., pp.3, 7.

[7] Martin McDonagh, *The Lieutenant of Inishmore* (London: Methuen, 2001), pp.13–14, 16. All other references are to this edition.

[8] Maya Slater, Introduction to *Three Pre-Surrealist Plays* (Oxford: Oxford University Press, 1997), p.xii.

[9] Charles Spencer, 'Devastating Masterpiece of Black Comedy', *Daily Telegraph* 28 June 2002.

[10] Sean O'Hagan, 'The Wild West', *The Guardian* 24 March, 2001.

[11] David Ian Rabey, *British and Irish Political Drama in the Twentieth Century* (Houndmills: Macmillan, 1986), p.4.

[12] W.A. Armstrong, 'The Irish Dramatic Movement', *Classic Irish Drama* (Harmondsworth: Penguin, 1964), p.10.

[13] Aleks Sierz, *In-Yer-Face Theatre: British Drama Today* (London: Faber and Faber, 2001). This has a section on McDongah's Leenane trilogy, pp.219–25.

[14] Ibid., p.xiii, 4.

[15] Quoted in Clare Bayley, 'A Very Angry Young Woman', *The Independent* 23 January 1995. See also Edward Bond, *Saved*, in *Plays: 1* (London: Methuen, 1977).

[16] Sierz, op.cit., p.206, 8, 6.

[17] Mark Lawson, 'Sick-Buckets Needed in the Stalls', *The Guardian* 28 April 2001; Susannah Clapp, 'Please Sir, I Want Some Gore', *The Observer* 20

June 2001.

18 'Animal Rights Campaigners Protest at Use of Live Cats in Play', *Ananova* 4 October 2002.

19 Lyn Gardner, review of *The Lieutenant of Inishmore*, *The Guardian* 29 June 2002; Brian Logan, '*The Lieutenant of Inishmore* at The Other Place, Stratford', *The Independent* 21 May 2001.

20 Ibid., p.6.

21 Martin McDonagh, *The Beauty Queen of Leenane* in *Plays: 1* (London: Methuen, 1999), p.33, and *A Skull in Connemara*, p.87.

22 Luckhurst, p.5.

23 Ibid., p.5.

24 Grene, p.211.

25 Sierz, p.221.

26 McDonagh, *Plays: 1*, pp.89, 154; and *Lieutenant*, p.58.

27 Luckhurst, pp.3-4, 7.

28 Aleks Sierz, p.243; and 'Cool Britannia? 'In-Yer-Face' Writing in the British Theatre Today', *New Theatre Quarterly* 56, (November 1998), p.333.

9 | Language Games: *The Pillowman, A Skull in Connemara*, and Martin McDonagh's Hiberno-English

Lisa Fitzpatrick

One of the most intriguing features of Martin McDonagh's *Leenane* and *Aran* trilogies has been the critical controversy that follows, and sometimes precedes, their staging. Read outside of their surrounding publicity, these texts appear to be simply clever, pop-culture comedies by a highly skilful pasticheur.[1] McDonagh's borrowing from other playwrights, including J.M. Synge, Harold Pinter, Samuel Beckett, and Franz Kafka, has been noted by both scholars and reviewers. His influences clearly include Quentin Tarantino, soap operas, and contemporary British playwrights like Mark Ravenhill and Sarah Kane, and he adapts conventional theatrical genres, devices and set-pieces for his own ends, as Nicholas Grene has noted[2]. Therefore, critiques of McDonagh's work as lacking in originality and capitalizing on sensational marketing tactics may seem justified, while his keen ear for the absurdities of domestic friction and sibling rivalry, his skill with comic stock characters, and his ability to blend elements from so many different sources provoke praise and critical interest. What is surprising is his acclaim as the *enfant terrible* of Irish theatre, and equally, the antipathy that his work evokes. While Fintan O'Toole reads McDonagh's plays as 'bridges over a deep pit of sympathy and sorrow, illuminated by a tragic vision of stunted and frustrated lives',[3] Mary Luckhurst argues that it is 'the sheer stupidity of McDonagh's characters that English audiences revel in', seeing the work as reviving colonial Victorian stereotypes of the Irish as brutish and stupid[4]. Vic Merriman's more layered critique reads the plays as pandering to neocolonial impulses within Irish society: the characters, he argues, play nature to the audience's culture, allowing the Celtic Tiger generation to laugh at sections of society left behind by the economic boom[5]. Yet both reactions – acclaim and denunciation – seem more like interpellations into contemporary debates about the rapidly changing nature of Irish culture and identity, than engagements with the actual plays.

Both Merriman's and Luckhurst's arguments are in part responding to the setting of McDonagh's plays in the West of Ireland: Aran and Leenane. Certainly, McDonagh's naming of these places raises the issue of the transfer of material from the actual world to the dramatic world. In his discussion of dramatic logic, Keir Elam addresses this transfer in relation to the inclusion of real people in the dramatis personae, and his argument is largely applicable also to place. Elam argues,

> In view of the flexibility of the 'as if' basis of the dramatic world, allowing the 'actual' to conjoin with the purely hypothetical in an imaginary state of affairs, it is not necessary to accept the Coleridgean notion of the audiences' 'suspension of disbelief' in the presented world. On the contrary, disbelief – i.e. the spectator's awareness of the *counterfactual* standing of the drama – is a necessary constant.[6]

The setting of the works and the playwright's use of certain markers of Irishness – the cottage scene, the crucifix on the wall, the characters' names, and their use of a dialect which seems, initially, to be a form of Irish-English – does not necessarily imply an attempt to represent or perform an actual Ireland, or an Irish identity. In their transfer into the theatrical space and into a fictional dramatic world, these clichés of Irishness take on other significances. Far from representing Ireland, McDonagh hangs the action of his plays on theatrical conventions and Bórd Fáilte imagery, using the fictionalized landscape familiar from tourism marketing campaigns to represent the alienation and stasis of the human condition. An examination of his use of language and the construction of his dialogues reveals considerable similarities between the supposed Irish-English of the earlier plays, and his 2003 play *The Pillowman*, set in a fictionalized central European country. Like the *Leenane* plays, *The Pillowman* draws upon clichéd conceptions of Eastern Europe that have very little to do with the events or histories of actual countries.

The Pillowman is in fact the first of McDonagh's plays, but it was only produced after the success of the *Leenane* trilogy, premiering in its revised form at the National Theatre in 2003. The play is set in an interrogation room, where the writer Katurian K. Katurian of Kamenice 4443, and his brain-damaged brother, Michal, are being held for questioning about a grisly series of child murders, that bear a striking resemblance to the murders in Katurian's short stories. The play takes its title from the story of a man made entirely of pillows, who goes about the world and encourages children to kill themselves before their lives become unbearable. This story is wound into the play in such a way that it becomes a metafiction about Katurian's own family history.

For the purposes of this essay, the exploration of the language and structure of the dialogue will focus on the second in McDonagh's multi-award-winning *Leenane Trilogy, A Skull in Connemara*, and *The Pillowman*. *A Skull in Connemara* opened in 1997, a year after *The Beauty Queen of Leenane*, as a co-production between Druid Theatre Company and the Royal Court. Like its companion pieces, this play in four scenes is an exceedingly dark, grim comedy. It is set in the cottage of Mick the grave-digger, and in the graveyard at night, and follows the annual exhumation of corpses to make room for the newly deceased. Mick is suspected of having murdered his wife seven years previously and passing off her death as a road accident. This year, the remains of Mick's wife will be among the disinterred bones, reawakening in the minds of the other characters – Mary Johnny, and her grandsons Mairtin and Thomas, who is a Garda – the suspicions surrounding her death. The play opens with Mary Johnny calling to Mick's door:

> **Mary:** Mick.
> **Mick:** Maryjohnny.
> **Mary:** Cold.
> **Mick:** Suppose it's cold.

Mary: Cold, aye. It's turning.
Mick: Is it turning?
Mary: It's turning now, Mick. The summer is going.
Mick: It isn't going yet, or is it now?
Mary: The summer is going, Mick
Mick: What month are we now?
Mary: (*Thinks*) Are we September?
Mick: We are, d'you know?
Mary: The summer is going.
Mick: What summer we had.
Mary: What summer we had. We had no summer.
Mick: Sit down for yourself, there, Mary (*Skull*, 63).

This exchange is a long courtesy that brings Mary from the door into the room and gets her seated: the main business of the visit should now follow. Instead, Mary sits down but the dialogue continues, ludicrously exhausting the question of the time of year, and gradually unfolding into a debate on the behaviour of school-children, whom she describes as 'a pack o' whores' (*Skull*, 64).

In her study *Green English*, Loreto Todd identifies certain specific grammatical and lexicographic particularities of Irish-English.[7] These include the tendency to use the continuous form of the verb; the use of 'after' followed by the verbal noun (e.g., I'm after seeing, I'm after hearing, etc.); the tendency to reply to a question using part of the question itself, rather than a simple 'yes' or 'no'; the use of 'and' to connect events occurring simultaneously (e.g., I saw her and she going past); the use of 'but' to emphasize a clause or phrase; the use of 'ye' or 'yous' for you plural; the use of 'a' in place of have, with the past participle; the use of 'them' as a demonstrative plural adjective or pronoun – typically, in place of 'those'; various uses of the verb 'to be' which are not found in standard English, notably the use of singular forms with plural subjects; the use of alternative past participles, often for comic effect, and the tendency towards hyperbole and oblique ex-pressions, again often for comic effect. Todd offers, 'them as raised you was fond of childer' or, 'them as raised you would drown nothing' as an example of the oblique insult which takes a few moments to decipher.[8] These examples also point to a tendency in Irish-English speech to hint at things, to communicate information largely by means of what is unsaid, or by opposites.

The dialogue above illustrates McDonagh's exaggeration of certain aspects of Irish speech, in particular, the tendency to respond to a question with the verb from that question: 'Is it turning?' 'It's turning.' In general in the *Leenane Trilogy* the markers of Irish-English that appear in the text are the use of the 'ín' (een) suffix from Irish as a diminutive, and a limited number of recognizably Irish-English words, notably feck, eejit, shite, get, and skitter, phonetic spellings like 'oul' for old, and occasional word-borrowings from Irish, including beag and poitín (spelt poteen). Some words and phrases that appear in the texts and are common in Irish-English, such as 'aye', the use of 'like' as a form of punctuation and contractions like 'd'you know', are also widely used in British-English dialects. But many of the key linguistic markers identified by Todd are absent. There is no reference to God in the greetings above, for example, few references to God or the saints in any of the plays, and very few alternative past participles. Even those quirks of dialogue construction that seem Irish, such as the repetition and inverted word order, occur also in *The Pillowman*, suggesting that they are typical of the rhythmic cadences of McDonagh's plays, rather than attempts to recreate Irish speech patterns.

Hiberno-English has, of course, a long stage history as a performative concept and marker of identity, being used on the English stage as early as Shakespeare's *Henry V* and Jonson's *Irish Masque*. These represent loyal Irish, although they are wild and exotic: MacMorris famously denounces his 'nation', while Jonson's Irish footmen, though dim-witted, are eager to declare their allegiance to King James, assuring him that he has 'very good shubzhects in Ireland ... Dat love dy mayesty heartily.'[9] Jonson's masque offers a justification for colonialism's civilizing mission in the final image of the Masquers casting off their mantles and appearing in English court dress, as 'new-born creatures all', while stressing the foreignness and inferiority of the un-Anglicized Irish, racializing what is otherwise the common comic device of using regional accents to denote stupidity or lack of sophistication. In the case of Irish dramatic characters, racially indistinguishable from the people at the imperial centre, the aural replaces the visual as a sign of difference: compare *The Irish Masque* with *The Masque of Blackness*, for example.

But although a performed inability to speak grammatical, Queen's English is a comic convention that often expresses both the stupidity of the character and the superiority of the audience, as Luckhurst notes, this is not all it does. Very many Irish playwrights use or create dialects, among them McDonagh's contemporaries Marina Carr and Enda Walsh. Walsh's *Disco Pigs* is an extreme example, where language and accent are used to build an almost impenetrable linguistic world around the two dramatis personae. Although Mary Harris notes that in the contemporary theatre the use of Stage-Irish dialects is sometimes 'for satirical purposes and tends to be associated with stupidity or cunning,'[10] the speech of Irish characters on stage often, even usually, reflects at least some of the grammatical and lexicographic peculiarities of Hiberno-English. This form of language, devised for the stage, has positive resonances as well, as is apparent in the example of Dion Boucicault's *The Shaughraun*.

In *The Shaughraun*, the picaresque Conn is the Stage Irishman who saves the day and charms the audience. With its stage-Irish playfulness, this text might seem to be representative of the 'buffoonery and easy sentiment'[11] criticized by the founders of the national theatre movement. However, the play is clearly not intended as a representation of Irish life: it is a romantic, pastoral comedy set in a fictional land of comely maidens, good-hearted rogues, and benevolent clergy. The play's conclusion, with a humorous dramaturgical device that fractures the distinction between stage and auditorium, relies upon the engagement of the audience with the characters. The performance ends with a direct address to the audience by the eponymous hero, Conn, the Shaughraun. He elicits the spectators' support for his cause in the form of their applause. Approaching the audience, he asks if they will 'go bail' for him, that is, will assure the priest that his intention to reform is genuine, so that he can marry the priest's niece, Moya:

> You are the only friend I have. Long life t'ye! – Many a time have you looked over my faults – will you be blind to them now, and hould out your hands to a poor Shaughraun?[12]

This is the audience's cue to applaud: the show is over. The spectator is drawn into a close sympathy with the dramatic hero, and the applause for the performance becomes inseparable from a display of faith in Conn himself. Boucicault's works elicit responses other than superiority to Stage-Irish characters and dialogue, feeding into a perception that persists into the present that Irish people are warm-hearted, charming, and friendly. The accent and dialect, therefore, are inevitably associated with these same qualities. Thus McDonagh's plays work in part against stereotype: the associations with this accent and language are contradicted by the violence and brutality of the action. These associations are more recent than the simian Irish of the *Punch* cartoons, to which Mary Luckhurst refers, and are surely the predominant ones.

McDonagh's plays depend only partially on their ability to evoke Irish-English, enlisting also visual aspects of performance to play with the conventions and clichés of Irish dramaturgy and theatre practice. *A Skull in Connemara*, like all of the *Leenane* plays, has a stereotypical Abbey set, described in the stage directions as a spartan room in a rural cottage, with a lit fireplace, simple furniture, and a crucifix and farm tools hanging on the back wall. Catholicism and rural life are iconically and indexically present on the stage, and the overall effect is of primitive poverty. It must be noted, however, that it is not clear how much of the set description in the printed text comes from McDonagh, and how much it reflects Druid Theatre Company's staging practice in *The Beauty Queen of Leenane*.[13] Together with the characters' names, Mick, Mairtin, and Mary Johnny, this initially creates the impression of a peasant play. McDonagh incorporates elements of the peasant play genre into a pastiche that includes elements from soap operas and television police shows. The characters acknowledge this: Thomas models himself on *Quincy*, while Mick remarks, 'I thought the way you do talk about it, just like *Hill Street Blues* your job is' (*Skull*, 89). Unlike Marina Carr, however, who also uses the peasant play, but who does so to open questions of power and gender, McDonagh does not delve into the genre but merely adapts its conventions for his own purposes. He does so, not to stage Irish identity or engage the audience in an emotional identification with the characters, but on the contrary, to create the distance that allows the audience to laugh at the horror he presents. The characters who populate Leenane are the stereotypical community of priests, rural bachelors, emigrants home for the holidays, grandmothers, young men, and marriageable girls. The departure from the peasant play is seen in the tone of the work and in the dramatic action. The business of the peasant play is normally the exchange of land, or marriage, or both. In the *Leenane Trilogy*, however, the main focus of the action is torture, suicide, and murder. Although the priest – who is referred to in the first two plays and who appears on stage in *The Lonesome West* – attempts to assert a kind of moral authority, he fails miserably, and is merely the butt of his parishioner's contemptuous humour. He finally commits suicide.

A Skull in Connemara includes a scene in which Mairtin and Mick, drunk on poitín, smash the skulls of the dead with a mallet; a story about 'Tinkers' cutting off the genitals of the dead to make dog-food, which evolves into a joke about the Famine; much discussion of Mick's unproven murder of his wife, Oona, and his attempted murder of Mairtin with the aforementioned mallet. The horror of this is largely obscured by the dialogue and charac-terization, which make it impossible to take any of it seriously. The characters' heart-break and despair rarely seems more than a pose, all the more so since it is so often motivated by such banal material objects as Tayto crisps, scrambled eggs, and cheap necklaces. Their violence and brutality is mitigated by their context: the world they inhabit is one in which grotesque death is normal and everyday. The play includes a discussion of people drowning on vomit – 'But sure, drowned on sick is nothing to go shouting about. Doesn't everybody drown on sick?' says Mairtin – and the story of a man from Salthill who drowned in urine – 'was it his own?' Mick asks (*Skull*, 106). The dramatic world is a charnel house, in which the living empty the ground so that it can be refilled with more corpses. The slurry and the lake are both full of the pulverized bones of the dead; they are brought into the domestic space of Mick's cottage and battered beneath the crucifix and the farm tools, and there are myriad bizarre ways of joining their ranks, of which drowning on sick is only one.

In this dramatic world, McDonagh uses the verbal tic of repetition to slow down the dialogue, creating these largely meaningless, ludicrous, and banal exchanges that may, nonetheless, be charged with rage and hatred and bitterness. These passages are interspersed with more conventional dialogue. Always sticho-mythic, they are sometimes phatic in function, like the opening sequence, where the chief purpose is to establish or maintain contact rather than to communicate information. Although this sequence provides an extreme example, shorter exchanges in which the same words and phrases are repeated over and over, recur regularly. Towards the end of scene one, a long sequence develops around the word 'aspersions' (*Skull*, 78-9), which recurs in a diluted form in scene two (*Skull*, 94-5), while scene three has a number of shorter exchanges about ways of dying (*Skull*, 105-7). Mick comments on these long pointless dialogues towards the end of the play, when he describes Mary Johnny's conversation as 'hour long weather bulletins' (*Skull*, 125).

An analysis of the sequence between Mick and Mairtin on ways of dying, shows how the dialogue gradually advances even as it circles the same repeated images and phrases. The two men are digging the graves when Mairtin explains that, though 'drunk as Jaysus', he often sobers himself up by putting his head in a bucket of water. Mick warns him not to drown. The word 'drown' reminds Mairtin of the man in Salthill who 'drowned on wee'. The dialogue circles this topic for seven exchanges, before Mick moves the conversation along to drowning on vomit, with the story of his three uncles who 'drowned on sick'. This introduces three new phrases: 'three uncles', 'in America' and 'drowned on sick', that both characters repeat. Each phrase recurs six times over the next page of dialogue.

A very similar pattern is evident in *The Pillowman*, where in scene one the central character, Katurian K. Katurian, is being inter-rogated by the two policemen, Ariel and Tupolski:

> **Tupolski:** All this story is to me, this story is a pointer.
> **Katurian:** A pointer?
> **Tupolski:** It is a pointer.
> **Katurian:** Oh.
> **Tupolski:** It is saying to me, on the surface I am saying this, but underneath I am saying this other thing.

Katurian: Oh.
Tupolski: It is a pointer. (*Pause*) It's your best story, you say?
Katurian: No. It's one of my best stories.
Tupolski: Oh, it's one of your best stories. You have so many.
Katurian: Yes. (*Pause*) My best story is 'The Town on the River' one. 'The Tale of the Town on the River'.
Tupolski: Your best story is 'The Tale of the Town on the River'? Wait, wait, wait, wait, wait, wait, wait, wait... (*Tupolski quickly finds the story.*) Hang on. Here we are. Ah-hah. This tells me something, 'This is your best story'.
Katurian: Why, what is it, is it a pointer? (*Tupolski stares at him.*) Um, it's the only one that was published (*Pillowman*, 18).

This stichomythic sequence revolves around the word 'pointer', a word repeated by both characters, but meaning different things to each of them. To Tupolski, it is proof of Katurian's involvement in the murders. Katurian is not quite sure what the pointer is pointing to, so he is initially hoping for an explanation – 'A pointer?' – then is sometimes wordless – 'Oh' – and sometimes attempts to guess the meaning of the term, assuring his captors, as the scene progresses, that he is not political, does not read the *Libertad*, does not hang around the Jewish district, does not have Jewish friends, but is not anti-Semitic either – all in an attempt to discover what he is accused of.

The process of denomination is explored by Veltrusky[14] in his study of dialogue. But where Veltrusky's analysis reveals the progression of the dialogue though a series of minor misunderstandings and clarifications, in McDonagh's dramatic worlds the effect is often the opposite. Although the dialogue about 'aspersions' in *A Skull in Connemara* does clarify the characters' meanings, thereby bringing them gradually into direct conflict with one another, other sequences in the same play do not function in this way. The various modes of death by drowning, for example, are in no way illuminated by the long sections of dialogue they instigate. Elaine Aston and George Savona discuss the work of Harold Pinter, Eugene Ionesco, and Samuel Beckett, and these authors' use of 'a conspicuous degree of 'small talk' which undermines the traditional expectation of external action moved forward through speech acts.'[15] Thus in *A Skull in Connemara*, our conventional expectations of exposition in the conversation of

Mick and Maryjohnny, once Mary is seated, are frustrated, and similarly, in *The Pillowman*, no explanation is offered for Katurian's arrest until more than half way through the first act. The repetitive exchanges, such as the one given here, do not provide any more information to either Katurian or the theatre audience; the function is not to clarify, but to create a sense of stasis and paralysis. Katurian is so unsure of the meaning of 'pointer' that he does not even venture to speak the word until near the end of the exchange, when he dares to hope for a clue in Tupolski's response to his story.

The exchanges between Katurian and his interrogators are imbued with a strong sense of threat. The opening scene of the play shows the author alone in an interrogation room, blindfolded. The dialogue immediately establishes his relative powerlessness and confusion. He has no idea what he is accused of, but is anxious to explain his willingness to help, assuring his interrogators that he 'will answer everything you want me to' (*Pillowman*, 4). Ariel replies:

> You will answer every question we want you to.' There was never a question, 'You will answer every question we want you to.' There *was* a question, 'How much are you going to make us fuck you up in the meantime?' was what the question was (*Pillowman*, 4-5).

Here, as in *A Skull in Connemara*, McDonagh uses repetition to slow the dialogue, this time to create a sense of threat, and to imbue Ariel and Tupolski with a kind of absolute power, that Katurian cannot hope to resist. In this scene, McDonagh draws upon Kafka, Pinter, and Havel, as well as American cop shows, to produce a pastiche that is a communicative short-hand for his audience: the characters and situation are already familiar to us, not from the actual world, but from other fictional worlds disseminated through the mass media and popular culture. Even the names of the characters, supposedly central or east European, are familiar from the multi-ethnic world of American television.

But where Pinter's obscurely frightened characters, Havel's nightmarish bureaucracies, and the plight of Kafka's Josef K. are disturbing reflections of modern life, *The Pillowman*, like the *Leenane* and *Aran* trilogies, provokes the audience to laughter rather than to fear. This in part is because the publicity surrounding the plays generally provides the audience with information that the characters do not have, informing them that the play follows an investigation of an author who has written 'dark fairy tales' or 'gruesome short stories'[16]. The audience, therefore – unlike Katurian – knows why he is in custody and what Ariel means by a 'pointer'. Since the audience do not share Katurian's confusion, and are placed in a position of superiority, his desperation appears funny rather than ominous, and the audience are drawn into a conspiracy with his torturers. The text alone does not clarify the charges against Katurian until after Ariel '*pulls him off his chair by the hair, kneels across him and gouges his face*', and Michal's screams as he is beaten have echoed across the stage. What might be a profoundly alienating play, becomes instead a violent comedy of mis-information and misunderstood communication.

Aston and Savona's discussion of communication in Beckett's *Endgame* labels these acts of miscommunication 'transgressive'. As in some of the exchanges in that play, in Ariel and Katurian's exchange about the 'pointer', there is 'no clarification of object reference', so 'the two speaker-listeners can engage in a series of illocutionary question-response acts which presuppose dis-ambiguity where none exists'. This is a parody of the normal rules of dialogue.[17] This parodying is an aspect of McDonagh's dramatic aesthetic, appearing also in *A Skull in Connemara*, where there is no ambiguity, but no progression either. In both plays, McDonagh uses verbal tics of repetition to create a sense of the absurd and comedic, in sharp contrast to the violence and brutality of the enacted events. Similarly, he makes use of inversions in word-order to force certain rhythms of dialogue, again heightening the atmosphere. In a very typical inversion of the usual word order, Tupolski says, '*The Libertad* it was published' (*Pillowman*, p.19); echoes of this sentence-structure are found throughout the *Leenane Trilogy*, where they suggest Irish-English. In this instance, it opens a sequence of fourteen exchanges, in which Tupolski repeats the name of the magazine, and Katurian avoids saying it.

A clue to *A Skull in Connemara*, I would suggest, is the title, which quotes Lucky's speech in *Waiting for Godot*: 'alas alas on on the skull the skull the skull the skull in Connemara'.[18] The graveyard scene in which Mick and Mairtin dig up the corpses recalls not only the gravedigger in *Hamlet*, but also Pozzo and Vladimir's descriptions of human life:

> Astride of a grave and a difficult birth. Down in the hole, lingeringly, the grave-digger puts on the forceps. We have time to grow old. The air is full of our cries. (*He listens.*) But habit is a great deadener (*Godot*, 91).

McDonagh's plays dramatize the short brutality of the cycle from birth to death, and the deadening effect of habit. His use of distinctive dialogue structures therefore becomes a tool for expressing the alienation of the characters from each other, and for creating a distance between stage and auditorium; the use of particular features of dialect are intended to heighten the required effect, more so than to produce an identification with a particular nation. This distance allows the audience to witness calmly the horrors depicted in the dramas, as the characters demonstrate the truth of Garcin's statement in Jean-Paul Sartre's *No Exit*, that 'Hell is other people'. McDonagh's dramatic worlds make use of theatrical clichés, staging conventions, and, in particular, repetitive patterns of dialogue to express, not contemporary Ireland, but the human condition.

---

[1] Michal Lachman, ' "From Both Sides of the Irish Sea": The Grotesque, Parody, and Satire in Martin McDonagh's *The Leenane Trilogy,' Hungarian Journal of English and American Studies* 10:1-2 (2004), pp.61-73.

[2] Nicholas Grene, 'Ireland in Two Minds: Martin McDonagh and Conor McPherson', *The Yearbook of English Studies* 35:1 (January 2005): pp.298-311.

[3] Fintan O'Toole, Introduction to *Martin McDonagh Plays: 1* London: Methuen, 1999.

[4] Mary Luckhurst, 'Martin McDonagh's *Lieutenant of Inishmore*: Selling (-Out) to the English', *Contemporary Theatre Review* 14:4 (2004): pp.34-41.

[5] Vic Merriman, 'Theatre of Tiger Trash', *Irish University Review* 29:2 (1999): pp.305-17.

[6] Keir Elam, *The Semiotics of Theatre and Drama* (London: Routledge, 1980, 1993), p.108.

[7] Loreto Todd, *Green English* (Dublin: O'Brien, 1999), pp.26-32.

[8] Loreto Todd, *The Language of Irish Literature* (Basingstoke: Macmillan, 1989),

   p.42.

[9] Ben Jonson, 'The Irish Masque', *Ben Jonson's Plays and Masques* (New York: Norton, 1979), pp.240-1.

[10] Mary N. Harris, 'Beleaguered but Determined: Irish Women Writers in Irish', *Feminist Review* 51 (1995), pp.26-40.

[11] Augusta Gregory, *Our Irish Theatre* (New York: Capricorn Books, 1965), p.9.

[12] Dion Boucicault, 'The Shaughraun', *Selected Plays of Dion Boucicault* (Gerrards Cross: Colin Smythe, 1987), p.326.

[13] Patrick Lonergan discusses the impact of Druid Theatre Company on McDonagh's career in 'Druid Theatre's *Leenane Trilogy* on Tour: 1996-2001', *Irish Theatre On Tour*, eds Nicholas Grene and Chris Morash (Dublin: Carysfort Press, 2005).

[14] Jiri Veltrusky, *Drama as Literature* (Lisse: Peter de Ridder Press, 1977), p.17

[15] Elaine Aston and George Savona, *Theatre as Sign System* (London and N.Y.: Routledge, 1991), p.66.

[16] http://www.nationaltheatre.org.uk/. National Theatre's online publicity material for *The Pillowman* at the Cottesloe Theatre, November 2003.

[17] Aston, 1991, p.66.

[18] Samuel Beckett, *Waiting for Godot* (London: Faber and Faber, 1956), pp.44-5.

'Like the Cat-astrophe of the Old Comedy': The Animal in *The Lieutenant of Inishmore*

Patrick Burke

One of the most engaging poems from the long Irish tradition is the early medieval 'The Scholar and His Cat', or, in the feline nomenclature by which it is more popularly known, 'Pangur Bán'. Together in the monastic cell, the scholar turns his eye on 'the great wall of knowledge,' while, with equal commitment, the cat prowls for mice. The untroubled togetherness and amity of monk and cat characterize the poem and explain its enduring appeal: 'Though we work for days and years/Neither the other hinders;/Each is competent and hence/Enjoys his skill in silence.'[1]

The dream of, or aspiration to such easy co-existence of human and animal is as old as the Book of Genesis and as recent as Kipling's 'Jungle' books or Burroughs' *Tarzan of the Apes*. It can take a more muted form, based less on experience than on memory, as we see in the instance of the middle-aged Owen Keegan in T.C. Murray's *Autumn Fire* (1924), bed-ridden and incapacitated because, ironically, of a fall from a horse:

> Up there in the stillness of the long day I do be listening to the humming and droning of the bees in the garden, and watching the swallows flying past the window, or hearing the cows gadding in the heat and they making a little boom of thunder with their hoofs on the sod and myself ... no better than a breathing corpse.[2]

In stark contrast, a manifest hostility towards, or cold indifference to animals may, within the *corpus* of Irish drama, betoken cruelty or even savagery in a maimed or diminished community, as in the well-known instance in J.M. Synge's *The Playboy of the Western World* (1907), just after Christy Mahon, newly arrived into the shebeen, has confessed to killing his father:

> You never hanged him the way Jimmy Farrell hanged his dog from the licence, and had it screeching and wriggling three hours at the butt of a string, and himself swearing it was a dead dog, and the peelers swearing it had life?[3]

Similarly, there is what modern audiences would see as the gratuitous cruelty shown by some of the island's 'hard m[e]n' in the following from Brian Friel's ironically titled *The Gentle Island* (1971): '… they tied two cats together and went chasing after them through the house, throwing hot water over them.'[4]

The killing of the donkey, as recounted by Bull McCabe in the first act of John B. Keane's *The Field* (1965) – 'Tadhg there beat him to death'[5] – might appear initially to be of a piece with those manifestations of cruelty. That play, however, invites us to consider that such action was at least partially justified in as much as the eating habits of the animal constituted a threat to the 'lush grass' of the field over which Bull believes he has proprietary rights, a threat, however exaggerated, to his livelihood and that of his son, Tadhg, in the future. Such threat, in turn, relates to one of mankind's primitive fears, that animals will somehow take over, take control of the human realm, the fear possibly most graphically depicted on film – a medium, incidentally, of which Martin McDonagh expresses himself more fond of than drama – for example, in *The Incredible Shrinking Man* (1957, directed by Jack Arnold) or Alfred Hitchcock's *The Birds* (1963), or Steven Spielberg's *Jurassic Park* (1993). Bull McCabe's rejoinder, when he hears, *apropos* the killing of the aforementioned donkey, that the local sergeant is 'investigatin' the death of an ass', is an articulation of that fear – 'There's more thought of donkeys in this world than there is of Christians.' And if Bull's sentiments are *ad hominem,* their sincerity suspect, a quiet statement in the final act of Gerald Healy's well-beloved 'famine play', *The Black Stranger* (1945), because of its unquestionable sincerity in emanating from Sean the

Fool, is frightening, even horrific vis-à-vis the primitive fear I describe:

> … Hetty with the golden hair. Lovely golden hair she had, soft an shiny … There was a dog on the road yesterday … I thought it was some kind of a big ball he had, but when I looked down at it, I saw what it was … There was no mistakin' the lovely golden hair. [6]

A variant on the fear outlined above, one central to drama, is that that the animal *element in man* will come to dominate and prevail. In tragic terms, this is the fear which underpins possibly the greatest play of all, Shakespeare's *King Lear*. voiced most explicitly by Albany in Act Four: 'It will come,/Humanity must perforce prey on itself,/Like monsters of the deep'.[7] In comic terms – and possibly from the same year as *King Lear* – the fear is dramatized in Ben Jonson's *Volpone*, a play in which very many of the characters' names derive from animals – 'volpone', the fox, 'mosca', the fly, 'corbaccio', the raven, 'peregrine', the falcon, etc. It may not be insignificant in that regard, that in *The Field*, already alluded to, one character is named 'bull' and another, 'bird', and that, in reverse, as it were, the comment made on the 'tinker's pony', the shooting of which by Bull has alienated his wife from him, is 'you'd swear he was human'.

Some of the foregoing may serve to illuminate the dramatic methodology of Martin McDonagh's most controversial play, *The Lieutenant of Inishmore,* first presented, following rejection by at least two other theatres, by the Royal Shakespeare Company at The Other Place, Stratford-upon-Avon, on 11 April, 2001. Like the monk in 'Pangur Ban' – though there the resemblance ends! – the young man, Padraic Osbourne, a member of a breakaway group from the Irish National Liberation Army (INLA), is passionately attached to his cat, Wee Thomas. When he learns that Wee Thomas has apparently been killed, his first suspicions are directed towards his own father, Donny, and a neighbouring boy, Davey, who try to cover up by painting over a substitute cat and pretending it is Wee Thomas. About to kill both of them, having peremptorily shot the substitute cat – which 'explodes in a ball of blood and bones' – Padraic is interrupted by three INLA members – Christy, Brendan, and Joey – who reveal that *they* had organized the killing of the cat, in retaliation for Padraic's crackdown on

INLA drug pushers, in particular 'Skank Toby', 'one of the big-time boys 'of the organization – whose nose Padraic had cut off and fed to a dog, which had choked on it! Padraic and his trigger-happy girl friend, Mairead (who specializes in shooting the eyes out of cattle and people), shoot Brendan and Joey, a relatively painless end in the light of what faces Christy when he admits that it was *he* who actually killed Wee Thomas:

> **Padraic:** (*to **Mairead***) Bring a knife, a cheese grater, a razor, an iron and anything to gag the screaming … (*Christy begins screaming hideously as Padraic tortures him, blood splattering*)[8]

Events move rapidly in the ensuing, final scene: the audience, confronted initially with the onstage dismemberment by Donny and Davey, under orders, of the bodies of Brendan, Joey, and, later, Christy, might be tempted to assume that the play will move towards a 'standard' happy ending with the prospect of marriage of Padrac and Mairead, apparently blissful lovers. When, however, Mairead learns that the substitute cat, shot earlier by Padraic , was in fact *her* cat, Sir Roger (named after Sir Roger Casement), she shoots Padraic! Finally, in a kind of *coup de théâtre*, a cat bounds onto the set, which we are quickly made to understand is the very alive, sexually predatory, Wee Thomas; in other words, all of the bloodshed had been for the wrong cat!

I suspect that that plot resumé, with some of the stage directions quoted, will convey something of the tenor of *The Lieutenant of Inishmore,* its black comedy, if one is an admirer of McDonagh, its cheap sensationalism, if one is not. In the inverted system of values presented by the play, Wee Thomas ('…[his] best friend in the world) matters more to Padraic, as does Sir Roger to Mairead, than anything else imaginable: in scene eight, Padraic discloses that his own seemingly imminent death will matter less to him than that of Wee Thomas. He has not the slightest misgiving about shooting his own father, whom he describes on one occasion as a 'fecking bastard', when he suspects him of com-plicity in killing his cat. Conversely, he leaves off the torturing of an INLA drug dealer, James, in the second scene, when the latter not only claims that *he* possesses a cat – Padraic commenting, evaluatively, 'I didn't know drug pushers had cats' (15) – but comes up with a cure for the putative ringworm that Wee Thomas might be experiencing. The non-drinking, non-drugtaking Padraic has no compunction about killing defenceless civilians – planting '…bombs in a couple of chip shops …because [they] aren't as well guarded as army barracks' (13), his basic cowardice in that respect matched by the callousness of Mairead who 'laugh[s] at' bombs going off in England! In terms of the play's moral schema, it is noteworthy that Padraic approaches such tasks with greater conviction, when he senses they are supported by Wee Thomas:

> No longer will his smiling eyes be there at the back of my head, egging me on, saying , 'This is for me and for Ireland, Padraic … ', as I'd lob a bomb at a pub , or be shooting a builder (15).

The nearest we get to a political manifesto from Padraic lends a proportionate priority to cats:

> … all I ever wanted was an Ireland free. Free for kids to run and play. Free for fellas and lasses to dance and sing. Free for cats to roam about without being clanked in the brains with a handgun … (60).

In this regard the moral status assigned to Christy is significant: his apparent killing of Wee Thomas, for which, as we've seen, he pays with a horrible death, provokes a rare paramilitary scruple in Mairead – 'Does it make you think twice about the INLA, so, that they let fellas like Christy in, who would do that to a cat?' (59) Earlier, Christy, having been presented as the ideological voice of the INLA, and posing the leading question, 'Is it happy cats or is it an Ireland free we're after?' (30), nonetheless concedes, on tactical grounds, the political importance of cats: '… won't the cats of Ireland be happier too when they won't have the English coming over bothering them no more?' (30) Cats are used also as the bench-mark by which to measure the core meaning and moral dimensions of notoriously painful events in Irish history, be they in the recent past: 'There's no guts involved in cat battering. That sounds like some-thing the fecking British'd do. Round up some poor Irish cats and give them a blast in the back as the poor devils were trying to get away, like on Bloody Sunday' (Joey in scene five) (28) – or further back historically: 'Do you know how many cats Oliver Cromwell killed in his time? … Lots of cats. And burned them alive. We have a long way to go before we're in that bastard's league' (30).

Even Ireland's proud record in creative writing is undermined by the importance Padraic attaches to feline-inspired bombing: in reference to Brendan and Dominic Behan, he observes: 'If they'd done a little more bombing and a little less writing I'd've had more respect for them.' (28)

With the possible exception of rare moments in *The Beauty Queen of Leenane* [Maureen and Pato] or *The Lonesome West* [Girleen and Father Welsh], the plays of McDonagh resolutely resist the intervention of conventionally humanizing affectivity, emotional softness, or of love familial or sexual: everything is hard-edged, even brutal. *The Lieutenant of Inishmore* takes that pattern to unprecedented extremes, presenting us with a world where sons threaten to kill fathers, who in turn dismember the sons' corpses, where girls deliberately try to shoot their brothers' eyes out, where sons trample on their own mothers, where lovers shoot lovers. The political, even religious icon of this ultra-Jacobean murderous world is the amoral, sensation-driven cat: as Davey so colourfully puts it, in the play's final moments: ' ... Four dead fellas, two dead cats ... All because that fecker [Wee Thomas] was after his hole?' (68) Recalling, then, the speculation with which I began, it would appear that McDonagh has combined a travesty of 'Pangur Ban', the communal savagery figured by the depiction of animals in *The Playboy of the Western World* or *The Gentle Island,* together with the primeval fear of animal dominance adumbrated in the structure of *King Lear* , and a definable trend in the Hollywood film canon (apropos of which, it may be noted that the most threatening animal in *The Incredible Shrinking Man* is a cat), for purposes of black satire directed, one presumes, against a perceived propensity towards blood-letting within Irish society and, specifically, against paramilitary violence. Such arguably reductive perception, in tandem with the *ersatz* feel of so much of McDonagh's work, has made him unpopular and artistically suspect with some not unenlightened critical opinion, which sees him as racially condescending, a Paddy-whacking entertainer for taste either formerly imperial (British and North American) or formerly colonized (Irish). I sympathize with that view. Finally, we may be tempted to ask, is anything salvaged in moral terms from what, it must be admitted, is very often a hilarious play? By way of rather less than final reassurance, Mairead, the sole female character of the play, is going to give up 'shooting fellas', albeit less from moral conviction than from boredom. A little more substantially, possibly in a pale echo of Albany and Edgar at the conclusion of *King Lear,* the stage is left at the end to Donny and Davey, the only two non-violent men of the play, as they consciously spare a life, asking history's most reiterated question, '... will it [the killing] never end?' (69) Our solace, however, in such prospective pacificism is undermined by the recollection that James, the INLA man of scene two, is still on the loose, and that the life which Donny and Davey agree to spare is not a man's but a cat's.

---

[1] Frank O'Connor, trans., *Kings, Lords, & Commons: an Anthology from the Irish* (Dublin and London: Gill and Macmillan, 1970), pp.14-5.

[2] Richard Allen Cave, ed., *Selected Plays of T. C. Murray* (Gerrards Cross, Bucks., and Washington, D.C.: Colin Smythe and Catholic University of America Press), p.23.

[3] Ann Saddlemyer, ed., *J. M. Synge: Plays* (London, Oxford, New York: Oxford University Press, 1969), p.115.

[4] Brian Friel, *The Gentle Island* (London: Davis-Poynter, 1973), p.14.

[5] John B. Keane, *The Field* (Cork: Mercier Press, 1966).

[6] Gerald Healy, *The Black Stranger* (Dublin: Duffy, 1950), p.43.

[7] S. Wells and G. Taylor, eds, *The Oxford Shakespeare: The Complete Works* (Oxford: Clarendon Press, 2005), p.931.

[8] McDonagh, M., *The Lieutenant of Inishmore* (London: Methuen Drama, 2001), p.54. (All further references will be given within the body of the text.)

11 | An Economy of Pity: McDonagh's Monstrous Regiment

Ashley Taggart

After first seeing *The Lieutenant of Inishmore* in the Garrick Theatre, London, my impression of the audience reaction was almost as enduring as that of the performance itself. For the first hour, they gazed on in discomfited silence, assailed as they were with images of feline slaughter, casual torture, cow blinding, all underpinned with escalating threats of ever more explicit and inventive brutality – finally attaining their expression in a grotesque coup de theatre of dismemberment and blood. Although the dialogue from the off was full of the trademark bulls, blarney, and begorrah which had characterized McDonagh's earlier work: 'Many's the time I trampled on my mam when she was alive. After she died I stopped. There seemed no sense.' (24) – still the audience remained mute.

More than that – as the night wore on a general unease became increasingly apparent. Individuals glanced around from their seats, more or less surreptitiously, to see just how others were reacting to this stuff. In an oddly theatrical gesture some actually lifted their hands to their mouths (in shock? To stop themselves laughing?), but then managed to compose themselves and carry on. Whilst no one actually walked out, they had the collective look of a group of tourists who had accidentally blundered into a strip-joint and were too embarrassed to leave, but by the same token very determined not to be seen to enjoy it.

This unease continued until late in the play, fed by the off-hand cruelties of the plot and (especially) the references to actual killings, such as Bloody Sunday or the political murder of Airey Neave, which barred any easy acceptance of the play as mere caricature. Faced with such a volatile dramatic mix, the reaction on the night was a kind of squirming politesse. Yet, as the absurdities and the corpses continued to pile up in front of us, this act of collective repression in the audience began to feel increasingly strained, until, finally, at the opening of scene nine

> Donny's house, night. As the scene begins, the blood-soaked living room is strewn with the body parts of Brendan and Joey, which Donny and Davey, blood-soaked also, hack away at to sizeable chunks. Padraic's two guns are lying on the table. In the adjacent bare room, Padraic is sitting on Christy's corpse, stroking Wee Thomas' headless, dirt soiled body …

the dam finally, belatedly, burst and the auditorium exploded with laughter. The last 15 minutes of the play rode a massively cathartic surge of (slightly hysterical) energy, powered by the very contraints which had once held it in check.

At the precise moment when the house gave itself permission to laugh, something became very clear. The evening, this particular performance, had been transformed, for whatever complex of reasons, into a performance of a different kind: a stress-test to near-destruction of the fundamental contract between dramatist and audience. McDonagh's ability to straddle the razor's edge between horror and humour had produced an intriguing meta-theatrical moment.

There were no doubt many cultural and political factors involved in this reception of *The Lieutenant of Inishmore* by an English audience. Within the limits of the space available what I would like to do is to focus attention on the general role of humour in the piece, and more specifically, the trade-off between humour and empathy. In Pirandello's celebrated essay 'On Humour' (1908) he makes a clear distinction between comedy and humour, using the analogy of 'an old lady whose hair is dyed and completely smeared with some kind of horrible ointment; [and] made-up in a clumsy and awkward fashion … like a young girl'.[1] He suggests that our initial response would be laughter: a comic 'perception of the opposite', i.e., that she is the opposite of what she is trying to appear. This however, is a superficial reaction. If, a moment later, reflection intervenes, we will be drawn closer to the old lady's predicament, begin to imaginatively identify with her and even start to speculate on the desperation and pain inherent in her situation. Once we have taken this step, we are no longer free to laugh at the initial 'perception of the opposite' but have shifted into a 'feeling of the opposite'. This leap, from comic perception (present in all of us, though characteristic of children) to humorous feeling, creates a problematic depth of affect. In purely emotional terms, as regards the spectator, humour inverts comedy.

Moreover, the special requirements of humour bring this new disturbing element to the birth of the work itself – reflection. Reflection which, according to Pirandello, would normally remain hidden at the moment of artistic creation, now becomes an additional complicating factor for the writer. And if, indeed, reflection has the capacity to reverse the audience *response* to a given character, it has an even more radical effect on the playwright at the point of conception.

Much of Pirandello's essay is given over to an effort to convey the deeply subversive nature of humorous reflexivity as it obtrudes into the spontanous act of creation. He makes several attempts to characterize it, ending up with this extraordinary simile:

> As a rule, when an emotion excites the spirit, all the ideas and images in harmony with that emotion are likewise aroused; in the case of humour, instead, because reflection is inserted into the seed of the emotion like a malignant viscous growth, only ideas and images conflicting with the emotion are aroused …This is why … humour could be considered a phenomenon of doubling in the act of artistic conception.[2]

A malignant viscous growth. Why such a threatening, even cancerous image (which the playwright is at pains to reiterate in the course of the essay)? He elaborates:

> Reflection, engaging in its special activity, comes to disturb and to interrupt the spontaneous movement that organises ideas and images into a harmonious form. It has often been observed that humoristic works are disorganised, disconnected, interrupted by constant digressions … [these] are the necessary and inevitable

consequence of the disturbance and disruption which are produced ... through the work of the active reflection.[3]

The Lieutenant of Inishmore displays innumerable examples of just
such disconnections, such digressions, and indeed appears to glory
in them. Padriac's rambling, faux-exculpatory monologue to his
torture victim, James, in scene two is only one such.

> **Padraic:** If I hadn't been such a nice fella I would've taken one
> toenail off separate feet, but I didn't, I took two toenails off the
> one foot, so that it's only the one foot you'll have to be limping on
> and not the two. If it had been the two you'd have found it a devil
> to be getting about. But with the pain concentrated on the one, if
> you can get hold of a crutch or a decent stick, I'm not sure if the
> General Hospital does hand them out, but they might do, I don't
> know. You could phone them up and ask, or go in and see them
> would be the best thing, and make sure them toes won't be going
> septic at the same time. I didn't disinfect this razor at all, I never
> do, I see no need, but they'd be the best people to ask, sure they're
> the experts. You'll probably need a tetanus jab too, oh there's no
> question. I do hate injections, I do (11).

And so on. The logical disconnections, the serpentine digressions are intrinsic to the humorous drama. They are not merely
comic window-dressing, but are an indispensable element in its
structure. It is not just that McDonagh's characters speak in non-
sequiturs, but that they wouldn't know a sequitur if it came up and
bit them on the arse (or, more accurately, shot them in the eye).
'Oh don't let me be killed by a girl, Sweet Jesus! I'll never live it
down', are the final lines of Brendan (51).

Pirandello's point is that, once admitted, reflection has a
violently unsettling effect on both the formal harmonies and moral
certainties within the universe of the play. Once again, he strains
for a suitably trenchant image to express the capacity of reflection
to invert, even corrupt every emotional response, to undermine
every narrative certainty: 'humour is art with a characteristic of its
own ... its source is a special activity of reflection, which decomposes the image created by an original feeling, in order that
from this decomposition a contrary emotion may arise and be
present.'[4]

And it is precisely this queasy sense of decomposition which
pervades McDonagh's work, right through from *The Beauty Queen of*

Leenane to the killing fields of *A Skull in Connemara*, the fratricidal squabbling and suicides of *The Lonesome West*, and beyond. His plays are populous with corpses, and even the living characters seem to be trembling on the brink of sudden and catastophic collapse. As Beckett before him, he has been targeted for his gallows humour, his melodramatic preoccupation with death and dysfunction, as if this is a tasteless case of playing to the gallery, whereas, in fact, this explicit focus on decay on 'decomposition', according to Pirandello, is nothing but the outward manifestation of something essential, something fundamental to humour itself.

In the climactic scene of *Lieutenant*, Donny and Davey sit astride the corpses of the ill-fated INLA unit, clumsily hacking at their joints with saws and knives. They chat (what else?) about the niceties of killing.

> **Donny:** Padriac has an entirely different style.
> **Davey:** Padraic goes all the way up to ya.
> **Donny:** Padraic goes all the way up to ya, then uses two guns from only an inch away.
> **Davey:** Sure, there's no skill in that.
> **Donny:** I think two guns is overdoing it. From that range, like.
> **Davey:** It's just showing off, really.
> **Donny:** Mairead sees more of the sport. (*Pause.*) Is he still sitting on the fella and stroking the dead cat?
> **Davey:** (*craning his neck*) He is. Morbid, that was, digging up his dead cat. After all the trouble we went to burying it, and without a word of thanks.
> **Donny:** I suppose it does help the mourning process.
> **Davey:** (*pause*) Digging up the corpse? (56)

And indeed, McDonagh is constantly 'digging up the corpse' and shoving our faces into it, much like the unfortunate Davey with the recently slaughtered Sir Roger in scene eight. Even setting aside such moments of dark knockabout (which play at times as if Joe Orton had joined the GAA) the playwright is happy throughout his work to unsettle the audience by a policy of transgressing conceptual taboos, setting-up in 'Lieutenant' a provocative equivalence of 'animal' and 'human' or even 'animate and 'inanimate' which is deeply unnerving: 'Them corpses won't be chopping themselves up, or d'ye think they will, Mairead?' (57)

As with all his previous work, there is an insistence on the brute physicality of existence, and its lamentable precariousness. 'What I want ye to remember, as the bullets come out through yere foreheads, is that this is all a fella can be expecting for being so bad to an innocent Irish cat', states Padraic (44). Or again, 'These guns are only circumstantial, so, and so too your brains'll be only circumstantial as they leave your heads and go skidding up the wall' (42).

Throughout all this the effects of the 'malignant viscous growth' of reflection are apparent, whereby 'only ideas and images conflicting with the emotion are aroused'. Small wonder that for long stretches of his drama, any audience is left wondering quite what the appropriate response to such material *could* be, as McDonagh takes repeated aim at sacred cows, left, right, and centre.

But such an obsession with death and decay is only the outward manfestation of any reflexive tendency. As with Beckett, the characters appear haunted by a self-consciousness which seems to undermine their very existence as autonomous entities, even as it contorts and 'decomposes' the feelings they express. In the same way that Johnnypateenmike in *The Cripple of Inishmaan* is hyper-aware of the status of his conversation as 'news' before he even opens his mouth, the characters in *Lieutenant* are subject to sudden reflexive attacks. They seem to blink, momentarily, in the full glare of the footlights. During these irruptions, (reaching into his post-modern bag of tricks) McDonagh, seems more than happy to conjure up a suspension of the 'suspension of disbelief'.

At the close of Padraic's torture monologue in scene two, delivered razor in hand, the heightened (stagey?) nature of his outpouring is underscored, first by Padraic himself, then, in a typically concretizing gag, by his victim.

> **Padriac:** …What a bad day you've had. (*Pause.*) But, em … I have lost me train of thought now, so I have.
> **James:** You've lost your train of thought? Uh-huh. As slow as that fecking train is, and you've lost it?
> **Padriac:** (*pause*) The next item on the agenda is which nipple of yours do you want to be saying goodbye to. The right or the left? (12)

Throughout the banter of the INLA team, McDonagh gets good mileage out of the very 'doubling' described by Pirandello, creating a 'hall of mirrors' effect on several semantic and performative levels.

> **Christy:** There's no talking to this fella.
> **Brendan:** Not on the subject of quotes, no.
> **Joey:** (*pause*) Ye've changed the subject on me.
> **Christy:** What was the subject? (28)

At other times, he chooses a more declarative approach – a bald statement of the speech-act itself.

> **Davey:** You *did* trample on your mam!
> **Donny:** Ten years ago that was!
> **Padriac:** There's no statute of limitations on mam trampling, Dad. Now shut up while I make me speech (43).

In Pirandello's summary formulation:

> humour consists of a feeling of the opposite produced by the special activity of reflection which does not remain hidden and does not become, as usual in art, a form of feeling, but its opposite, though it follows closely behind the feeling, as the shadow follows the body. The ordinary artist pays attention only to the body: the humorist pays attention to both, and sometimes more to the shadow than the body: he notices all the tricks of the shadow ... [5]

A concept of dramatic humour which goes some way to elucidate one source of the crippling self-consiousness affliciting McDonagh's blighted universe of killers and colleens, figurine-melters and mam-tramplers, and our sense of unease beholding it. As humorist, he is as concerned with the shadow of a gunman as with the gunman himself.

Freud in *Jokes and the Species of the Comic* (1905) comes at the issue from quite a different angle, beginning with a broader definition of the comic. Freud's contention is that the grounding for comedy (in his use of the term) is empathy.

> The comic that is found in someone's intellectual and mental characteristics is ... the outcome of a comparison between him and my own self ... it becomes comic if [a character] has spared himself expenditure which I regard as indispensable (for nonsense and stupidity are inefficiencies of function) ... The comic effect depends on the difference between the two cathectic expenditures. [6]

So, at the simplest level, Donny and Davey's efforts to turn a (suspiciously) orange cat black with the aid of bootpolish is a case where the two men have spared themselves the mental 'expenditure' of thinking the plan through, something which becomes increasingly apparent as the scene progresses, finally threatening even their desperate and foundless optimism.

> **Donny:** It does have a tag. What's it's name now … ?
> **Davey:** Sir Roger.
> **Donny:** Sir Roger. That's a funny name for a cat.
> **Davey:** It is. It was probably some mental case named that cat.
> **Donny:** Will I take his name tag off, Davey? Else that'd give the game away straight off.
> **Davey:** Take it off, aye, else Padraic'd be reading it and know straight off by the name it wasn't Wee Thomas. That was intelligent thinking, Donny.
> **Donny:** I know well it was. I don't need your opinion on my intelligencientiousness (25).

In such examples of what might be dubbed the 'comedy of innocence', part of our pleasure derives from watching the clunky machinations of their thinking exposed to view. As with, say a Laurel and Hardy film, the frisson we get derives partly from the latent threat of violence facing the pair, and partly from a smug comparison between their thinking and ours. In short, according to this view, our pleasure in comedy derives from 'an economy in expenditure upon ideation'.

Psychoanalysis places considerable emphasis on the 'un-masking' nature of the comic, focusing on an aspect of comedy (as already seen) prevalent in McDonagh's work, i.e., 'the dependence of the mental on the physical'. Freud sees this as a 'method of degrading the dignity of individuals by directing attention to … the dependence of their mental functions on bodily needs. The unmasking is equivalent here to an admonition …'[7]

The Lieutenant of Inishmore is a darky comic object-lesson in the dependence of the mental on the physical, from the opening scenes angry debate about scraping Wee Thomas's skull off a bicycle wheel; Padraic forcing his victim to decide exactly how his own torture will progress; the three blinded gunmen shooting wildly at imagined targets, through to Mairead finally blowing out Padraic's brain; we are caught in a sharp contrariety – perceiving at once the vulnerable, corporeal nature of mind and its vicious potential for harm.

The general tendency to self-aggrandizement by elevating the abstract above the everyday is thoroughly satirized here in a political context, with Padraic repeatedly launching into flights of rhetoric, only to land with a bathetic thump.

> **Mairead:** The girls must be falling over themselves to get to you in Ulster so, if them's the kind of compliments you be paying them.
> **Padraic:** A few have fallen but I paid no mind. Not while there was work to be done ridding Erin of them jackboot hirelings of England's foul monarchy, and a lot of the girls up North are dogs anyway, so it was no loss' (33).

But the play is not content just to bring empty concepts crashing down to earth. At its very heart lies an extended analogy between human life and animal life which is pushed to its logical limit and beyond. Freud gives over much time to the question of analogy, concluding that, as with the comparison of oneself with a comic figure, the reason for our amusement is a kind of psychic labour-saving,

> ... analogies are capable of a use which brings with it a relief of intellectual work – if, that is to say, one follows the usual practice of comparing what is less known with what is better known or the abstract with the concrete ...[8]

One of McDonagh's main tricks is to off-set an adherence to the brutal abstractions of terrorism with a maudlin attachment to a particular pet:

> **Padraic:** I will plod on, I know, but no sense to it will there be with Thomas gone. No longer will his smiling eyes be there in the back of me head, egging me on, saying, 'This is for me and for Ireland, Padriac. Remember that,' as I'd lob a bomb at a pub, or be shooting a builder. Me whole world's gone, and he'll never be coming back to me (44).

The above quotation also serves to illustrate a key point in relation to McDonagh's work in general, and *The Lieutenant of Inishmore* in particular. Freud is concerned to focus our attention on what creates comedy, but, more than that, what interferes with its reception. As he puts it, 'The comic is greatly interfered with if the situation from which it ought to develop gives rise at the same time to a release of strong affect …The generation of affect is the most intense of all the conditions that interfere with the comic.'[9]

And of course, this play is full of highly-charged events, from the insouciant mention of bombings and 'acts of terror' to the onstage depiction of torture, maiming and murder – any one of which might cause the 'release of strong affect' in the audience. It is as if the playwright here is deliberately shoring up the emotional resistance to his own comic material, only to finally prove that he can break through the very same. Again, Freud is explicit,

> The release of distressing affects is the greatest obstacle to the emergence of the comic. As soon as the aimless movement does damage, or the stupidity leads to mischief, or the disappointment causes pain, the possibility of a comic effect is at an end.[10]

At least initially, during the London performance of the play, the audience were pinioned by this very dilemma. They could not accept the comedy as such because they were investing feeling in the victims (seen and unseen). Consider the phone-call Padraic has with his father while he is in the act of torturing James. He is discussing drug dealers:

> **Padraic:** They *are* terrible men, and it's like they don't even know they are, when they know well. They think they're doing the world a favour, now. (*Pause*) I haven't been up to much else, really. I put bombs in a couple of chip-shops, but they didn't go off. (*Pause*) Because chip shops aren't as well guarded as army barracks. Do I need your advice on planting bombs? (*Pause*) I was pissed off, anyways. The fella who makes our bombs, he's fecking useless (13).

Setting aside the rich irony of his first two sentences, it is the lightness of delivery and treatment that chills here. Any audience might well be thrown by it, find itself unable or unwilling to react with laughter, whilst still recognizing the inherent comedy.

And yet, says Freud, there is one psychic event which would allow us to overcome this state of horrified inhibition – to cut loose – and that is an appreciation of *humour*. In his view, too, humour is quite distinct from the comic. Unlike the rest of comedy it does not depend on 'saving ideation', but rather, 'saving feeling'. Humour will only arise in very specific circumstances:

> The conditions for its appearance are given if there is a situation in which, according to our usual habits, we should be tempted to release a distressing affect and if motives then operate upon us which suppress that affect *in statu nascendi*.[11]

That is to say, we are suddenly freed from the burden of empathy. We are liberated from the obligation to care.

Unlike comedy *per se*, humour is not reliant upon an (initially) empathetic comparison between 'self' and 'other':

> With humour it is no longer a question of two different methods of viewing the same subject-matter ... The situation is dominated by the emotion that is to be avoided, which is of an unpleasurable character.[12]

By the final scene of *The Lieutenant of Inishmore* ('*the blood-soaked living room is strewn with the body parts of Brendan and Joey, which Donny and Davey, blood-soaked also, hack away at* ...) the audience on that night in London reached a tipping point between (blocked, edgy) comedic identification with the victims and humorous dispassion; the extravagant gore on display prompting a sudden and irreversible shift. Due to the unreleased comic pressure of the preceding scenes, and the fact that the victims in this case are the very terrorists we have been encouraged to despise, an outpouring of repressed energy took place. The audience understood clearly for the very first time that they need not invest in or empathize with the suffering confronting them:

> As a result of this understanding, the expenditure on the pity, which was already prepared, becomes unutilizable and we laugh it off.[13]

If comedy saves us ideation, humour saves us feeling, and in a world as morally twisted as the one McDonagh's depicts, an 'economy of pity' as Freud dubs it, might just be a suitably perverse source of laughter.

---

[1] Luigi Pirandello, '*On humour*', trans. Antonio Illiano and Daniel P Testa (North Carolina: University of North Carolina Press, 1960), p.112.
[2] Ibid., p.120.

[3] Ibid., p.120.
[4] Ibid., p.121.
[5] Ibid., p.145.
[6] Sigmund Freud, *Jokes and their Relation to the Unconscious* (London: Pelican, 1983), p.254.
[7] Ibid., p.263.
[8] Ibid., p.273.
[9] Ibid., p.284.
[10] Ibid., p.293.
[11] Ibid., p.293.
[12] Ibid., p.301.
[13] Ibid., p.295.

12 | War on Narrative: *The Pillowman*[1]

Eamonn Jordan

> Tell me a story, tell me a story
> Tell me a story, before I go to bed
> You promised me, you said you would
> You got to give in, so I'll be good
> Tell me a story, before I go to bed.

Introduction

Martin McDonagh's first three plays, collectively known as *The Leenane Trilogy*, all had Irish premières, even if they were co-produced by Druid Theatre, Galway, and the Royal Court, London. The other two plays *The Cripple of Inishmaan* (1997) (RNT) and *The Lieutenant of Inishmore* (2001) (RSC) opened in London. Yet, all five of his performed plays, prior to *The Pillowman* (2003) (RNT) were set in notional West of Ireland locations. *The Pillowman*, set in an unspecified totalitarian state, shows considerable tonal and dramaturgical consistency with much of his other work, but at the same time, it was to be a surprise in a way, given it was not trapped in some Irish dystopic sensibility and it was not a feck-fest; so it is less easily seen as re-imaginings, re-workings, and re-constitutings of the Irish tradition – the generation of 'copies that have forgotten their originals' as Christopher Morash describes *The Leenane Trilogy*.[2] Dominic Dromgoole puts it slightly differently, arguing McDonagh's 'greatest talent is as a pasticheur, he is able to produce perfect forgeries' at will of writers in this tradition.[3] Rather than seeing it in terms of copies or forgeries, I would prefer to read his work as palimpsest, that is layered, interconnected, intertexual, and dialogical. In that way, McDonagh's work both recognizes and disacknowledges a notional idea of a tradition, is read critically against this tradition, regardless of direct influence, and is keen, when aware to jeopardize and overwrite it with alternative sensibilities, without adoration. Thematically and formally, much of McDonagh's work can be set within a trajectory of tradition, however, the sensibility of McDonagh's work cannot be aligned with anything within that same Irish tradition. This is how the anomalies and contradictions establish distinctiveness. While the earlier plays contained a great deal of brutality and cruelty, the challenges *The Pillowman* sets in terms of violence and staging are a good deal more confrontational and challenging – more in line with the work of his British contemporaries[4] Mark Ravenhill and Sarah Kane or the threatening and harrowing sensibility of the Hollywood serial killer on the rampage.[5] (The curious irony of course is that *The Pillowman* was substantially drafted in 1993-4 before any of his Irish plays.) By the end of this article I will be interested in connecting McDonagh to the Irish tradition of narrative, while at the same time interlinking his work with that of the two previously mentioned writers of his own generation.[6]

What is remarkable is the number of international performances that *The Pillowman* has received since 2003, including productions in London, a short tour in Britain and Ireland, four in Germany: Munich, Berlin, Hamburg, and Mainz; and others in Holland, Austria and Japan. The best known is the Broadway production in New York, which starred Jeff Goldblum and Billy Crudup.[7] And of course, even if *The Pillowman* denies any specific context, it must be kept in mind that it was first performed in late 2003 as the War in Iraq (War on Terror) was ongoing, with democracy as one of its key motivations. Indeed, the interrogation techniques, notionally in the name of democracy, deployed by American army forces in Abu Ghraib prison in Iraq find many parallels with the McDonagh play.[8] For some, democracy is the prize and not a weapon in a war on terror. For many, McDonagh is entering indirectly this contemporary debate, not as some political theorist, but as someone who is reflecting on the fabrication of narratives of enablement, forgery, and disruption and the justification of state terror.

The Pillowman maps the interrogation of Katurian Katurian Katurian (KKK), a writer whose stories seem to be the templates for a series of gruesome murders involving children. He is the chief suspect, and has been detained along with his brain-damaged brother, Michal. It is not so much that tactics of the totalitarian state are taboo to democracies, but that the play focuses on brutal interrogation techniques and on the murder of children and not adults as is the usual methodology of most narratives, especially Hollywood's, which remain for the most part weary of serial child killers.

The McDonagh play considers the circulation of ideology in a contemporary, we are to assume, unnamed totalitarian state. The drama establishes the regimes through which citizens are recruited, indoctrinated, and interpellated by systems and structures. It considers how institutions, totalitarian and democratic, through narratives socialize, discipline, and induce re-enactment, most especially within the boundaries of family life. It is not so much that families simply imitate the configurations of the state; more-over, it is the difficulties of those units to evade the distinctive practices of the state, which ultimately foist positive aspirations and false realities and illusions before its populace. Such citizens become most likely both misguided and beguiled agents of the state. For Ciarán Benson:

> Family is the crucible in which self is forged. Whether directly by incorporating or indirectly by rebellion, the family and its associates (the church to which the family belongs, the schools it chooses for its children, its various loyalties in politics and play) supply and edit the self-constituting narratives available to its offspring, and power-fully influence the structuring of their identities.[9]

Nation as family is an on-going 'pervasive metaphor' as Benson reminds us, but its opposite family as nation is also apposite.

Staging Totalitarianism and Democracy

Unlike the totalitarian states, democracies are based notionally on the entitlement of its citizens to certain freedoms, equalities, and rights.[10] The USA, western European, and Australasian states, and an increasing collection of other countries across Africa and South America are all waving the banner of democracy.[11] Anthony Giddens proposes that 'democracy is the most significant innovation in the twentieth century' and he highlights the fact that in this century 'there is not just a gradual expansion of democracy; something has happened that is radically pushing forward the democratization of political systems across the world' as people have 'discovered that communism and a command economy doesn't work'.[12]

Unnatural, fundamentally restraining or inhibiting socio-political structural dynamics are not truly acknowledged within this democratic model and such forces are associated only with undemocratic societies. However, democracies function, in part, by means of ranked relationships and they normalize inequitable distributions of wealth and social inequality by disguising certain injustices, social immobility and repression, in terms of gender, race, and class, all in the guise of a freedom to choose, exercise human will, and to endeavour.[13]

Noam Chomsky argues that:

> The selective eye of the West picks out just those rights that benefit the rich and powerful: freedom of speech is of great value to those who can use it to achieve their ends, confident that unwanted thought will be marginalised and the mass of the population left effectively voiceless.

He continues:

> For similar reasons, the privileged insist upon political rights. The social and economic rights of the Universal Declaration are peripheral concerns for those whose wealth and privilege guarantees them these amenities, and who profit from the denial of the rights to others. Accordingly, the West adamantly rejects the universality of the Universal Declaration. For the poor and suffering, all of these rights are values to be treasured, but they scarcely enter the debate or commentary on it.[14]

In contrast, Giddens presses for an increasing process 'demo-cratizing democracy' and envisages great progress due to the procedures of 'transnational democratization'.[15] And it is this 'transnational democratization' which fuels globalization and of course a war on terror. Indeed, the unnamed totalitarian state of

The Pillowman offers on the surface the ultimate point of contrast with contemporary democracies.

Clearly, non-identical formations such as Italian Fascism under Mussolini, Hitler's national socialism in Germany, Russia under Stalinist rule, Mao's China after the communist victory in 1949, and Fidel Castro's rule in Cuba since 1959 have all been equated with totalitarianism, as has either single-personed dictatorships or a 'dictatorship of the proletariat'[16]– the rule of the people in another guise. Associated with either extreme right-or left-wing ideologies, and far more potent than either absolutism or autocracy, citizenship within totalitarian states is generally equated with powerlessness, unerring regimentation, fragmentation, centralized rule, and ideological control of culture, education, judicial, religious, political, and interpersonal relationships. The mass media, art, pedagogy, and technology are tools of subordination and regimentation, as is popular culture.

In this notional unitary state, there is no truly oppositional voice countenanced, and it is thus seen in pejorative terms by most, especially those who espouse liberal democratic values. Bracher adds that although totalitarian states

> reject the pluralist system of representative democracy, they simultaneously present themselves as a higher manifestation of popular sovereignty, of the people's democratic consensus and unity.[17]

He calls it 'plebiscitary acclamation' because it 'manipulates assent to the exercise of power by a leader or a monopolistic party'.[18] There is not only the promoted sense of benign rule, but that any violation of human rights serves a higher order, thus a lack of accountability permeates the system. A higher evolving, freedom beyond democracy is hailed as a sort of utopia fantasy of equality. Thus the elimination of personal freedoms is a normalized price and worthwhile sacrifice of such activities, resulting in what Bracher describes as 'exalted submission'.[19] Such a state certainly debilitates and reduces self-confidence, whereas, for an example, Hollywood movies typically promote heroic individuality that finds individual and not collective solutions, where justice is realized. Within democracies, individuality is not perceived as corrupt *per se*, but as a natural unit of recognition, whereas within totalitarian states there is the obvious overriding of individuality for the benefit of the greater good. Risk and the taking of initiative would not be necessarily encouraged. Totalitarian coercion is even more sophisticated than monarchic, dictatorial or imperial rule.[20]

Leonard Schapiro, discussing Hannah Arendt's *Origins of Totalitarianism*, notes that the key strengths of her book are to identify that 'totalitarian lawlessness is lawlessness of a particular, and novel, kind, since it is lawlessness masquerading as constitutionalism: the state machine, emasculated and manipulated by the party.[21] Secondly, he notes that 'ideology in the totalitarian state had little to do with ideas or beliefs, but was an instrument for manipulating the population', and thirdly, that the function of terror for a totalitarian leader

> is not merely to frighten people into submission, but rather to isolate each individual, to leave him enclosed by a wall of loneliness, shut off from the support and comfort of his family, his friends and, of course, any kind of free association of his fellows. This is regarded by many as a process of 'atomization.[22]

It is more the spirit of totalitarianism[23] that McDonagh is after, and not the preciseness of the socio/political parameters, which some London critics found lacking. The totalitarian state has dramaturgical, metaphorical as well as symbolic significances.[24] McDonagh offers a truncated totalitarianism writ small,[25] where totalitarianism symbolizes anything from imperialism, state oppression, repressions, even perhaps academic/critical interrogation of theatre itself. The flexibility, even portability of the concept is hugely significant. Of course, McDonagh grew up in London and presumably has no direct experience of totalitarianism, however writers can extrapolate and make sense of oppression and violence in different ways. (The connection between totalitarian and British imperialism will not be pursued here.) I am less interested in the factual content and pervasiveness of totalitarianism and more concerned with the contextual subjugations and the fantasy of the writer/child oppressed by institutional restraint.

McDonagh pursues the legal processes, police interrogation, and the creativity of a specific writer, in order to reflect upon the fears and anxieties and lack of freedom therein. Katurian's tales[26] are parables or fables that warn about the dangers of interpersonal encounter and are full of negative experiences and foreboding, partly about the threat of individuality in the face of apparent state or parental omnipotence. Katurian's stories are almost anti fairy tales, like the one that ends Georg Büchner's *Woyzeck*. It is persuasive to suggest that the oppressive totalitarian state is the springboard for Katurian's negative imaginings, but to restrict McDonagh's play to such a world view is to miss the point, as his work is more playful and elusive than that. The general political interrogation is so full of recurrent ironies that cannot be side-stepped by critical interpretation. Likewise, the role of the writer in the totalitarian state has been romanticized and McDonagh ironizes that a great deal. This is evident in Tupolski's comment:

> [...] We like executing writers. Dimwits we can execute any day. And we do. But, you execute a writer, it sends out a signal, y'know? (*Pause.*) I don't know what signal it sends out, that's not really my area, but it sends out a signal (30).

In order to give further substance to the sensibility of the play in performance I would like to briefly identify some of the staging choices made for the original Royal National Theatre, Cottesloe production. The music composed by Paddy Cunneen is dominated by eerie Eastern European tones[27] and the scenography by Scott Pask[28] brought the play into alternative territory. (The production relied on distinctly English accents in the London performance and not voices with some Eastern European inflection.) John Crowley directed the piece in the spirit of a carnivalesque Grand Guignol,[29] which ultimately, is about destabilizing the gaze, perspective, and presence of the spectator. Mikhal Bakhtin in two books, *Rabelais and His World* and in the *Problems of Dostoevsky's Poetics*, explains the concept of Carnival. Carnival is of course about the festivalization of the real, while making space for difference, desire, and the imagined. The underworld space itself is liminal, and 'paintoverable', transgressive and other. (The feast of the pig.) The body is fundamental to its tradition as is the notion of both the violated and the reproducing body. Likewise mock trials, mock kings (The Pillowman character), mock deaths (the survival of the little mute girl) are substantial components. The play then is a Show-trial of sorts. The play revels in misrule and in surreal sensation, through the crucifixion of the little girl. (London audiences in 2003, especially, experienced the play, perhaps sensitive to the trial of Ian Huntley, who was found guilty of the murders in 2002 of the young girls, Holly Wells and Jessica Chapman, in Soham. (The Soham murders gave rise to a frenzied sensibility around the safety of children in a culture.)[30]

Sue Vice articulates the parameters of Bakhtin's thinking on Mésalliances, which leads to strange combinations, 'lofty with the low, the great with the insignificant, the wise with the stupid'.[31] This is the world of McDonagh. The playwright instead of presenting an audience with the innocence and pure body of a child gives us the abject body of the violated child and dead children. For Julia Kristeva, death is a site of 'abjection' – 'The corpse, most sickening of wastes, is a border that has encroached upon everything.'[32] As Vice argues, 'the abject confronts us … with those fragile states where man strays on the territories of animal'.[33] Reverence or empathy for a child's suffering is not so much contested as moved into an alternative space. In earlier work, McDonagh has the corpse of Mag Folan on stage in *The Beauty Queen of Leenane*, motioning in her rocking chair, the ears of a dead dog appear in *The Lonesome West*, the skull of Mick Dowd's dead wife, Oona, is present on stage in *A Skull in Connemara*, and many bodies are littered around the stage towards the end of *The Lieutenant of Inishmore*, but it is the figures of violated and mutilated children and the crucified child in *The Pillowman*, however distanced and theatricalized, which potentially shocks most. This is the space where unease is generated, where the darkness begins to glow. In addition, corpses in McDonagh are carnivalized through the notion of dark play.[34] And this is a play full of narrated, re-enacted, and performed carnage.

The past and the acting out of narratives are accommodated in *The Pillowman* through a sort of monstrous and transgressive, almost carnivalesque, summation in a way that casts aside any notion of verisimilitude in favour of the grotesque, inhumane, cartoon-heightened style. In the play's first production, these scenes of excess and torture initially took place on elevated platforms, backstage left and right, with the bedroom spaces opening up from behind screens. The audience witnessed the electrocution sequences, with the grotesque rather than the real as the reference point. (The actor performing as Michal played the teenage Katurian in the flashback/narrative sequences and a young boy played the young Michal.) However, the play's dramatic present was played out within a relatively realistic representation of a prison cell, with the exception of 'The Little Jesus' narrative. So this dominant theatrical space was governed by the conventions of naturalism, whereas the alternative spaces were guided by a very different stylistic approach; it was in the re-enactment sequences where realism could be seen to be the inappropriate mode of absorption and comprehension. It is the melding of both realities which seriously skews the coordinates of the real, as the re-lationship between cause and effect begins to break down.

When the audience came into the theatre, they saw a stage curtain with the play's title projected onto it. As Katurian pre-sented his first re-enacted narrative, he delivered the voices of the parents, while the actors playing the parts enacted the gestures. As Katurian destroyed his best story, there was the burning of the story in both spaces. (In reality no detainee is going to be left with a lighter in his possession.) For the 'Little Jesus' story, the re-enactment happened, not up high as in the previous acting out of a narrative, but mid-stage towards the back of the performance area. A screen rotated behind the actors illustrated key scenarios. Both the nice parents and the cruel foster-parents in 'The Little Jesus' story were played by the actors who initially played the cruel Katurian parents, and the character shifts were indicated only by a 'slight costume' change (67), as the script suggests. The little girl in this story believes that she is the 'second coming of the Lord Jesus Christ' (68) and thus wore an exaggerated false beard. No beating sounds were heard; only blows were visible, which again was an attempt to break the verisimilitude.

The text suggests that the Blind man should be performed by the actor playing Katurian, while in performance it was the actor playing Michal who took the role. The little girl in the 'Little Jesus' story was resurrected as the girl in the 'Little Green Pig' tale. For the final moments of the production, the set was altered. The light that hung over the interrogation table was whisked away, altering the interrogation space and making free a space for the imagination.[35]

Re-enactment

As the play opens, Katurian is hooded and duly disorientated, awaiting the arrival of his interrogators/ torturers. The catalogue of strategies, emotional, psychological, and physical, used to extract 'the truth' during cross-examination, is similar to those listed in any Amnesty International Report on prisoner mistreatment. Katurian cannot understand why he has been arrested, believing that he only tells stories and that he has 'no axe to grind, no anything to grind. No social anything whatsoever' (7). However, Katurian is fearful that if 'something political came in by accident, or something that seemed political came in', he is willing to remove it straight away (7-8). In *The Pillowman*, Katurian's relating of stories becomes one of the initial modes of interrogation. He is invited to tell a story, not knowing why he has been asked to recount it. The hope is that through interrogation, narrative intelligence can lead someone to 'actionable intelligence' to use a phrase from current United States military parlance.

At the basis of Katurian's stories is the idea that a child is treated badly, according to Tupolski. Ariel's whole justification for torture is premised on the exact same thing: 'I may not always be right, but I stand on the right side. The child's side' (78). Ultimately, he believes that in his old age, 'Little kids are gonna follow me around and they're gonna know my name and what I stood for, and they're gonna give me some of their sweets in thanks' (78). Likewise, Tupolski's story 'The Story of the Little Deaf Boy on the Big Long Railroad Tracks. In China' captures his own world view and that of the state itself: 'I shall save that idiot from that train, I shall save my fellow man from those criminals, and I won't even get a word of thanks for it' (90). The perversity of it all is that totalitarian states are never on the 'child's side'. Moreover, Katurian's actions, in killing his parents, are about the 'child's side'. However, the re-enactments carried out by Michal, are not from the child's side. There are huge contradictions to be followed through in both plays around the rights of children and the status of innocence and how violence is used to disable innocence. The

Katurian family guarantees neither the security nor innocence of their children.

Katurian's 'The Tale of the Town on the River', which was published in *The Libertad*, is set in Hamelin. A boy's toes are cut off by a stranger, despite the child's act of kindness. The injury saves him later, when he is unable to keep pace with all of the other children as they are lured away by the Pied Piper of Hamelin, who was chasing the children all along. The non-payment for the removal of an infestation of rats was just an excuse to inveigle the children away. Again innocence is violated, but the initial act of brutality brings with it perverse redemption. The drama duplicates or plays with this constant notion of contrary justice or redemption.

Katurian wonders: 'What, are you trying to say that I'm trying to say that the children represent something?' (12) In that sense, not only is this a comment on the processes of representation, but also on how children have been used in literature, parables, and fairy tales as ways of gaining access to certain root values and emotions. On a broader scale while the patriarchal family is a perverse and perverted agent of the state, it cannot be a simplistic representative of the state. The child's revenge on the destructive, gluttonous father in 'The Little Apple Men', who is tempted into eating the razor blades hidden inside hand-carved pieces of apple in the shape of men, cannot be read simply as an anarchic or subversive gesture of violation, directly either towards a character or towards the state. However, it can be indicative of it. (Ariel's murder of his own abusing father can add perspective to all of this.) The 'comeuppance' for the father in the above story is followed by another act of sadistic revenge. The little girl is also forced to swallow razor blades. This stylistic twist shifts the usual register of fairy tales, making destruction not just interpersonal, but indicative of a pattern of repeated, cyclical violation.

'If there are children in them, it's incidental. If there is politics in them, it's incidental. It's accidental', Katurian claims, in relation to 'The Tale of the Three Gibbet Crossroads' (16). In this story the rapist and the murderer are offered compassion and some comfort, but the unidentified and unforgivable crime of the third criminal, who knows he is guilty of some crime, but can not remember what it is: we can assume child abuse or murder of some horrific type is why he is incarcerated (16). Indirectly, Katurian's stories are very much about abuse and violation, where the family, as a primary agent of socialization, discipline, and punishment, becomes the cruel arbiter of fates. On the one hand, the parents of the Katurian family decide on totally different childhood realities for two brothers: Katurian gets the privileged lifestyle, full of love, encouragement, and admiration, and Michal is gifted all of the negative experiences, whereby he is ritually tortured and abused, as part of some grotesque artistic experiment. Katurian sees Michal as a 'child' (24). But that doesn't stop Ariel from threatening to 'put something sharp up inside him and then turn it' (25). The state that notionally sides with innocence, still threatens to violate. The torture doled out to Michal duplicates almost exactly how the police state tortures at will, perhaps, randomly, in order to maintain order. Despite all that Katurian has to say about his own innocence, Andrea Jovacovic has been killed, recovered on a heath with blades down her mouth, and Aaron Goldberg is dead, found in a dump behind the Jewish quarter, while his toes were discovered in the Katurian home. A third child, a little mute girl, is now missing.

When an audience first encounters Michal in *The Pillowman*, he is alone in a second police cell. Katurian is being tortured nearby, but Michal is de-sensitized to such an extent that he has little or no empathy for his brother's suffering. Indeed he mimics his brother's screams with a good deal of disassociative impatience. For years previously, Michal had suffered and Katurian was the observing party, and now McDonagh very skilfully plays out the reversal of roles. In *The Pillowman*, neither policeman acknowledges the dysfunctionality of his own interrogative routines. Both cower behind the protection offered to them by narratives of justification and by the state.

Likewise, while Katurian, under interrogation, spurns any deconstruction of his own writing for inherent values or as reflections on justice, in reality, to a considerable extent, he is writing out of the horrors of his past. Moreover, his refusal to read into his own stories is strategic in the face of his interrogators, but disingenuous, in terms of his own psyche. The relentless and morbid content of his stories, and the violation of children at the core of almost all of his work, cannot be evaded. This is Katurian's particular fantasy:

> Well … I kind of hate any kind of writing that's even vaguely autobiographical. I think people who only write about what they know only write about what they know because they're too fucking stupid to make anything up (76).

Writing needs the imagination more than personal experience, Katurian argues, but attempts by writers, in general, to deny contexts and the potential of experiences even as indirect influences or to hide behind the fiction of purely imaginatively driven work are clearly false in most instances. (In the film, *Shakespeare in Love*, William Shakespeare is inspired to write, prompted by a failed, loving relationship, whereas Katurian suggests in 'The Shakespeare Room' that Shakespeare stabs with a stick a 'little black pygmy lady in a box … every time he wants a new play wrote' (62). Katurian may deny any direct influence that his personal past has had on his writing, but what he cannot rebuff is its impact on the actions of himself and his brother. Katurian brutally kills both parents. Katurian acts out the fantasy of the Pillowman, the core narrative about a figure who can bring a graceful ending to the suffering of children, and Michal acts out the stories of his brother, narratives that are filtered through the trauma of their growing up.[36]

Scene Two of Act Two proves somewhat problematic. The written text suggests that the actor playing Katurian sits on a bed in 'an approximation of a child's room' and he 'narrates the short story which he and the mother, in diamonds, and father, in a goatee and glasses, enact' (31). That production choice changes the meaning of this scene, moving it from participative re-enactment to something more distant. The note reads:

> They have loved you and tortured me for seven straight years for no reason other than as an artistic experiment, an artistic experiment which has worked. You don't write about little green pigs any more (32-3). (We can identify the 'little green pig' fascination from an early age in the writings of Katurian.)

What the parents perceive as an 'artistic experiment' is far more than that. Of course, the story twists when Katurian at fourteen tries to rescue his brother only to find his parents waiting for him as if they were staging everything. Years later, the writer returns to his former home place, only to discover the 'horrific corpse of a child' (33) and a story written in blood that displays a talent vastly superior to his. (Creativity from the imagination and nurturing is trumped by lived experience of trauma, in this instance.) The truth is as far fetched as the fiction. At fourteen Katurian did discover the body of his brother, who was still alive despite the torture. Katurian murdered his parents that evening, exhibiting the core violence of his parents, but unlike them, he takes care of the abused Michal. No comfort can erase Michal's trauma. His re-enactment of his own violation, and his use of his brother's stories as prompting narratives, confirm this.

When Michal confesses his deeds to Katurian the sheer perversion of re-enactment is fully realized. For Michal, '[…] The little boy was just like you (Katurian) said it'd be' (48). Michal's stated motivation for doing such gruesome deeds is because Katurian 'told' him through the stories to do so (49). Michal rejects the accusation that he is like his cruel parents. 'Michal: I'm not like them. I didn't want to hurt anybody. I was just doing your stories' (55). This indirectly raises issues about imitation, copycat murders and films like Oliver Stone's *Natural Born Killers*. He also argues that he was just 'testing how far-fetched' the stories are (50), but really he is experimenting, just like his parents. Through these exchanges the spectator gets the measure of the madness. Re-enactment is not agency, but perversion.

Legacy

Michal had told Katurian earlier that the latest missing girl, Maria, had been crucified like the main character in 'The Little Jesus' story (echoes of Snow White and the glass coffin – in a way the story mingles the world of the fairy tale with religious parable in the form of the life of Jesus Christ). The police go out expecting to discover the enactment of that tale. The investigators don't find a crucified little girl. Instead, as his last hurrah, as a serial killer of children, Michal re-enacts 'The Little Green Pig' story and the rescued girl appears on stage, covered in green paint. In the initial rendition of this story, the little green pig is pink and very different from all the other pigs on the farm that happen to be green. The farmers (society) repaint the pink pig with green indelible ink, so that he will not be different. However, one evening after a heavy shower, perhaps divine intervention, all the green pigs turn pink, except of course the once pink pig, whose permanent green colour cannot be erased. His uniqueness is re-affirmed. It also suggests that individuality cannot be obscured, despite the broad strokes of an ideologically repressive society.

Having confessed to all of the murders, Katurian's account is found wanting. Despite the girl's survival and the fact that Katurian had nothing to do with the deaths of the other children, he is still executed. (Likewise, the expectations and ultimate closure associated with the classic fairy tale are not revealed in Katurian's work; the twists at the end of each narrative find obvious parallels in the manner through which Michal refracts the stories, putting his own spin on them.) And while Katurian's stories may have an impulse towards 'fashionable downbeat' endings, they still retain some innate sense of fundamental legitimacy that moves way beyond either natural or poetic justice.

Although the totalitarian state cannot offer even-handed and unbiased justice, McDonagh, through 'The Pillowman' story offers a different type of twisted redemption. 'The Pillowman' tale is a redemptive fantasy, something that ensures that little children don't die alone, for he is a 'soft person' to hold the hand of a child close to death. (Tupolski's own child drowned while fishing alone.) *The Pillowman* urges the child to commit suicide in order to avoid pain in the future. If they agree, *The Pillowman* would stage 'tragic accidents'. However, the Pillowman's job makes him unhappy, so he decides to visit his younger self and to end his suffering. The little Pillowboy sets fire to himself and

> the last thing he heard was the screams of the hundred thousand children he'd helped to commit suicide coming back to life and going on to lead the cold, wretched lives that were destined for them (47).

Michal identifies with the Pillowman, regarding him as somewhat of a hero: 'He reminds me a lot of me' (52). When Katurian tells 'The Pillowman' story, he impersonates the description of the Pillowman. Katurian slays both his parents, covering their faces with a pillow, and he sees his suffocation of his brother as a mercy killing,[37] hoping to avoid for him the pains of torture and the trauma of preparing to die. (Ariel also killed his father with a pillow, in an act of self-defence.) In the story of the 'The Writer and the Writer's Brother',[38] the notional writer survives, the suffering brother dies, but it is the writing of the tortured brother that is better; positions are reversed, so the dead child is the author and Katurian becomes the writer's brother, as he has the lesser talent.

Neither life nor death matters; 'it is about what you leave behind', according to Katurian (60). He reflects further: 'They're not going to kill my stories. They're all I've got' (60). On the other hand, Michal enacts all too literally the gory physical violations at the core of Katurian's stories, without having any respect for the symbolic structures of the stories. If one really wants to pursue the connections between the child, pain, the body and violation, one needs to draw fundamentally on the traditions of carnival. It helps make sense of the gruesome details of the drama, as it highlights an inversion of sensibilities and moral imperatives.

Michal uses shaping narratives of Katurian's fictional stories for his own purpose and to justify their behaviour on a conscious level. But the playwright wants his audiences to interrogate the unconscious compulsions as well. In the case of Michal, the pain he suffered as a child finds some expression or articulation through mimicry in his murdering of children. There was no state intervention to stop the savage parents, despite the screams. McDonagh gives Katurian an alternative ending, bringing him back from the dead and allows him to re-write the finale of the drama. This time Ariel puts out the flames that envelop the output of the writer, placing the work in the case file where they will remain unopened for fifty years. In the final narrative, Michal, as a child, is visited by the Pillowman, and given the chance to die, but Michal opts for life, and the degradation and suffering it entails, so that his brother can live his dream and be a writer. Michal sacrifices his sanity and agrees to bear the burden of nightly torture out of kindness and love. Instead of offering one of his usual downbeat endings, Katurian tenders an unfashionably optimistic one. This of course is Katurian's ultimate fantasy of carnivalesque redemption. Katurian's final narrative, from the realm of death, is a fundamental plea to grant meaning to the pain and suffering of his brother and, of course, to himself.

Agency

Katurian, once his interrogation begins, acknowledges that his destiny is not within his own authority. Can literature perform a subversive activity that confronts with subtlety or otherwise the imposed order or does most writing serve as a means of perpetuating values, and of subliminally and aggressively conditioning the citizen? Either way, literature as text or state rule delivers suggestive and counterfeit narratives that cannot be without ideological imperatives and inhibitions. The Katurian parents experiment in a way gives spurious legitimacy to the violence, which is tolerated by social structures. Michal is sacrificed by his parents to see if they can produce perfection and evil, and the state itself corrals individuals almost along the same lines, dividing its citizens between those who support the state or are dissenting. Katurian through his belief and false optimism that his stories will survive cannot relinquish the myth of agency. Decency and truth do not prevail, thus undermining the fallacy of agency.

What at first may seem like a futile opposition between democratic freedom and the compulsion and control of totalitarianism is not so clear-cut. Under the banner of freedom all kinds of discord are negated, legitimate queries invalidated, and different needs other than material ones subordinated. The redemptive entrepreneurial and cultural narratives of Willy Loman in Arthur Miller's *Death of a Salesman* (1949) and the justice-driven literary ones of Katurian have their own pathologies. Like the salesman, a writer has 'got to dream', as 'it comes with the territory' (138). Miller understands Willy's need to leave some mark on the world, describing it as a 'need for immortality, and by admitting it, then knowing that one has carefully inscribed one's name on a cake of ice on a hot July day'.[39] Katurian's fantasy is that his work will one day be unearthed from an archive and perhaps revered as a work of genius or at least merit in its own time, which is conceivably the fantasy of every failed writer. Katurian's final narrative, from the grave, is a fanciful victory over *The Pillowman* or the state.

McDonagh's previous work has had a great populist appeal, dealing as it does with the perversity of the pastoral and the irrationality and dysfunctionality of certain family dynamics within notionally Irish contexts. Some critics have confronted McDonagh for his disingenuity and for his perpetuation of negative Irish stereotypes, while many other international critics wish to refract the gore, sensation, and violence of McDonagh's work through the frame of Irishness. McDonagh himself prefers to be considered as neither Irish nor English, but both. However the two indications of Irishness in the play are hugely significant. No other nationality is mentioned in the play. The town Kamenice has no specific geographic location (towns by that name can be found in Northern Albania and in the Czech Republic.) There is of course mention of a Jewish quarter (Lamence, whose dictionary meaning is in 'layman's terms'), but that is more a matter of ethnicity than nationality. When asked to describe the little Jewish boy, Katurian states that he had 'browny-black' hair. However, the boy was half-Irish – 'It's a shame his mum was fucking Irish, and her son closely resembled a red fucking setter,' according to Tupolski (97). (The little green pig 'really liked being green … liked being a little bit different, a little bit peculiar' (65), and is 'peculiar' whether it is green or pink.)

The colour green has also a fundamental association with Irishness, and, secondly, classical British stereotypes have long associated the Irish with pigs. Victorian representations of Ireland used illustrations of the Irish families sharing living spaces with pigs, as indications of the lack of civilization amongst the Irish, rather than reading the fact of shared accommodation as having more to do with grave economic lack. McDonagh is not so much leaving to one side an Irish tradition but recalibrating it. The play's emphasis on narrative, places it in part within a tradition of Irish plays fixated on storytelling ranging from Brian Friel's *Faith Healer* (1979) and Tom Murphy's *Bailegangaire* (1985) to Frank McGuinness's *Someone Who'll Watch Over Me* (1992). It is with Conor McPherson that McDonagh is most closely allied, and the relationship between *The Pillowman* and McPherson's *The Weir* (1997) is substantial; the interrogation room replaces the public house of the latter, and tales of child murder in gory detail are swapped for tales of the supernatural and dead children, without too much gore. Both deal with the violation of innocence in the form of children to a significant degree; innocence has been the cultural fantasy of Irish theatre and the presumption of innocence at the core of most of Irish theatre is utterly shattered. Instead, McDonagh exposes the tyranny of innocence. In a way, Katurian is guilty until proven guilty. (Like McPherson's *The Weir*, *The Pillowman* owes a great deal to the film, *The Usual Suspects*.)

Conclusion

Sarah Kane's *Blasted* (1994) achieved a certain notoriety because of a scene where a character eats a child, and of course Edward Bond's *Saved* (1965) contains a scene where a child is stoned in a pram by a group of youths, which is one of the crucial moments in British Theatre. Indeed, Mark Ravenhill, claims that in hindsight, the murder of Jamie Bolger, almost three years old, by the young boys Robert Thompson and Jon Venables, both ten at the time, in February 1993 was the incident that prompted him to write plays. He describes it as 'somehow something had shifted, that a tear in the fabric had happened … Shop, videos, children killed by children. It wasn't a project I set out to write. But it became one'.[40] Such a tragedy motivated Ravenhill, and he speculates on how others of his generation, including McDonagh, were moved by the same incident. That said, as Ben Brantley notes, *The Pillowman*

> is about, above all, storytelling and the thrilling narrative potential of theater itself. Let's make one thing clear: Mr McDonagh is not preaching the power of stories to redeem or cleanse or to find a core of solid truth hidden among life's illusions.[41]

However, make narrative not war is not the slogan.

In *The Pillowman* totalitarianism becomes both grotesque and perverse in the spirit of Grand Guignol. *The Pillowman* brings about cycles of abuse and a legacy of violation. If it is the figure of the writer who contests the reality of the totalitarian state, and such a state symbolizes the corruption of patriarchy and familial authority, the sacrosanct nature of family unit within democracy is just another enabling fairy tale. (The family that narrates [prays] together stays [preys] together.) It is the series of indoctrinating parables and serial narratives of democracies which shape motivate and inhibit its citizenship. Ultimately, however, to be told that story at bedtime, doesn't always guarantee that the citizen will be 'good' in not so much the prison-house of the real, but the haunted house of moral ambivalence. Narrative is a battlefield, given the globalization of the media and its communication through images of laceration, carnage, trauma, and death. If terrorism is, in part, the fate of the first world countries, child murder is the ultimate depravity. Democracies will do anything to stop it. All kinds of horrors can be validated and storied. Democracies become additionally morally ambivalent in the face of horror and war, paedophiles and the destruction of the innocent. Due process, civil liberties, and the rule of law are often subjugated. The relative security and sanctuary that democracies offer is often just a fairy tale, when greater things are at stake, like political stability, national security, institutional, party and individual reputations. Democracy can be at times just a demotic freak show – a pathology of innocence. Today, in its war on terror, first world democracy has devised its own theatre of cruelty, with its black prisons and phantom states, – democracy is aligned with Christianity, and evil, often ever so bluntly, with Islam.

On the one hand, the mercy killings of *The Pillowman* seem preferable to a cycle of rape, trauma, violation, and suffering. Yet on the other hand Michal's self-sacrifice in his willingness to live in order that his writer brother can fulfil his potential, which is Katurian's ultimate fantasy, gives ultimate merit to suffering, which has strong Christian overtones. These are crucifixion and martyrdom fantasies that coexist as both optimism and perversion. Yet, Katurian's resurrection and the irony of the 'Little Jesus Story' captures McDonagh's contestation, dismissal, or at least perversion of Christianity myth and iconography. Narrative is both playground and the battleground. Cut your teeth on that cross, that corpse or Habeas corpus, invites McDonagh.

---

[1] A version of this essay titled 'The Fallacies of Cultural Narratives, Re-enactment, Legacy and Agency in Arthur Miller's *Death of a Salesman* and Martin McDonagh's *The Pillowman*' has been published in *Hungarian*

Journal of English and American Studies 11.2 (2005).

[2] Christopher Morash, *A History of Irish Theatre 1601-2000* (Cambridge: Cambridge University Press, 2002), p.269.

[3] Dominic Dromgoole, *The Full Room: An A-Z of Contemporary Playwriting* (London: Methuen, 2000), pp.199-200.

[4] Aleks Sierz identifies offences, sensation, and shock tactics as part of a new style of theatre in the 1990s in Britain. See *In-Yer-Face Theatre: British Drama Today* (London: Faber and Faber, 2001).

[5] See movies like *Copycat, Basic Instinct* and *Urban Legend.*

[6] Fintan O'Toole in his Program Note suggests that '*The Pillowman* reminds us that he has an English ear as well as an Irish one. In his dialogue, Harold Pinter and Joe Orton blend seamlessly with Tom Murphy and John B. Keane to create a vibrantly original mixture of absurd comedy and cruel melodrama.'

[7] http://www.pillowmanonbroadway.com/ photogallery.htm. Viewed September 2005.

[8] Most recently, shocking revelations were made about so called Black sites, covert CIA run prisons where human rights violations and torture are deployed in order to gain intelligence.

[9] Ciarán Benson, *The Cultural Psychology of Self: Place, Morality and Art in Human Worlds* (London: Routledge, 2001), p.212.

[10] William Su, 'Academic Definitions of Democracy' http://www.lse.ac.uk/Giddens/RWDDemDef.htm

[11] Constitutional democracies stress majority rule, the rights to fair elections and public representatives, the presumption of innocence within the legal system; morality, the absence of terror, the rights to privacy, free speech, freedom of assembly and association, and legitimate the capacity to dissent. An emphasis on freedom, ranging from individual choices, through free speech and the freedom of the press are notional prerequisites. These are all the variables that are supposedly absent under totalitarian rule.

[12] Anthony Giddens, *Reith Lectures* 1999, http://www.lse.ac.uk/Giddens/RWDlectures.htm .

[13] See Paul Treanor, 'Why Democracy is Wrong,' http://web.inter.nl.net/users/Paul.Treanor/democracy.html

[14] Noam Chomsky, 'Human Rights and the United States: Letter From Lexington June 18, 1993', *Creative Resistance*, 2003, http://www.designandpeople.org/crone/noam.html

[15] Giddens.

[16] Karl Dietrick, Bracher, 'The Disputed Concept of Totalitarianism:

Experience and Actuality' in *Totalitarianism Reconsidered*, ed. Ernest A. Menze (Kennikat Press: New York and London, 1981), p.16

[17] Ibid., p.15.

[18] Ibid., p.15.

[19] Ibid., p.17.

[20] Winston Churchill in a telegraph on 21November 1943 wrote: 'The power of the executive to cast a man into prison without formulating any charge known to the law, and particularly to deny him the judgment of his peers, is in the highest degree odious and is the foundation of all totalitarian governments whether Nazi or communist.' See Andrew Sullivan, 'Waging war on terror abroad and on freedom at Home', *The Sunday Times* 13 November 2005.

[21] Leonard Schapiro, *Totalitarianism* (London: Pall Mall, 1972), pp.102-3.

[22] Ibid., pp.102-3.

[23] Bracher summarizes it as:

'an absolute and exclusive ideology; legalized terror legitimized by chiliastic promises; through control of political and social life by means of pressure and threats, fear and coercion; the creation of the 'new man' to fit the new and perfect totalitarian order; the preclusion of future conflict by means of suppression of all opposition in favour of ideological political cohesion and effective technological function; lastly, as the basis for a legitimisation of this unprecedentedly brutal extermination of individual freedom, the identification of oligarchic dictatorial leadership with the interests of the "whole", the "community of the people" (volksgemeinschaft) or the "class of workers and peasants", an identification as fundamental as it is fictitious', p.20.

[24] In theatre, all too often police/militaristic states are a simplistic short-hand for totalitarianism, especially in adaptations of Greek classics.

[25] The map is not the territory. The socio/political realities or totalitarianism are not the substantial ingredients; it is the psychic territory of threat, mayhem, absence of cause and effect and due process, and the individual vulnerability of all concerned.

[26] Caryn James in her article on the New York production relates 'descriptions by John Crowley, the Director of the London and New York productions, of how McDonagh "had actually written the stories that became Katurian's before tackling the play" (he created them for possible screen versions that never materialized) and in its first incarnation *The Pillowman* resembled "stories strung together" … In its revised form, those same stories "keep looping back on themselves", as a detail dropped here later pops up there, to create "a wilderness of

stories" ', 'Critic's Notebook: A Haunting Play Resounds Far Beyond the Stage', *New York Times* 15 April 2005.

27 See Paula Rego's, *The Pillowman Triptych*.
http://www.tate.org.uk/britain/exhibitions/rego/theme3.shtm

28 Scott Pask's account of his set design for the New York Production, which won him a Tony Award.
http://www.nytimes.com/packages/khtml/2005/06/15/multimedia/20
050615_PILLOW_AUDIOSS.html (Viewed September 2005).

29 See Pierron http://www.grandguignol.com/history.htm

30 The Moors murders carried out in the 1960s by Myra Hindley and Ian Brady carried a similar type of focus.

31 Sue Vice, *Introducing Bakhtin* (Manchester: Manchester University Press, 1997), 152.

32 Ibid., p.175.

33 Ibid., p.174.

34 Richard Schechner argues: 'Dark play occurs when contradictory realities coexist, each seemingly capable of cancelling the other out, as in the double cross ... Dark play subverts order, dissolves frames, breaks its own rules, so that playing itself is in danger of being destroyed ... Unlike the inversions of carnivals, ritual clowns, and so on (whose agendas are public), dark play inversions are not declared or resolved: its end is not integration but disruption, deceit, excess, and gratification'. See *The Future of Ritual: Writings on Culture and Performance* (Routledge: London and New York, 1993), p.36.

35 Christine Madden notes, commenting on the production of *The Pillowman* at the Deutsches Theater, Berlin, during the Heidelberger Stüchkemarkt festival, that 'Far from being presented naturalistically, everything in the play converged on the idea of a world gone wonky, from the ingenious set – an Irish drawing room, complete with typical doors and wall mouldings, tilted 90 degrees to the left – to the cartoon like yet sinister presence of the actors. In its sharp absurdity the production felt like Flann O'Brien on cocaine', *The Irish Times* 24 May 2004.

36 According to James, 'For two preview performances in London, Mr Crowley also had an actor in a pink Pillowman costume onstage. 'I thought it would be quite spooky and scary, but it wasn't,' he said of that experiment. For one thing, that Pillowman too closely resembled an English cartoon character called Mr Blobby. For another, people said it looked nothing like *The Pillowman* of their imaginations, even though the costume had faithfully reproduced Katurian's description.'

37 See Marina Carr's *By the Bog of Cats ...* in *Plays: 1* (London: Faber and

Faber, 1999) and John Steinbeck *Of Mice and Men* (London: Penguin, 2000, originally published in 1937). Both texts include mercy killings of sorts.

[38] Martin McDonagh's brother John wrote the screenplay for the film *Ned Kelly* (2003).

[39] See *The Theatre Essays of Arthur Miller*, ed. Robert A. Martin (New York: Viking Press, 1978), p.142

[40] Mark Ravenhill, 'Tforum: A Tear in the Fabric', *Theatre Forum*. 26 (Winter/Spring 2005), p.90.

[41] Ben Brantley, 'A Storytelling Instinct Revels in Horror's Fun', *New York Times* 11 April 2005.

13 | Martin McDonagh's Blend of Tradition and Horrific Innovation

Laura Eldred

Critics of Martin McDonagh's work seem unable to decide whether the young playwright is Dr Jekyll, Mr Hyde, or both. On the one hand, McDonagh is Jekyll: a good writer descended from a long line of adept playwrights, spinning yarns that utilize the best of a distinguished tradition (namely the dramatists of the Irish Renaissance), altering these structures and tales slightly to fit a new milieu. Many critics have compared McDonagh to his forebears – to Synge, to O'Casey, to Lady Gregory – with the sense that McDonagh is, however occasionally offensive, part and parcel of an illustrious tradition, a talent to be proud of and claim as an Irish playwright. On the other hand, McDonagh is Hyde: a hack cannibalizing the talents of his forebears, mutilating their subtle themes and deft wordplay with lazy disrespect, a pretender to the throne of Irish dramatist. His satire tips over into bloody excess; his characters lose any pretence of realism; gore becomes an end in itself.[1]

The best answer, however, is that McDonagh is both Jekyll and Hyde, that he interweaves tradition with horrific innovation – a sensibility partially derived from the horror genre, which has been popular in fiction and film in the last century. McDonagh participates in the tradition of Irish drama, and he also seeks to update that tradition through his integration of contemporary violent films and horror entertainment. Certainly, there is a tradition represented by figures such as Synge and O'Casey of disturbing an audience in Irish drama, a tradition that embraces the 'brutal' as a tool for engaging an audience. There are extensive ties between Martin McDonagh and these literary predecessors; their portrayals of the people of rural, western Ireland are strikingly similar and rely upon analogous images of violence and brutality.[2] However, little work has been done on McDonagh's more contemporary influences, despite the importance that he places on film and television in his interviews. Joseph Feeney's analysis notes that McDonagh, when young, spent most of his free time 'watching films and television, and reading and writing voraciously';[3] 'He was also affected by such violent films as *Taxi Driver* and *Night of the Hunter*';[4] furthermore, McDonagh admits that 'I'm coming to theatre with a disrespect for it. I'm coming from a film fan's perspective on theatre'.[5] Despite McDonagh's insistence on a literary background that owes a great deal to contemporary popular culture, much discussion of McDonagh either focuses on his relationship with Synge or merely dubs him 'the Quentin Tarantino of the Emerald Isle'.[6] Nicholas Grene places Martin McDonagh and Patrick McCabe under the umbrella of the 'black pastoral' that 'is formed by analogy with black comedy' and 'involves a similar kind of travesty on the pastoral mode';[7] the source of that darkness and travesty, in McDonagh's case, often seems to be violent films. If, as Vic Merriman notes, McDonagh's works provide 'a kind of voyeuristic aperture on the antics of white trash whose reference point is more closely aligned to the barbarous conjurings of Jerry Springer than to the continuities of an indigenous tradition of dramatic writing',[8] then perhaps some analyses of McDonagh need to consider the 'barbarous conjurings' of popular culture alongside J.M. Synge. These analyses gesture toward the importance of popular culture and specifically of disturbing film in comprehending McDonagh's work; in fact, a consideration of the filmic horror genre in the late twentieth century, especially the slasher film, has a great deal to contribute to the understanding of McDonagh's characters and plot structures in *The Lieutenant of Inishmore* and *The Pillowman*, and of these plays' peculiar relationships with their audiences. While McDonagh follows the precedents of the literary greats of the Irish

Renaissance in his use of disturbing material, he updates that tradition with innovations imported from late-twentieth-century horror film.

Contemporary writers like Martin McDonagh and Patrick McCabe are part of the tradition – reaching back at least to Synge and O'Casey – of using violence and brutality to disturb an audience, often to show the limitations of Irish society. Playing Dr Jekyll, Martin McDonagh relies upon these precedents in his plays, focusing on the lives of rural, Western, fast-talking Irish people, and reactions to his plays have sometimes been similar to those of J.M. Synge.[9] Declan Kiberd interprets *The Playboy of the Western World* as 'the monstrous spectacle of a deformed colonial life' that anxious nationalists converted 'through vilification and hearsay into a genuine "monster"'; notably, this accusation could also be levelled at Martin McDonagh.[10] Popular responses to and criticism of Synge's plays revolved around his failure to properly idealize the figure of the Irish peasant, which landed him the charge of un-realism. One should note here that these same critics found the peasant plays of Colum and Gregory quite realistic. William Boyle chose to remove his works from Abbey circulation following the furore over *The Playboy of the Western World*, writing to the *Freeman's Journal* to protest

> against any present attempt to set up a standard of National Drama based on the vilification of any section of the Irish people, in a theatre ostensibly founded, for the production of plays to represent real Irish life and character.[11]

Clarke notes that Boyle here 'voiced the feelings of a large section of the Abbey audience who were staunch Nationalists.[12] In his 1907 diaries, Holloway called *Playboy* the 'outpouring of a morbid, unhealthy mind',[13] a quote that Shaun Richards repeats in '"The outpouring of a morbid, unhealthy mind": The Critical Condition of Synge and McDonagh', which investigates the ties between the two playwrights. The *Freeman's Journal* labelled the play an 'unmitigated, protracted libel upon Irish peasant men, and worse still upon Irish girlhood'.[14] Certainly, a great many people were furious at Synge's portrayal of the Irish peasantry.

In *The Theatre of Nation*, Ben Levitas discusses Synge's reaction to the riots, quoting Synge's comment to W.G. Fay before the production of *Playboy*, 'the next play I write I will make sure I annoy them'.[15] Levitas notes that 'Synge, for his part, was frustrated by petty bourgeois nationalism, annoyed at the League's policy of standardizing Irish, and impatient with the conservatism of the Catholic Church'.[16] The Irish people resented Synge's satiric impulse and strongly preferred optimistic peasant plays that depicted the Irish people favourably. Maureen Waters understands the riots in the following terms:

> The Irish were hardly pleased by images of themselves as ignorant, backward, weak-spirited fools ... Maurice Bourgeois observed in 1913 that the Irish people as they are portrayed in *The Playboy* 'are anything but fit for self-government. Synge's comedy when viewed in this light, certainly constitutes the most tragic exposure of his fellow-countrymen's besottedness'. Quite understandably, the strongest reaction to Synge's play came from nationalists like Arthur Griffith, who were carefully developing the image of the heroic and high minded patriot.[17]

Synge's particular blend of the comedic and horrific alienated audience members who viewed the theatre as a vehicle for recovering the lost glory of the Irish people; they wanted to visualize the Irish peasantry through images of nobility, as seen in the witty, intelligent rogues of Yeats's works about Hanrahan or Lady Gregory's play *Spreading the News*. Most of the plays of the Irish Renaissance fall between the poles of portraying the people realistically, on the one hand, and attempting to compensate for centuries of cruel misrepresentation by portraying the people in a more idealized sense. Lady Gregory's Irish are generally quick-witted, jovial, imaginative, patriotic, and optimistic – charming peasant rogues and young ladies. Synge's are certainly quick-witted, but he pairs his sense of Irish wit with what Maureen Waters calls the 'darkness and vitality of the folk' – a representation that was not always favourable.[18] Christy gains a reputation as a charmer with a way with words, but this is, in part, because of his power as a skull-cracker and his winning ways with a loy.

This willingness to present the rural people of the West of Ireland in less than idealized terms is a characteristic shared by Synge and McDonagh. However, if Synge's Christy receives a burnt leg, McDonagh's Christy in *The Lieutenant of Inishmore* is tortured with a cheese grater, and the audience is treated to screams and spurting blood. McDonagh is quite conscious of his predecessors, and he consciously attempts to surpass them with more violence, gore, and disturbing material. These violent and bloody excesses land McDonagh with the charge of being Mr Hyde – the cannibalizing and unworthy hack. However, McDonagh blends Jekyll and Hyde – literary tradition and horrific innovation – in the creation of his Irish plays. Many of these new spins are imported from the horror genre, which has been very popular and prolific throughout this century, producing classics such as *Psycho, The Exorcist, Halloween,* and *Alien,* brilliant movies that are only recently receiving serious attention.[19]

Perhaps the best-known subgenre of horror film is the slasher, represented by such infamous series as *Nightmare on Elm Street, Friday the 13th,* and *Scream.* These films invariably begin with a group of teenage friends, often heading out for a raucous vacation far from civilization. Their shenanigans are interrupted, however, when the villain appears, leaving a trail of dead teenagers in his wake. The group of teenagers will be whittled down to one girl – 'The Final Girl' – who is stronger, smarter, more practical, and somehow a bit more masculine than the other females in the film; the final girl will endure an extended fight with the killer, and she generally emerges victorious, often dispatching her erstwhile murderer with his own weapons. Carol Clover suggests that this inescapable plot structure provides a convenient framework to initially destabilize traditional gender dynamics in order to ulti-mately vindicate masculine strength and resourcefulness through the masculine final girl's victory over a feminized villain.[20]

In *Lieutenant,* the plot follows a similar structure to the slasher film. The killer comes to the remote community; murders begin; blood, gore, and body parts are strewn about; the murderer is dispatched by a female using his own weapons. The basic plot structure maps onto the slasher film easily. However, the most interesting and significant similarities between the play and slasher films actually occur in the nuances of character development. These highly formulaic horror films require a particular sort of villain and a particular kind of heroine; the twisted gender dynamics of the average slasher feature a somehow feminine, but male, killer and a rather masculine, but female, final girl. This is not a totally new plot development; Declan Kiberd notes that *Playboy* features 'the masculinization of women and a corresponding feminization of men'.[21] While this trend is present in Synge's work, Martin McDonagh expands on it and uses the established patterns of the slasher film to do so.

McDonagh's use of these slasher films' characters in the service of destabilizing traditional gender roles fits clearly within his overall project of destabilizing all the traditional foundations of Irish society. Stereotypes of rural, western, Irish life invoke a warm hearth with a loving family gathered around it, a life of hard work in the farm fields and the garden, a trusting faith in God's goodness, and a caring relationship with the other members of the rural community. These ideals of the family, religion, and community meet with harsh treatment in McDonagh's plays; families are the source of all hatred and murder; people sit around watching TV rather than pursuing any employment; any show of religion is based on self-interest and misunderstanding; the community merely looks out for good gossip and interesting feuds. In *Lieutenant*, McDonagh turns his satiric gaze to traditional gender roles – the strong, masculine Republican and the feminine, demure, rural Irish girl. The use of slasher film characters allows McDonagh to destabilize both sides of this traditional gender dichotomy.

Padraic, the mad and sadistic member of the INLA, fits the profile of the slasher villain; he is sexually underdeveloped and frustrated, with a very conservative moral outlook. For example, in *Halloween*, Michael Myers begins his illustrious career by killing his sister as she has out-of-wedlock sex with her boyfriend. Hitchcock's *Psycho* features Norman Bates, so twisted by his unresolved Oedipal complex and his subsequent inability to consummate a relationship that he murders any young woman he finds attractive. Most slasher villains are actually very conservative; as Stephen King puts it in *Danse Macabre*, 'the horror story, beneath its fangs and fright wig, is really as conservative as an Illinois Republican in a three-piece pinstriped suit'.[22] Indeed, the first victims in the slasher film are generally those teenagers who have seen fit to consume massive quantities of alcohol or to sneak to the shed for sex. The slasher film villain is the punishing agent of conservative morality; he eliminates undesirable or lascivious characters before he is eliminated himself.

Padraic matches this outline perfectly. While torturing James, the pot dealer for the local college, Padraic becomes furious when James swears. He uses jingoistic anti-drug rhetoric, accusing James of 'Keeping our youngsters in a drugged-up and idle haze'.[23] He has a low estimation of women, and he initially refuses to consider Mairead's entrance into his paramilitary group, suggesting instead 'Let your hair grow out a tadeen and some fella's bound to be looking twice at you some day, and if you learn to cook and sew too, sure that'd double your chances. Maybe treble' (36). Padraic's character thus combines the torturing murderer with conservative morality, and it is a conjunction common in the slasher film.

Furthermore, the slasher villain reveals an underdeveloped and frustrated sexuality. As Clover writes, 'violence and sex are not concomitants but alternatives, the one … a substitute for and a prelude to the other'.[24] Padraic's affections, prior to his involvement with Mairead, had been confined to an unnatural attachment to his childhood cat, Wee Thomas. When Mairead asks Padraic about his previous love life, he reveals a lack of interest in women:

> A few have fallen but I paid no mind. Not while there was work to be done ridding Erin of them jackboot hirelings of England's foul monarchy, and a lot of the girls up North are dogs anyways, so it was no loss (33).

For him, as for most slasher villains, torture and sadism take the place of sex. In Clover's analysis, this stunted sexuality and conservative morality reveal a killer whose 'masculinity is severely qualified', despite his violent and aggressive nature.[25] Certainly Padraic, with his proclamations on the dangers of marijuana and the proper place of women, along with his lack of interest in girls and his strange obsession with his cat, fits this paradigm quite well.

The opposite and enemy to the slasher villain is the final girl. Carol Clover describes her as 'boyish, in a word';[26] if the killer is somehow feminine, not fully male, then the final girl is somehow masculine, not entirely female. In *Lieutenant*, Mairead is described clearly as just this sort of tomboy: 'Mairead is a girl of sixteen or so, slim, pretty, with close-cropped hair, army trousers, white Tshirt, sunglasses. She carries an air-rifle and starts kicking Davey's bicycle into the ditch as he gets up' (17). Furthermore, one of Mairead's favourite hobbies has been shooting out cows' eyes; this is hardly the equivalent of going shopping for makeup at the mall. This characterization also invokes Synge's Pegeen, the able country girl who has the guts to burn Christy's leg. However, in the overall context of *The Lieutenant of Inishmore*, with its mad sadistic murderer and its pile of dismembered corpses, this tomboy also invites comparison with the final girl of slasher films.

The eventual conflict between these two horror film types will end in the killer's destruction, often with his own weapons. In this battle between a feminized male and the masculine female, the girl wins every time. Viewers generally identify with the plight of the final girl and applaud her eventual victory over the murderous and emasculated villain. When Mairead kills Padraic, she uses not only his guns, but his particular style. As Donny points out, Padraic has a preferred method of killing: 'Padraic goes all the way up to ya, and then uses two guns from only an inch away' (56). Upon discovering that Padraic killed her cat, Mairead uses exactly this method on him: '*Mairead reaches down behind him, picks one gun up in each hand, slowly raises them and points them one on each side of Padraic's head*' (65). The use of guns in these scenes certainly does recall actual sectarian executions, rendering this violence more affective and realistic than a pile of dismembered body parts. However, within the overall hyperreal excesses of the play, these moments of political realism are fleeting; they add to the general violence of the play without making any coherent, independent statement on sectarian murder. And Mairead's use of Padraic's guns places her, once again, within the slasher film tradition. Carol Clover describes the final confrontation between the killer and the final girl as

> the castration, literal or symbolic, of the killer at her hands. The Final Girl has not just manned herself: she specifically unmans an oppressor whose masculinity was in question to begin with.[27]

This figurative castration comes through in *Lieutenant* not only in Mairead's murder of Padraic, but also in her final emasculating gesture of placing the barrels of both guns in his mouth.

It may also be interesting to consider Davey's role in this dynamic. In Padraic and Mairead, McDonagh introduces his concern with gender, especially with characters that cross gender boundaries or combine gender characteristics. Davey furthers this theme, as his masculinity is constantly and directly questioned. He begins the play as a weakling with a 'girl's mop' of long hair, which contrasts with Mairead's boyishly short hair (4). When he is too sensitive to steal a cat from a group of children, Donny suggests that his failure is due to his ambiguous masculinity:

> And if you were any kind of a man at all you'd've walked up to them mams and said 'I'm taking yere kids' cat', and if they'd put up a show you could've given them a belt, and then trampled on the bitches! (23).

Finally, he still has a strong bond with his mother: 'I love my mam. Love her more than anything' (26). Certainly, Donny and Padraic question Davey's masculinity throughout the play, and this serves to further highlight McDonagh's overall destabilization of gender. However, this gender ambiguity also suggests the influence of horror films; Davey's strange bond with his mother invokes Hitchcock's *Psycho*. Furthermore, Clover posits that the audience for horror films is primarily adolescent males, young men troubled by their own gender ambiguity at a time of transition. The ambiguously gendered Davey fits into this category. Clover suggests that these young men, in the viewing of the slasher film, symbolically reject the feminine within themselves through the death of the feminized villain and embrace the masculine through the triumph of the masculine final girl. As the play progresses, Davey becomes much more masculine. Padraic cuts off Davey's long hair, and Davey increasingly stands up to Padraic, willing to question his methods and motives. He also progresses from a timid boy who would not steal a cat to someone who very seriously considers shooting a cat; the violence of the play has apparently made him into more of a 'man' than he was at the opening. By rendering the viewer more clearly masculine, the horror film has done its work. The characters and gender dynamics of *Lieutenant* map onto a slasher film easily, revealing the multiplicity of sources that McDonagh draws from in his works – turning *Lieutenant* into the incestuous offspring of *The Texas Chainsaw Massacre* and *The Playboy of the Western World*.

However, these characters are not the only correspondences between McDonagh's work and horror films. The trajectory of his plays moves toward more violence, more bodies, and more gore. This is characteristic of the horror genre, and especially of the slasher, where the highly formulaic nature of the plot and characters leaves little room for variance – the differences between films tend to be the number of bodies and the bloodiness of the special effects. This emphasis on special effects leads to constant one-upmanship, each film gorier than the last. As Carol Clover notes,

> what can be done is done, and slashers, at the bottom of the category, do it most and worst. Thus we see heads squashed and eyes popped out, faces flayed, limbs dismembered, eyes penetrated by needles in close-up, and so on.[28]

In the mid- and late-twentieth-century, the horror film, especially the slasher, has become *the* source of grotesque and bloody special effects. McDonagh's works, especially *Lieutenant* and *The Pillowman*, necessitate a significant amount of technical skill and special effects work. *Lieutenant* features several torture scenes, involving a bloody man suspended upside down without some toenails and a man enduring torture with a cheese grater who begins spraying blood. Not only does the play entail spurting blood, but a cat must explode '*in a ball of blood and bones*' onstage (40). Several people are shot at point-blank range. Furthermore, scene nine requires that '*As the scene begins the blood-soaked living room is strewn with the body parts of Brendan and Joey, which Donny and Davey, blood-soaked also, hack away at to sizeable chunks*' (55). Any theatre with a limited budget could not produce these effects; they require money, significant technical skill, and the special effects knowledge of an expert. Furthermore, though these scenes seem difficult, *The Pillowman* surpasses them, requiring, among other things, a little girl to be crucified onstage. Any sequel must have a higher body count than its predecessor.

The excessive, meaningless violence of *The Lieutenant of Inishmore* and its characters Padraic, Mairead, and Davey all point toward the horror genre, especially toward the slasher. However, another subgenre, called the regional Gothic, is interesting to consider alongside McDonagh's work, and, in fact, these horror subgenres often overlap, so that a slasher may well include aspects of the regional Gothic. In *The Texas Chainsaw Massacre,* Leatherface is not only an emasculated serial killer, but also a member of an isolated and impoverished family that lost its livelihood when the local meatpacking plant began to use machines to slaughter cattle. Daryl Jones suggests that the genres of horror, Gothic, and melodrama often revolve around the perceived cultural margins of the time and culture:

> This is certainly the paradigm of what I would want to call 'regional Gothic', and thus in the ideological rhetoric of horror, Catholics, Welshmen, hillbillies and cannibals are all pretty much the same.[29]

Leenane, Inishmore, and Inishmaan all provide distinctly rural and lonely locations that offer ideal settings for the regional Gothic and ideal settings for bloody rural murders; as Clover describes,

> Going from city to country in horror film is in any case very much like going from village to deep, dark forest in traditional fairy tales … The point is that rural Connecticut (or wherever), like the deep forests of Central Europe, is a place where the rules of civilization do not obtain.[30]

Regional Gothic plays on possible fears that the people out in the country are lawless, violent, and very possibly incestuous or cannibalistic, which certainly seems to apply to McDonagh's rural settings, replete with murderers of all sorts getting away with their crimes in a setting without sufficient law or religion to rein them in.

The Ireland of Leenane, Inishmore, and Inishmaan in these plays is a bankrupt state; family, religion, culture and law are powerless to provide coherence. Empty and bored people turn to violence because they have nothing else to do. While this blend of 'nihilism and gore' (as Jones describes modern horror)[31] may be a useful framework through which to critique the stereotypes and ideals of the nation, it raises questions about the future of McDonagh's art. If McDonagh continues to play this game of one-upmanship with his predecessors and his own plays, we can expect only bloodier and gorier works as his career progresses. Gore can be powerful, and it can even be beautiful, but there is a danger in mistaking body count for artistic merit.

McDonagh's newest play *The Pillowman* also depicts excessive violence, and this violence is directed at the most vulnerable in society, children. This sadistic violence always results in twisted adults incapable of relating to other people with empathy. This world is essentially horrific, and there's no escape – as described in Katurian's story 'The Pillowman':

> See, when the Pillowman was successful in his work, a little child would die horrifically. And when the Pillowman was unsuccessful, a little child would have a horrific life, grow into an adult who'd also have a horrific life, and *then* die horrifically.[32]

In this play, life can only be horror. That horror, furthermore, is often explored in terms that are familiar from genre films. When Michal is being tortured by his parents, the description resembles nothing more than a mad scientist's lab in the tradition of Dr Frankenstein: Katurian listens to the 'low whirring of drills, the scritchety-scratch of bolts being tightened, the dull fizz of unknown things electrical, and the muffled screams of a small gagged child began to emanate through [the room's] thick brick walls', and audience members are able to see '*In the nightmare semi-dark of the adjoining room, it appears for a second as if a child of eight, strapped to the bed, is being tortured with drills and sparks*' (31–32). The torture of Katurian's brother Michal, furthermore, is only one of many horrific stories told within *The Pillowman*; horror piles upon horror as tale piles upon tale. The cyclic nature of history in this play – in which adults torture children who then grow up to torture others – is replicated in the play's structure. Horrific stories repeat, over and over, and the close of the play suggests that those stories will repeat again, indefinitely, in the future. This emphasis upon endless repetition without escape finds expression in both *The Lieutenant of Inishmore* and in *The Pillowman*; the one uses piles of variously murdered corpses, while the other uses a litany of horrific stories. In neither does there seem to be any legitimate hope for escape from this widening gyre. Mairead may form her own paramilitary group, and Katurian's stories will find a new audience in a younger generation.

Certainly, as one might expect, horror films lend themselves to a pessimistic outlook. As Stephen King posits,

> When we turn to the creepy movie or the crawly book, we are not wearing our 'Everything works out for the best' hats. We're waiting to be told what we so often suspect – that everything is turning to

shit. In most cases the horror story provides ample proof that such is indeed the case.[33]

David Skal elaborates on this in reference to the American horror film tradition: 'One place the [American] dream is permitted to perish, with noisy, convulsive death rattles, is in horror entertainment'.[34] McDonagh shares this emphasis on pessimism and national critique, as Heath Diehl recognizes:

> Ultimately McDonagh's voice is pessimistic, offering readers/spectators neither a means of escape nor a hope for a future lived differently. For me, this is the most provocative aspect of the playwright's voice. In a moment when glib sentiment and simpleminded morality predominate on the world's leading stages, McDonagh has gained international fame for realizing in his work what Synge opined in 1909: that 'before poetry can be human again it must learn to be brutal'.[35]

McDonagh's pessimistic voice, filtered and crystallized by his use of horror, thus provides a useful tool to express despair about the state of the nation – everything is turning to shit, and those cultural foundations that should help have instead become quagmires. Horror offers a convenient framework through which to express feelings of hopelessness, failure, and lack of control – it can provide an excellent critique of a nation's idea of itself. McDonagh tears very large holes in the ideals of religion, family, community, and nation dear to popular conceptions of Ireland. However, he always presents this decay of the state as a zombie vaudeville show – decomposing representatives of the Irish family, community, and religion stagger across the stage, dropping body parts along the way. Audiences have learned what to expect from McDonagh, and he always delivers it: violence, gore, pessimism, and camp, self-conscious humour in plots that seem to be more variations on a theme than individual and distinct texts. And this characteristic – this joyous laughter that revels in repetition – is one that McDonagh shares with the average slasher film, which fills theatres with audiences ready to boo the villain, cheer the final girl, and laugh at over-the-top scenes of blood and gore. He incorporates accepted canonical references to J.M. Synge and other Irish literary greats alongside nods to *Psycho* and *Frankenstein*, thus displaying a postmodern integration of high and pop culture.

McDonagh has taken the critique of cultural nationalist art implicit in J.M. Synge's works, as well as his uses of violence and humour, and combined them with the plots and characters of late-twentieth-century horror films. He unites these influences into works that are both traditional and innovative. McDonagh's Dr Jekyll is always poised to transform into Mr Hyde, and a good, violent, blood-soaked Hyde is what today's audience wants.

---

[1] Of course, as Robert Louis Stevenson's *The Strange Case of Dr Jekyll and Mr Hyde* suggests, a colonized identity can create a partition of personality, the respectable surface and the rebellious underbelly, so this metaphor also proves apt for considering how McDonagh both invokes and satirises Irish stereotypes.

[2] Scholars such as José Lanters and Shaun Richards demonstrate the strong ties between McDonagh and the greats of the Literary Revival, especially J.M. Synge. As they have done superlative work already on this topic, my overview here will be brief. See José Lanters, 'Playwrights of the Western World: Synge, Murphy, McDonagh', in *A Century of Irish Drama: Widening the Stage* , eds Stephen Watt, Eileen Morgan and Shakir Mustafa (Bloomington: Indiana UP, 2000), pp.204–22, and Shaun Richards, '"The outpouring of a morbid, unhealthy mind": The Critical Condition of Synge and McDonagh', *Irish University Review* 33.1 (2003), pp.201-16. Accessed online via InfoTrac. 8 June 2004.

[3] Joseph Feeney, 'Martin McDonagh: Dramatist of the West', *Studies* 87 (1998), p.25.

[4] Ibid., p.29.

[5] Ibid., p.28.

[6] *Financial Times*, qtd. in Feeney, p.24.

[7] Nicholas Grene, 'Black Pastoral: 1990s Images of Ireland', *Litteraria Pragensia* 20.10, 2004. <http://komparatistika.ff.cuni.cz/litteraria/no20-10/grene.htm>, paragraph 3.

[8] Victor Merriman, qtd. in Richards, 2003, paragraph 3.

[9] While McDonagh insists that he was not familiar with Synge's work when composing his most famous plays, I find this nearly impossible to believe. These comments seem to be Brendan Behan-esque performances designed to generate controversy.

[10] Declan Kiberd, *Inventing Ireland* (Cambridge: Harvard UP, 1995), p.167.

[11] Qtd. in Brenna Katz Clarke, *The Emergence of the Irish Peasant Play at the*

Abbey Theatre (Ann Arbor: UMI, 1982), p.160.

[12] Clarke, p.161.

[13] Qtd. in Clarke, p.161.

[14] Qtd. in Clarke, p.161.

[15] Ben Levitas, *The Theatre of Nation: Irish Drama and Cultural Nationalism, 1890–1916* (Oxford: Oxford UP, 2002), p.115.

[16] Ibid., p.119.

[17] Maureen Waters, *The Comic Irishman* (Albany: Suny Press, 1984), p.79.

[18] Ibid., p.81.

[19] Books like Carol Clover's *Men, Women, and Chainsaws*, Darryl Jones's *Horror*, Stephen King's *Danse Macabre*, and David Skal's *The Monster Show* investigate the complexity of these films and their relevance to cultural norms and anxieties. My analysis below will primarily rely on Carol Clover's text, as she offers the best overview of the slasher film's plot and characters. See Carol Clover, *Men, Women, and Chain Saws: Gender in the Modern Horror Film* (Princeton: Princeton UP, 1992).

[20] Clover suggests that the gender of the 'final girl' is actually a sort of feint; the final girl's masculinity, as opposed to her friends or to traditional ideals of young femininity, makes her final triumph a problematic one to claim for feminist goals. She wins only because, and to the degree that, she's like a man.

[21] Kiberd, pp.175–76.

[22] Stephen King, *Danse Macabre* (New York: Berkeley, 1983), p.395.

[23] Martin McDonagh, *The Lieutenant of Inishmore* (London: Methuen, 2001), p.12. Henceforth cited parenthetically.

[24] Clover, p.29.

[25] Ibid., p.47.

[26] Ibid., p.40.

[27] Ibid., p.65.

[28] Ibid., p.41.

[29] Darryl Jones, *Horror: A Thematic History in Fiction and Film* (London: Arnold; New York: Oxford, 2002), p.18.

[30] Clover, p.124.

[31] Jones, p.161.

[32] Martin McDonagh, *The Pillowman* (London: Faber, 2003), p.45. Henceforth cited parenthetically.

[33] King, p.32.

[34] David J. Skal, *The Monster Show: A Cultural History of Horror*, rev. ed. (New York: Faber, 2001), p.354.

[35] Heath A. Diehl, 'Classic Realism, Irish Nationalism, and a New Breed of Angry Young Man in Martin McDonagh's *The Beauty Queen of Leenane*', *JMMLA* 34.2 (2001), pp.112-13.

14 | Grotesque Entertainment: *The Pillowman* as Puppet Theatre

Ondřej Pilný

The 'Irish' plays of Martin McDonagh were all dark, violent comedies, irreverent and hilarious. All of them were extremely skilfully plotted and included some exquisite dialogue. *The Leenane Trilogy*, *The Cripple of Inishmaan*, and *The Lieutenant of Inishmore* also productively engaged in an ironic manner with the conventions of canonical Irish drama. They may moreover be viewed as an ironic send-up of the entire discourse of Irish identity and all those who are still seriously concerned, in the post-nationalist context, with coining and/or maintaining a firm definition of Irishness.[1] *The Pillowman*,[2] McDonagh's first 'non-Irish' play, raised high expectations not only due to the enormous success of the playwright's earlier work: quite a portion of the playwright's audiences were beginning to feel that it was high time for a talent of McDonagh's calibre to change the subject and prove his worth by going now for 'something completely different'.

Set in a fictitious totalitarian state, probably some time in the mid-twentieth century, *The Pillowman* concerns a writer who has been arrested for the content of his stories. It is again a black comedy which features graphic violence, frequent vulgarities, and moments of irresistible humour. As with McDonagh's previous plays, much of its effect is based on sudden, unexpected twists, while significant aspects of the plot are conceived basically as 'a puzzle without a solution' (17) – in the end, you will never know, for instance, whether Katurian's mentally handicapped brother Michal really killed the little girl and the little boy, an act for which he ended up murdered by Katurian.

Moreover, McDonagh once more utilizes elements of naturalist theatre within a grotesque framework in order to play with audience expectations. The opening scene initially seems fairly realistic: a writer suffers politically motivated violence from a couple of plain-clothes policemen. Nonetheless, the interaction grows gradually clichéd to the point of hyperbole. The linguistic mélange of names only underscores the fictitious nature of the setting: the writer's name appears to be Armenian in overdose ('Katurian Katurian Katurian;' 8); his hometown is called Kamenice which is Czech, but features a Jewish quarter with the non-Czech name of Lamenec (besides, Jewish quarters vanished from Czech towns after the Holocaust). The brother is called Michal – Czech, Slovak, or Polish; the victims are Andrea Jovanovic – Serb, Croat, or Slovene, and Aaron Goldberg – a credible Germanic/Jewish name for the Central European region. The detectives' names, Tupolski and Ariel, blend Polish with Shakespeare. Finally, Katurian's address of 'Kamenice 4443' lacks a street name (the town is too large for the streets not to be identified) and sounds more like a linguistic joke which concerns the writer's name: the four which echoes in his appellation, three times. Is the play supposed to be an allegory or a travesty, one is made to ask?

Despite this uncertainty, the violence in *The Pillowman* is always offered in a gruesome, naturalist fashion which tends to regularly disrupt any hyperbolical pattern. To blur things even further, there are scenes which seem to bring in symbolical elements, most remarkably the re-enactment of the story of the writer and his brother staged in a *'child's room, next door to which there is another identical room, perhaps made of glass, but padlocked and totally dark'* (31), a scenery symbolically suggestive of the writer's unacknowledged secrets, or perhaps his unconscious. The dialogue oscillates throughout in the same manner between realistic conversations, captivating storytelling, and stand-up comedy routine (Katurian: 'Yeah, like I bet you gave my brother his rights too.' Ariel: 'I gave him his rights alright.' Katurian: 'I bet you did. I bet you fucking did.' [...] Ariel: 'No, *I* bet I fucking did.' Katurian: 'Yeah, I bet you fucking did.' Ariel: 'No, *I* bet I fucking did!' etc. [27-8]).

Apart from the blending of genres, *The Pillowman* is characterized by an incessant switching of themes. The initial motif of the totalitarian oppression of artists gets swiftly modified as it transpires that the problem with Katurian's writing has nothing to do with politics, and the interrogation turns out to be a murder inquiry. At the same time, the grave issue of authorial responsibility is raised: if an author writes stories which feature vivid descriptions of violence and slaughter, is he/she to blame when people take them up as a set of instructions and proceed to actual murder? The question remains unanswered though, while the play swerves to focus on Katurian's brother Michal, the story of the brothers' childhood and the writer's sadistic Muse (i.e., his parents and their revolting experiment). Yet another theme surfaces through Katurian's story 'The Pillowman,' one of 'nipping some young doom in the bud'; but this theme gets quickly forgotten as well due to Michal's confession to the killings of the children. Finally perhaps the play seems to start focusing on Katurian as an instance of a writer who values his work more than human life, including his own and his brother's. However, even this important issue gets qualified by a series of final shifts in the plot, and ultimately by Katurian's triumphant resurrection from the dead, an uncanny moment which indicates that the whole story of Katurian's interrogation may have been sheer fiction from the start. Indeed, as a reviewer has noted, the play may appear to deal with some grave matters of ethics and authorship but in fact backs out of any such considerations almost as soon as they emerge.[3]

If there is no consistency of genre and theme in *The Pillowman*, while the characters appear to be as shifty as the play itself (particularly the supposedly 'retarded' and infantile Michal, who at times exhibits rather surprising skills as a speaker and thinker), and the plot abounds in digressions, what is it that holds the play together? Clearly, it is the mere power of the story. The play features numerous absurd turns and unabashed lies; every time the audience gets close to piecing the plot together and being able to predict what may follow, the play leaves everyone baffled again. Paradoxes are plenty, including a striking example at the heart of the eponymous tale of 'The Pillowman': the Pillowman is said to be a creature who comes to tell adults to kill themselves when they were children because their ensuing suffering in this world is not worth living for (43-47). This story cannot be dismissed simply as a bizarre yarn, as its peculiar treatment of time has in fact a well-known parallel in mythical narratives of primitive societies; the existence of the precedent indicates that the story might also be viewed as a mock-mythical tale explaining away child suicides. Due to such feats of dark narrative magic, and despite all the wild turning points, one remains captivated by what he/she is told to believe. It is indeed as if the play were an extended illustration of Katurian's (and McDonagh's)[4] borrowed thesis that 'The only duty of a storyteller is to tell a story', and to tell it well (7).

The Pillowman invites – not merely by its title – an interesting analogy with the famous story by E.T.A. Hoffmann, 'The Sandman'.[5] For the start, there are a number of similarities in detail, in particular between the fantastic bogey-like characters of the Sandman and the Pillowman and the fatal consequences of encountering them, or professor Spalanzani's daughter, Olympia, being kept locked in a room behind a glass door like Michal in McDonagh's play. What is of more consequence though is that Hoffmann's tale is also one of a writer, Nathaniel, who tells a story of the Sandman; at the same time, those around Nathaniel claim that the horrific Sandman is really a product of the darker side of Nathaniel's mind. Despite the fact, the power of the fantasy is such that it eventually produces lethal effects in reality: because of the metonymic telescope given to him by the Sandman/the optician Coppola, Nathaniel first falls in love with Olympia, who is a mechanical puppet, and then is driven to suicide. Similarly, the fantastic tale of the Pillowman is transferred into reality by Katurian's suffocating of his brother with a pillow and thus acting out the role of the phantom produced by his own sinister mind.

The very core of the analogy lies however in the way 'The Sandman' and *The Pillowman* make use of the uncanny and our eerie fascination with it. Nicholas Royle claims that the uncanny

> is concerned with the strange, weird and mysterious, with a flickering sense (but not conviction) of something supernatural. The uncanny involves feelings of uncertainty, in particular

regarding the reality of who one is and what is being experienced....
It can take the form of something familiar unexpectedly arising in a
strange and unfamiliar context, or of something strange and unfamiliar unexpectedly arising in a familiar context.[6]

The uncanny is the innermost focus of Hoffmann's tale: indeed,
he comes to introduce an authorial narrator in the middle of his
story in order to do justice to the extraordinary power the uncanny
has over Nathaniel. The authorial narrator opens by stating that his
task is to persuade the reader about the actual existence of the uncanny as this is the only way of gaining credibility for Nathaniel's
fate. In order to do that, he says, the story must be told in a
manner as inspiring, original, and striking as it is possible. Hence,
'The Sandman' is revealed to be really an exercise in telling
uncanny tales, by different narrators, in the most persuasive and
effective way.

The similarity of this fundamental aspect of Hoffmann's tale to
the concerns of *The Pillowman* is remarkable. McDonagh employs
all his skills to make the uncanny palpable, giving control over the
plot to different characters in turn and excelling in the per-
suasiveness of their tales and perspectives. As in 'The Sandman',
the blurring of the borderline between reality and fiction is an
essential device: in the words of Sigmund Freud, 'an uncanny
effect is often and easily produced when the distinction between
imagination and reality is effaced'.[7] As indicated above, the
audience of *The Pillowman* can hardly ever be sure about the status
of what they are told – but fact or fiction, they still find themselves
deep in the tenets of the tale which unravels in front of them, as
the lure of the uncanny is enormous and we essentially *want* to
believe in it.

Royle shows in his comprehensive study of the subject that the
uncanny can often 'be felt in response to dolls and other lifelike or
mechanical objects'.[8] This brings me to my central thesis: I wish to
suggest that *The Pillowman* is best viewed as a particular kind of
puppet theatre. Jan Švankmajer, Czech artist, puppeteer, and
filmmaker has stressed that puppet theatre is primarily characterized by the puppeteer's scot-free manipulation, while the
puppeteer's actions are in fact very much childlike. He claims that:
'The child-puppeteer is then really a shaman, god and creator, the

Great Mover, but also a judge who decides on the fate of the characters manipulated by him. And at the same time, his actions are not liable to judgement, being absolute'.[9]

Manipulation is an overall defining feature of *The Pillowman*. Despite the fact that Katurian is introduced as someone who is being victimized, already Scene 2 – the re-enactment of the story of the writer and his brother – shows him to be pulling the strings of the other characters in the story (a fact comically stressed also by the child's corpse sitting 'bolt upright in bed' [34]). A similar situation occurs in act Scene 2 (the drastic re-enactment of 'The Little Jesus'), and ultimately at the very end of the play which, in a feat of unabashed authorial ventriloquism, unravels Katurian the puppeteer to be merely a puppet himself as his corpse with a 'bloody, bullet-shattered head' stands up and delivers the de-nouement (102). The finale demonstrates in this way what one should have really suspected all along: the point is that all the characters in the play are puppets, swung around by their mani-pulative creator, while the ultimate aim seems to be to shunt the audience to and fro in a similar way without losing a firm grip over it. Or in Tupolski's words, the objective is to 'Disconcert and de-stabilize the prisoner' (82). In this context, then, it is obviously no problem that characters lack consistency, get killed and resurrected freely, and that the play features any kind of improbable turning points.

Heinrich von Kleist's masterful ironic sketch 'Über das Marionettentheater' presents a bold proposition: puppets are more graceful than live dancers. The self-consciousness of humans and the fact that they are subject to the laws of nature (as represented by gravity in Kleist's essay) prevents human dancers from executing a truly graceful dance. This is why Kleist's interlocutor concludes that 'Grace appears most purely in that human form which either has no consciousness or an infinite consciousness. That is, in the puppet or in the god' (12).

Paul de Man has pointed out that in 'Über das Marionetten-theater' Kleist targets Schiller's idealistic aesthetic, in particular the latter's notion of the aesthetic state.[10] Schiller has likened the perfect aesthetic society to 'a well executed English dance, com-posed of many complicated figures and turns' featuring 'an infinite variety of criss-crossing motions which keep decisively but arbitrarily changing directions without ever colliding with each other.'[11] Kleist's essay replaces this image of a graceful dance with the dance of puppets, in order to demonstrate the mechanistic, formulaic and essentially dehumanized nature of Schiller's ideal. The interlocutor in 'Über das Marionettentheater' first provides the narrator with a detailed mock-scientific explanation of the puppets' movements. He then admits that in spite of the geometrical precision of movement, residual traces of human volition still appear in the puppet dance, those represented by the puppeteer. If these were removed, the whole spectacle could in fact be produced by 'turning a handle' as if it were a barrel organ (2-4).

Although the context of Kleist's essay has to do with the dangerous political implications of a specific aesthetic ideology,[12] de Man has demonstrated that Kleist's strategy may indeed be plausibly used against any kind of 'aesthetic formalization' (de Man's term),[13] i.e., against any kind of aesthetic which may be reduced to a series of formulae (and potentially peopled with puppets). On this note I would like to return to *The Pillowman*.

The Pillowman really exemplifies the recent genre of what I would term grotesque entertainment. Apart from the puppet-like nature of its characters and action, the play builds on a number of formulae which it shares with many other contemporary plays and films – a lot of 'in-yer-face theatre', American plays such as Tracy Letts's *Killer Joe*, most films of Quentin Tarantino and his epigones, a number of recent gangster movies, and to an extent also McDonagh's own earlier plays. The formulae of the grotesque entertainment include – to repeat my earlier list – the staging of graphic, often gratuitous violence, offensive language, ubiquitous black humour (including rather cheap laughs at the expense of, let's say, mentally deficient characters). To this should be added the lack of depth of character psychology, and – in accordance with the traditional notion of the grotesque – the mixing of disparate genre and thematic elements.

Grotesque entertainment also features strategic deployment of the uncanny as its central device. The violent aspect of the plays and films is not merely about the buckets of blood and the severed body parts (although these of course tend to be profusely in evidence); what is more important is the exploitation of what Victoria Nelson has called the audiences' 'unconscious desire' to believe in the supernatural.[14] Hence, inexplicable interventions from outside the presented reality abound, fantastic tales produce fatal effects, characters miraculously survive what seem to be mortal wounds or diseases in order to unexpectedly reappear, and even the dead get occasionally resurrected.

Finally, grotesque entertainment often raises seminal questions of ethics, justice, and artistic responsibility but as a rule, these issues get swiftly – for some viewers, cynically – swept aside by the outrageous shenanigans of the particular piece. Moral, political and artistic dilemmas indeed seem to be introduced merely for the sake of being deemed, sooner or later, irrelevant.

The aesthetic similarity of all such works is striking, and turns one back to Kleist's image of the puppets: what we are watching is in fact a clattering puppet dance, distinctly manipulative and largely dehumanized. To be sure, it may be quite hilarious at the same time: as the interlocutor in 'Über das Marionettentheater' puts it, 'Often, shaken in a purely haphazard way, the puppet falls into a kind of rhythmic movement which resembles dance' (2) – and we laugh. However, the general repetitiveness of the pattern only stresses its fundamental emptiness. We should be grateful on the whole for the remaining 'traces of human volition' on the part of the puppeteers, that is authors like McDonagh whose skilful plotting makes yet another piece still watchable, even though the handle of the same old barrel-organ is clearly being turned again.

There is no need for general statements regarding what the immense popularity of such grotesque spectacle says about the condition of the contemporary Western society: more alarming social and cultural tendencies are surely to be addressed by those who see themselves qualified. What I can offer instead is a mere aphoristic postscript:

— Kleist's 'Über das Marionettentheater' shows that the 'graceful dance' of a formulaic aesthetic will always be executed by puppets and idols only, as such grace 'appears most purely [...] in the puppet or in the god.' (12) Kleist's sardonic observation clearly comments on worship: unless the dancers be gods, the fanciers of the formulaic dance worship puppets.

— Nathaniel, the romantic hero of Hoffmann's tale of the Sandman, falls in love with the puppet Olympia while dancing with her. His infatuation with the creature whose eyes only mirror his desire nearly deprives him of his wits.

— The Sandman throws sand into children's eyes, taking away their sleep, and eventually pokes their eyes out. But, like thePillowman, he is an uncanny work of morbid imagination. Isn't he?

---

[1] For a more detailed discussion see my earlier article, 'Martin McDonagh: Parody? Satire? Complacency?', *Irish Studies Review* 12.2, 2004, pp.225-32.

[2] Martin McDonagh, *The Pillowman* (London: Faber and Faber, 2003). Premièred in the Cottesloe auditorium of the National Theatre, London, 13 November 2003. Further references appear in parentheses in the text.

[3] Toby Lichtig, 'It Must Be the Way He Tells Them', *The Times Literary Supplement* 5252, 28 November 2003, p.20.

[4] 'It's definitely easier to write about things from a distance – especially when you just want to tell stories, which is all I want to do.' Martin McDonagh quoted in Joyce Flynn, 'Stage, Screen, and Another Ireland', *American Repertory Theatre News* 20 January 1999. '[I]t's always, first and last, about story. Story is everything. Story and a bit of attitude.' Martin McDonagh quoted in Sean O'Hagan, 'The Wild West', *The Guardian* 24 March 2001.

[5] E.T.A. Hoffmann, 'The Sandman' in *Tales of Hoffmann*, trans. R.J. Hollingdale (Harmondsworth: Penguin, 1982), pp.85-125.

[6] Nicholas Royle, *The Uncanny* (Manchester: Manchester University Press, 2003), p.1.

[7] Sigmund Freud, *The Uncanny*, trans. James Strachey, *Pelican Freud Library*, 14 (Harmondsworth: Penguin, 1985), p.367.

[8] Royle, *The Uncanny*, p.2.

[9] Jan Švankmajer, 'Apoteóza loutkového divadla' [Apotheosis of Puppet Theatre] (1998), eds Eva Švankmajerová, Jan Švankmajer, *Jídlo* [Food] (Praha: Arbor vitae, 2004), p.187; my translation.

[10] Paul de Man, 'Aesthetic Formalization: Kleist's *Über das Marionettentheater*', *The Rhetoric of Romanticism* (New York: Columbia University Press, 1984), pp.263-5, and *passim*.

[11] Friedrich Schiller, *On the Aesthetic Education of Man in a Series of Letters*, eds and trans. E.M. Wilkinson and L.A. Willoughby (Oxford: Clarendon Press, 1967), p.300. De Man's essay opens with an extended quotation of this passage.

[12] An important discussion of Kleist which links Schiller's 'aesthetic state'

with the mechanisms of totalitarian societies appears in Martin
Procházka, 'From "Affirmative Culture" to the "Condition of Justice": A
Reading of a Czech Post-Communist *Hamlet*', forthcoming 2006.

[13] De Man ultimately focuses on the principles of textual hermeneutics
which he views as formalised precisely in this manner. De Man,
'Aesthetic Formalization', pp.282ff.

[14] Victoria Nelson, *The Secret Life of Puppets* (Cambridge, Mass. and London:
Harvard University Press, 2001), p.170. See also Chapters 1, 7, and
passim.

15 | 'When it's there I am, it's here I wish I was': Martin McDonagh and the Construction of Connemara

John McDonagh[1]

> The latest in the Royal Court's amazing run of exciting discoveries is Martin McDonagh, another fine Irish playwright. He's only in his mid-twenties, damn him, and his first play, *The Beauty Queen of Leenane*, is an absolute cracker. The extraordinary achievement is that it is wildly funny, deeply affecting and grotesquely macabre all at the same time. During its most potent scenes, you don't know whether to laugh, cry or gasp with horror.[2]

Charles Spencer's review for the *Daily Telegraph* (8 March 1996) of Martin McDonagh's play *The Beauty Queen of Leenane* typifies the critical euphoria that greeted the Royal Court/Druid Theatre co-production on its London debut in 1996. Having premiered in the Town Hall Theatre in Galway on 1 February 1996, McDonagh's play has been described as 'astonishing'[3] and this specific production has garnered numerous prestigious allocades, including four Tony Awards after its Broadway run in 1998, one of these the first ever award for a female director, Garry Hynes. The play catapulted McDonagh into the unenviable role of the latest in a long line of 'the next big thing' amongst Irish playwrights, despite the fact that his distinctly Anglo-Irish heritage calls into question the very nomenclature used by critics to categorize him. The play has been performed by various theatre companies throughout the world and the cast of Anna Manahan, Kate Burton, Ruaidhri Conroy and Peter Gowen embarked on a sell-out 13 venue, 4 month tour of the UK and Ireland in 2000. The critical and commercial success of the play, however, belies the inherent inconsistencies in both its dramatic and linguistic constructions that crucially undermine the cultural authenticity that it so obviously craves. The play's loose structure, within which McDonagh allows a significant and unsettling chronological gaffe to occur, develops in a traditional tragicomic fashion, culminating in the none-too-astonishing murder of Mag by her daughter, Maureen. McDonagh's combination of melodrama, naturalism and black comedy, coupled with a distinctive Irish background, has obviously struck a chord with audiences and critics desperate for a Syngean successor yet the dramatic effect of the play serves merely to highlight the traditional nature of the *oeuvre* within which McDonagh has chosen to operate.

McDonagh, however, treads on dangerous ground because he has attempted to dislocate a stock tragicomic form and setting by subverting some of the central elements of the tragic-comic genre, such as the clear delineation of the tragic and the comic. One obvious technique is the running gag of the smell of urine from the sink, a comic interlude that is regularly used to alleviate a potentially explosive encounter. The danger in this is that too often McDonagh appears to be merely tinkering with the genre, happy to include a few contemporary references to recognizable icons of popular culture while maintaining the predictable plotline of the standard tragicomic dramatic construction, thereby creating the suspicion that the genre is not being dislocated at all. Charles Spencer's inability to know whether to 'laugh, cry or gasp with horror' says less perhaps about McDonagh's dramatic abilities than it does about the critic's obvious lack of knowledge of the basic tenets of black comedy, a dramatic form which extracts its laughter precisely from chance, cruelty, suffering and death, all of which are clearly signposted in McDonagh's play. In the first description of Mag Folan, for example, he emphasizes that 'her left hand is somewhat more shrivelled and red than her right',[4] a clear reference to some previous sinister and perhaps violent past event. That Maureen should eventually kill her mother should really come as no surprise to an audience drip-fed details that obviously herald the violent climax of the play while the eventual murder weapon, a heavy iron poker, makes its appearance in the opening setting of scene one. The oft-noted critical reaction of shock at the murder of Mag fails to take account of the clear early indications that all is not and has not been well with Maureen Folan for some time.

Equally, the deliberate setting of the trilogy in Connemara undoubtedly places certain dramatic and linguistic pressures on McDonagh. *The Beauty Queen of Leenane* is overtly set in a specific West of Ireland location in a particular time, 1989, and McDonagh goes to a good deal of trouble to specifically relate the action with the setting and the chronological time, a task that is somewhat foisted upon him by the conscious foregrounding of Connemara at a particular time in its evolution. In an overtly conscious attempt to capture the grammatical, syntactical, and idiomatic language of Connemara, McDonagh has recreated a speech pattern reminiscent of Synge and *The Playboy of the Western World*, a work to which McDonagh's play pays linguistic homage. The realism of the dialogic exchanges between Maureen and Mag, peppered as it is with cutting wit and sharp rivalry, is skewed by McDonagh's somewhat tortured syntactical constructions, consciously fore-grounded in an attempt to present an authentic snapshot of Connemara speech. However, on closer analysis, the speech patterns used by McDonagh appear to owe more to a semantically romanticized Syngean legacy than an accurate portrayal of the linguistic patterns of Connemara. For example, in one typical exchange in scene eight, Maureen and Mag communicate in their usual linguistic *modus operandi*, composed of equal measures of accusation, reprimand, bitter recollection and ironic admonish-ment. Maureen is reflecting on a night spent with her lover, Pato, and comments to her mother 'Aye, a great aul time me and Pato did have' (44). When translated into Connemara Irish, the phrase reads 'Sea, bhí an-time agam fhein agus ag Pato'.[5] However, when this Irish is translated back into the English common to Connemara, it reads as follows: 'Ah, Pato and meself had a great time'. Therefore, a more realistic portrayal of Connemara speech, based on the translations of renowned author, life-time native speaker and Connemara resident, Padraig Breathnach, would have

Maureen recalling the night in the somewhat more prosaic construction of the translation rather than a more consciously staged Irish linguistic construction operated by McDonagh. While translations are notoriously idiosyncratic and open to myriad interpretations, there are countless examples throughout *The Beauty Queen of Leenane* in which McDonagh departs from his much sought-after authenticity in favour of a somewhat contrived linguistic construction that appears to trace its heritage more from John Ford's 1952 film *The Quiet Man* than the dialogic exchanges that would be noted in Leenane in the late 1980s. Indeed, Father Jack from *Father Ted* would have been proud of the nine consecutive 'fecks' that Ray somewhat absurdly manages at the beginning of scene six in expressing his exasperation at the tardiness of Maureen's expected return. This artificiality, masked as it is under a veil of brash realism, undermines McDonagh's play to the extent that the dramatic events, as they unfold, also appear to hark to a previous dramatic age rather that tilting towards a fresh and much needed appraisal of the chronic immaturity and emotional illiteracy that would appear to characterize the relationship between Mag and Maureen. This is the contested space that McDonagh occupies in contemporary Irish theatre and it is the varying interpretations as to the subversive nature of his plays that arouses such heated debate between those who see him as a challenging postmodern deconstructor of rural Ireland and those who, in Declan Kiberd's words, see him as a playwright who 'traduces rather than represents western people'.[6]

By choosing a linguistic construction that pays homage to a clearly bygone dramatic age rather than attempting to recreate contemporary speech, perhaps unwittingly McDonagh admits that the themes of his play, however dressed up, also belong to a somewhat hackneyed theatrical past rather than the abrasive, confrontational future so cherished by his critics. Indeed, Patrick Kavanagh's epic poem *The Great Hunger*, first published in 1942, provides a far more realistic and depressing portrayal of rural Irish familial relationships without relying upon the shock-horror tactic of direct physical violence. McDonagh has claimed that he is more influenced by Martin Scorsese's 1976 film *Taxi Driver* than *The Playboy of the Western World*, yet *The Beauty Queen of Leenane* certainly borrows heavily from Synge in both structure and dialogue, and the troubled Travis Bickle carries an immense menace and un-predictability that is notably absent from McDonagh's theatrical creation. Equally, Bickle's troubled existence is essentially urban, played out against the stifling heat of the city of New York and it tackles a range of political and social issues that are utterly lacking in McDonagh's claustrophobic Leenane.

This linguistic construction is not, however, without its sup-porters. Ireland's leading drama critic, Fintan O'Toole, likens McDonagh's writing to Harold Pinter and David Mamet, holding 'in perfect tension ... the rhythms and structures, the twists and elisions of Irish speech',[7] and certainly the language of McDonagh's plays undermines the binary opposites of the lin-guistic constructions of both Irish and English. He grew up in a house where both languages were spoken and within the strong Irish community in the Elephant and Castle in London he was exposed, at an early age, to the inflections, elisions and cadences inherent and exclusive to the two traditions, and it is precisely in this confused confluence of cultures that McDonagh can be per-ceived as offering something new, rather than the general critical acclaim that has been heaped on his plotlines and dialogue. In a telling article in *The New York Times* in 1999, Declan Kiberd draws a close parallel between McDonagh and Synge, acknow-ledging that his (McDonagh's) plays 'capture also the lyricism of Yeats and Gregory, as well as the bleakness picked up upon by Synge and Gregory',[8] a tacit acknowldgment of the of the linguistic duality of Mc Donagh's dialogue.

It is important to explore the idiosyncratic aspects of an accent because one of the central claims of authenticity that a play can aspire towards is an accurate reflection of the accent and dialect of the location of the action, particularly if that location is referred to as specifically as it is in McDonagh's play. If McDonagh is prepared to utilize the motif of the Australian television soap opera in an attempt to capture how people really live, then it equally behoves him to attempt to replicate, as accurately as possible, the rhythms, phonetics and intonations of Connemara if this sense of cultural authenticity is to be maintained. Surely the accurate detail of the popularity of Australian soaps should be carried over into the construction of dialogic exchanges if McDonagh is to maintain his grip on his audiences willing suspension of disbelief. However, the introduction of *Sons and Daughters* as the choice of viewing in the Folan household appears to be almost too much for Michael Billington of *The Guardian* who (8 March 1996) describes the introduction of this particular programme into the play as 'a postmodern irony', the Aussie soap immediately establishing, in his opinion, 'a global village as the characters stare at the Australian soaps on the box'. It would appear that here, once again, the Syngean dupe has been played on a critic desperate for a successor to emerge from the shadow of the master. The reference to *Sons and Daughters* is brief and Ray's expressed liking for the fact that a lot of the girls in the programme wear swimsuits again introduces a lighter note into a scene charged with the classic tension of the about-to-be-delivered note. Again, this apparent postmodern irony could extend to Mag's 'often expressed preference for Kimberley biscuits', a relatively exotic biscuit introduced to the Irish market in the 1970s. Unfortunately, Kimberley's also flatter to deceive, tasting more like mouldy cardboard filled with silicone bath sealant. However, McDonagh's appreciation of the nuances of rural taste, perceptive as it is, does not make it naturally or automatically subversive, in that these economic changes endemic in Irish society cannot easily be perceived as indicative of a generation unable or unwilling to put up with the interference of the previous generation. McDonagh's overt references to Complan, Kimberley's, *Sons and Daughters*, and Swingball are not enough to make his play notably postmodern or indeed even conventionally challenging, merely culturally perceptive. It is when a character like Maureen has the courage and, more importantly, the ingenuity to change her life without destroying both herself and the perceived cause of her troubles in the process that a play like *The Beauty Queen of Leenane* can begin to claim the status that so many critics appear willing to ascribe. Blood on the floor is no longer shocking, even in the theatre. The nature of a good deal of the lives lived in rural Ireland throughout the middle decades of the twentieth century was arguably best described by Patrick Kavanagh as the wishy-washy way of true tragedy[9] and it is certainly arguable that McDonagh's play would have achieved a greater deal of dramatic intensity if Maureen could have avoided the inevitable and clearly signposted killing of her mother. Patrick Maguire, the anti-hero of Kavanagh's long poem, is cut to the quick by his mother's shrill commands and her bitter longevity is something that he has to bear until he is an old man himself:

> A year passed and another after it
> And still Patrick Maguire was six months behind life –
> His mother six months ahead of it;
> His sister straddle-legged across it: –
> One leg in hell and the other in heaven
> And between the purgatory of middle-aged virginity –
> She prayed for release to heaven or hell.
> His mother's voice grew thinner like a rust worn knife
> But it cut more venomously as it thinned,
> It cut him up the middle till he became more woman than man,
> And it cut through his mind in the end. [10]

The setting of the West of Ireland places McDonagh as one of the latest in a long line of playwrights to favour this particular, if often loosely described, landscape. The melancholic nature of the allure of the West typifies the exilic conundrum, where a perception of being forced away from home by economic circumstances is compounded by the physical beauty and isolation of the landscape. Indeed, one of the key moments in the play arrives in scene four when Maureen is forced to admit that she has spent some time in a mental institution in England in the late 1960s. She proceeds to describe the England of Paul Brady's popular 1981 song *Nothing But The Same Old Story*: menial labour and racial abuse being the order of the day. Pato, however, offers a more sophisticated reading of the experience, in which his articulation of life in England points to the complexities of emotions experienced by those who work abroad:

> **Pato**: … when its there I am, its here I wish I was, of course. Who wouldn't? But when it is here I am … it isn't there I want to be, of course not. But I know it isn't here I want to be either (21-2).

His confusion perfectly captures the inherent challenge of any contemporary portrayal of a place like Connemara. The 2002 census in Ireland shows the rapid increase in population that has occurred in Ireland over the past five years. Isolated counties have shown large increases in population in line with the national 11% increase in population to almost 4 million (3, 917,336 to be exact) the highest level since the 1880s and up a phenomenal 290,000 between 1986 and 2002 alone.[11] Areas like Connemara have benefited from this influx with a 9.9% increase in population since 1996, and the establishment of large American multinational companies in the Galway area have pushed property prices and population in Connemara to unprecedented levels. While McDonagh's play is clearly set in a more economically and socially depressed 1989 (indeed, previous census figures echo this economic malaise with a national decrease in population of 15,000 between 1986 and 1991), its first production in the mid-1990s would have coincided with the economic boom that was experienced in many parts of Ireland. Consequently, the Folan kitchen, bereft as it is of mod cons (with the notable exception of the TV), would appear increasingly remote to an audience whose experiences of material advancement and economic prosperity would undoubtedly alter their appreciation of the dramatic environment. By failing to tap into the zeitgeist of change that characterized Irish society, McDonagh's play appears to be even more reliant upon a reworking of an older theatrical tradition and plot than any challenging of its formal central elements. Indeed, this challenge would appear to be more apparent in the work of, amongst others, Brian Friel and Tom Murphy, more sophisticated creators of a subtler dramatic environment, nonetheless challenging in their themes than McDonagh but prepared to allow their audience some hermeneutical flexibility. McDonagh has been described as the Tarantino of Theatre, and this clever alliterative title is one that has been used more than once. In a review of the play in July 1999, Kamal Al-Solaylee noted that 'it is all too easy to think of *The Beauty Queen of Leenane* as a Quentin Tarantino movie transplanted to a remote West of Ireland village'[12] with 'more than enough torture, blood and petty but amusing thuggery to pass the most rigorous Tarantino-wannabe test'. According to these criteria, one wonders what the reviewer would have made of Brendan Kennelly's contemporary version of *Medea*, in which the heroine murders her brother and chops his body into bits, cuts the throats of her beloved two sons, and orchestrates the painful deaths of two other innocent parties, escaping scot-free from the high body-count. This loose equation of two very different genres is clearly an attempt to spice up the public perception of a theatre under threat from the dominance of the cinematic genre.

In McDonagh's Leenane, it rains incessantly, and the dreary backdrop of the endless sheets of rain provide a somewhat pre-dicable environmental reinforcement of the claustrophobic at-mosphere of the main setting, the kitchen of the Foley household. Once again, McDonagh follows a favoured theatrical device of the kitchen setting with its potential for violence (cookers, ranges, pokers, hot oil, etc) and the original Druid production utilized a stage which certainly appeared more 1880s that 1980s.

One of the most glaring errors in the play occurs over the argument about Mag's confiscation of Ray's Swingball. Again, McDonagh uses a contemporary cultural reference to overtly place his characters at a particular time in their development. Swingball was an immensely popular children's game in the 1980s and the fact that it has reached Leenane is testament to the fact of the changing nature of rural Irish society, a society which is rapidly being homogenized through the proliferation of icons of popular culture, including Australian television soap operas. Ray accuses Maureen of confiscating the ball of his Swingball in 1979 (38), what he refers to as 'ten years ago', and is incensed when he spots the confiscated ball sitting on a shelf in Maureen's kitchen. Maureen's sad apology, in which she admits that 'me head was in a funny oul way in them days' (58) is not well received and leads to Rays often repeated accusation that Maureen is 'a loon'. Now this clearly places the play in 1989, ten years after the confiscation of the ball. However, in an earlier exchange in the same scene, when Ray casually tells Maureen the devastating news of her lover Pato's engagement to Dolores Hooley, he notes that their impending wedding will take place in America 'July next' (57), that is, 1990. However, Ray is concerned that the 'Yankee bastards' (57) will not have 'the European Championships on telly' because 'they don't care about football at all'. He twice mentions the name of this particular football event, which he worries, will clash with his brother's wedding. Dramatically, his interest in the football is clearly designed to heighten Maureen's despair at the news of Pato's betrayal and Ray's complete lack of interest in Maureen's plight and merely reinforces the futility of her mother's murder. Ray's much loved swingball becomes a focus for the depiction of the futile nature of much of Maureen's life, an icon of ensnared hope and shattered dreams. However, the effectiveness of this scene is somewhat skewed when one considers the fact that the World Cup took place in Italy in July 1990, and not the European Championships (they had already occurred in Germany in 1988). There are, of course, two ways of looking at this particular error. Firstly, it could be indicative of Ray's lack of awareness, but the fact that he says he is going to write to his brother about postponing his proposed wedding would indicate that he cares deeply about football and therefore would be unlikely to confuse two such important sporting events. Secondly, it can be construed as sloppy writing from McDonagh, a major sequential confusion in a play that relies a good deal upon the portrayal of specific social, cultural, and environmental detail clearly designed to reinforce the authenticity that the play clearly attempts to recreate. If, as Kate Stratton declares, 'McDonagh is a superb technician' and his play is 'full of gritty, realistic detail',[13] then this error has to stand as an example of authorial negligence that sits uneasily with the expected sympathy for the duped Maureen, occurring as it does in the same speech in which Maureen learns that her future has, once again, been taken from her. In his review, Michael Billington refers to the play as 'a model of rustic realism', but surely McDonagh's mistake, if that is what it is, is one that could have been easily avoided with a little careful editing. It might appear churlish to focus on a detail that does not appear to overtly affect the overall dramatic development of the play, but such an error, occurring as it does at a crucial dramatic moment, undermines the play's effectiveness and places the audience into a curious time warp where real events and real dates do not coincide. If the audience is to believe that the Complan is indeed lumpy then other details should be what McDonagh says they are. McDonagh overtly uses real television programmes and real consumer products in his attempt to present the real Folan household, but this chronological gaffe unfortunately undermines this authenticity at a potentially fatal moment.

The Beauty Queen of Leenane is a powerful play that deals with important social, personal, and cultural issues but it is important to question the overwhelming critical response to the play as shocking, postmodern, innovative, and indicative of a bright, brash future for Irish theatre. The *mise-en-scène* (dreary kitchen, audible rain, run-down furniture, claustrophobic design) appears to immediately immerse the play into the world of a generalized and recognizable Irish misery. The incessant rain parallels the incessant bitterness of the exchanges between Maureen and Mag and with virtually no chinks of light in this abusive mutual tirade it is difficult to see any change in pace over the course of the play. Indeed, the violent conclusion is clearly indicated by McDonagh from the very first stage direction. Mag's murder becomes almost a theatrical *fait accompli*, firmly posted in scene four when Mag tells Pato that Maureen burned her hand over a hot range and poured boiling oil over her for good measure. The pressure is built effectively but without a break – the killing appears almost inevitable. Whacking Mag on the head with a poker appears to be an overtly dramatic gesture that is relatively easy to achieve. It is ironic that the violent conclusion conforms to the soap opera genre of a narrative cul-de-sac: if the narrative is flagging, stick someone in hospital, or better still, murder them!

---

[1] A version of this article appeared in *Working Papers Irish Studies* 2, 3-2, 2002.

[2] Charles Spencer, *Daily Telegraph* 8 March, 1996, found at http://www.royalcourttheatre.com/reviews/beautyqueen.html. All of the reviews mentioned can be found at this site.

[3] *The Guardian* 8 March 1996.

[4] Martin Mc Donagh, *The Beauty Queen of Leenane* (London: Methuen, 1986), p.1. All subsequent references will be from this edition.

[5] The noted Connemara author, lecturer and native speaker, Padraig Breathnach, carried out this translation.

[6] Declan Kiberd, 'The Real Ireland, Some Think', *The New York Times* 25 April 1999.

[7] Fintan O'Toole, *Plays 1: The Leenane Trilogy* (London: Methuen, 1998), p.x.

[8] Kiberd, *The New York Times*.

[9] See 'Self-Portrait in *Collected Poems* (London: Martin Brian and O`Keefe, 1972).

[10] *The Complete Poems of Patrick Kavanagh*, ed. Peter Kavanagh (New York: Kavanagh Hand Press Inc., 1996), pp.98-9.

[11] See http://www.cso.ie/census/preliminary-details.html.

[12] 'Reservoir Broads: Reid Shines in Tarantino-esque Beauty queen' at http://www.eye.net/issue_10.07.99/arta/beauty queen/html.

[13] *Time Out* 10 December 1996.

16 | Genuinely Inauthentic: McDonagh's Postdiasporic Irishness

Aidan Arrowsmith[1]

> Weren't all immigrants shadows? Immigration blocked out the sun as it stretched back over their family. There was no return from its plunge into darkness. The Irish, and generations of the once Irish ... vanished absolutely. (Moy McCrory, 'Aer Lingus', 1985)

> Ever since I had begun to identify my subjects I had hoped to arrive, in a book, at a synthesis of the worlds and cultures that had made me. (V.S. Naipaul, *The Enigma of Arrival*, 1987)

Migration, Jonathan Rutherford has argued, removes the 'spatial and temporal coordinates' deemed necessary for personal and cultural identity.[2] Migrant identities, as a result, tend to be ambiguous and problematic, especially for the second generation, for whom a sense of migrant in-betweenness is exacerbated. This postdiasporic generation is faced with a situation 'simultaneously easier and more difficult' than that of their parents, as Liam Greenslade argues:

> Isolation, in the sense of a deeply felt or experienced, classical alienation is ... characteristic of these people. They belong completely to neither one culture nor the other and are caught between their parents' heritage and their present context, rendered invisible and inaudible from the point of view of recognition.[3]

Postdiasporic writings like Maude Casey's 1987 novel *Over the Water* encapsulate the experience of second-generation Irishness in England: 'We live in England', announces Casey's protagonist Mary,

> but all year long we are preparing for the journey home ... I wonder, for the hundredth time of wondering, why is it that [Mammy] never thinks of *this* house as being her home. And why she should feel so foreign here, when she's been here for years and Ireland is so near. And I wonder ... in which if them is *my* true home ... I do not know where I belong.[4]

In the eyes of exclusive nationalisms from both sides of the water, hybrid identities such as Mary's are doubly inauthentic: not quite English, not quite Irish. By the same token, critiques of emigrant nostalgia[5] tend to ridicule the postdiasporic search for identity as angst-ridden special pleading, the sentimentality of the second generation. Benedict Anderson sketches the comical figure of the 'determinedly "Irish" Bostonian'.[6] And in Glenn Patterson's novel *Fat Lad* (1992), these 'Irish wannabees' are represented by Kelly, born in Leicester 'though my great-grandparents on my mother's side were from Ireland, which is where I get Kelly'.[7] Michael O'Loughlin plays it for laughs in his short story 'Traditional Music', depicting Ciaran's desperation to belong within a group of Irish workers in Germany:

> 'You're Irish, aincha? So am I.' This was in an outrageous cockney accent, the kind that tends towards falsetto ... He was a big-boned, swarthy fellow, as English as the Old Kent Road.'[8]

When novelist Joseph O'Connor declares that 'the whole world longs to be oppressed and post-colonial and tragically hip and petulantly Paddy, and *we Irish* just want to be *anything* else', the inauthenticity of second-generation Irish identities is confirmed. These 'plastic paddies' do not belong within O'Connor's Irish 'we'; they are unfit to claim the authenticity upon which his argument unwittingly rests. The charge of plastic paddyism is developed to a disturbing, and simplistic, degree by some critics who equate such assertions of identity the '*dangerous* nostalgia' (as Roy Foster sees it) of support for republican terrorism.[9]

If the position of the second generation *vis-à-vis* the 'authentically Irish' is blurred, they disappear completely in British race and ethnicity debates. Cultural difference, as Trinh T. Minh-ha has shown,

> does not always announce itself to the onlooker; sometimes it stands out conspicuously, most of the time it tends to escape the commodifying eye. Its visibility depends on how much one is willing to inquire into the anomalous character of the familiar.[10]

Even so, comparison with identities such as Black-British or Asian-British shows up clearly the contradictions, tautologies and oxymorons of Irish-Englishness. As Eamonn Hughes puts it:

> Because writers whose background is Asian or Afro-Caribbean appear to be less easily assimilable – due to factors such as race, social and kinship structures, language and culture and because they come from countries with a more conventionally colonial history – than writers whose background is Irish, there is a sense to using a hyphenated phrase which indicates the merging and/or yoking together of different social and cultural experiences in those cases. In the Irish case, merging seems, on the one hand, to be too weak a word – Irish society and culture have contributed for so long to the British socio-cultural entity as to be a constitutive part of it (and vice versa) – and, on the other hand, is far too strong a word in suggesting that social and cultural experiences which have for so long been defined on both sides as irreconcilable could ever be brought together in any fruitful way.[11]

Ethnicity is defined almost exclusively in terms of colour by the British 'race relations industry'. Not until 1995 were 'the Irish' (however defined) there recognized as an ethnic minority group by the British Commission for Racial Equality.[12] The effect of this lack of recognition has been that assertions of Irish ethnicity in Britain, and especially second-generation Irishness, are prob-lematized or silenced. As, of course, are claims – legitimate or not – of anti-Irish discrimination.[13]

Definitions of 'the Irish', then, are deeply confused. The diaspora historian Donald Akenson is as critical as O'Connor or Foster of the 'exclusivist mentality lunacy' which he sees retaining a strong currency in 'the enclaves of the Irish diaspora'.[14] For Akenson, the only 'historically defensible' definition of Irish identity would be that of someone 'who either was born in Ireland or was a permanent resident of Ireland before embarking for some New World'.[15] However, Akenson then illustrates the general confusion over such identities by seemingly contradicting himself:

> a person is part of the Irish ethnic group – whether he or she is of the first generation or the fifth or anything in between – as long as his or her primary sense of ethnic identity is Irish. ... [The] term – 'The Irish' – should be employed when dealing with the new homelands only to refer to the entire multigenerational ethnic group.[16]

Akenson's inclusivist sweep bypasses complications such as cultural hybridity or 'double consciousness'. In his attempt to simplify, he appears to ignore the confusion of identity within diasporic contexts – an experience documented in second-generation writing such as Casey's and Moy McCrory's, where fundamental questions are posed of simple identifications with an idealized Irishness. These writers explore the postdiasporic desire articulated by Ien Ang, 'to assimilate, a longing for fitting in rather than standing out'.[17] And yet, as we see in McCrory's story 'Aer Lingus' (1985), when Kitty and Nora seek to shine a light into the shadowy void of immigrant family history, what they find is 'real distance':

> Immigration blocked out the sun as it stretched back over their family. There was no return from its plunge into darkness. The Irish, and generations of the once Irish, roamed all over the globe rolling soil between their palms and cursing the blight that had packed them like cattle into coffin-ships ... They vanished absolutely (*WE*, 172).[18]

The distance and disconnection of postdiasporic identities also underpins the work of Britain's most celebrated second-generation Irish writer, Martin McDonagh. Seamus Deane's 1996 review of Frank McCourt's bestselling memoir of migration, *Angela's Ashes*, criticized the author for 'believ[ing] too much in the reliability of memory, as if that were enough in itself'.[19] Such a charge is not applicable to McDonagh's plays, which show the impossibility of accessing authentic memory, history or identity.

McDonagh has himself been subjected to the discourses of authenticity, the British media having great fun with this 'awfentic Cockney Oirishman'. As evidence for charges of simple nostalgia and plastic Paddydom, critics cite his apparently unproblematized self-location as an 'Irish' playwright within a coherent tradition of Irish drama (revolving particularly around J.M. Synge and Tom Murphy). McDonagh's concern, however, is more with the paradoxes of cultural memory – the inevitable yet futile desire to access the vaults of history, truth, and identity. His plays deal less with seamlessness and coherence than with rupture and untruth. They revolve around misinterpretation, misrepresentation, and the distortion of 'reality'. Characteristically, narratives of history and identity are severed in McDonagh's work and in this way, plays like *The Beauty Queen of Leenane* (1996) and *The Cripple of Inishmaan* (1997), respectively the first instalments of his Leenane and Aran Islands Trilogies, evoke the processes of second generation identity construction. In Fintan O'Toole's suggestive description, McDonagh's drama has 'the ghostly, dizzying feel of a superimposed photograph':[20] both of these plays expose postdiasporic identity construction as an excavation of a troubled palimpsest, made up of generations of embroidered family narratives and distorted images of 'home'.

McDonagh's Leenane is an apparently conventional image of authentic, if backward, rural Ireland – likened by O'Toole to a 'black-and-white still from a bad Abbey play of the fifties'.[21] But it turns out to be a place of intense communication problems. All messages and stories are shown to be mediated and distorted here, none can be trusted. Emphasizing this sense of mediation, McDonagh overlays his 'photograph' of rural Connemara with a 'postmodern landscape' of media saturation, a dripfeed of cheap television and American popular culture. The consequently twisted and torn communication cord has ultimately fatal consequences in *The Beauty Queen*'s dramatic climax:

> **Mag:** (*Terrified*) A letter he [Pato] did send you I read!
> Maureen slowly and deliberately takes her mother's shrivelled hand, holds it down on the burning range, and starts pouring some of the hot oil over it, as Mag screams in pain and terror. ...
> **Maureen:** Where is the letter?
> **Mag:** (*Through screams*) I did burn it! I'm sorry, Maureen!
> **Maureen:** What did the letter say? ...
> **Mag:** (*Through screams*) Asked you to go to America with him it did! ... But how could you go to America with him? You do still have me to look after.[22]

Mag's deliberate interference with this communication ultimately drives Maureen to murder her desperate mother.

In McDonagh's world, reality is always mediated, history always compromised, memory always distorted. Unsurprisingly, migration is shown to be a particularly strong fount of such distortions and idealizations, as evidenced by the temporary returnee Pato:

> it's beautiful here, a fool can see. The mountains and the green, and people speak .... hopping across to that bastarding oul place every couple of months .... when I'm over there in London and working in rain and it's more or less cattle I am, and the young fellas cursing over cards and drunk and sick, and the oul digs over there, all pee-stained mattresses and nothing to do but watch the clock ... when it's there I am, it's here I wish I was, of course. Who wouldn't? (*BQ*, 21-2)

Pato's memory is shown as an idealization through tense juxta-position with the reality that initially drove him away: 'But when it's here I am ... it isn't *there* I want to be, of course not. But I know it isn't here I want to be either' (*BQ,* 22).

As Benedict Anderson says: 'home' as it emerges for the second generation is 'less experienced than imagined, and imagined through a complex of mediations and representations.'[23] These mediations are the ambivalent emigrant narratives constituting the unstable layers of second-generation identities; they are the palimpsest of 'photographic' misrepresentations which have been touched up, airbrushed to improve and conceal. The view 'home' from a second-generation vantage point is through a lens always already tinted by idealizations, selections, and distortions – themselves pressurized by the historical contexts of migration.

The trope of photographic (mis)representation and the desire for elsewhere appear centrally in *The Cripple of Inishmaan*. Distance in time and space seems only to reinforce the desire for an authenticity that is always inaccessible because fictionalized – as in the Irish-American Robert Flaherty's 1934 film *Man of Aran*, an infamously embroidered depiction of the ruggedly 'authentic' Irishness of the Aran Islands. In one of the film's central scenes, the natives are shown shark-fishing, and McDonagh's play delights in debunking Flaherty's primitivist fantasy: 'It's rare that off Ireland you do get sharks', comments Bartley gently; 'This is the first shark I've ever seen off Ireland.' More forthright is Helen, for whom Flaherty's 'documentary' is 'a pile of fecking shite': 'It wasn't even a shark at all, Mrs,' she points out. 'It was a tall fella in a grey donkey jacket.'[24] Bartley is seduced by the hegemony of American capital and culture in Ireland, and uses his telescope to try to see across space to the 'authenticity' of America. In parallel with this, 'Cripple' Billy tries to see back through time in order to trace his family narrative and uncover the truth about his parents' fatal attempt to emigrate from Inishmaan. As Stuart Hall says, however,

> the homeland is not waiting back there ... There is a past to be learned about, but the past is now seen, and has to be grasped as a history, as something that has to be told. It is narrated. It is grasped through memory. It is grasped through desire.[25]

In his quest to discover his parents' story, Billy is tormented by the indeterminacy of history, accidental distortion and deliberate fictionalization. Echoing the processes of second generation identity construction, Billy encounters multiple, unreliable versions of the past, all of which demonstrates the absence of an un-mediated communication cord by which one's 'spatial and temporal coordinates' might be identified.

The play not only exposes some of the mechanics of emigrant desire, but also debunks the stereotype of Irish emigrant nostalgia. During the filming of *Man of Aran*, Billy is 'discovered'. The Irish Americans value him especially for his high level of 'authenticity', being a poverty-stricken, orphaned Irish cripple. When he travels to Hollywood for a screen test, the audience sees Billy indulging in that most stereotypical of Irish nationalist reactions to migration, a sentimental backward look driven by the misery of life abroad, and infused with a nostalgic nationalism. He mourns the loss of his mother (Ireland):

> can't I hear the wail of the banshees for me, as far as I am from me barren island home? A home barren, aye, but proud and generous with it, yet turn me back on ye I did. ... An Irishman! *(Pause) Just* an Irishman. With a decent heart on him, and a decent head on him, and a decent spirit unbroken by a century's hunger and a lifetime's oppression! (*CI*, 52 – 3)

To cap this image of emigrant nostalgia in the classic way, McDonagh has Billy sing 'The Croppy Boy' before gently dying. Like Flaherty's film, however, and like the stories Billy hears of his parents, this conventional representation of the Irish abroad in terms of sentimentality and nationalism is exposed as wholly constructed. Billy's is shown to be performing a role scripted for him as part of his screen test. Rejecting the film offer, Billy's distaste for such a stereotyped representation is clear:

> To tell you the truth, Bartley, it wasn't an awful big thing at all to turn down Hollywood, with the arse-faced lines they had me reading for them. 'Can I not hear the wail of the banshees for me, as far as I am from me barren island home ... An Irishman I am, begora! With a heart and a spirit on me not crushed be a hundred years of oppression. I'll be getting me shillelagh out next, wait'll you see.' A rake of shite. And had me singing the fecking 'Croppy Boy' then (*CI*, 63).

McDonagh's dramatization of uncertainty of nation and identity springs, as O'Toole suggests, from his experience of 'living between two cultures'.[26] Postdiasporic identity is shown to be formed from a narrative inheritance which is inevitably shaped by the experiences, desires, repressions of those who tell the tale. And such unreliability of memory and history invalidates any notion of 'authentic' identity for the second generation. Rather than a stereotypical, naïve clinging to singularity and racial essence, the second-generation experience requires an awareness of the constructedness and hybridity of identities. McDonagh acknowledges these not only as inevitabilities but as legitimate and productive. In this way, his work points towards a sense of postdiasporic identity that is genuinely inauthentic.

---

[1] A version of this article appeared in 'Plastic Paddy: Negotiating Identity in Second Generation "Irish-English" Writing', *Irish Studies Review* 8.1 (2000), pp.35-43.

[2] Jonathan Rutherford, 'A Place Called Home', in *Identity: Community, Culture, Difference*, ed. Jonathan Rutherford (London: Lawrence & Wishart, 1990), p.24.

[3] Liam Greenslade, 'White Skin, White Masks: Psychological Distress

Among the Irish in Britain', in *The Irish in the New Communities*, ed. P. O'Sullivan (Leicester: Leicester University Press, 1992), p.220.

[4] Casey, *Over the Water*. Subsequent page references will appear in parentheses within the main text thus: (*OW*, 1, 4, 60).

[5] For Roy Foster, amongst emigrant communities, 'the perspective over one's shoulder must remain identical to that recorded by the parting glance – even if that moment happened two (or more) generations back.' Roy Foster, Introduction to *Paddy and Mr Punch: Connections in Irish and English History* (Harmondsworth: Penguin, 1995), p.xiii.

[6] Benedict Anderson, 'Exodus', *Critical Inquiry* 20 (Winter 1994), p.325.

[7] Glenn Patterson, *Fat Lad* (London: Chatto and Windus, 1992), p.1.

[8] Michael O'Loughlin, 'Traditional Music', in *Ireland in Exile: Irish Writers Abroad*, ed. Dermot Bolger (Dublin: New Island Books, 1993), p.26.

[9] Foster caricatures and critiques the 'emigrant community' for their nationalism and ignorance of Irish historical revisionism. He regrets that this academic work: 'carr[ies] little resonance in Camden Town – where one is told that the only work of 'real history' to have come out of Ireland is Gerry Adams's *Falls Memories,* and where any discussion of the (largely unknown and unwritten) history of 1916-22 will be deflected into sentimental reminiscences of 'the songs we sang in my auntie's front room'. Foster, 'We Are All Revisionists Now', *The Irish Review* 1, 1986, p.3.

[10] Trinh T. Minh-ha, 'Bold Omissions and Minute Depictions', *When the Moon Waxes Red: Representation, Gender and Cultural Politics* (New York and London: Routledge, 1991), pp.159-60.

[11] Eamonn Hughes, '"Lancelot's Position": The Fiction of Irish-Britain', in *Other Britain, Other British: Contemporary Multicultural Fiction*, ed. A. Robert Lee (London: Pluto, 1995), pp.142-43.

[12] See Floya Anthias and Nira Yuval-Davis (in association with Harriet Cain) *Racialized Boundaries: Race, Nation, Gender, Colour and Class and the Anti-Racist Struggle* (London: Routledge, 1992).

[13] As Mary Hickman has pointed out, the attempted homogenisation of the 'British nation' around a notion of whiteness underpins the conventional view of simple and painless and unprobmatic Irish assimilation – an assumption which is then built upon with the assumption of 'no problem of discrimination'. See Mary Hickman and Bronwen Walter, 'Deconstructing Whiteness: Irish Women in Britain', *Feminist Review* 50, (1995), p.8. Elsewhere, Hickman argues: 'There is evidence of second and third generation Irish youth being socially disadvantaged, having something to do with their Irishness.' See Madeleine Casey, 'Focus

Interview: Dr Mary Hickman', *British Association for Irish Studies Newsletter* 13 (January 1998), p.4.

14 Donald Harman Akenson, *The Irish Diaspora: A Primer* (Queen's University, Belfast: Institute of Irish Studies, 1993), p.7.

15 Akenson, *The Irish Diaspora*, p.8.

16 Ibid., p.10.

17 Ien Ang, 'On Not Speaking Chinese: Postmodern Ethnicity and the Politics of Diaspora', *New Formations*, 24, 1994, p.9. Original emphasis.

18 For a fuller discussion of these writers' work, see Arrowsmith, 'Plastic Paddy: Negotiating Identity in Second Generation 'Irish-English' Writing', *Irish Studies Revie*, 8.1 (2000), pp.35-43.

19 Seamus Deane, 'Merciless Ireland', *The Guardian 2*, 12 December 1996, p.12.

20 Fintan O'Toole, 'Martin McDonagh', *The Guardian 2*, 2 December 1996, p.11.

21 Ibid., p.11.

22 Martin McDonagh, *The Beauty Queen of Leenane* (London: Methuen, 1996), pp.47-8. Subsequent page references will appear in parentheses within the main text: (*BQ*, 47-8).

23 Benedict Anderson, 'Exodus', p.319.

24 Martin McDonagh, *The Cripple of Inishmaan* (London: Methuen, 1997), pp.55-61. Subsequent page references will appear in parentheses within the main text: (*CI*, 55-61).

25 Stuart Hall, 'The Local and the Global', in *Culture, Globalization and the World System*, ed. Anthony D.King (London: Macmillan, 1991), p.38.

26 O'Toole, 'Martin McDonagh', p.11.

17 | 'The Outpouring of a Morbid, Unhealthy Mind': The Critical Condition of Synge and McDonagh[1]

Shaun Richards

Martin McDonagh's *The Beauty Queen of Leenane* (1996) was hailed by Fintan O'Toole as 'the most brilliant debut in modern Irish theatre since Tom Murphy and Noel O'Donoghue's *On the Outside* in 1959'.[2] Other judgements as to McDonagh's qualities were equally positive: he was the recipient of three major British theatre awards: the *Evening Standard* Award for Most Promising Newcomer, Writer's Guild Award for Best Fringe Theatre Play, and the George Devine Award for Most Promising Playwright. The transfer of *Beauty Queen* to Broadway saw it win four coveted 'Tony' awards, including Best Director for Garry Hynes – the first time it had been won by a woman. An intense period of exposure from 1996 to 1997 saw three further plays premiered which, in 1997, were simultaneously available on the London stage – *The Leenane Trilogy* (*The Beauty Queen of Leenane*, 1996; *A Skull in Connemara*, 1997; *The Lonesome West*, 1997) in repertory at the Royal Court and *The Cripple of Inishmaan* (1997) at the National Theatre. While O'Toole reported that the National Theatre had 'plans to do the other two parts [of a projected Aran Islands trilogy] over the next 18 months'[3] it was four years until *The Lieutenant of Inishmore* (2001) was produced by The Royal Shakespeare Company after what appeared to have been a series of acrimonious wrangles with both the National Theatre and the Royal Court; McDonagh stating that their reasons for not staging the play 'smacked of crass stupidity and gutlessness.'[4] Nothing, however, appeared to have dampened the commercial and critical enthusiasm for McDonagh's work: the play progressed from The Other Place, the RSC's experimental space at Stratford, via The Barbican, to a West End run at The Garrick. And, as with *The Leenane Trilogy*, commercial success was matched by critical praise: *The Guardian*'s Michael Billington speaking of a 'boldly brilliant play'[5] while his colleague, Lyn Gardner, described it as 'terrific', McDonagh's 'best play to date'.[6]

Analysis of McDonagh's work, while divided, is almost unanimous in comparing it with the major figures of Irish drama, most frequently those working within the genre of what we might term 'the western play', specifically J.M. Synge. For Michael Billington, McDonagh's work 'constantly alludes to the great Irish tradition.'[7] Jose Lanters compares McDonagh with Synge and Tom Murphy, each one reflecting 'the concerns and anxieties of his age',[8] while Karen Vandevelde judges that 'McDonagh's *Leenane Trilogy* is undoubtedly a canonical work with echoes of Synge, Beckett, O'Casey and many more.'[9] However there is a discernible critical counter current: Susan Conley argues that McDonagh simply provides an opportunity for 'smug, superior chuckling at those ignorant culchies who haven't got the spunk to get out and make it in the big city',[10] while Vic Merriman sees McDonagh as marking a self-serving reversion to a theatre of 'Gross caricature [whose] appeal to the new consumer-Irish consensus lies in their appearance as ludicrous Manichaean opposites – the colonized simian reborn.'[11] But while Merriman's language evokes that of early-twentieth century nationalist critics for whom the Abbey was a 'degraded and anti-national theatre' in which the country was 'held up to ridicule',[12] their villain is his hero: 'The journey from Synge to McDonagh takes us all the way from images which challenge the submerged ideological positions of a neocolonial class to those which collude in reinforcing them.'[13] And both challenge and collusion are related to the playwrights' images of the West of Ireland, the cornerstone of the Literary Revival which Maud Gonne MacBride described as the 'hidden spring'[14] from which, as Douglas Hyde phrased it, 'future generations can draw for ever.'[15] It was this location 'of pure, Catholic, native Ireland'[16] which was the defining stage-set of the Abbey theatre between

1902 to 1908 when it 'produced twice as many peasant plays as poetic plays.'[17]

Christopher Murray has argued that

> in modern Irish dramatic history [...] each successive writer rewrites his/her predecessors. This is not just another way of defining tradition but is also a useful way of describing the procedures of Irish writing in a post-colonial world [...] An Irish dramatic text tends to assimilate other and earlier material.[18]

This could perhaps legitimize McDonagh's recycling of Syngean tropes were it not for the fact that in 1997 he announced his relative ignorance of, and complete lack of interest in, any Irish theatrical tradition of which he might be a part. Coming to theatre with what he termed 'a film fan's perspective' he asserted that after writing the first scene of *A Skull in Connemara*

> I realized it was completely fresh for me and I wasn't harking back to anything I had seen or read. I can see similarities now – I read *The Playboy of the Western World* and the darkness of the story amazed me [...] At the time, though, I didn't know it at all.[19]

And even should he have known Synge's work there is no suggestion that he would have sought to locate himself within any specifically Irish dramatic tradition:

> It always struck me as kind of dumb, any kind of pride in the place you happen to be born in. Even culturally, I don't think you can take too much pride in what your predecessors in your country have written. If you haven't written it yourself, you're as close to it as an Eskimo.[20]

However, and despite denials of awareness and influence, the use of the trope of the west firmly locates McDonagh within a critical paradigm in which Synge has now 'emerged ever more convincingly as a type of the post-colonial artist'[21] while McDonagh, his Manichean 'other', is judged to offer merely 'a kind of voyeuristic aperture on the antics of white trash whose reference point is more closely aligned to the barbarous conjurings of Jerry Springer than to the continuities of an indigenous tradition of dramatic writing.'[22] Despite the differing critical judgements, however, the onstage reality is that of the chronologically divided, though geographically unified, location of the West of Ireland; an image

with which Irish audiences are also familiar from the work of M.J.
Molloy and Tom Murphy, both of whom, along with Synge and
McDonagh, formed part of the repertoire of the Druid Theatre
Company of Galway. And it is the implicit claims of both Synge
and McDonagh to present a realistic staging of the west to their
audiences which needs to be first examined.

In noting that 'Synge took care to give his action a local
habitation and a name: the characters' references to place are
convincingly authentic for people living on the Benmullet
peninsula',[23] Nicholas Grene illuminates a central issue with regard
to the 1907 audiences' perception that *Playboy* was a profoundly
damaging mis-representation of the western world. For disputes
over the dramatized content were exacerbated by Synge providing
Playboy with a geographical and historical specificity with their
implicit claims for the 'reality' of the action dramatized within that
context. The query as to whether Christy Mahon has been 'fighting
bloody wars for Kruger and the freedom of the Boers'[24] positions
the play at the onset of the twentieth century. Audiences of 1907
were then being presented with an Ireland which was clearly
claimed to be contemporary. While Leenane's geographical actuality is not expanded on in terms of a network of neighbouring
towns and villages as in *Playboy* it has an even more precisely
defined historical moment. The whole *Trilogy* is set across a matter
of months from the summer of 1995 to that of 1996; a movement
mapped through Ray Dooley's *Beauty Queen* anxiety that his brother
Pato's wedding in America 'next year' will 'coincide with the
European Championships'[25] and *The Lonesome West*'s disparage-
ment of Packy Bonner's goalkeeping errors in those same matches.
And the same tight chronology runs through the texts of all three
plays. In *A Skull in Connemara*, which is set in the September of
1995, Mick Dowd notes that the funeral of Mag Folan (of *The
Beauty Queen*) was 'last month'[26] and the failure of the incompetent
Garda, Thomas Hanlon, to convict Mick of murder leads to his
suicide in *The Lonesome West*. Just as Synge seeks to create the
'mental land-scape of a small community' through his use of
patronymics or toponymics[27] so McDonagh adds density to his
characters' world through an almost endless listing of products and
programmes from Taytos and Kimberly biscuits to *Star Wars* and

afternoon soap-operas. Moreover, McDonagh's staging, like Synge's, observes the detail of naturalism. This is significant with regard to their intentions (and audience's perceptions) for, as noted by Keir Elam, 'Even in the most detailed of naturalistic sets what is actually presented to the audience's view stands for only part of the dramatic world in which the action takes place.'[28] Further to this grounding of the plays in a precise social locale McDonagh's close intertextual referencing, in which characters and incidents seen in one play become the topic of conversation in another, heightens the extent to which, for all its excesses and eccentricities, Leenane is not being presented merely as a vague 'Craggy Island' backdrop to comic iconoclasm. As in Synge, this is Ireland, this is now. And the condition, and more specifically the cause (and correctability) of that condition becomes crucial, specifically as it is linked to the socio-historical particularities within which the nominal plot-line, Christy's courtship of Pegeen is set; namely what Bernard Beckerman calls the play's 'contextual envelope [...] the background or ground of the action'[29] which must be considered in all its specificity of moment, location and action; both mimetic and diegetic.

The world into which Christy enters is one threatened by 'the harvest boys with their tongues red for drink' and 'the thousand militia [...] walking idle through the land' (63). This is a world of violent instability before news of Christy's (attempted) parricide, and even in the community there has been the 'sneaky kind of murder' of her husband by Widow Quin who 'hit himself with a worn pick, and the rusted poison did corrode his blood the way he never overed it and died after' (89). McDonagh's plays are also replete with violence, from matricide in *The Beauty Queen*, death through drink-driving, attempted murder, and the desecration of the bones of the dead in *A Skull in Connemara*; parricide and the suicide of a priest in *The Lonesome West*. But the world of *Playboy* has a range of violence whose cruelty of action and expression makes Mairtin Hanlon's microwaving a hamster in *A Skull* appear modest. Coleman in *The Lonesome West* has cut the ears off his brother, Valene's dog, but Jimmy Farrell in *Playboy* hanged his dog 'and had it screeching and wriggling three hours at the butt of a string' (73).

Matching the violence and madness of the plays is the pervasive sense of bodily functions, sexual desire, blasphemy, and general degeneracy. Pegeen might be 'a lovely, handsome woman' (111) in Christy's poetic courtship but she is also 'a girl you'd see itching and scratching, and she with a stale stink of poteen on her from selling in the shop' (127). In *Beauty Queen* Mag Folan pours her infected urine into the kitchen sink – the source of comedy when it comes to her facing porridge stirred with a spoon taken from there. And while McDonagh might have gone further than Synge, particularly in *A Skull* where Mick Dowd tells Mairtin Hanlon of the custom of cutting the penises off corpses for selling as dog food to tinkers and, during the Famine, 'You would see them riding along with them, munching ahead' (27), Synge was equally alert to the vitality, and contemporary impossibility, of this Bakhtinian grotesque comedy: 'The wilder – the Rabelaisian side of the Irish temperament is so wild it cannot be dealt with in book or periodical that is intended for Irish readers.'[30] Synge was concerned to restore 'the sex-element to its natural place',[31] and while his work does not match the explicitness of Maureen's declaration that 'You'll have to be putting that thing of yours in me again before too long has past, Pato. I have a taste for it now, I do' (28), Widow Quin's rhapsody of desire for 'the gallant hairy fellows are drifting beyond, and myself long years living alone' (127) leaves little to the imagination.

The drunken destruction of the bones of the dead in *A Skull in Connemara* is blasphemous, but hardly more so than Michael James's evocation of Kate Cassidy's wake when 'there were five men, aye, and six men, stretched out retching speechless on the holy stones' (151). Mairtin Hanlon's 'Feck God so! And his mother too!' (32) in *A Skull*, and Girleen's rejection of her given name of Mary (in *The Lonesome West*) because it was the name of God's mother and 'It's the reason she never got anywhere for herself' (37) mark the brutal and comic extremes of McDonagh's blasphemy. Perhaps even more shocking for their time, however, are the thirty-seven occasions on which the name of God is invoked in Act I of *Playboy* alone, along with the ultimate blasphemy of Christy's acknowledgement that he killed his father: 'With the help of God I did surely' (73).

Both playwrights also recognize the extent to which an absence of social purpose, and social significance, produces an often perverse desire for sensation, particularly among the young. Indeed, as in Ray Dooley's attempt to purchase the Folan's poker in order to take out 'half a dozen coppers' and then 'clobber them again just for the fun of seeing the blood running out of them' (39) it is the amoral sense of 'fun' which is to the fore. Similarly, in *A Skull* Mairtin Hanlon is eager to join Mick Dowd in dispatching the bones of the exhumed corpses: 'You hit them with a hammer and you pegged them in the slurry? Can I do that now Mick?' (13). An equivalent longing is found in Pegeen's lament for the loss of those like 'Daneen Sullivan knocked the eye from a peeler, or Marcus Quin, God rest him, got six months for maiming ewes': 'Where will you find the like of them, I'm saying?' is her scornful riposte to Shawn's suggestion that 'we're [...] as good these times as we were for ever' (59). And lacking any adequate stimulation she scours the newspapers for 'the fearful crimes of Ireland' (113). This desire for stimulation is what drives the young girls of the parish to see Christy, whose reputation as a man that killed his father launches him into the realm of celebrity enjoyed by 'the man bit the yellow lady's nostril on the northern shore' (97) whom Sara Tansey drove the ass cart ten miles to see; her response to a crime of such banality serving to highlight the desperation with which stimulation is sought. Lack is then what unites Synge and McDonagh, above all a lack of emotional and economic opportunity captured in Ray Dooley's *Beauty Queen* confession 'I be continually bored' (53) to Maureen who, while older, shares the younger man's frustrations. When her mother accuses her of being a whore her response encapsulates a whole community's desire:

> **Maureen:** 'Whore'? (*Pause*) Do I not *wish*, now? Do I not wish?
> (*Pause*) Sometimes I *dream* ...
> **Mag:** Of being a ... ?
> **Maureen:** Of anything! (*Pause. Quietly*) Of anything. Other than this (16).

The world of 'hunger' so vividly rendered in Patrick Kavanagh's epic poem is prefigured in Synge and reprised in McDonagh, where Coleman's lascivious but euphemistic desire to touch the nuns 'both upstairs and downstairs' (55) along with Girleen's observation that he and Valene would have no need of condoms 'unless they went using them on a hen' (39) suggests that 'the sex-horrors' seen by Synge which, if told, 'would wither up your blood'[32] are not the preserve of early twentieth-century Ireland alone.

McDonagh's west in *The Leenane Trilogy* is then not so far removed from that of Synge's *Playboy* as might initially appear; violence, deprivation and desperation span the century dividing them. But McDonagh's work is even more tragic. For while Maureen Folan might share the final anguished isolation of Pegeen Mike's keening, at least the latter and her community had a possibility of correcting their condition from within; all that was on offer to Maureen was the possibility of escape, not correction. And frustrated with that she becomes, as noted by Ray Dooley, 'The exact fecking image of your mother you are, sitting there pegging orders and forgetting me name!' (60). In the Connemara of McDonagh there is no Playboy and no possibility of his emergence. A father is killed in *The Lonesome West* – over a comment on a haircut. But instead of projecting Coleman into a 'romping lifetime' he continues a life of violent bickering with Valene, for McDonagh's characters are condemned to continue in a condition captured in Tim Robinson's comment that 'Connemara still lives in the aftermath of millennial famine of age-old physical and psychic deprivation,' a landscape where cottages have been replaced by mail-order haciendas and the flora and fauna stripped away through 'over grazing by [the] grant-driven multiplication of under-nourished ewes, too weak to feed their lambs'.[33]

While McDonagh's critics are prone to disparage *The Leenane Trilogy* as stage-wise but shallow, a theatrical experience for the habitués of soap-opera entertainments which cynically recycles worn stereotypes, his gaze is as unforgiving as that of Synge and just as alert to the condition of those idealized on stage but marginalized in reality. As a comparative reading of the detail of their work indicates, McDonagh is as engaged in challenging his audiences as were Synge, Molloy, and Murphy, and most specifically on the basis of the economic desolation of the west and its negative impact on the lives of his characters.

According to Seamus Deane, *Playboy* demonstrates Synge's 'disengagement from history'[34] in not placing issues such as the 'broken harvest and the ended wars' (69) at centre stage. But while, in Ronan McDonald's phrase, 'the plays can only bear to cast a sidelong glance at surrounding political circumstances'[35] there is still a comprehensive recognition of the actuality of various states of deprivation, specifically the economic realities of the west. The western world recorded by Synge at the time of his tour in 1905 was one being driven ever deeper into the condition of economic dependency and exploitation in which its indigenous vitality would be progressively extinguished by 'an ungodly ruck of fat-faced, sweaty headed swine'[36] whose self-serving class base is captured in his image of 'the groggy-patriot-publican-general-shop man who is married to the priest's half-sister and is second cousin once-removed of the dispensary doctor'. It was this emerging bourgeoisie which, according to Synge, was 'swindling the people themselves in a dozen ways'[37] and the stark reality of the concentration of economic power in a few hands is captured in *Playboy* in the character of the 'strong farmer', Shawn Keogh, who attempts to use his wealth to first buy off Christy and then enlist Widow Quin's help in ridding him of Christy as a competitor for Pegeen. Shawn's marriage to Pegeen, moreover, is founded on a dowry, as Shawn reminds Michael, of a 'drift of heifers and my blue bull from Sneem' (155).

Synge's disdain for 'the cosy alliance of commerce, parliamentary politics, religion and the professions' which was advancing 'the mean-spirited sectional interests of middle Ireland'[38] is repeated in M.J. Molloy's *The Wood of the Whispering* (1954) where Sanbatch responds to the suggestion that the community wait for the next election to provide a solution to their penury with the comment:

> Isn't that what we're doing all our lives, and each gang we elected turned out to be worse than the last? Sure, they don't know how we're living at all and how could they? Wance in every five years they come down to draw our votes, halting their cars at the crossroads for five minutes, with big detectives all around them, for fear they'd see or hear us.[39]

And in an anticipation of the contemporary condition of Connemara described by Tim Robinson, Molloy's 'Preface' to the play argues that it is this national heartland which must be preserved against the encroachment of agribusiness, for 'neither cattle nor combine harvesters have ever fought for their country as small farmers have been known to do'.[40] Three decades later Tom Murphy's *Conversations on a Homecoming* (1985) continued to underline the despoliation of the west by 'those men of prudence and endeavour who would sell the little we have left of charm, character, kindness and madness to any old bidder with a pound, a dollar, a mark or a yen'.[41] This is localized in Liam, 'the worst of the worst type of a ponce of a modern fuckin' gombeen man' (72) whose exploitation of the need of the community has some of them 'living with the hens, to make room for tourists' (60).

This critical stance which looks to expose the class-based inequalities affecting the economic decline of the west is then the legacy of Synge. But McDonagh's plays are not acknowledged by Merriman as a extension of these critiques; rather than being seen as a challenge to contemporary orthodoxies they are judged to be their confirmation:

> In each belly laugh which greets the pre-posterous malevolence of [their] actions there is a huge cathartic roar of relief that all of this is past – 'we' have left it all behind.[42]

This, however, is to ignore the fact that in line with the analysis advanced by his predecessors in the genre of 'the western play' McDonagh too sees the west as surviving on the leavings of more prosperous economies; now even that of Ireland's own Celtic Tiger. While the young men of Leenane are unemployed and spend their days waiting for the screening of Australian TV soap-operas, the only opportunities for employment among the young is selling poitin like Girleen, temporary work in the graveyard like Mairtin Hanlon, or operating as a tour guide until, like Ray Dooley in *Skull*, the job is lost through 'pegging shite at Americans [...] And cracking Vietnam jokes' (53). Leenane may be part of a post-modern world which is open to all the images of the global economy, but its condition is as functionary rather than bene-ficiary. Both playwrights are then opposed to the sentiment-talization of the harsh realities of the life of the west. Synge set himself against what he found to be 'senile and slobbering in the doctrine of the Gaelic League', and in place of their 'gushing, cowardly and maudlin' perceptions of Ireland which rendered a once mighty people fearful of 'any gleam of truth'[43] he wished to revive realities of possibility to counter actualities of fact. McDonagh's target is equally sharply focused on the triumph of the 'maudlin' image of Ireland which gained state-approved funding in Robert Flaherty's *Man of Aran* (1935). When the islanders in *The Cripple of Inishmaan* (which is set at the time of the film's production) are provided with a screening, the precocious Slippy Helen greets the 'authenticity' of the shark fishing sequence with

> Ah they're never going to be catching this fecking shark. A fecking hour they've been at it now [...] If it was *me* had a role in this film the fecker wouldn't have lasted as long. One good clobber and we could all go home',[44] welcoming the film's end with a relieved 'Oh thank Christ the fecker's over. A pile of fecking shite (61).

A denunciation expanded on to include all such filmic excesses of 'Irishness' in the death-scene which Cripple Billy performs while in Hollywood; one he condemns as full of 'arse-faced lines' (63).

The argument to date has focused on *The Leenane Trilogy* as the projected trilogy set on the Aran Islands is incomplete, and the two extant plays, *The Cripple of Inishmaan* and *The Lieutenant of Inishmore*, have a setting divided by some four decades and lack the intertextuality which was so marked a feature of the first trilogy. However *The Lieutenant* has been advanced by Mary King as further evidence of McDonagh's radical relevancy as a critic of the Irish body politic who matches Synge in terms of rigor and seriousness; indeed McDonagh's work, she suggests, provides a lens through which Synge could be viewed afresh and seen as just as provocative since

> [*The Playboy*] takes the gloves off completely, to contest bare-fisted the sentimentalised versions of 'The West' ... Bullying, whinging, double-dealing, incest, decadence, sexual perversions and torture are shown to be part and parcel of 'The Western World'.[45]

King regards *Lieutenant* as worthy of staging alongside what she describes as a postmodern *Playboy*, seeing an equivalence of quality and intent between the two works; *The Lieutenant* she describes as

[an] excoriatingly highly intelligent contextualized dramatization of the politics and psyche of sentimental ultra-right wing republican violence in the midst of today's 'Celtic Tiger' which echoes Synge's prescient anatomy of the disease afflicting the Irish body politic one hundred years ago.[46]

As indicated by the argument developed above, this article is concerned to advance the case for a serious consideration of McDonagh's work as a contemporary engagement with the world staged by Synge. The extent to which this can be evidenced through *The Lieutenant* is open to question, however, and, more-over, demands reflection on the precise terms in which *The Leenane Trilogy* itself can be valued in regard to Synge's work. The extent to which McDonagh, despite his claims to the contrary, was working within a genre largely defined by Synge has been acknowledged. More open to question, in terms of a full critical engagement with McDonagh's work, is the degree to which it can be disassociated from that particular influence and still retain critical, as opposed to purely commercial, credibility.

The Lieutenant was one of four plays which McDonagh had completed at the time that *Beauty Queen* was first staged: the other two being *The Pillowman*, produced by the English National Theatre in 2004, and *Dead Days At Coney* which is still unproduced; neither of which is set in Ireland. *The Lieutenant* has all of McDonagh's trademark black humour and Grand Guignol effects, but what it lacks is not only a sense of a meaningful geographical location but also, crucially, the intertextual actualities and Syngean echoes which placed *The Leenane Trilogy* within a tradition whose critique of the west provided a sense of depth and critical purpose. The Inishmore location was, in fact, purely pragmatic for, as McDonagh told Penelope Dening, his plot demanded 'a place in Ireland that would take a long time to get to from Belfast' and, as she noted, 'Inishmore fitted the bill.'[47] The casualness with which Inishmore was selected is matched by the fact that it was merely the numerical equivalence of the three Aran Islands with a dramatic trilogy which 'prompted the idea', rather than any overt commitment to a thematically and dramatically unified exploration of a community and culture. A similar lack of plot-based necessity applies to time: 1993 as it is first given on one page or circa 1993

on another, which does little beyond suggest that this is a contemporary world; there is no greater historical specificity. As a
result of this imprecision, the play lacks the substantive echoes of
Synge and of the world he evoked, which in *The Leenane Trilogy*
(and *Cripple of Inishmaan*) provided 'the depth model' for
McDonagh's work. The phrase is Fredric Jameson's, and indeed it
is Jameson's critique of postmodernism (the form with which
McDonagh's work is most frequently – and favourably –
associated) which provides a theoretical basis for an evaluation of
the totality of his debt to Synge.

For Jameson, the inadequacy of the postmodern is that its
relationship to the works whose styles it 'quotes' is that it has
moved from 'parody', defined as having some serious conviction,
and become simply 'pastiche' which is 'blank parody, a statue with
blind eyeballs'.[48] Jameson's distinction between parody and
pastiche is critiqued by Linda Hutcheon – for whom parody and
pastiche (or ironic quotation, appropriation or intertextuality) are
synonyms – on the grounds that postmodern parody can offer a
way in to the investigation of the politics of representation.
However, both she and Jameson subscribe to the view that in the
postmodern the critical relationship is that between the contemporary work and those precursors on which it performs, for
Jameson, its acts of 'random cannibalization',[49] or, for Hutcheon,
its 'parodic representational strategies'.[50] The point, however, is
that there is a precursor without which Hutcheon's 'strategies' or
Jameson's valued 'parody' cannot fulfil what he terms their
'vocation'. In this context the key issue is raised by Hutcheon:
'What if we do not recognize the represented figures or the
parodied composition?'[51] For without recognition of the 'original'
on the part of the audience then there is no possibility of the work
signalling 'how present representations come from past ones and
what ideological consequences derive from both continuity and
difference'.[52]

This literally 'critical' relationship between McDonagh's stage
world and the Syngean original is identified by Christopher Morash
who describes The Leenane Trilogy as 'copies that have forgotten
their originals'.[53] For the plays to function in the terms which I
have argued above that they can, however, depends on the

audience's ability to read them in the context of the genre of 'the western play' – their 'original'. And as Morash develops his argument the point about working within a defined and identifiable genre is deemed crucial:

> By creating an image that audiences are invited to see as 'traditional', and then removing from it the last vestiges of 'traditional' values, the plays stage the contradictions of a society that continues to nurse images of itself in which it no longer believes.[54]

In other words, while all audiences have the potential to respond positively to the shock techniques McDonagh employs in terms of language and action, enjoying them on the titillating level of Tarantino-type terror if nothing else, only audiences familiar with the genre in which he is working are capable of analyzing and evaluating the plays as critiques of the society whose western 'source' they so rigorously explode.

However, as Fintan O'Toole has noted, the critical question with regard to McDonagh is 'when does the laughing stop and the thinking begin?'[55] For what is most striking about *The Leenane Trilogy*'s violence and depravity is the absence of any informing moral structure on which authority itself rests. When the law is both ignorant and criminally inclined in the pursuit of convictions, as in *A Skull in Connemara*, and the church is valued, as in *The Lonesome West*, only for the quality of the vol-au-vents provided at funerals ('It seems like God has no jurisdiction in this town. No jurisdiction at all' [6] is the comment of the ineffectual and finally suicidal Father Welsh/Walsh), then previously clear parameters within which actions could be either approved or denounced have been removed. The problem, and hence the frequent difficulty of interpreting McDonagh's work, is that while exploring a world that has imploded, in which order has collapsed, he does not stage 'some basis for the new morality he seems to be seeking, some ground for reconciliation'.[56] And if that crucial perspective is to be supplied it can only be by audiences who recognize the Syngean 'originals', most notably *Playboy*, which contained vital, if marginalized characters whose dynamism was an explicit condemnation of the multiple failures in the community. In other words, only audiences able to read 'across' the dysfunctionality of McDonagh and Synge's characters are able to mobilize readings of the former's plays as social critique – and this is above all dependent on a recognition that the one thing missing from otherwise complete echoes of their Syngean antecedents is a vibrant protagonist capable, like Christy, of condemning 'the fools is here' (173) and establishing a dynamic on-stage counter to social degeneration. While one might argue that McDonagh credits his audience with the capability of providing this critique unaided, the problem here is that audiences can too easily avoid the harsh facts towards which the on-stage 'raisonneur' can direct them and opt, instead, for the easy option of entertainment alone. The crucial Syngean referents are lacking in *The Lieutenant of Inishmore* where McDonagh's stylistic tic of juxtaposing graphic violence with comic bathos amuses audiences through its audacity but ultimately fails to engage their intellects; the presentation of a Republican gunman more concerned with the death of a pet cat than the suffering of his multiple victims, not confronting the complexities of an Irish situation which, to English audiences, is all too often perceived as that of the reductive extremes in which McDonagh couches his nominal 'satire'.

Condemnation of McDonagh has frequently been couched in terms of a falling away from the achievement of Synge who, in his time, was condemned in terms remarkably similar to those now directed at McDonagh: Vic Merriman's judgement that McDonagh offers only 'a sustained dystopic vision of a land of gratuitous violence, craven money grabbing and crass amorality'[57] echoes Joseph Holloway's description of *Playboy* as 'the outpouring of a morbid, unhealthy mind ever seeking on the dunghill of life for the nastiness that lies concealed there'.[58] As argued above, however, there is a case to be made for McDonagh as being more than an astute purveyor of meretricious, crowd-pleasing 'entertainments', but it is one which is dependent on the audience's ability to perceive the Syngean connection and read McDonagh's work within that particular generic frame. In the search for authentic props for his Abbey Theatre productions Synge was normally dependent on his Aran Island friend, Martin McDonough. It is a nice irony of theatrical history that the dependency is now reversed, the contemporary McDonagh being indebted to Synge for a critical 'authenticity' within which his plays can be read, not as crowd-pleasing mobilizations of redundant stereotypes, but as serious interrogations of the gap which has opened up between the west idealized in the period of the Literary Revival and its re-maindered actuality in the time of the Celtic Tiger.

[1] This essay was first published in *Irish University Review* 33 (Spring/Summer 2003).

.[2] Fintan O'Toole, 'A brilliant début', *The Irish Times* 24 December 1996.

[3] Fintan O'Toole, 'Nowhere Man', *The Irish Times* 26 April 1997.

[4] Penelope Dening 'The Scribe of Kilburn', *The Irish Times* 18 April, 2001.

[5] Michael Billington, '*The Lieutenant of Inishmore*', *The Guardian* 4 January 2002.

[6] Lyn Gardner, 'The Lieutenant of Inishmore', *The Guardian* 29 June 2002.

[7] Michael Billington, Rev.of *The Lieutenant of Inishmore*, *Irish Theatre Magazine*, 2.9 (2001), p.98.

[8] José Lanters, 'Playwrights of the Western World: Synge, Murphy, McDonagh', in *A Century of Irish Drama, Widening the Stage*, eds Stephen Watt, Eileen Morgan, and Shakir Mustafa (Bloomington: University of Indiana Press, 2000), p.221.

[9] Karen Vandenvelde, 'The Gothic Soap of Martin McDonagh', in *Theatre Stuff: Critical Essays on Contemporary Irish Theatre*, ed. Eamonn Jordan (Dublin: Carysfort Press, 2000), p.293.

[10] Susan Conley, 'Rev. of The Beauty Queen of Leenane', Irish Theatre Magazine, 2.5 (2000), pp.63-4.

[11] Vic Merriman, 'Decolonisation Postponed: The Theatre of Tiger Trash', *Irish University Review*, 29.2 (1999), p.313.

[12] Editorial, *The United Irishman* 8.193, 8 November 1902, p.1.

[13] Merriman, p.316.

[14] Maud Gonne MacBride, 'A National Theatre', *The United Irishman* 243, 24 October 1903, p.2.

[15] Quoted in Terence Brown, *Ireland: A Social and Cultural History* (London: Fontana, 1981), p.93.

[16] Fintan O'Toole, 'The Lie of the Land', in *Black Hole, Green Card* (Dublin: New Island Books, 1994), p.28.

[17] Brenna Katz Clarke, *The Emergence of the Peasant Play at the Abbey Theatre* (Ann Arbor: UMI Research Press, 1982), p.1.

[18] Christopher Murray, 'The State of Play: Irish Theatre in the 'Nineties', in *The State of Play: Irish Theatre in the 'Nineties*, ed. Eberhard Bort (Trier: Wissenschaftlicher Verlag Trier, 1996), p.21.

[19] O'Toole, 'Nowhere Man'.

[20] O'Toole, 'Nowhere Man'.

[21] Declan Kiberd, *Synge and the Irish Language* , end ed. (Basingstoke: Macmillan, 1993), p.xxix.

[22] Merriman, p.314.

[23] Nicholas Grene, *The Politics of Irish drama: Plays in context from Boucicault to Friel* (Cambridge: Cambridge University Press, 1999), p.98.

[24] J.M. Synge, *Playboy of the Western World*, in *Collected Works, Vol. IV, Plays Book II,* ed. Ann Saddlemyer, (London, Oxford University Press, 1968), p.71. Subsequent references are entered directly in the text in parenthesis.

[25] Martin McDonagh, *The Beauty Queen of Leenane* (London: Methuen, 1996), p.57. Subsequent references are entered directly in the text in parenthesis.

[26] Martin McDonagh, *A Skull in Connemara* (London: Methuen, 1997), p.11. Subsequent references are entered directly in the text in parenthesis.

[27] Grene, p.98.

[28] Keir Elam, *The Semiotics of Theatre and Drama* (London: Methuen, 1980), pp.26-7.

[29] Bernard Beckerman, 'The Artifice of 'Reality' in Chekhov and Pinter', *Modern Drama* 21 (1978), pp.153-4.

[30] Synge, *Collected Works*, Vol. IV, *Plays*, p.xxv.

[31] J.M. Synge, *The Collected Letters of John Millington Synge, 1871-1907*, Vol.I, ed. Ann Saddlemyer (Oxford: Clarendon Press, 1983), p.74.

[32] Synge, Collected Letters, p.76.

[33] Tim Robinson, *The Leenane Trilogy*, Souvenir Programme, Druid Theatre Company/Royal Court Theatre, 1997.

[34] Seamus Deane, 'Synge and Heroism', in *Celtic Revivals: Essays in Modern Irish Literature 1880-1980* (London: Faber and Faber, 1985), p.55.

[35] Ronan McDonald, 'A Gallous Story or a Dirty Deed?: J.M. Synge and the Drama of Guilt', in *Reviewing Ireland*, eds Sarah Briggs, Paul Hyland, and Neil Sammells (Bath: Sulis Press,1998), p.139.

[36] Synge, *Collected Letters*, p.330.

[37] Synge, *Collected Letters*, p.116.

[38] P.J. Mathews, 'The Irish Revival: A Re-appraisal', in *New Voices in Irish Criticism*, ed. P.J. Mathews (Dublin: Four Courts Press, 2000), p.16.

[39] M.J. Molloy, *The Wood of the Whispering*, in *Three Plays* (New York: Proscenium Press, 1975), p.173. Subsequent references are entered directly in the text in parenthesis.

[40] Mary King, 'Focus Interview: Mary King on John Synge', *British Association*

for Irish Studies Newsletter 27 (2001): 125.

41 Tom Murphy, *Conversation on a Homecoming* in *Plays: 2* (London: Methuen, 1993), p.80. Subsequent references are entered directly in the text in parenthesis.

42 Merriman, p.313.

43 Synge, *Collected Works*, Vol. II, *Prose*, pp.399-400.

44 Martin McDonagh, *The Cripple of Inishmaan* (London: Methuen, 1997), p.56. Subsequent references are entered directly in the text in parenthesis.

45 See Mary King.

46 Mary King, p.5.

47 Dening, 'The Scribe of Kilburn'. With thanks to Patrick Lonergan for drawing this point to my attention.

48 Fredric Jameson, Postmodernism or, The Cultural Logic of Late Capitalism (London: Verso, 1991), p.17.

49 Jameson, p.18.

50 Linda Hutcheon, *The Politics of Postmodernism* (London: Routledge, 1989), p.100.

51 Ibid., p.105.

52 Ibid., p.93.

53 Christopher Morash, *A History of Irish Theatre 1601-2000* (Cambridge: Cambridge University Press, 2002), p.269.

54 Ibid., p.269.

55 Fintan O'Toole, 'Murderous Laughter', *The Irish Times* 24 June 1997.

56 Ibid.

57 Merriman, p.313.

58 Quoted in *Modern Irish Drama*, ed. John P. Harrington (New York: W.W. Norton, 1991), p.455.

18 | Decolonization Postponed: The Theatre of Tiger Trash

Victor Merriman[1]

> … as colonialism manifests itself, post-colonial desires for reconfiguring power relations and modes of representation develop and interlock with structures of domination. As integral discourses, they rely on the other for coherence and strategy. This immediately means post-coloniality is not necessarily after colonialism, but the cultural foundation on which an alternative society is conceptualised and lived. Caught in this concept's trajectory are issues of decolonization, anticolonialism and independence, nationalism and neocolonialism[2]

This essay offers some thoughts on contemporary Irish theatre provoked by Dr. Awam Amkpa's paper to the Dublin Institute of Technology Shaw Arts Festival, Shaw's *Pygmalion*: Drama and the Languages of Post-colonial Desires.[3] What follows is organized in two parts. In the opening section, Amkpa's model for social development in formerly colonized societies is described and elaborated. The second section offers a discussion of trends in contemporary Irish theatre production facilitated by reflection on that model. The discussion attempts to explore the success of Martin McDonagh and Marina Carr in terms of what it may tell us of cultural politics in independent Ireland at a time of increasing affluence.

Wherever colonialism has been and is resisted, anti-colonial activists see themselves as working toward decolonization. The teleology implicit in their analysis might be represented as follows:

Colonization–anticolonialism-decolonization

Experience teaches that their struggles tend to result in the replacement of one elite by another, as the departing colonizers give way to a nascent bourgeois class. This outcome thwarts the achievement of a decolonized social order, and typically results in disillusion, voluntary exile or even incarceration for some of the most radical persons and groups in the new social order. The evolving society itself is deprived of the insouciant energies of such persons, thus hastening the triumph of bourgeois social organization and curbing the movement toward full indigenous democracy.

Awam Amkpa proposes an iterative process of struggle between orders of domination and movements for liberation as follows:

> Colonization–anticolonialism–neocolonialism–
> post-colonialism– decolonization

His phased model of social, cultural and political development accommodates a more sophisticated account of social change, and enables us to read the process by which those involved in anti-colonial struggle experience frustration and fatigue under conditions of independence. If the model were to be rendered as follows, it might make more explicit Amkpa's understanding of decolonization as less a destination than a journey:

colonization ⬅➡ anticolonialism
limited decolonization as anticolonial raison d'être
neocolonialism ⬅➡ post-colonialism
ongoing decolonization as utopian project

The struggle to decolonize is as much a part of neocolonial experience as it is of anti-colonial effort. The model suggests that the crisis in colonialism which produces anti-colonial consciousness is effectively reiterated in the emergence in the neocolonial social order of post-colonial critique. Recalling Ngugi,[4] Amkpa directs inquiry toward issues around democracy, citizenship and identity as constituents of an ongoing moral imperative to decolonize. From an Irish perspective, one of the most fertile aspects of Amkpa's discussion lies in its potential to expose the slackness with which the concepts *neocolonial, post-colonial* and *decolonized* are routinely confused. The most serious consequence of this lack of conceptual rigour is in the way it enables the refusal of the term neocolonial. That refusal disables the kind of critique which might animate decolonization as a critical democratic project.

I begin with an elaboration of and commentary on Amkpa's developmental model. Colonization is a state of being. For Amkpa, the fully realized human subject is capable of personal agency and social action. In his discussion of Shaw's *Pygmalion*,[5] Amkpa reads the colonization of Eliza's mind as a metaphor for bourgeois culture's colonization of the bodies, minds and geographical spaces that constitute society itself. Colonization is thus a process of separation, of alienation from oneself, in which the minds, bodies, spirits and languages of the colonized are abused. In order to present herself as a bourgeois, Eliza must define herself in terms set by others. She must come to know her desired self as other to her actual self. Her submission to reconstruction by Higgins is a manifestation of the self-despising colonized subject's desire for abnegation. Colonial education is a process of co-option into contradiction[6] which corrupts one's notion of belonging and suppresses possibilities of becoming. Groups and individuals are presented as other to themselves, and are thus dominated. Self-naming, self-description, and the search for one's own place in which to realize subjectivity are rendered impossible. In Amkpa's account of the message of colonial education, to be is to be like; to be like is to be like the colonizer.

Amkpa identifies anti-colonial consciousness as the moment of being able to critique, of realizing that there is another option in articulating one's humanity. This becomes the organizing stance of emergent countercultural narratives. In this, his position maps on to the work of Freire and Boal: awareness of the actually existing situation enables the realization that there is an option to act for change. A further step is to choose that option, and to develop material practices which enable its enactment. A key concern for Amkpa is the potential of theatre as material cultural practice. Emphasizing art as public meaning-making, he assigns a potentially key role to theatre in critiquing and transforming democratic participation in the nation state. This 'high ambition' for theatre will inform the discussion of contemporary Irish theatre which forms the second part of this essay. Amkpa sees dramatic metaphor as the unit of communication of meaning in theatre. Misreadings, and by this Amkpa means readings which are not open to metaphor, which remain at a level of the literal, or the crudely symbolic, are culturally very costly indeed. Rather than positioning content for significance, misreadings cause its location to be circumvented, avoided, or ignored as theatre-as-spectacle is assumed to be all there is to see, and its forms are avidly consumed. For Awam Amkpa, his fortuitous[7] exposure to *Pygmalion* constituted a first step toward realizing his own power to appropriate dramatic narrative to his subjective needs. His oppositional reading of the film amounted to a cultural and political awakening: he identified wholly with Eliza's 'savage tongue', with the oppositional potential of her socially unacceptable forms of speech, and with her anxiety to domesticate it to civilized bourgeois norms.

Amkpa understands anti-colonial struggle as social and cultural actions and practices arising from moments of critical insight. This phase of endeavour is as replete with contradiction and brutality as the domination which makes it inevitable. Anti-colonial movements typically posit a unified people engaged in an onward journey toward self-determination. The people's destiny is typically – in Irish experience, specifically – aligned with the achievement of an independent state (ideally, a nation-state). Difference is set aside in the service of a greater, nobler plenitude of oppositional identifications. As an ideology of struggle, cultural nationalism inaugurates a self-contradictory process in which the act of imagining a social order which has yet to be brought into being is presented as a task of recovering and reinstating an ancient community already constituted in a reified narrative of a common past. This mobilizing narrative of nationhood denied also engenders what Luke Gibbons has called 'a national longing for closure',[8] which compromises the public's willingness to acknowledge the persistence of social problems after independence.

Apparently convincing and simple solutions to actually complex and intractable issues will evoke a mass surge for narrative closure rather than a rigorous commitment to disclosure, negotiation and agreement. In achieving this, the circumstances of the present are unlikely to co-operate, which is why appeals to essential values encoded in images of a past characterized by commonality of purpose are so useful. Rowlands observes, 'It is a remote past that best symbolizes the nation's sacrifice, rather than the recent past that exemplifies the realities of conflict and power.'[9] In the immediate aftermath of anti-colonial struggle, this could be rewritten as 'a recent past best symbolizes the nation's sacrifice, rather than a present that exemplifies the realities of conflict and power'. Lawson and Tiffin warn against practices which attempt to erase difficult socio-cultural problems by means of recourse to 'a spurious claim (or capitulation) to 'native' authenticity, since this has the effect of itself foreclosing on difference'.[10] A refusal to engage with actual historical experience of difference is fatal to the project of developing a decolonized state. In these circumstances, the establishment of the nation state will do no more than enshrine the aspirations and desires of a community which is itself no more than a fantastic projection of an unrealizable homogeneity – a return to the patterns of colonialism itself.

One of the strengths of Amkpa's theoretical model is the distinction it enables between 'anti-colonial' and 'liberationist'. The exigencies of struggle forge a powerful sense of group *solidarity*. Building on this base, the resultant independent state further legitimizes itself as the embodiment of popular *liberty*. In proclaiming common cause in liberty, the new entity actually enforces a denial of difference as a condition of inclusion in its orthodoxy. Valorization of difference is essential to *equality* in the social order. To the extent that it undervalues or actively excludes this ethic from its practices, the democratic imperative, encoded in signatures of 'belonging' is fatally compromised in the new state. With the fallacy of independence-as-deliverance in place, the inevitability of a divided society, and an ultimately conflictual social order is engendered. In tandem with this, the tendency 'to produce a native subject locked in a prehistoric and hence apolitical past'[11] as the organizing motif of citizenship, sets the stage for a neo-colonial body politic. In this social order, all sites of resistance, apart from the (now-vacant) anti-colonial position, are rigorously delegitimized. With analyses based on the consequences of economic, race and gender inequalities rendered mute, the possibility of confronting the contradictions they would expose – the *sine qua non* of a process of decolonization – is all but negated.

Neocolonialism is a bourgeois social project. As a state of being it is effectively nameless, and is almost never acknowledged in public discourse[12] in the neocolonial state. The felt contradictions of neocolonialism may be even more acute than those of colonialism itself, not least because of the sense of betrayal experienced by the excluded. However, its ability to manipulate the symbols and rhetoric of resistance, make it highly complex and difficult to engage on anything other than its own terms, which never countenance shortcomings in the common project. It is by means of such rhetorical strategies that emergent elites posit, legitimize and enforce a selective definition of identity, culture and citizenship. Amkpa is clear on the internal weakness of newly independent states: 'Those who lead the anti-colonial revolution frequently take the place of the colonizers and in fact repeat the processes of colonization.' Such is the power of the state to demand loyalty, naming its failures – not to speak of denouncing them as a negation of liberationist aspirations – becomes somehow a greater betrayal than acquiescence in a new paradigm of domination. This prohibition notwithstanding, Amkpa's model suggests that even as the neocolonial state repeats the tropes, dynamics and administrative practices of colonialism, so it will produce a countervailing social consciousness – the post-colonial critique.

Just as anti-colonial consciousness emerges at that point in colonial relations where its contradictions are subjected to critique, and utopian imaginings begin, Amkpa understands post-colonialism as the assertion of critical subjectivity under neocolonial conditions. The 'post' in post-colonial is read as a strategic epistemological stance, not as a periodization of consciousness, or characterization of experience. For Amkpa, the post-colonial moment is one in which the material circumstances of the social order which has been settled for are subjected to sustained critique. It marks the emergence of a realization that there are other options in articulating humanity, beyond what is envisaged in the independent state. Post-colonialism, thus understood, emphasizes processes of becoming over the condition of having arrived. Neocolonialism posits and institutionalizes bourgeois liberalism as identical with the aspirations of the mass of the people in the former colony. This involves subordinating the aspiration to equality in the social order to the right to economic liberty under capitalism. While it is represented as a natural outcome, rooted in a quasi-mythic account of the struggle of an ancient people for self-determination, and supported by the rhetoric of homogeneous community, it is in fact a choice. The fact that the public were not offered such a choice does not diminish the possibility of imagining a world trans-formed, an achievable, utopian social order.

Amkpa advocates decolonization 'as a transitional process, a national event, a perpetual process of challenging internal and external domination'. In Amkpa's analysis, decolonization is not an event, but a language of inquiry, a constant process. It is marked by practices which acknowledge hybridity and difference in the constitution of the social order. In this way, decolonization an-nounces the potential for, and underpins the practice of demo-cratic citizenship. Identity and citizenship are formed and experienced in negotiating the problematic relations between the interests of individual subjects and those of the nation state and its neocolonial projects. Such projects are usually articulated by, and seen as synonymous with the concerns of the indigenous elite which emerges out of the anti-colonial struggle. These concerns are often at odds with that which might be called 'the common good', the historical basis for the legitimacy of the state's claim on citizen allegiance. As inscriptions of the new hegemony, however, they can function as powerful symbolic manifestations of com-munal identity: to reject such projects is not simply to oppose a point of view, it is to repudiate consensus. To exclude oneself from consensus is an effective renunciation of one's rights to full social participation.

The stalemate produced by alienation of persons and groups in the neocolonial social order does not necessarily create conditions for change. Ngugi suggests a reason for this phenomenon: '(neocolonial) cultural control today has blunted perceptions, and moreso the feelings about those perceptions.'[13] With the development of globalized capital and its wonderful efficiencies, practices of consumption are deliberately posited as the location of social participation. Inclusion in the social order is then predicated on economic capital, disposable income and lifestyle. These processes are further enabled by the emergence of virtual identifications as stabilizers of human identities.[14] Because all systems proclaim a vision of the good life, and because capitalist corporations have the resources[15] to communicate their formulations more extensively and with remarkable effectiveness, the contemporary social order sees the proliferation of tropes, discourses and rhetorical figures which serve to align the very goals of liberal democracy in the nation state with the elaboration of capital as a global system. The weight of the contradictions attending the reconciliation of this paradox may be evident, but it is of great value to the failing neocolonial social order. While consumers derive satisfaction from dispersed loyalties easily gratified in acts of consumption, with one bound the state can shed its contradictions, evade its day of reckoning and embrace a new world order which emerges as the national destination transmogrified and writ large: The Land of the Spree. Independence is retrospectively revealed not as a destination in itself, but as the ante-room of a global economic order. The revised neocolonial teleology may be figured as follows:

Colonialization–anticolonialism – autonomy in globalization

This account of social development enables anxieties about social liberation to be laid aside in the self-evident triumph of full incorporation in consumption.

Irish theatre and the project of decolonizing a neocolonial social order in Amkpa's model provides opportunities to open up discussion about the current state of neocolonialism, post-colonial consciousness and the prospects for decolonization in contemporary Ireland. As outlined above, he accords great significance to theatre as a transformative cultural practice. That said, there are many great difficulties attending the responsibilities of artists and intellectuals in a neocolonial state. Their historical roles require that they accept responsibility for naming and opposing inconsistencies, contradictions and injustice in the social order. Even as they set about discharging that role in independent Ireland, the state responded with the institution of censorship of artistic works. Self-censorship is never far behind, as people internalize the new orthodoxy, and applies perhaps more acutely to publics for art works than it does to artists themselves. There is an apocryphal story of a young woman attending a play at the Abbey Theatre with her mother in the 1950s. As a plaster image of Christ is shattered in an act of frenzied violence on the stage, she whispers loudly, 'It's all right mother, I have my eyes closed.' This episode illustrates the greater perceived transgression involved in acknowledging difference and contradiction than in colluding in their denial, and acquiescing in the consequences. What then of current trends in Irish theatre? What savage metaphors are currently figured as 'symbols adequate to our predicament'?

Many contemporary plays stage moments of violence and breakdown of human relations from the deeply intimate to the broadly social, in ways which enable a deepening of audience understanding of the complexities of their conditions. Billy Roche's *Amphibians*[16] represents a community in turmoil in the shadow of economic change, in which communal values are under fatal strain. The tensions produced cohere in the tortured figure of Broaders, and result in a night of crazed violence, and his flight into exile. By carefully positioning the dramatis personae relative to each other, their economic situation and their stance on communal values, *Amphibians* both problematizes and reasserts solidarities around blood relationship, place and labour. Johnny Hanrahan's and John Browne's *Craving*[17] employs a metaphor of sexual relations as a site for performing class inequities in staging the moral emptiness accompanying the first roars of the tiger economy. The play, a problematic but fascinating multi-media text, fictionalizes and occupies Cork city as a liminal space: a site without co-ordinates, but fully implicated in the everyday concerns and projects of what independent Ireland is becoming. Both plays were well received in their places of origination, which they fictionalize, but were staged in Dublin as fringe events.

Among the most celebrated Irish playwrights of the late 1990s are Marina Carr and Martin McDonagh. In an apparently bold oppositional stance, their successes have been built around plays which stage Ireland as a benighted dystopia. At a time of unprecedented affluence, Carr and McDonagh elaborate a world of the poorly educated, coarse and unrefined. The focus is tight, the display of violence inhering in the people themselves, grotesque and unrelenting. Carr's *By the Bog of Cats...* and *Portia Coughlan* take as their point of departure the condition of being poor in contemporary Ireland. Both plays travesty the experiences of the poor, urban and rural. Introducing a category of internal outsider known in the United States of America as 'white trash', they posit worlds in which material poverty and moral bankruptcy map on to one another, eerie partners in a dance of death. In McDonagh's case, *The Beauty Queen of Leenane*, *A Skull in Connemara*, *The Lonesome West* and *The Cripple of Inishmaan* stage a sustained dystopic vision of a land of gratuitous violence, craven money-grubbing and crass amorality. No loyalty, either communal, personal or familial can survive in this arid landscape. Death, affection, responsibility appear as meaningless intrusions in the self-obsessed orbits of child-adults. Amkpa's model suggests that neocolonialism repeats the practices of colonialism, and these plays demonstrate the cultural logic of such repetitions. While dystopic visions of Ireland are nothing new in theatre – The Love Scene in Tom Murphy's *Famine* being perhaps the most fully realized – such stagings populated by violent child-adults repeat the angriest colonial stereotypes as a form of communal self-loathing. The dramatis personae of these plays specifically mark out figures of the poor which are overdetermined in their Irishry. Gross caricatures with no purchase on the experiences of today's audi-ences, their appeal to the new consumer-Irish consensus lies in their appearance as ludicrous Manichaean opposites – the colonized simian reborn. In each belly laugh which greets the preposterous malevolence of its actions there is a huge cathartic roar of relief that all of this is past – 'we' have left it all behind. The plays' constitution of an apparently homogeneous community around a feared and despised negative is a blatant reinscription of colonial relations. The problem, from a post-colonial point of view is clear: these plays implicate audiences in particular stances toward the poor, the past and Irishness. Their emergence at a time of economic boom exposes the *embourgeoisement* of contemporary culture, and invokes Amkpa's sense of 'the futility of organizing social progress within bourgeois value systems.'[18]

The appearance in wedding dress of the traveller woman, Hester Swane at the monstrous petit bourgeois wedding of Carthage, her daughter's father in *By the Bog of Cats…* evoked no closed eyes in the auditorium of the Abbey Theatre. On the contrary, the mother-in-law's racist epithet 'Ya piebald knacker!' brought the house down. The moment when the bride's father shoves a loaded shotgun under Hester's skirt is an image of gross brutality so gratuitous that it risks rupturing the boundaries of the fictional world altogether. A dangerous and amoral woman, even Hester's marginal economic status turns out to have been attained by means of fratricide. The dénouement will see her slit her daughter's throat from ear to ear. Her association with violence, deceit and unnatural urges is specifically grounded in her identity as a traveller. Hester Swane, traveller, is beyond the pale, a constant figure in a mutating social order desperate for points of otherness against which to imagine its own impossible consistency.

The entirety of *The Leenane Trilogy* stages not one moral voice, save that of the ludicrous Father Walsh …Welsh, referred to in the first two plays and finally encountered in *The Lonesome West*. His contribution ends in a suicidal walk into the fjord at Leenane, leaving the fictional world of the West of Ireland with nothing to counter the craven barbarity of its inhabitants, except the strong possibility that they will one day wipe each other out. No Syngean anthem to robust paganism this. These plays offer a kind of voyeuristic aperture on the antics of white trash whose reference point is more closely aligned to the barbarous conjurings of Jerry Springer than to the continuities of an indigenous tradition of dramatic writing. Importantly, the repellent figures presented turn out to be representations of those most fully betrayed by indigenous self-rule: emigrants, undereducated peasants, bachelor smallholders, women abandoned in rural isolation by economic collapse. By othering representations of their near-selves, and scorching them in the heat of their derision, McDonagh and Carr offer bourgeois audiences course after course of reassurance, of the kind offered to the upwardly mobile when 1980s economic neoliberalism provided them with the prone form of the homeless to step over on their way to the stock exchange.

Bertolt Brecht recognized the reality that even theatre that compromises its content and eschews its responsibility to engage with the world can be enormously seductive: 'the theatre can stage anything; it theatres it all down.' McDonagh's plays, in particular, are commercially very successful. There are good reasons for this, in that they have been served by the resources of the Royal National Theatre, the Royal Court and Druid Theatre Company. What is not at issue here is the quality of the productions. Brian F. O'Byrne's work in the *Leenane Trilogy*, brilliantly brought to the stage by Garry Hynes, was excellent. No one can gainsay the performances of Marie Mullen, Anna Manahan, Ray McBride or Mick Lally. In Carr's case, *Portia Coughlan* was staged at the Peacock Theatre, *By the Bog of Cats...* was directed at the Abbey by Patrick Mason, who cast Olwen Fouéré in a finely-crafted performance as Hester Swane. Those critics who confine them-selves to accounts of performance which privilege categories such as sense of place, ear for dialogue, fine observation, quality of star acting/ensemble performances, appropriateness of design and technical precision do a good job in recording the high production standards of the plays as originally performed. Criticism that goes no further than documenting the quality of the spectacle, is wholly inadequate to critique what these plays amount to as cultural interventions. The resources of the most successful of Irish theatre companies have been deployed in the service of deeply problematic work, to the extent that their theatricality – their ability to operate as spectacle – overpowers engagement with their significance as dramatic art. What is at issue here is the meaning of these representations as constitutory events in the evolution of civil society. What is being played – about whom, to whom and in whose interests? What are its meanings, and their consequences?

For some, the perceived importance of Carr's work rests on a claim that she brings feminist perspectives to the stage. Others

celebrate the perceived boldness of her literary achievement. If this
is feminist writing, it is of the kind which has been challenged by
those outside the cultural economies of Western bourgeois
circulation. Hester Swane demonstrates in an Irish context the
limited egalitarianism of such a cultural stance. The most fully
female of all the dramatis personae on show, she is also the most
comprehensively damned *in and of herself* for her unnaturalness.
And this is a crucial point. The application of referents in classical
and renaissance drama upon which Carr tends to draw, results in
the unproblematic ascription of fatedness to the poorest and most
vulnerable in the social order. Such a manoeuver, in which class
and entitlement is ignored inaugurates not questioning, but evasion
of the social meaning of their position. In a truly ironic inversion
of a powerful feminist slogan, Swane is obliged to play 'nature' to
the audience's 'culture'.

There is a view that McDonagh's work is in some postmodern
sense metatheatrical, that the whole project is a wonderful jape in
which the jaded repertoire of Boucicault, Synge, and the 'lesser'
Abbey playwrights has been plundered as an antique hoard of
quirky, dated images. Such theatrical freaks have no currency in an
urbane present, so to parade them in all their benightedness is a
big joke, in which the laugh is on the naïve drama of a past which
really must be left behind. From the point of view of the art form
itself, one of the casualties here is the radical potential of those
theatrical figures from the past. Significant theatre is as much
about the reinterpretation of existing work as it is about the
creation of the new. Patrick Mason's interpretation of *The Well of
the Saints*[19] raised important questions of integrity, truth and
spirituality while heightening the pagan rhythms of Synge's language and worldview. If the target is Boucicault, then Garry
Hynes's powerful reappropriation of the colonial textuality of *The
Colleen Bawn*,[20] and Conall Morrison's playful clarity with the ironies
of the same play[21] assert that such work, intelligently textualized
can perform Amkpa's task of challenging the contra-dictions of
neocolonialism as it reiterates colonial relations of domination.
The easiest target of all, so ruthlessly raided for cheap effect by
both Carr and McDonagh, the small town bourgeoisie, can be
staged to critical satirical effect, as Gerard Stembridge's production

for Barabbas ... the Company of Lennox Robinson's *The Whiteheaded Boy* demonstrates.

McDonagh's plays are often greeted as parodies of the works of John Millington Synge. This needs to be challenged. In staging peasant life, Synge unambiguously confronted the ideological project to which it had been co-opted: a travesty serving the need felt by a resurgent nationalist bourgeoisie for a foundational myth. What Lawson and Tiffin would identify from a post-colonial perspective as the danger of 'a spurious claim to 'native' authenticity foreclosing on difference' was grasped intuitively by Synge, and, his exposure of this cultural fraud was all too apparent to the audience for *The Playboy of the Western World*. That audience clearly recognized his representation of an actually existing peasant world as an act of subversion of their project of enthroning an idealized peasant as a trope of cultural nationalism. Synge's work, in other words, is a self-consciously provocative cultural intervention. His plays are written, against the position of his audience, into the heart of the myth-making project of emergent bourgeois nationalism at its most exclusive. Far from being an early, naïve version of McDonagh, *The Playboy of the Western World* or *The Well of the Saints* embody a cultural project which could hardly be more different. Such plays vigorously assert the dignity and spirit of people whose image, emptied of their life experiences, would be mobilized in the service of bourgeois neocolonialism. This is a hallmark of art engaged in cultural decolonization. McDonagh's work – notably *The Cripple of Inishmaan* – parades the emptied shell of peasant life for smug dismissal by a metropolitan[22] audience. The journey from Synge to McDonagh takes us all the way from images which challenge the submerged ideological positions of an emergent neocolonial class to those which collude in reinforcing them.

The success of Carr's and McDonagh's plays has little to do with the loss of relevance of older worlds and their inhabitants. *Portia Coughlan, By the Bog of Cats...*, *The Cripple of Inishmaan* and *The Leenane Trilogy* come from, and perform something else. A neo-colonial society in the throes of globalization is a peculiarly inhospitable location for post-colonial critique. The argument that the apparent ironic playfulness of McDonagh's work marks an ability on the part of the nation to laugh at itself claims cultural significance for the plays as manifestations of a coming of age, a type of post-colonial[23] maturation. In reality, the comfortable echelon of a nakedly divided society is confirmed in its complacency, as it simultaneously enjoys and erases the fact that 'our' laughter is at the expense of 'them'. This phenomenon both illustrates and deploys the confusions about the status and meaning of post-colonialism to which Amkpa's model draws attention. The movement of the dramatis personae of *By the Bog of Cats...* and *The Leenane Trilogy* to central positions in Irish theatre enables such figures to occupy and redefine the coordinates of cultural space. In celebrating the new Irishness of the audience for such spectacles, they simultaneously negate the interrogation of the conditions in which such images are produced and have points of reference. In this way, they point to a turn away from public inquiry, a willingness to settle for a divided society, a fatal refusal of the difficult process of decolonization itself. A spurious post-coloniality of chronological severance institutes a lesser public role for theatre itself, in which its credentials as spectacle overpower its ethical obligation to critique and thus renew the social order.

---

[1] This essay was previously published in *Irish Univesity Review* 29.2 (1999).

[2] Awam Amkpa, *Framing narratives of post-coloniality* in http://www.mtholyoke.edu/-aamkpa/Framing.Questions.html

[3] Awam Amkpa, *Shaw's Pygmalion: Drama and the Languages of Post-colonial Desires*, paper to the Dublin Institute of Technology Shaw Arts Festival, 9 April 1999. The paper gave rise to a lengthy response session, chaired by Dr Anthohy Roche (UCD). Many of the references in this essay refer to that discussion rather than the published text of Dr Amkpa's paper itself.

[4] 'For as in the days of colonialism, the African people are still struggling for a world ... in which they will control the economy, politics and culture to make their lives accord with where they want to go and who they want to be.' Ngugi wa Thiong'o, *The writer in a neocolonial state*, in his *Moving the Centre: the struggle for cultural freedoms* (James Currey, 1993), p.73.

[5] Amkpa refers to the film by Asquith, *Pygmalion* (b/w 1935) with Leslie Howard and Wendy Hiller.

[6] Amkpa cites personal experience of being required to learn poems in

English about winter and snow even though living in sub-tropical conditions during his boyhood in Nigeria.

[7] Interestingly, the British Council in Nigeria presented *Pygmalion* as a film of the work of an important British playwright, Bernard Shaw.

[8] Luke Gibbons, in *Nation, Narrative, History*, closing address to *Nationalisms: visions and revisions* (Conference organised by RTÉ and the Film Institute of Ireland. Dublin, November 1998).

[9] Michael Rowlands, 'Memory, Sacrifice and the Nation' in *Cultural Memory* (*New Formations*, No 30), p13.

[10] Alan Lawson and Chris Tiffin, eds, *Describing Empire: Post-colonialism and textuality* (London: Routledge, 1994), pp.232-233.

[11] Ibid., p.233.

[12] Roland Barthes, (*Mythologies* (Paladin 1980))states: 'the bourgeoisie has obliterated its name in passing from reality to representation, from economic man to mental man', p.138. 'The flight from the name 'bourgeois' … is the bourgeois ideology itself, the process through which the bourgeoisie transforms the reality of the world into an image of the world, History into Nature', p.141.

[13] Ngugi wa Thiong'o, *Freeing Culture from Eurocentrism*, op.cit., p.49.

[14] Coverage in Summer 1999 of Manchester United plc's tour of China featured shots of local supporters of the British team wearing club shirts and consuming related merchandise. The power of virtual imagery in constructing contemporary identities across time and space is clearly illustrated.

[15] Henry Armand Giroux, in *Fugitive Cultures: Race, Violence and Youth* (London: Routledge, 1996) refers to capitalist cinema and television as 'popular teaching machines'.

[16] Billy Roche, *Amphibians* (London: Warner Chappell, 1992) was staged at YMCA Wexford and Andrews Lane Theatre, Dublin (Dublin Theatre Festival Fringe) during 1998.

[17] Johnny Hanrahan, and J. Browne, *Craving* (Unpublished) was staged during 1998 at Everyman Palace Theatre, Cork, Project at the Mint, Dublin (Dublin Theatre Festival Fringe), and Watergate Theatre, Kilkenny.

[18] Amkpa, p.5.

[19] Abbey Theatre, 1996.

[20] Royal Exchange Theatre, Manchester 1995.

[21] Abbey Theatre, 1998.

[22] In this case, 'metropolitan' denotes not a location but a colonial or neocolonial mindset.

[23] The 'post-' in this case is intended to indicate a caesura: a clean break with an unsophisticated past.

19 | Is Martin McDonagh an Irish playwright?

Sara Keating

The question that the title of this article poses is almost incidental to the argument it will make. It is at the same time, however, the crucial issue that makes the following argument important: critical responses to the issue of Martin McDonagh's 'Irishness' indicate some key concerns and problems in contemporary Irish theatre studies. The apparent paradoxes generated by the plays of Martin McDonagh do not issue from the plays themselves, but stem from the ambiguity of the critical response that has accompanied them; it is the reception of his work, rather than the work itself, that makes Martin McDonagh an interesting figure.

By making McDonagh's Irishness or non-Irishness the focal point of the critical discussion of his plays, Irish theatre scholars have immersed McDonagh's work in a post-colonial discourse of national authenticity completely inappropriate to the postmodern politics of his plays. Examining this anxiety of reception, then, is far more illuminating about the critical conditions of contemporary Irish theatre criticism than it is about McDonagh's plays.

This article will discuss the dominance of post-colonial discourse in the field of Irish theatre studies, and the particular problems that arise when this discursive tradition is confronted by the transnational politics of postmodern representation. Taking the critical anxiety surrounding the work of Martin McDonagh as a case study, this article aims to show that the reluctance to move beyond the limited 'identitarian politics'[1] of post-colonial concerns inhibits the discursive development of Irish theatre studies in line with the dilution of such constructs in the contemporary globalized world.

Writing Ireland: Colonialism, Nationalism, Culture, published in 1988 by David Cairns and Shaun Richards, introduced post-colonial thought into mainstream practises of cultural politics in Ireland, aligning Irish cultural discourse with post-colonial scholarship through reading 'the ways in which the making and re-making of the identities of colonized and colonizer have been inflected by their relationship'.[2] In their investigation of the conditions for the invention of Irish cultural identity, Cairns and Richards apply a Gramscian logic of class liberation, suggesting that the creation of 'a 'counter-hegemony' to combat the ideological control of the dominant class'[3] is the only means through which cultural and national liberation is possible. Describing how British colonial identity was established through a process of 'othering', Cairns and Richards then turn to the 'othering' processes of cultural identity construction in Ireland, whereby cultural constructions of 'Ireland' and 'Irishness' were defined in oppositional relationship to colonial constructions, and in opposition to the colonial culture itself.

The final chapter in the Cairns and Richards' book borrows from Seamus Heaney in defining the post-colonial project in *Writing Ireland* as a search for 'symbols adequate to our predicament'. Citing Seamus Deane, Declan Kiberd and Tom Paulin as the key intellectual figures in the contemporary critical debate, Cairns and Richards conclude their study with a call for the re-invigoration of cultural critical practices through the re-writing (or re-reading) of cultural and political practises: that is through its alignment with the post-colonial project of reclamation, whereby homogenous cultural constructions of colonial (and anti-colonial) discourse might be replaced by a celebration of cultural diversity. Cairns and Richards use Deane to argue that this 'will enable new writing, new politics, unblemished by Irishness' (that is in its previous construction) yet still 'securely Irish'[4] (but as they define it) to emerge.

Declan Kiberd certainly responded to the call in his 1995 study *Inventing Ireland: Literature and the Modern Nation*. Following an investigation of the cultural construction of Ireland as 'a fiction created by the rulers of England in response to specific needs at a precise moment in British history',[5] Kiberd turns to Franz Fanon and Ashis Nandy for an examination of Irish literature through the post-colonial framework. Kiberd's political agenda in this literary study is exemplary of the post-political project: the dismantling of 'the hegemonic boundaries and the determinants that create un-equal relations of power based on binary oppositions such as 'us and them'[6] and the celebration of 'the hybridity of the national experience'.[7]

Kiberd's study moves through the canon (in theatre, Synge, Yeats, O'Casey, Friel) and ends with a short meditation on the future of Irish cultural studies. Kiberd states that the development of a 'comparative method' of analysis[8] is imperative. This will place Ireland and Irish studies within a wider framework of cultural studies (or, more specifically, within the international framework of *post-colonial* studies), and will acknowledge the politics of influence that have worked both ways.

Both Kiberd's book and the Cairns and Richards study helped to inscribe Irish critical discourse within the post-colonial framework of cultural criticism, encouraging the reading of Irish literature through the deconstructive practices of: firstly, anti-colonial cultural formations; secondly, neocolonial ideology whereby the practices of colonial hegemony were repeated in the interests of the 'Nation'; and thirdly, the post-colonial texts of resistance. While both turn to post-colonial literary practices to deconstruct colonial imaginings of Ireland and Irishness they neglect, however, to investigate the potential essentialism of the (essentially national)[9] post-colonial literary practices that they investigate, nor, for that matter, the potential essentialism of their own post-colonial critical position. While post-colonial *theory* on a global level may operate with the careful transparency of post-structuralist discourse,[10] post-colonial *practice* in the Irish context, it appears, does not.

An essay by Victor Merriman entitled *Decolonization Postponed: The Theatre of Tiger Trash*, published in the *Irish University Review* in

1999, brings us straight to the (problematic) point. Following a discussion of the post-colonial trajectory through the phased model of Nigerian scholar Awam Amkpa, Merriman approaches the project of decolonization (the process of liberation from colonial terms of reference and influence) through an analysis of contemporary Irish theatre. Following Christopher Murray's idea that 'in Ireland the nation is staged',[11] Merriman proposes an important public role for artists in the post-colonial state, which requires that they 'accept responsibility for naming and opposing inconsistencies, contradictions and injustice in the social order'.[12]

Responsibilities assigned, Merriman then introduces two key figures in contemporary Irish theatre, Marina Carr and Martin McDonagh. Far from fulfilling the critical role that he has assigned them, however, Merriman insists that they implicate themselves in the neocolonial project resisted by post-colonial literary and political practises. Rather than being fully 'implicated in the everyday concerns and projects of what independent Ireland is becoming',[13] he argues, Carr and McDonagh not only oppose an engagement with contemporary Ireland, but the 'Ireland' with which they engage is an Ireland that never even existed in the first place. The Ireland of their plays, Merriman continues, is an Ireland that was invented for the defence of colonial superiority, and Carr and McDonagh are complicit in preserving *this* view of Ireland and Irishness rather than one of 'authentic' contemporary experience.

Thus Merriman takes on the ethical position of the post-colonial critic, which Smyth would cite as a responsibility to reclaim 'both the historical realities of colonial oppression and the experience of those who either suffered its effects or protested its injustice':[14] contemporary Ireland must be saved from the negative cultural portrayals of its representational oppressors on the stage.

Using the value-laden logic and language of the moral commentator, Merriman judges the Carr and McDonagh plays as 'amoral'[15] travesties of contemporary Ireland that have 'no currency in an urbane present'.[16] In their plays, he insists, the 'colonized simian' is reborn. By being 'over-determined in their Irishry' and by 'implicat(ing) audiences in particular stances toward the poor, the past and Irishness',[17] the plays, he argues, set themselves up within the neocolonial project. If neocolonialism merely repeats the practices of colonialism, Merriman continues, 'these plays demonstrate the cultural logic of such repetitions.'[18]

Merriman's critical discomfort, however, implicates him in the charges that he brings against the reviled playwrights: if McDonagh and Carr repeat colonialist practices of representation, his own position as post-colonial critic reveals a logic of ideological and cultural dominance within post-colonial literary practices that is analogous to the social anxiety of colonial and neocolonial cultural censorship. For if post-colonialist critical practise, as Merriman himself defines it, is the 'assertion of critical subjectivity under neocolonial conditions',[19] by denying Carr and McDonagh critical subjectivity under the conditions of the post-colonial cultural order, Merriman effectively hangs himself and martyrs precisely those playwrights he sets out to oppose.

To follow Colin Graham's assertion that nationalist Ireland is a future always posited but never attained,[20] the 'Ireland' of post-colonial cultural and ideological discourse, which Merriman's argument seems to depend on, becomes continuously suspended by its own reflexivity. Decolonization is, indeed, as Merriman's title suggests, endlessly deferred: but the responsibility must fall equally on the shoulders of the critics who mediate its continuing process, not just on the artists with the power to represent it.

Merriman's position follows Smyth's diagnosis of (national) post-colonialism as a 'reverse discourse … implicated in the re-production and survival of that which it disdains'.[21] Smyth's study in fact aims to foreground the reflexive tendencies of the post-colonial theorist involved in the process of decolonization. By foregrounding the 'metadiscursive principle' Smyth problematizes the 'processes of national subject formation in contexts beyond the usual notion of criticism as textual commentary'.[22] His study then goes on to bring post-colonial theory into conversation with Irish critical practices of the period of 1950s, and it is essential to apply this kind of transparent discursive logic to contemporary con-ditions of cultural (and theatre) criticism. For, if the post-colonial theorist must ask 'When does the post-colonial begin?',[23] in the context of Celtic Tiger Ireland the contemporary cultural critic must ask, 'When will the post-colonial end?' The issue of what it will be replaced by, however, is one that can only be suggested through a self-reflexive critical practice that moves beyond the limits of 'the logic of identity', and here I would specify national identity, that, as Lloyd would argue, merely 'maintains the post-colonial moment'.[24]

Merriman's use of McDonagh as a scapegoat for his own critical anxiety about Celtic Tiger Ireland's position within the trajectory of post-colonial discourse is revealing about the necessity for the reinvention, not just of the cultural construct of 'Ireland', as a 2002 book of essays entitled *Reinventing Ireland: Culture and the Celtic Tiger* suggests,[25] but a re-invention of the discourses through which contemporary cultural practices in Ireland are mediated. The widespread ambiguity with which the plays of Martin McDonagh have been received has revealed the inadequacies of post-colonial theory in the postmodern context of a globalized Ireland.

McDonagh's plays illuminate this argument on three separate levels: (i) by provoking critical controversy they reveal the in-adequacies of the continued critique of contemporary culture through the *post-colonial* framework; (ii) by both absorbing and challenging the preceding canon of post-colonial texts they assume the intertextual characteristics and functions of *postmodern* re-presentation; and (iii) through their success on an international level, they contribute to the reading of contemporary 'Irishness' as a cultural construct that functions as a commodity of negotiation and exchange in the *globalized* world, not as an essential concept of national identity.

As a child of Irish parents living in England, McDonagh occupies a liminal space that is neither part of the colonial nor the neocolonial cultural order; nor, for that matter, do his plays form part of the post-colonial project of cultural decolonization. Yet the tendency in contemporary Irish cultural discourse is to place his plays within a conservative nationalist post-colonial framework that denies McDonagh's texts the critical paradigms that their representational strategies demand. From their intertextuality and visual citation of an entire century of Irish drama to their in-corporation of popular cultural references like soap-opera, McDonagh's plays place Ireland on an international, intercultural, intertextual map that eschews the very idea of cultural authenticity that these conservative critical frameworks demand.

Steve Wilmer acknowledges the problem and narrows the focus of McDonagh's problematic status within a national theatre history to one of nationality.[26] Indeed in the immediate reaction to his plays McDonagh's nationality is nearly always mentioned (although the classification is often contradictory). American reviews, for example, classify McDonagh almost unreservedly as an Irish playwright (whether that be a 'London-based Irishman' or a 'Roscommon County native')[27] while British commentators draw atention consistently to his cultural hybridity, in case his subject matter should suggest that he is actually Irish, rather than a British citizen.

Irish cultural critics, however, have wavered between positions, using McDonagh's cultural hybridity to defend their own particular ideologies. Thus, Fintan O'Toole can call *The Beauty Queen of Leenane* 'one of the most auspicious debuts by an Irish playwright in the past 25 years'[28] and Nicholas Grene can assert that *The Beauty Queen* may be an 'Irish made play', but it is an 'Irish made play' '*made in London by a London-Irish dramatist*'.[29] Grene's insistence on exposing McDonagh's national hybridity is a deliberate position that questions the representational 'legitimacy' of *The Beauty Queen of Leenane*. But by denying McDonagh authority on the grounds of a nebulously defined cultural 'authenticity' such critical conservatism merely exposes its own insularity.

In a transnational, globalized age where the very concept of cultural authenticity has become problematized, and arguments about 'nationality' have been replaced by more expansive argments about citizenship, the suggestion that McDonagh is not Irish enough to write a play set in Ireland is absurd. It is not, however, just McDonagh's nationality that creates a problem for the Irish post-colonial cultural critic. The *ideologies* of 'Irishness' that McDonagh's *texts* perform further alienate him from the cultural discourses espoused by post-colonial critical practices (Merriman's 'urbane' present).

First produced in 1996, when Celtic Tiger Ireland was just beginning to roar, McDonagh's *The Leenane Trilogy* concerns a late twentieth-century Ireland which affronts the conservative national values underlying the critical position of Irish scholars. Leenane is a liminal world, a pitiless rural wasteland set on the periphery of modern Ireland. It is not unaware of Ireland's recent, rapid modernization; but it is not engaged with it, for modern Ireland does not engage with those who are stuck in the rural Western outpost. Televisions, fancy stoves, and the conveniences of modern life have reached them, but the civilized urbanity that Merriman sees in contemporary Ireland has not: daughters kill mothers, brothers try to kill brothers, and the only possible moral arbiter of their world (Father Welsh-Walsh-Welsh) kills himself. The only boom that McDonagh's Ireland experiences is the one caused by the explosion of a brother's precious stove when his only sibling takes a loaded shotgun to it.

All three plays of *The Leenane Trilogy* take place in a country kitchen in the West of Ireland, providing an immediate visual signification of its engagement with the Irish theatrical tradition. The onstage world of Leenane, however, is not merely recognizable: it is deliberately over-familiar. This is going to be another Irish play, the set says, and the plays in *The Leenane Trilogy* do indeed follow the theatrical tradition that the plays' physical setting suggests, quoting everyone from J.M. Synge to J.B. Keane to Tom Murphy along the way.[30] The dialogue that McDonagh's plays open up with their predecessors, however, is not merely parasitic, it is also subversive, posing a challenge to both the theatrical tradition that it feeds off and the critical conditions that nurture it.

The anxiety with which the plays are received, however, cannot be reduced to an issue of content: from the violent inter-familial uprisings familiar from Murphy's *A Whistle in the Dark* to the specific form of patricide in *The Lonesome West,* invoking Christy Mahon's failed attempts to kill his father in *The Playboy of the Western World*, McDonagh is not exactly covering new dramatic territory. Nor can the problem be reduced to one of style: the melodramatic excess of his plays has proved wildly successful with both national and international audiences. It is to the critical context, then, that we must look to for the answers to the problems that McDonagh's work appears to pose, and for this we must examine the difficulties of reconciling the political purposes of post-colonial thought with postmodern representation in contemporary Ireland.

This debate echoes the contentious critical conversation between post-colonial and postmodern discourse that has engaged critical theorists from both sides. The overlapping theoretical strategies of post-colonial and postmodernist practices have been well documented – from their challenge to power and history and their resistance of homogeneous discourse to their structural concern with mimicry (duality) and multiple points of view.[31] At the slippery level of identity politics, however, post-colonialism and postmodernism (and, for Gerry Smyth, post-colonialism and post-structuralism) part theoretical ways.

The debate has not, however, just concerned issues of discursive supremacy, ideological hegemony and cultural appropriation, as the post-colonial theorist, forever engaged in shaking off vestiges or reappearing strands of colonial repression, would suggest. Hutcheon and Dirlik[32], for example, have brought a deeper, fundamentally political, level of concern to the tension that defines the post-colonial/postmodern relationship. Both theorists observe that postmodernisms fundamental disconnection from the material reality of political situations makes it ahistorical in a way that frustrates the post-colonial agenda and threatens post-colonialisms fundamental function as a discourse of resistance.

Furthermore, postmodernism's fragmented and multiple identities pose a serious challenge to the basic premise of post-colonial nationalism and post-colonial cultural practices: the coherent subjectivity that post-colonialism ultimately strives for through the processes of decolonization is continually disrupted and denied in the postmodern context.

The grotesquery, the intertextuality, the parody and pastiche of the McDonagh plays all align themselves with the postmodern politics of representation. Christopher Morash borrows from Baudrillard in his diagnosis of the plays' postmodern politics when he asserts that they are 'copies that have forgotten their originals',[33] but to leave the analysis of *The Leenane Trilogy* at that would be to succumb to the charge of depthlessness that is often levied against the McDonagh plays by the very same cultural critics that would question the validity of his representations of Ireland. McDonagh deliberately invites the audience to view his plays through the lens of the Irish theatrical tradition, but, by exaggerating and satirizing the characters, languages and forms of the tradition, he removes the very (anti/post-colonial) moral and ethical values on which that tradition was cultivated and which it espoused. McDonagh's plays' do not so much *forget* their originals, as Morash would argue, but they *empty* those originals of their cultural signification, and their contemporary cultural significance.

More importantly, however, McDonagh empties out the cultural construct of contemporary '*Ireland*', refilling it with nothing more than the cultural signification that its own reified forms take (hence the charge of depthlessness). While such canny commercialized markers as Kimberly, Mikados and Tayto crisps do indeed become shorthand signifiers of Irishness in the play, the very absurdity of their invocation as part of some shared heritage exposes the ensuing debate about the authenticity of Leenane, or the authority of McDonagh, as ridiculous.

This is not, however, to deny that McDonagh's plays are wholly removed from the conditions of reality in contemporary Ireland. Such a suggestion would be both dishonest and naïve. But it is more interesting to examine McDonagh's plays through their engagement with the discourses through which 'Ireland' has existed in the literary, ideological, and critical discourse of the twentieth-century stage. By refusing to replace the cultural constructions that he deconstructs, McDonagh's plays expose the very shallowness of their construction: depthlessness, then, is precisely the point. Furthermore, the critical reaction that has accompanied his plays is revealing about the critical reality of contemporary Irish criticism, characterized by its preoccupation with the politics of post-colonialism despite the fact that 'culture as social critique has given way to culture as economic commodity' in contemporary Ireland.[34] Merriman's view that McDonagh's plays postpone the process of decolonization, must be replaced with a view that the nationalist rhetoric of the post-colonial position in the 'deterritorialized' culture of contemporary Ireland[35] infers critical complicity in the continuing deferral of decolonization. Merriman may look to McDonagh's position as an artist for the resolution of his own anxiety about the complexities of a postmodern Irish identity, but he needs to look to his own ideological position for a resolution to the representational anxiety that McDonagh's plays provoke. For the 'Ireland' that Kiberd diagnosed as a 'fiction created … in response to specific needs at a precise moment in British history' is an 'Ireland' that is being constantly re-invented by contemporary cultural and critical practices, and the cultural critic and the consumer, not just the artist, must take responsibility for the role that criticism and consumption plays in the process of 'national' representation.

In a review of *The Cripple of Inishmaan* at the New York Irish Arts Centre, the first of McDonagh's plays to arrive on (or, rather, just off) Broadway, Fintan O'Toole asks 'Can McDonagh's work survive outside its native element?' The answer he gives is an 'unquestionable yes'.[36] For McDonagh's work has less currency with post-colonial nativism, than with the social and cultural formations of the transnational postmodern globalized world. If, as the post-colonial position exemplified by Merriman suggests, effective strategies of decolonization are still wanting, the cultural critic as well as the artist must engage with the politics of the globalized world, whereby post-colonial nativism is replaced by hybrid multinationalism that can be accommodated on both the local and the global level.

The ambiguous critical response to McDonagh's plays, then, as well as the postmodern strategies of representation that McDonagh employs, expose the narrowness of national self-definition in Ireland, the narrowness of the representational strategies of the theatrical tradition, and the narrowness of the post-colonial critical tools that have been employed to deconstruct and de-legitimate the 'authenticity' of his plays.

But McDonagh has lately turned away from Ireland as a site of representation towards Eastern Europe, and the critical reaction to his most recent play *The Pillowman* has been (surprise, surprise) highly ambiguous. McDonagh's refusal to specify the exact site of the play's location, however, adds another layer of significance to the argument. Whether interpreted as a deliberate strategy to avoid the controversy that surrounded his Irish plays or as a strategy of reinforcement of his postmodern position, his plays demand to be read from the position of the contemporary globalized world, where 'the local is not a site of liberation but manipulation'[37] and culture is not an essentialized strategy for the representation of an authentic national self, but a commodity of negotiation and exchange.

Dirlik would agree, and he prescribes the way forward through a return to the fundamental reality that drives all discursive ideologies: power. Dirlik insists that post-colonial criticism needs to shake off 'the cover of culture'[38] and look to contemporary material reality, where it will find that the politics of post-colonial subjectivity have been transcended by the transnational politics of global capitalism. Dirlik insists that global capitalism is of fundamental importance to both the 'social and political formations' and the 'cultural/epistemological formations' of contemporary post-colonial reality[39]: but it is only through engaging with changing social and political formations that the cultural and epistemological tools that we use to understand the world can be reformulated for contemporary reality.

---

[1] Gerry Smyth, *Decolonisation and Irish Criticism: The Construction of Irish Literature* (London: Pluto Press, 1998), p.20.

[2] David Cairns and Shaun Richards, *Writing Ireland: Colonialism, Nationalism and Culture* (Manchester: Manchester University Press, 1988), p1.

[3] Ibid., p.14.

[4] Seamus Deane, as quoted in Cairns and Richards, p.148.

[5] Declan Kiberd, *Inventing Ireland: The Literature of the Modern Nation* (London: Vintage, 1995), p.2.

[6] Helen Gilbert and Joanne Tompkins, *Post-colonial Drama: Theory, Practice, Politics* (London: Routledge,1996), p.3.

[7] Kiberd, p.7.

[8] Kiberd, p.641.

[9] See Smyth, pp.10-14 for the implications of nationalism in a post-colonial context.

[10] See Ania Loomba, Chapter 1, *Colonialism/Post-colonialism* (London: Routledge, 1998) for an analysis of the potential critical fallacies of post-colonial practice; or Gayatri Spivak in *The Post-colonial Critic: Interviews, Strategies, Dialogues*, ed. Sarah Harasym (New York; London: Routledge, 1990), who incorporates the idea of 'strategic essentialism' into the fabric of her post-colonial position. For other critics who take on these

limitations as part of their own theoretical practice see Arif Dirlik, *The Post-colonial Aura: Third World Criticism in the Age of Global Capitalism* (Boulder: Westview Press, 1997) or Bob Hodge and Vijay Mishra, 'What is Post (-) Colonialism?' in *Colonial Discourse and Post-colonial Theory: A Reader*, eds., Laura Chrisman and Patrick Williams (New York: Columbia University Press,1994), pp.276-290.

[11] Christopher Murray, *Twentieth Century Irish Theatre: Mirror up to Nation.* (Manchester; New York: Manchester University Press, 1997), p.7.

[12] Victor Merriman, 'Decolonisation Postponed: The Theatre of Tiger Trash', *Irish University Review* 29:2 (Autumn/Winter 1999), p.311.

[13] Ibid., p.312.

[14] Smyth, p.26.

[15] Merriman, p.312.

[16] Merriman, p.314.

[17] Ibid., p.314.

[18] Ibid., p.312.

[19] Ibid., p.310.

[20] Colin Graham, *Deconstructing Ireland: Identity, Theory, Culture* (Edinburgh: Edinburgh University Press, 2001), p.ix.

[21] Smyth, p.15.

[22] Smyth, p.98.

[23] Loomba, p.9.

[24] David Lloyd, *Anomalous States: Irish Writing and the Post-colonial Moment* (Dublin: Lilliput, 1993), p.56.

[25] Michael Cronin, *Reinventing Ireland: Culture and the Celtic Tiger*, eds Luke Gibbons and Peader Kirby (London: Pluto, 2002).

[26] 'Martin McDonagh creates problems in that he grew up in London and visited Ireland only occasionally. But because his parents are Irish, and his plays are about Ireland and are regularly produced in Ireland, McDonagh is included in the recent *A History of Irish Theatre: 1601- 2000* by Christopher Morash.' Steve Wilmer, 'On Writing National Histories' in *Writing and Rewriting National Theatre Histories*, ed. Steve Wilmer (Iowa City :University of Iowa Press, 2004), p.19.

[27] Blake Green, 'New Directions', *Newsday* 7 June 1998.

[28] Fintan O'Toole,'Review of the *Beauty Queen of Leenane*', in *Critical Moments: Fintan O'Toole on Modern Irish Theatre*, eds Julia Furay and Redmond O'Hanlon (Dublin: Carysfort Press, 2003), p.159.

[29] Nicholas Grene, *The Politics of Irish Drama* (Cambridge: Cambridge University Press, 1999), p.262.

[30] See particularly José Lanters, 'Playwrights of the Western World: Synge, Murphy, McDonagh' in *A Century of Irish Drama: Widening the Stage*, eds. Stephen Watt, Eileen Morgan, Shakir Mustafa (Bloomington: Indiana University Press, 2000), pp.204-290 and Michal Lachman, 'Happy and in Exile' in *Engaging Modernity: Readings of Irish Politics, Culture and Literature at the End of the Century*, eds. Michael Boss and Eamon Maher (Dublin: Veritas, 2003), pp.194-204.

[31] Loomba, p.240.

[32] See Dirlik, 1997, and Linda Hutcheon, 'Circling the downspout of empire' in *Past the Last Post: Theorising Post-colonialism and Postmodernism*, eds Jan Adam and Helen Tiffin (Hemel Hempstead: Harvester Wheatsheaf, 1991), p.167-189.

[33] Christopher Morash, *A History of Irish Theatre 1690-2000* (Cambridge: Cambridge University Press, 2002), p.269.

[34] Kirby, Cronin, Gibbons, p.2.

[35] Patrick Lonergan, 'Recent Irish Theatre: The Impact of Globalisation' in *New Voices in Irish Criticism : 4*, eds. Fionnuala Dillane and Ronan Kelly (Dublin: Four Courts, 2003), p.28.

[36] Fintan O' Toole, 'Review of *The Cripple of Inishmaan*', in *Critical Moments: Fintan O'Toole on Modern Irish Theatre*, eds Furay and O'Hanlon, p.183.

[37] Dirlik, 1997, p.96.

[38] Ibid., p.68.

[39] Ibid., p.73.

20 | Martin McDonagh, Globalization, and Irish Theatre Criticism[1]

Patrick Lonergan[2]

> The Laughter Will Come of Itself. The Tears Are Inevitable.

Introduction: the McDonagh enigma

At the 2003 annual conference of the International Association for the Study of Irish Literatures (held in Debrecen, Hungary, in July 2003), a special panel discussed the works of Martin McDonagh. The event was well attended, and the papers presented in it were of the highest quality, yet there was an unmistakable sense of frustration and weariness in the debate that ensued – one participant even proposed that, owing to the impossibility of gaining agreement on the quality, authenticity, or importance of McDonagh's work, no further discussion of it should take place until his *oeuvre* had developed sufficiently to allow for greater critical consensus.

Such frustration has been evident in discussions about McDonagh since shortly after *The Beauty Queen of Leenane* premiered in Galway in 1996, with opinion about his work usually falling into one of two apparently irreconcilable extremes: the belief that he is cleverly subverting stereotypes of the Irish, and the conviction that, on the contrary, he is exploiting those stereotypes, earning a great deal of money by making the Irish look like a nation of morons. Discussing the literature on this subject, John Waters neatly frames this polarization as involving a clash between those who think that McDonagh's work represents 'the search for truth' and those who state that it instead serves 'the appetite for delusion'.[3] Any review of these debates will quickly show why discourse about McDonagh appears to have become exhausted: there is strong evidence to support both sides of the argument.

Those who believe that McDonagh's plays facilitate a search for truth might point to Irish audiences' enthusiastic responses to the original Druid Theatre/Royal Court co-production of *The Leenane Trilogy* (1997). There are many ways of explaining that enthusiasm. The plays can be seen in the context of the Irish comic tradition of absurdism combined with gallows humour – a striking feature of the novels of Flann O'Brien and the drama of Samuel Beckett, and an important presence throughout Irish literature, as discussed by Vivian Mercier in *The Irish Comic Tradition*. Furthermore, they cover thematic ground very familiar to Irish audiences: their treatment of emigration, for example, locates them firmly in the tradition of such plays as Brian Friel's *Philadelphia, Here I Come!* (1964) or Tom Murphy's *Conversations on a Homecoming* (1985).

However, the plays' popularity may best be explained by the way in which they allowed Irish audiences to confront many of the changes that occurred during the 'Celtic Tiger' period of economic prosperity and social transformation in Ireland. Each play in *The Leenane Trilogy* represents one of the major authorities in Irish life – *The Beauty Queen of Leenane* deals with the family, *A Skull in Connemara* with the law, and *The Lonesome West* with the church – at a time when the power of those authorities in Ireland was being eroded by revelations about political corruption, child abuse, and institutional incompetence. It is unlikely that any member of McDonagh's audience in Ireland would have mistaken his representations of the country as accurate or authentic, but the popularity of *The Leenane Trilogy* can be understood in terms of its skewed representation of these – and many other – uncomfortable truths to Irish audiences. The plays presented the music of Dana as if it were irrelevant Irish kitsch two years before that singer became a Member of the European Parliament for a constituency that includes Leenane and the Aran Islands, where all but one of McDonagh's plays are set. They presented familial murder in a

pseudo-gothic style at a time when the Irish media were dubbing
Catherine Nevin a 'black widow' during her trial for the murder of
her husband in March 1996.[4] The plays' dramatic power was based
on the revelation of deeply buried secrets – something they had in
common with the legal tribunals established to dig into the pasts of
some of Ireland's most prominent politicians. *A Skull in
Connemara's* presentation of an inept policeman coincided with a
growing Irish anxiety about the ability of the Irish police force to
cope with organized crime, particularly after the assassination of
Veronica Guerin in June 1996. And in Father Welsh, a well-
intentioned priest whose sense of his growing obsolescence leads
him to suicide, *The Lonesome West* presents audiences with an
interesting analogy for the status of the Irish Catholic Church,
which had been declining throughout the 1990s: like the plastic
figures of saints in that play, the Church was experiencing a form
of meltdown. Judged from the perspective of the society in which
– and for which – they were first produced, McDonagh's plays
certainly do not appear to have facilitated escapism, delusion, or
any of the other responses that critics would later attribute to Irish
audiences.

The notion that McDonagh's work might serve an appetite for
delusion did not gain currency until Irish commentators began to
consider productions of his work overseas – where, occasionally,
his plays *did* appear to reinforce negative ways of thinking about
the Irish. As Fricker puts it, many thought that McDonagh's depiction of the Irish is 'particularly problematic when it's exported',
because 'it feeds the whole *Angela's Ashes* view of Ireland. When it
travels, it's taken at face value'.[5] Some of those reactions may be
explained by the prevalence of popular misconceptions about
Ireland. Yet even as distinguished and well-informed a critic as
Michael Billington could tell his *Guardian* readers that McDonagh's
aim in *The Trilogy* was not to challenge Irish stereotypes, or to
critique contemporary Irish society, but to suggest bluntly that 'the
reality [about Ireland] [...] is *murder,* self-slaughter, spite, ignorance
and familial hatred' (emphasis added).[6] It is hardly surprising that
such (deluded) commentary generated coverage in Ireland and, as
early as January 1997, an *Irish Times* article was already drawing the
public's attention to what critics, referring to the divergence of

responses to McDonagh's work, were calling the 'McDonagh Enigma'.[7]

Views about McDonagh continued to diverge between 1997 and 2001, when an increased focus on the authenticity of his work provoked a critical and popular backlash in Ireland and Great Britain. Richard Eyre (former artistic director of the Royal National Theatre, which premiered McDonagh's *The Cripple of Inishmaan*) and Nicholas Wright relate this decline directly to the British public's concern that McDonagh was exploiting Irish stereotypes: '[W]hen McDonagh, in his many media appearances, turned out to be a chic young guy, wearing the nicest Armani suit you've ever seen and sporting a marked South London accent, bemusement turned to fury. 'If this is an Irish playwright, I'm a banana,' cried the chorus'.[8] Leaving aside this interesting opposition of the terms *chic young guy* and *Irish playwright*, these comments encapsulate British attitudes to McDonagh very well.

Such attitudes appeared to strengthen in the late 1990s, as both the Royal Court and the Royal National Theatre refused to stage *The Lieutenant of Inishmore*, with many commentators interpreting this absence of McDonagh's plays from London's stages as evidence that his career was already over. Writing in 2001, Aleks Sierz declared:

> After [McDonagh] compared himself to the young Orson Welles, claiming to be 'the greatest' and attacking older playwrights for being 'so ugly' and 'really badly dressed,' his sudden decline seemed like a comeuppance.[9]

Such reports proved premature, however, as first *The Lieutenant of Inishmore* (2001) and then *The Pillowman* (2003) were produced in England and elsewhere to acclaim.

With the production of *The Lieutenant*, the divergence between Irish and non-Irish interpretations of McDonagh became more marked. Premiered by the Royal Shakespeare Company in April 2001, McDonagh's play about terrorism provoked controversy for its treatment of animals when it debuted, but became unexpectedly pertinent after the 11 September 2001 attacks in the United States – following which it transferred from Stratford to a hit season in the West End. Subsequent productions took place outside the United Kingdom, where the play's mercilessly satirical treatment of terrorism often resonated with – and perhaps reassured – audiences in countries being affected by the emergence of the so-called 'war against terror'. For example, in December 2003, Mehmet Ergen directed his own translation of the play in Turkey, only weeks after a series of devastating terrorist bombs in Istanbul. The reception of the play was therefore strongly conditioned by Turkish audiences' actual confrontation with terrorism. Indeed, Susannah Clapp writes that 'some of the cast thought they should cancel [the production]. They had all heard about people picking up body parts in the streets; the play ends with body parts strewn over the stage'.[10]

Similarly, in September 2003, Australia's Company B produced *The Lieutenant* at the Belvoir Street Theatre in Sydney. One context for the production was, undoubtedly, the October 2002 terrorist bombings of a Bali nightclub frequented mainly by Australians. But the director of the play, Neil Armfeld, included *The Lieutenant* in a season that addressed his sense that Australia's political direction under Prime Minister John Howard was 'shameful'. Armfeld stated that, in Australian society, 'we're being taught values that don't seem to represent good parenting – where is the sense of the primacy of tolerance, understanding, sympathy, generosity? [...] We've been yoked to the preemptive assertion of power, and it doesn't seem the right way to go. It's about fear, not trust'. [11] This reference to the 'pre-emptive assertion of power' is an obvious allusion to Australia's participation in the war against Iraq, suggesting that the reception of *The Lieutenant* in that country was conditioned by Armfeld's critique of his government's militarism in Afghanistan and Iraq.

While Ireland was not isolated from these events, an Irish audience at *The Lieutenant* would inevitably receive the play more as a direct statement about the Troubles in Northern Ireland than an exploration of the post-9/11 geopolitical map. Accordingly, the Irish premiere of the play in October 2003 generated many negative reactions. Programmed for only five performances during the Dublin Theatre Festival, word of mouth seems to have led to diminishing interest in the production, with the result that its final performances were poorly attended. The healthy advance sales for the play imply that this decline was probably due as much to the inadequate standard of acting in the touring Royal Shakespeare Company production, as to audiences' difficulties with the play's theme. Nevertheless, it is possible to raise many objections to its content. McDonagh's representation of Irish terrorism as arising from primitive, tribal barbarism – rather than politics, economics, class, or colonialism – might appeal to some audiences in countries on the front line of the 'war against terror', but in Ireland, the representation of terrorists as mindless butchers is thought to be an impediment to the resolution of conflict.[12] It might therefore have seemed to an Irish audience that the most primitive aspect of *The Lieutenant* was not the mindset of the terrorists on stage, but McDonagh's representation of Irish politics.

More importantly, however, most Irish audiences must have been aware that many of the 'jokes' in *The Lieutenant* refer to actual IRA atrocities. McDonagh's line about the terrorist murder of children[13] might play as an outraged authorial attack on terrorism outside Ireland – but in the country itself, it seems a deeply tasteless reference to the 1993 IRA bombing of Warrington, which caused the death of two children. Similarly, the play's references to the murder of Australians, and to Padraic's loss of his list of 'valid targets' on a bus, seem an attempt to make Irish audiences laugh at real events in recent Irish history. The problem here, it could be argued, is not that the play is inauthentic, but that it is insufficiently respectful of actual victims of real terrorist atrocities.

The productions in Istanbul, Sydney, and Dublin all appeared within four months of each other, but provoked a variety of responses. Audiences in Istanbul must have seen the play in relation to the atrocities carried out within a very short distance of the theatre itself. Conversely, audiences in Sydney were invited to see it in the context of Armfeld's protest against the foreign policy of the Australian government. McDonagh says that *The Lieutenant* was written from a position of 'pacifist rage' and that it is a 'violent play that is wholeheartedly anti-violence').[14] It is interesting that the play was presented in Istanbul mainly in the context of terrorist violence, whereas in Australia it was presented as a condemnation of state violence. Yet in Ireland itself, the play's presentation seemed not to condemn terrorism, but to be a glib trivialization of it.

The Leenane Trilogy may have resonated with Irish audiences' preoccupations in the late 1990s, just as audiences in Australia and Turkey found *The Lieutenant* relevant to their societies' confrontation with terrorism. Conversely, international reactions to *The Lieutenant* and *The Leenane Trilogy* can, from an Irish perspective, seem deluded. Perhaps, then, the solution to the 'McDonagh enigma' does not involve deciding whether his works facilitate the search for truth or the appetite for delusion, but in the acceptance that they facilitate *both*: that they mean different things to different audiences at different times.

So, although McDonagh's plays travel freely throughout the world as examples of 'Irish' drama, and although they have attracted attention mainly from scholars of Irish literature, their production and reception are nevertheless often determined by factors that have little to do with Irish history, culture, or politics. Hence, the difficulty for critics is not with establishing the truth of McDonagh's plays, but in our insistence on applying the term *Irish* to work that can be fully understood only in a global context.

Accordingly, I want to suggest that the impact of globalization on the production and reception of theatre requires new ways of thinking about Irish theatre criticism. And from that suggestion arises an important question: how can a theatre criticism that styles itself as national – as Irish criticism currently does – meaningfully address the work of such writers as McDonagh, whose reputation and reception are so strongly predetermined by global factors?

Globalization and theatre

Although the term *globalization* is widely used, little consensus exists about what it ought to define,[15] or about whether it can operate usefully as a critical category. As Roland Robertson observes, the term is 'often used very loosely and, indeed, in contradictory ways'. For Marshall McLuhan, globalization could be represented as a 'global village', but for Michael Hardt and Antonio Negri, it is 'Empire'. Some believe that we live in a 'new international information order', others that we are trapped in a 'McWorld', and being 'coca colo-nized'.[16] We are told that globalization represents something new, yet both Christianity and Islam showed globalizing tendencies, as did sixteenth-century conquest and nineteenth-century imperialism. And, as Tom Standage shows in *The Victorian Internet*, a process of technology-driven global compression has been underway since the middle of the nineteenth century – initiated by the invention of the telegraph, accelerated by the development of aviation, radio, and television, and firmly established with the growth of the Internet.

When faced with this mass of confusing and frequently contradictory information, 'globalization' can, as Zygmunt Bauman notes, often appear to be little more than

> a fad word fast turning into a shibboleth, a magic incantation, a pass-key meant to unlock the gates to all present and future mysteries. For some, 'globalization' is what we are bound to do if we wish to be happy; for others 'globalization' is the cause of our unhappiness. For everybody, though, 'globalization' is the intractable fate of the world.[17]

This term therefore seems generally problematic. In an Irish context, its use might also seem pointless. As Nicholas Grene writes, since at least the time of Boucicault, Irish drama has been 'created as much to be viewed from outside as from inside Ireland',[18] and this remains the case at present, as the global popularity of Martin McDonagh attests. The international elements of Irish literature may be explained in relation to many historical phenomena – colonialism, transatlantic exchange, the spread of Christianity, and so on. One might therefore wonder what can be gained from adding a poorly defined concept to an already crowded discursive framework.

Although the international profile of McDonagh may be compared to that of Boucicault, it may also be considered in the context of a growing mobility of theatre practitioners everywhere. Since 2000, Neil Labute and David Mamet have produced new work in London, the British directors Richard Eyre, Trevor Nunn, and Nicholas Hytner have premiered work in New York, and Edward Bond first produced *The Crime of the Twenty-First Century* in Dublin. Such cases show that the historical mobility of writers and companies in Ireland is comparable to that currently pertaining in many other countries. This mobility cannot be explained exclusively in terms of Ireland's status as a small or post-colonial country, since it is a feature of theatre not only in such countries as Denmark or India, but also in Britain and the United States.

Robertson's definition of globalization is useful here. 'Globalization', he writes, 'refers to both the compression of the world and the *intensification of consciousness* of the world as a whole' (emphasis added)[19]; that is, globalization does not just transform geographical relations, but alters the manner in which the world is perceived. Harvey defines this phenomenon as 'time-space compression', a process that 'so revolutionize[s] the objective qualities of space and time that we are forced to alter, sometimes in quite radical ways, how we represent the world to ourselves'.[20] Accordingly, globalization may be defined as a 'social process in which the constraints of geography on economic, political, social and cultural arrangements recede, in which people become increasingly aware that they are receding and [...] act accordingly'.[21]

Globalization does not alter geography, but instead produces a *phenomenology of compression*: the world is not becoming physically smaller, but our understanding of the relations between different physical and temporal spaces *has* altered. This means that, although globalization has resulted in increased opportunities for some theatre practitioners to travel, its most significant effect has been that the production and reception of theatre is now increasingly determined by global factors, rather than national or local ones. This has many consequences, but its main effect is that the growth of opportunities for international touring – coupled with audiences' and critics' increased access to global media – has altered the way that plays are produced and studied.

I propose that it is possible when analysing these developments to note six tendencies in the globalization of world theatre. This grouping is necessarily formulaic but, to varying degrees, each of the following characteristics will be found in theatre productions that are produced for international diffusion:

The use of branding to manage risk
The abrogation of localizing references
The promotion of reflexivity rather than universality
The promotion of mobility, which leads to localization
The emergence of a globalized discourse about theatre
The inhibition of intercultural exchange.

The economies of scale involved in international theatre productions bring large financial rewards, but also carry financial risks. As a way of offsetting these risks, production companies often use instantly recognizable markers that encourage audiences to visit a production without knowing anything about the play being produced, or the culture from which it emerged. Such markers frequently include the presence of celebrity actors in the cast, or the inclusion in the crew of a director who has won internationally recognized awards, such as Oscars or Tonys. Frequently, the national origins of a play are emphasized as a way of signifying its content. For example, plays from the developing world are often marketed for their authenticity.[22] I want briefly to sketch the way in which nationality becomes part of the branding process by examining the way in which plays from England are increasingly marketed for their sophistication when presented in the United States.

In 2003, Vanessa Redgrave's performance in *Long Day's Journey into Night* and Simon Russell Beale's appearance in *Uncle Vanya* and *Twelfth Night* were widely praised – with the *New York Times*'s Ben Brantley declaring (apparently without irony) that Beale's 'posture alone makes two trips to the Brooklyn Academy a necessity for connoisseurs of acting'. The thematic complexity of the many English plays produced or toured in America during the year is also noteworthy. Peter Nichols' *A Day in the Death of Joe Egg* is about a couple raising a disabled child; Nicholas Wright's *Vincent in Brixton* is about Van Gogh; *Continental Divide* by David Edgar is an anatomization of American politics since the 1960s; and *Humble Boy* by Charlotte Jones includes astrophysics among its themes. American theatregoers' admiration for the acting of Redgrave and Beale, together with the thematic complexity of these four plays, offers a useful indicator of the kinds of English work currently being produced in America: plays that include refined, elegant acting best appreciated by 'connoisseurs', and a plot that cites – but does not elaborate upon – such weighty themes as astrophysics or modern art. This may be seen as an example of theatre being driven by branding.

Another consequence of risk management is the abrogation from theatre of localizing references that might impede audiences' appreciation of the action presented onstage. Hence, many producers now emphasize visual spectacle over language. Franco Moretti's analysis of the recent success of Hollywood action movies offers a useful model for what is happening in theatre:

> [S]tories travel well because they are largely *independent of language.* [...] This relative autonomy of the story-line explains the ease with which action films dispense with words, replacing them with sheer noise (explosions, crashes, gunshots, screams ...); while *this brisk dismissal of language, in turn, facilitates their international diffusion,* ... (second emphasis added).[23]

A third tendency is for plays to be received reflexively. Miriam Bratu Hansen usefully describes reflexivity in relation to classical Hollywood cinema, which

> succeeded as an international modernist idiom on a mass basis [...] not because of its presumably universal narrative form but because it meant *different things to different people, and publics, both at home and abroad.* We must not forget that these films, along with other mass cultural exports, were consumed in locally quite specific, and unequally developed, contexts and conditions of *reception* (emphases added).[24]

The growth of a global touring circuit has led to the development of a growing number of plays that do not attempt to be universal or local, but, rather, attempt to make themselves sufficiently open to interpretation to be understood in different ways by different audiences. Examples of such varying interpretations are the international responses to *The Lieutenant*, discussed above.

The abrogation of localizing references and the promotion of reflexivity allow companies to capitalize on opportunities for touring and joint production, to free themselves from what director Adrian Noble termed 'the tyranny of buildings'.[25] This may lead to conflict because, at a time when theatres want to be mobile, local communities need theatres to be firmly focused on their immediate environment. '*Local transformation* is as much a part of globalization as the lateral extension of social connections across time and space', notes Giddens,[26] implying that globalization leads also to *localization*. As Bauman explains, '[L]ocalities are losing their meaning-generating and meaning-negotiating capacity and are increasingly dependent on sense-giving and interpreting actions which they do not control'.[27] The growth of global touring means that theatres may now determine their success not by the satisfaction levels of local audiences, but by their ability to tour overseas – an understandable if unsustainable situation. Hence, although British journalists write with pride about the successes of British drama in America (implying that American approval still matters in England), they are increasingly uncomfortable with the presence in the West End of so many American actors and plays, which is seen not only as a form of dumbing down, but often as cultural imperialism, or specifically, as Americanization.[28] Just as Britishness is invoked on Broadway as a signifier of sophistication, so is America invoked in the West End to explain commercialization, despite the fact that the development is driven by British theatre consortia, producers, and audiences.

Fourth, discourse about theatre is globalized, but not internationalized. With the globalization of media, British newspapers may easily report upon the success of English drama on Broadway – but rarely report on developments in American drama. Such reportage is thus not directed towards the promotion of links between American and British culture, but exists merely to give British audiences a broader perspective on issues that are of local importance to them. Furthermore, professional discourse about theatre is increasingly being written for an 'international reader' – a euphemism to describe an editorial process in which facts that require local knowledge in order to be widely understood are cut from texts. While this process may in some cases facilitate greater levels of understanding between cultures, its overall effect is to homogenize: the decision about what constitutes localized or specialized knowledge is almost always based on the decision of an editor, whose choices inevitably will be grounded in personalized and/or institutional notions of the constitution of 'normality'. Those notions frequently will be underwritten by corporate policies founded in competitive practices. The concept of the 'international audience' thus involves the use of universalist assumptionism within the rhetoric of borderlessness that comes with globalization. This development should be regarded with caution.

Finally, international touring tends to inhibit rather than promote intercultural exchange. As Patrice Pavis writes,

[O]ne may say that contemporary theatrical or choreographic production has become international, often for simple economic reasons: in this way artists and producers stand a much greater chance of making a profit, since their productions can be understood everywhere without adaptation. This may seem to justify them, but it also risks reinforcing national stereotypes. There is a great temptation to produce immediately exportable productions [...] But the internationalization of festivals and productions and the cosmopolitanism of certain groups [...] do not necessarily result in an intercultural experience. [29]

This is true of the Simon Russell Beale *Uncle Vanya*, toured by the Donmar Warehouse to America in 2003. The play is adapted by Brian Friel – an Irish writer – from a Russian text, produced in London by an English director (Sam Mendes) who had recently won an Oscar, before touring to New York, moving freely from one cultural centre to another with a set of instantly recognizable selling points. As such, it is an almost perfect blend of internationalization, commercialization, and mobility – three key features of globalization. Yet it would be wrong to exaggerate the level of cultural exchange occurring here: no specialized knowledge of British society or culture was required of American audiences to appreciate the play, nor was such knowledge imparted. American audiences were not asked to consider their relationship to Ireland, Britain, or Russia; nor were members of the original London audience encouraged to compare Britain under Blair to pre-revolutionary Russia, or to consider their place in the analogy between pre-independence Ireland and Russia. It would be insulting to those audiences to assume that none of them independently explored such issues. Nevertheless, *Uncle Vanya* shows that, despite the rhetoric of borderlessness that accompanies globalization, the production's mobility took place as a result of the exchange of a great deal of capital, but very little culture. Indeed, it could be argued that the mobility of the production mitigated against the exchange of culture.

The axes charted above are between global and local: events in London theatre are unlikely to be consequential in provincial Britain, any more than Broadway affects culture in middle America. Yet the national remains a definite presence in this discussion – not as a collection of characteristics requiring recognition and enumeration, but rather as a commodified abstraction, used for the purpose of branding a commercialized product. In order to establish whether this means that the national has no real bearing on theatre in a globalized world, I want to turn my attention now to the globalization of Irishness in world theatre.

Otherness and Irish theatre

The economics of the Irish stage are such that Irish writing has always been conditioned by the need to be accessible to audiences abroad. Grene's *The Politics of Irish Drama* explains how this has resulted in the figuration of Irishness as *other* in our theatre since (at least) the middle of the nineteenth century. To be viewed from inside Ireland, a play's action must be meaningful to an Irish audience; to be successful abroad, the central 'Irish' narrative must be framed or mediated in a way that will provide an interpretative or moral anchor for an urbanized, cosmopolitan audience assumed to be lacking in specialized knowledge of Ireland. In the nineteenth century, this involved the use of 'stage interpreters', such as the English gentlemen who populate Boucicault's Irish plays: characters whose interaction with feckless Irishness was not just the occasion of comedy, but also fulfilled an interpretative and mediative function for non-Irish audiences.[30]

However, an engagement with otherness may also stimulate the development of the self, and so the dramatists of the Irish Revival recalibrated Boucicault's presentation of otherness so that it could be used to construct an emergent national identity, with a 'stranger in the house' motif (a reference to Yeats' *Cathleen Ní Houlihan*) being the most common example of this strategy. The transformative power of otherness is a feature of the drama of many countries; but its purpose within the context of the Irish Revival was to imagine the possibility of a transformed Ireland, independent of colonial rule.

Despite the fact that Ireland achieved partial independence from Britain over eighty years ago, this motif has persisted into contemporary Irish drama. As Grene notes, '[O]n the whole Irish drama has continued to look to social margins for its setting, whether the western country districts or the working class inner city. It is thus typically other people that a largely middle-class urban audience watches in an Irish play, other people who speak differently – more colloquially, more comically, more poetically'.[31]

While it makes sense for a colonized culture to deploy ideas of otherness as a counter-hegemonic device, it is surprising that Irish drama continues to use this strategy. In some cases, it is used positively: many of the plays of Frank McGuinness turn on the dramatic consequences of the appearance of an outsider in a claustrophobic social setting, allowing McGuinness to posit gay sexuality as liberating and restorative of social justice. Given that homosexuality was decriminalized in Ireland only in 1993 – a decade after McGuinness's first works premiered – his drama is also an example of the capacity of theatre to counter oppressive legislation. However, the persistence of otherness may also have negative effects: Victor Merriman notes that many recent Irish plays use otherness to present a version of rural Ireland as a 'benighted dystopia'[32] and argues that the purpose of these presentations is to allow middle-class audiences to avoid facing their responsibilities for the genuinely marginalized members of Irish society.

There are many ways of understanding how otherness functions in Irish drama, but for the present purposes, its most important is the way in which it facilitates the international diffusion of Irish writing. The appeal to non-Irish audiences of such drama may be illustrated by Mikhail Bakhtin's consideration of otherness:

> In the realm of culture, outsidedness is a most powerful factor [...] We raise new questions for a foreign culture, ones that it did not raise for itself; we seek answers to our own questions in it; and the foreign culture responds to us by revealing to us its new aspects and new semantic depths. Without one's own questions one cannot creatively understand anything other or foreign. Such a dialogic encounter of two cultures does not result in merging or mixing.[33]

The inherent otherness of much Irish drama allows other cultures to answer their own questions creatively, without having to merge or mix with Irish culture itself: this was true in the time of Boucicault, and remains true for the reception of many Irish writers at present. The result is that the historic otherness of Irish drama has now been reconfigured to correspond with an inter-nationalized branding of Irishness as a consumable commodity.

This process has been underway for over a decade in the marketing of Irish popular music, international tourism, the production of food, clothing, and drink, and, most notably, in the spread of the 'Irish' pub.[34] This commodification of a nationalized abstraction is – unlike the Nike logo or the Intel Pentium noise – not a copyrighted brand owned and controlled by a centralizing authority, so it is difficult to define precisely. But it is possible to identify five characteristics in plays marketed internationally as 'Irish'.

First, Irish plays are frequently presented as undisciplined but not transgressive. These forms of ill discipline can be linguistic – so that Irish speech is received not as language in its own right, but as a deviation from standard speech; or they may be formal, so that (for example) although Gar in *Philadelphia, Here I Come!* is performed by two actors – one portraying his private thoughts, while the other enacts his public persona – audiences tend to respond most positively to the naturalism and authenticity of the play's rural Irish setting, rather than Friel's experimentation. And this ill discipline can be perceived in many ways, all of which tend to allow the audience to *reinforce* their sense of normality.

A second tendency is for Irish plays to be perceived as representing 'authenticity' or primitivism, so that, to borrow a phrase from Merriman, the work on stage is received as 'nature' to the audience's 'culture'.[35] This can occur in many ways: Irish violence is represented as being primal or tribal, as discussed above in relation to *The Lieutenant of Inishmore*. Many Irish plays are set in the least populated parts of the country, locating the action not in a society but in a landscape. And a naturally poetic quality is frequently attributed to Irish speech.

Perhaps the most common example of this phenomenon is the cliché that the overdependence on textuality in Irish drama arises not from a lack of investment in production, but from a natural Irish ability to tell stories – which the rest of the modernized world has apparently lost, we are told. Such interpretations may be understood as indicators of audiences' desire for escapism, with 'Ireland' being offered as a reassuring counterpoint to the world to which audiences will return when they step from the theatre into the urbanized, prosaic, and commercialized space of Broadway, the

West End, or theatreland in any city's downtown (including, it is worth noting, the cities of Ireland itself).

Third, Irish work is typically received as reflexive rather than universal. This means that an Irish play will not promote one theme that everyone agrees upon, but that the play's theme will be sufficiently vague for audiences to relate the action to their own lives and localities. An excellent example of this is Friel's *Translations* (1980). The play is a success because it can allow people in such cities as Prague and Barcelona to explore their own different linguistic histories and their relationships to other dominant linguistic traditions nearby (though this of course is not the only interpretation possible in such places). On the other hand, audiences in countries where language is less contested – such as the United States or England – can respond to the play's exploration of the instability and flexibility of identity, which are important issues in those countries. The strength of the play – as is the case with many of Friel's works – is not that it presents a universal situation, but that, to return to Hansen's phrase, it 'meant different things to different people',[36] or that, as Grene writes, audiences everywhere 'loved it, though, for significantly different reasons'.[37]

The fourth feature of the reception of Irishness on the globalized stage is that it is arbitrary: it is in no way dependent for its currency on any form of Irishness that actually exists. Not all Irish plays will be marketed for their Irishness, as the Gate Theatre have shown in their international tours of work by writers such as Ayckbourn and Pinter.[38] Similarly, not all plays marketed as Irish are from Ireland – so that *The Weir*, *The Steward of Christendom*, and *The Cripple of Inishmaan* all played down the high level of British involvement in their productions when they visited New York, whereas *The Pillowman* emphasized its origins in London.[39]

Finally, the Irish brand is commodified – it has market value in relation to other products, and that value can rise and fall. So in 2003, Simon Russell Beale's posture was considered to be a more marketable aspect of *Uncle Vanya* than Friel's script – yet a decade earlier, Friel was being held up as an example of precisely the kind of work to which the British theatre should aspire.

These five features are not necessarily applicable to every Irish play, but they offer a useful way of understanding many of the important debates in recent Irish drama. Although it is possible for an Irish play to do good business overseas without having its Irishness emphasized, plays that actively challenge audiences' preconceptions about 'Irish' work will usually be received with hostility, as was most recently shown with the American premiere of Marina Carr's *On Raftery's Hill*.[40] And, as is illustrated by the example above of Michael Billington's interpretation of McDonagh's work as representative of Irish 'reality', responses to Irish plays may sometimes appear to be grounded in an understanding of the country that is shallow or sentimentalized, even from critics who write brilliantly about other writers. It is noteworthy that responses to 'Irish' plays rarely involve a consideration of technique or politics, but instead focus on the emotional elements of the production – finding primitivism rather than simplicity, authenticity rather than poverty, nostalgia rather than regret. Or – as Billington has it – finding 'murder, self-slaughter, spite, ignorance and familial hatred' where an Irish audience may find a complex representation of a transforming Ireland.[41]

This might help us to understand the reception of Martin McDonagh. His work clearly feeds into preconceptions about Irish ill discipline and primitivism. The market value of his work between 1996 and 2006 has risen, fallen, and been resurrected again, with his Irishness appearing and disappearing from media discussions of his plays' significance. But the actual Irish qualities of the work itself – the cultural references, the linguistic idiosyncrasies – generally appear not to be very well understood abroad; nor do audiences appear particularly interested in understanding them. This can be illustrated from a comparison of two international productions of *The Cripple of Inishmaan* – one in Illinois, the other in New Zealand.

A central, if neglected, feature of McDonagh's theatre is how it explores the divergence between representation and reality. One of the finest examples of this divergence occurs in *The Cripple of Inishmaan*. The audience is moved by the apparent death of the play's protagonist Billy, whose last words are given in detail:

Mam? I fear I'm not longer for this world, Mam. Can't I hear the wail of the banshees for me, as far as I am from me barren island home? A home barren, aye, but proud and generous with it, yet turned me back on ye I did, to end up alone and dying in a one-dollar rooming-house, without a mother to wipe the cold sweat off me, nor a father to curse God o'er the death of me, nor a colleen fair to weep tears o'er the still body of me. A body still, aye, but a body noble and unbowed with it. An Irishman! (52)

This scene includes huge levels of stage-Irishry and is a good example of many of the tendencies referred to above, particularly in McDonagh's use of language, and his inclusion of references to banshees, fair colleens, and barren island homes. Yet audiences are being primed to receive this representation as authentic and to react emotionally to the action's sentimental qualities. Those audiences are then challenged by the realization that what they had taken to be reality was in fact a screen test for a Hollywood movie, and that Billy was not only unsuccessful in his attempts to gain the part for which he'd been auditioning, but contemptuous of the lines he'd been speaking:

> **Billy:** [...] it wasn't an awful big thing at all to turn down
> Hollywood, with the arse-faced lines they had me reading for them.
> 'Can I not hear the wail of the banshees for me, as far as I am from
> me barren island home.'
> **Bartley** *laughs*
> **Billy:** 'An Irishman I am, begora! With a heart and a spirit on me
> not crushed for a hundred years of oppression. I'll be getting me
> shillelagh out next, wait'll you see.' A rake of shite. And had me
> singing the fecking 'Croppy Boy' then (63).

McDonagh's point here is clear: he is neither creating nor exploiting images of stage-Irish characters; rather, he is drawing attention to his audiences' willingness to accept such images uncritically. This offers clear evidence against the proposition that McDonagh is exploiting Irish stereotypes.

The difficulty, however, is that the persistence of globalized images of Irishness means that many theatre producers appear unaware of these elements of McDonagh's work. For example, in a program note for the Theatre of Western Springs 2003 production of *The Cripple of Inishmaan*, director Dorothy Parlaw introduces the play as follows:

> Beautiful Ireland ... the modulations of the light, the surprising moments of the rain. Tonight we are telling a great little story; one-half laughter, one-half tears [...] When two or three Irishmen get together ... whether in the kitchen or a pub, a song-fest is inevitable. As in a junket of storytelling, these song-fests reveal two sides of the Irish: the laughter and the tears. They create a beautiful whole, like the weaving together of the glorious colors in an Irish shawl, the purples, the roses, the greens, and the blues. So sit back and relax, and enjoy the Cripple's adventures. No great lesson, no great theme – just a story. The laughter will come of itself. The tears are inevitable.

When we discover the words *rain* and *surprising* in the same sentence, it becomes apparent that the writer's understanding of Ireland might be deficient in some important respects; nevertheless, she considers herself qualified to direct her audience's reception of the play. There is 'no great lesson' in this 'little story', Parlow writes, promising to use the 'Cripple's adventures' to show audiences the two halves of the Irish character – laughter *and* tears – that together make up our beautiful, shawl-like, whole. This clearly is not the kind of language likely to encourage an audience to go looking for a sophisticated interplay of images, clichés, and stereotypes.

There are, however, many positive treatments of the play. *The Cripple of Inishmaan* was produced by the Court Theatre in Christchurch, New Zealand, in 1998 – but with an entirely different approach. That theatre's program (2003)[42] for the production included background information about McDonagh, the Aran Islands, Robert Flaherty, and many other aspects of the play, drawing attention to its resemblances to the works of both Synge and Pinter. The theatre also produced an education resource kit, which included an interesting 'before and after' exercise: student audiences were asked before the show to write down three stereotypes commonly associated with the Irish; they then had to consult their list at the end of the show and consider how McDonagh had undermined their preconceptions. Drawing attention to the difference between the world that 'we live in' and the 'world [that] is imagined by others', the booklet asked student audiences to consider how the play might apply to New Zealand (10).

This is an example of how, with the mediation of well-informed theatre professionals, a globalized theatre product such as *The Cripple of Inishmaan* may stimulate a localized response of meaning-generation. As Appadurai puts it, 'There is growing evidence that the consumption of the mass media throughout the world often provokes resistance, irony, selectivity, and, in general, *agency*'.[43] The audiences at Christchurch probably learned little of lasting significance about Ireland, but McDonagh's playful use of that audience's familiarity with globalized images of Irishness did appear to inspire agency: they were able to respond to the play as a work of art that allowed them to refocus their relationship with their own locality. That the production at the Theatre of Western Springs appears to have been sold on a mass-mediated piece of Celtic schlock is regrettable. But the example of Christchurch suggests that there is a need to avoid simplifying the international reception of McDonagh's work. I want therefore to conclude by considering how the globalization of Martin McDonagh's drama might inspire agency in Ireland.

McDonagh and Irish theatre criticism

Ireland is not unique in being stereotyped on the global stage. Nevertheless, a resolution of the 'McDonagh enigma' requires a focus on the possibility that non-Irish audiences' reception of Irish plays may be influenced by stereotypes and simplifications. McDonagh's use of language, for example, plays into contradictory stereotypes: his characters' dialogue is engaging but inarticulate, which means that audiences can simultaneously believe that the Irish are a nation of poets while also believing we are a nation of feckin' eejits. It is important to avoid simplistic responses to this situation: it would be too easy to describe it as involving a clash between Irish audiences' 'correct' interpretations and foreign audiences' 'mistakes'. In a globalized environment, there is little basis for privileging Irish interpretations over anyone else's – especially since only three of McDonagh's six plays (*The Leenane Trilogy*) were originally conceived for an Irish audience (the other three having been premiered in England).

The question of whether McDonagh is exploiting or subverting stereotypes is not so much unanswerable as irrelevant. As demonstrated by the discussion above of *The Cripple of Inishmaan*, it is possible to prove that McDonagh is doing a great deal to challenge the reception of Irishness abroad, since he places that issue at the centre of his work. The difficulty for Irish theatre critics appears to be that, although we can convincingly argue that McDonagh is attacking globalized Irishness, audiences throughout the world may continue to receive his plays in ways that reinforce negative thinking about Ireland. The problem, therefore, is not with what McDonagh's intentions as a writer may be, but with the absence of an Irish criticism that could deconstruct the conditions that lead to the proliferation of the globalized Irish brand that makes the (mis)interpretation of his work possible.

A good starting point for such a criticism might involve a consideration of why there is so much Irish interest in the reception of McDonagh abroad. As a result of economic growth, Northern Irish peace, and many other factors, Irishness since the early 1990s has become increasingly indeterminate, leading us to attempt to reconcile, or at least accommodate, the many contradictory versions of Irish identity that are now available. We want to be seen as cosmopolitan but distinctive, traditional but not backward, authentic but not alien, forward-looking but not amnesiac. We want our present to be prosperous and our past to have been oppressive. And perhaps most difficultly, we continue to seek a single narrative to explain an identity that has become diffuse. McDonagh's work touches off the nerves made raw by the clash of these desires, blending versions of Irishness that expose their contradictions. His plays give us the Irish male as an inexplicably violent rural caveman, while his public persona is the 'chic' cosmopolitan Anglo-Irishman, a combination that places him at the fault line between Ireland's traditional past and its postmodern present. Irish responses to his reception abroad must be viewed as a sign of Irish anxiety about a lack of control over the discourse surrounding Irish identity, and this may explain some of the animosity directed towards McDonagh personally.

As such, it is not surprising that McDonagh is routinely attacked for things that earn other Irish theatre practitioners praise. It is interesting, for example, to note the reluctance of Irish critics to question the role of Garry Hynes, the Tony Award-winning director of *The Leenane Trilogy*, in the construction of McDonagh's reception. Noted for her love of Synge (whose *Playboy of the Western World* gives *The Lonesome West* its title), Hynes's work on John B. Keane could be subjected to many of the criticisms that have been applied to McDonagh's plays. As the person who discovered him, and did most to construct his aesthetic, Hynes is exposed to many of the criticisms leveled against McDonagh. The fact that no one has tackled Hynes's work on the terms used to criticize McDonagh suggests that some of the attacks directed towards him may be disingenuous or unfair.

There are many other explanations for this fear of tackling McDonagh on Irish ground. It may be that the desire to celebrate the success abroad of Irish plays, while natural, is undermined by the knowledge that such celebration might be politically ir-responsible. The success of Irish drama internationally has been celebrated by the Irish media. When *The Beauty Queen of Leenane* opened on Broadway, the *Sunday Times* declared that McDonagh's achievement proved that it was 'hip to be Hibernian',[44] while the *Irish Times* emphasized the play's value by including quotes from Mick Lally and Jennifer Aniston (Mulkerns) – an unusual blending of Irish soap *Glenroe* with *Friends* that interestingly resonates with McDonagh's own mix of tradition and postmodernity. The celebratory tone of these reports on the success of Irish literature abroad contrasts depressingly with the fact that, during the 1990s, Irish illiteracy rates were shown consistently to be among the highest in the West (OECD, *Education; Literacy*).[45] Any attempt to cheer the progress of Irish drama abroad thus seems an irresponsible distraction from life on the ground in Ireland. It is similarly difficult to celebrate Irish drama unambiguously when most of its biggest successes abroad would not have occurred without British money, British expertise, and England-based critics. It could thus be argued that the success of McDonagh has allowed Irish theatre agencies to sidestep legitimate questions regarding underperformance, and this again may account for some of the animosity that his work provokes.

Whether McDonagh is subverting stereotypes or not, he is benefiting enormously from the prevalence of those stereotypes – but so are Brian Friel, Marina Carr, Conor McPherson, and most other major Irish dramatists, with the possible exception of Tom Murphy. And, so, too, is virtually every other person currently resident in Ireland. The stability of the Irish economy is at least partially dependent on the global proliferation of myths about Irishness: the tourism that results from it accounts for a significant proportion of Irish GDP, and Irish-branded exports – including cultural exports – play a significant role in the Irish economy. Perhaps it could be said that, to consider the reception of McDonagh on serious terms would involve a move towards considering the basis of Irish economic prosperity. Might this explain Irish critics' unwillingness to tackle his work?

These arguments lead to a number of conclusions. The first and most important is that Irish drama is changing. The question of whether work such as McDonagh's – which originates either in or for another country – can be regarded as genuinely 'Irish' will no doubt continue to provoke discussion but, perhaps, as we examine the global context, it is a debate that will no longer provoke anxiety. It is important that focusing on issues such as Ireland's historical relationship with Britain does not obscure the fact that institutions around the world now share many of the dilemmas historically faced by Irish theatres – and, in fact, may learn from the strategies that Irish theatres have been employing for more than a century.

Globalization presents theatres with opportunities for dialogue and growth, and it exposes audiences to work by practitioners from elsewhere. While such developments are welcome, there is a risk that when theatres or scholars concentrate excessively on the global, they lose sight of the needs of the communities from which their work springs. It is vital that there is more discussion about the local and civic function of theatres – and theatre critics and scholars – in a globalizing world.

The commodification of theatre in particular, and literature generally, could be regarded as a negative development. However, globalization cannot simplistically be invoked as the cause of all contemporary problems facing theatre: globalization is not, after all, a phenomenon that produces change, but a set of processes to which individuals and institutions must react. An awareness that globalization inspires agency can point to the opportunities it presents; it also makes clear that it imposes responsibilities on individuals working within theatre.

In the absence of a sustained critical discourse in Ireland about theatre, representation, culture, and society – and about Martin McDonagh as an Irish playwright – the decision to criticize him might seem like scapegoating: the problem is not with what his plays *really* mean, but with the lack of a criticism that would facilitate more sophisticated responses to his work, or undermine the stereotypical presentations of Irishness that make superficial approaches to his work possible. It is easy to criticize the sentimentalized or stereotypical approaches to Irish drama employed by such companies as the Theatre of Western Springs, but it is worth observing that almost no Irish criticism of the play exists that can refute such interpretations.

This, I would suggest, is where the category of nation becomes relevant in a globalized theatre discourse. Clearly, what is required for Irish drama is for a theatre criticism with a specifically national remit. Such a criticism could begin to tackle the misrepresentation of Irishness abroad – and could, more importantly, begin to understand what its misrepresentation might mean for people living in Ireland. Such a criticism would not be inward-looking, but would instead be *rooted*, and therefore well positioned to address the theatre of other countries on a dialogic basis – rather than considering other countries' cultural output only insofar as it confirms our sense of who we think we are. To do so would be to refocus Irish attention on issues of strictly Irish importance: literacy, the role in Irish life of intellectual and creative activity, the responsibilities of those involved in Irish culture as promoters and beneficiaries of globalization, and so on. But the function of this criticism would also be to mediate the relationship between local theatre audiences and global theatrical productions. Friel's notion that Irish dramatists are talking to themselves and being overheard abroad may no longer be relevant to Irish dramatists. But it must now be adopted by Irish theatre critics.

[1] This article first appeared in *Modern Drama* 47:4 (Winter 2004), and was edited by Karen Fricker and Brian Singleton. It arose from a conference organized by *irish theatre magazine* in October 2003, which was supported by the Arts Council of Ireland.

[2] I wish to acknowledge the assistance of the Irish Research Council for the Humanities and Social Sciences, which provided a Government of Ireland Scholarship in support of the research from which this paper derives. I also wish to thank Shaun Richards, whose comments on a previous paper about McDonagh encouraged me to explore some of the issues considered herein, and Karen Fricker who worked editorially on this paper with me, providing invaluable advice, as always.

[3] John Waters, 'The Irish Mummy: The Plays and Purpose of Martin McDonagh' in *Druids, Dudes and Beauty Queens: The Changing Face of Irish Theatre* ed. Dermot Bolger (Dublin: New Island, 2001), p.54.

[4] Niamh O'Connor,.*The Black Widow: The Catherine Nevin Story* (Dublin: O'Brien, 2000).

[5] Karen Fricker, 'Ireland Feels Power of "Beauty"', *Variety* 21-27 August 2000: p.27+.

[6] Michael Billington, 'Triple Whammy', *The Guardian* 28 July 1997: T12.

[7] The phrase was introduced to Irish discourse by White, but was first used by Charles Spencer. See Victoria White, 'Critics Cry "Heartless"', *Irish Times* 16 January 1997, p.14.

[8] Richard Eyre, and Nicholas Wright, *Changing Stages: A View of British Theatre in the Twentieth Century* (London: Bloomsbury, 2000), p.277.

[9] Aleks Sierz, *In-Yer-Face Theatre: British Drama Today* (London: Faber, 2001), p.225.

[10] Susannah Clapp, 'Pack Up Your Troubles ...', *Observer* 30 November 2003, p.6.

[11] Sandra McLean, 'Armed for A Laugh', *Courier Mail* (Queensland, Australia) 13 March 2004, BAM; p.M04.

[12] Ronan Bennett wrote about these representations, drawing particular attention to the recurrent use of the abattoir as a metaphor to describe Northern Ireland, as long ago as 1994. See Ronan Bennett, 'An Irish Answer', *The Guardian* 16 July 1994.

[13] At the end of the play, Mairead says that she will try not to murder any children, but will make 'no promises' (p.57).

[14] Qtd. in Sean O'Hagan, 'The Wild West', *The Guardian* 24 March 2001, p.32.

[15] Roland Robertson, *Globalization: Social Theory and Global Culture* (London: Sage, 1992), p.8.

[16] See Marshall McLuhan and Quentin Fiore, *War and Peace in the Global Village: An Inventory of Some of the Current Spastic Situations that Could Be Eliminated by More Feed Forward* (New York: Bantam, 1969) and Michael Hardt and Antonio Negri, *Empire* (Cambridge: Harvard UP, 2000).

[17] Zygmunt Bauman, *Globalization: The Human Consequences* (Cambridge: Polity, 1998), p.1.

[18] Nicholas Grene, T*he Politics of Irish Drama: Plays in Context from Boucicault to Friel* (Cambridge: Cambridge UP, 1999), p.3.

[19] Roland Robertson, *Globalization: Social Theory and Global Culture* (London: Sage, 1992), p.8.

[20] David Harvey, *The Condition of Postmodernity* (Oxford: Blackwell, 1989), p.240.

[21] Malcolm Waters, *Globalization*, 2nd ed. (London: Routledge, 2001), p.5.

[22] See also Rustom Bharucha, *The Politics of Cultural Practice: Thinking Through Theatre in an Age of Globalization* (Hanover and London: Wesleyan UP, 2000).

[23] Franco Moretti, 'Planet Hollywood', *New Left Review* 2nd ser. 9 (May/June 2001), p.94.

[24] Miriam Bratu Hansen 'The Mass Production of the Senses: Classical Cinema as Vernacular Modernism', *Reinventing Film Studies*, ed. Christine Gledhill and Linda Williams (New York: Hodder Arnold, 2001), p.335.

[25] Quoted in John Peter, *Sunday Times* 20 May 2001.

[26] Anthony Giddens, *The Consequences of Modernity* (Cambridge: Polity, 1990), p.64.

[27] Baumann, pp.2–3.

[28] For example, David Hare describes Billington's attitude to the West End as follows: 'Michael Billington wrote recently about his fear that the British theatre was turning into the American. We were, he said, developing the mentality of hit and flop that makes the culture of New York so alien and unsatisfactory.' Billington is one of many critics expressing this view. See 'Why I Hate Star Critics', *The Guardian* 20 January 2004: p.4.

[29] Patrice Pavis, ed., *The Intercultural Performance Reader* (London: Routledge, 1996), p.5.

[30] This formula was famously reversed by Shaw in his presentation of Broadbent and Doyle in *John Bull's Other Island* (1904).

[31] Grene, p.264.

[32] Vic Merriman, 'Settling for More: Excess and Success in Contemporary Irish Drama', ed. Bolger, p.59.

[33] Quoted by Debbie Ging, 'Screening the Green: Cinema under the Celtic Tiger', *Reinventing Ireland*, eds Peadar Kirby, Luke Gibbons, and Michael Cronin (London: Pluto, 2002), p.184.

[34] For a particularly useful discussion of the spread of consumable versions of Irishness see Colin Graham, *Deconstructing Ireland: Identity, Theory, Culture* (Edinburgh: Edinburgh UP, 2001) pp.132-50.

[35] Vic Merriman, 'Decolonisation Postponed: The Theatre of Tiger Trash', *Irish University Review* 29.2 (1999), p.315.

[36] Hansen, p.335.

[37] Grene, p.35.

[38] The Gate Theatre toured Alan Ayckbourn's *Taking Steps* to Bombay and Calcutta in 1984, and curated the 2000 Lincoln Center Pinter Festival in New York.

[39] Conor McPherson, *The Weir* (Royal Court Theatre, 1997), Sebastian Barry, *The Steward of Christendom* (Royal Court Theatre, 1995), *The Cripple of Inishmaan* (Royal National Theatre, 1997).

[40] Marina Carr's *On Raftery's Hill* toured to the John F. Kennedy Center for the Performing Arts as part of the Island: Arts from Ireland festival (13–18 May 2000).

[41] Billington, p.12.

[42] I wish to acknowledge with thanks the assistance of Beth Dunn, Education Co-ordinator, Court Theatre, who provided information and documentation about the production.

[43] Arjun Appadurai, *Modernity at Large: Cultural Dimensions of Globalization* (Minneapolis: U of Minnesota P, 1996), p.7.

[44] Michael Ross, Mick Heaney, Gerry McCarthy, Marian Lovett, and Brian Boyd, 'Be Here Now', *Sunday Times* 10 May 1998, Eire 2.

[45] During the late 1990s, numerous policy initiatives were launched by the Department of Education to tackle illiteracy. Illiteracy rates among the workforce (ages 16-65) had been found to be relatively higher in Ireland than in many other countries, with one in four Irish adults rated completely illiterate in the findings of the International Adult Literacy Survey (IALS). The IALS was a survey of literacy in twenty-two industrialized countries, carried out between 1994 and 1998. For a full description of the survey and Ireland's position relative to other OECD

countries, see OECD, 1997 and 2001. OECD, *Education at a Glance.* Paris: OECD, 2001 and *Literacy Skills for the Knowledge Society.* Paris: OECD, 1997.

21 | Domesticating a Theatre of Cruelty: The Plays of Martin McDonagh on the Hungarian Stage[1]

Péter P. Müller

There is a paradox in reviewing and mediating the Hungarian theatrical reception of a contemporary Anglo-Irish playwright to an Irish and international professional public who might not know very much about Hungarian theatre in general and contemporary Hungarian theatre in particular. Interpreting and reviewing the meaning and significance of these plays for the Hungarian theatre and its audience place the critic into the position of a mediator who makes efforts to connect two distant and different worlds, trying to explain the familiar through the unfamiliar, to bring Hungarian theatre closer to the Irish and vice versa. This is not the place to summarize Irish-Hungarian cultural/theatrical relations, but let me just refer to the symbolic fact that in spite of the above paradox there is a reason to search for the relevance of Irish culture for the Hungarians, e.g., there is a metaphorical name for Irish people in Hungary, they are called Hungarians of the West.[2]

By the end of 2005 in Hungary there have been ten productions of five of Martin McDonagh's plays, the first Hungarian premiere having taken place in October 1997. Notably, the Hungarian reception did not follow the sequence and structure of the British premieres. Not all three plays of *The Leenane Trilogy* have been produced so far. *The Beauty Queen of Leenane* had three premieres (in

1997, 1998, and 2004), *The Lonesome West* had one (in 2004), while *A Skull in Connemara* has not reached the Hungarian stage yet. Beside the success of *The Beauty Queen of Leenane* the other plays whose reception is worth attention, *The Cripple of Inishmaan* with three premieres (two in 1998, and one in 2001), *The Lieutenant of Inishmore* with two productions (in 2002 and 2003), and the recent premiere of *The Pillowman* (in October 2005).

Coinciding with the fact that 'McDonagh's international profile grew throughout 1998',[3] this was the year when most Hungarian premieres of McDonagh took place with two productions of *The Cripple of Inishmaan* and one of *The Beauty Queen of Leenane*. After two years of no premieres there was one each year in 2001, 2002, 2003, two in 2004, and one in 2005. These figures are too low to give a firm basis to any kind of generalisation, and do not confirm whether McDonagh's plays have got into the repertoire of Hungarian theatre or they will disappear through the trap door as fast as they burst onto the stage. But even these low figures make him the most frequently produced contemporary Irish playwright in Hungary, if we identify him as such, leaving Brian Friel behind.

Although this is a minor element in McDonagh's reception it is worth mentioning that only one of his plays is available in Hungarian translation published in a contemporary Irish drama anthology, entitled *Pogánytánc: Mai ír drámák* (*Dancing at Lughnasa: Irish Plays of Today*). The plays included in the anthology are, Brian Friel's *Dancing at Lughnasa*, Tom Murphy's *The House*, Sebastian Barry's *Prayers of Sherkin*, Paul Mercier's *Down the Line*, Marina Carr's *On Raftery's Hill*, and Martin McDonagh's *The Lieutenant of Inishmore*. The volume was selected and edited by László Upor, and published by Europa Publishing House in Budapest 2003.

The context of the McDonagh reception in Hungary can be connected to the phenomenon we call New European Drama. McDonagh's plays arrived as representatives of New European Drama, which is mainly the extension of a trend in recent British drama.[4] McDonagh has been seen as a member of this new generation of playwrights, labelled by different terms, as new brutalists, representatives of in-yer-face theatre etc. This young generation of playwrights appearing in the mid-1990s was immediately acclaimed internationally, primarily in Central Europe. Malgorzata Sugiera, a Polish scholar, has written on their influence:

> The first ones to be imported were the British plays of Mark Ravenhill, Sarah Kane and Martin McDonagh. They were soon followed by the works of German authors such as Marius von Mayenburg, Dea Loher and Theresia Walser. ... These works inspired a debate on the problems of the (realistic) plausibility of the action and the characters; the extent to which they could be treated as representative of society; and the potential harm that the contents of these texts pose for society. They tend to be regarded as too explicit in terms of both subject-matter and means of expression to be produced by institutional theatres, financed by taxpayers' money, who usually prefer their 'art' to be somewhat more edifying.[5]

As the above citation states these new plays have been received in Central Europe as representatives of today's society which view has been very much true for Martin McDonagh, whose plays have been considered primarily as representations of Irish reality. One of the very first critics to debate this realistic approach has been Fintan O'Toole, noting on McDonagh's first production ever that, '[a]ll the elements that make up the picture are real, but their combined effect is one that questions the very idea of reality'. And declaring that, 'the whole idea of theatrical realism becomes itself the biggest double take of all'.[6]

One basic reason why the representational interpretation of his plays can be challenged is the universality and extent of violence as a permanent motif and ingredient of these works. The savagery of the plays has been inspired by the mass media, images of accidents, wars, catastrophes, gangster movies etc. The exaggeration of brutality, the depth of violence, the quantity of bloodshed in McDonagh's plays testify to the influence of or at least an affinity with such films as *Pulp Fiction*, *Desperado* or *Fargo*. The amount of violence in these films turns them into a parody of their own genre, which happens in the case of the McDonagh plays as well.

In spite of these features, the majority of the Hungarian theatrical reception has been characterized by the representational approach to these plays. Even those few exceptional productions that have used stylized acting and/or directing primarily, demonstrated the representational perspective as well.

Some of these ten Hungarian McDonagh productions have not reached a satisfactory aesthetic level; therefore it is not necessary to discuss each premiere respectively. Besides, instead of following the chronology of premieres, a more perspicuous view can be offered if the reception is discussed on the basis of plays, making it possible to draw some comparison between the different Hungarian productions of the same drama.

The presence of Martin McDonagh's works in Hungary has inspired only a theatrical reception so far. Literary criticism has not discovered his plays yet, except for the comments of a few experts in Irish studies. Although the less than a dozen premieres of his in Hungary have to be linked to the playwright as author of these plays, the works of art mentioned in the present essay are Hungarian stage productions, being part of the directors' *oeuvre* first of all, the actors' career, the companies' season more than the literary works of McDonagh.

The very first Hungarian McDonagh premiere on 16 October 1997 took place in the tiny studio room of Vígszínház (Comedy Theatre) in Budapest. Critics identified *The Beauty Queen of Leenane* somewhere between psychodrama and social drama. They praised first of all the description of the atrophied mind of the characters. The first professional review stressed the abnormality of the characters under the title, 'Who is Nuts?'. Comparison to contemporary Hungarian drama already appeared in the reviews, relating McDonagh to such Hungarian dramatists as György Spiró, Péter Kárpáti, and István Tasnádi who can hardly be described either as belonging to the same group, or to the same generation.[7] The translator of the play, László Upor (b. 1957, dramaturg, translator), was among the very first bringing McDonagh into the horizon of Hungarian theatre. A few months later, residing in New York City, it was Upor who reported on McDonagh's American success and introduced the Anglo-Irish playwright via New York to the Hungarian theatre professionals in their monthly *Színház* (*Theatre*).

The direction of Balázs Simon (b. 1968) adapted the play to Hungarian conditions and expectations, making it softer, more consumable, lighter than the original. The style selected for the production was that of a detective story interlarded with comic

elements. Even the cast was less harsh than the instructions demand: both Maureen and Mag were played by actresses who could
be hardly seen as cruel or wicked. The space of the premiere was a
small black box room with limited stage techniques, hosting some
fifty-sixty spectators. The narrow, limited space worked against
naturalistic performance, and stressed the grotesque features and
motives of the play.

The second Hungarian premiere of *The Beauty Queen of Leenane*
took place in Kaposvár on 10 December 1998. The theatre of
Kaposvár was the leading artistic theatre in Hungary in the 1980s
and early 90s and it is still among the better companies of the
country. The direction of Radoslav Mileković (Serbian guest
director) avoided making the play either a melodrama or a detective story and stressed its realistic and poetic features. The set
design of Juraj Fabry (Slovakian guest designer) suggested the
experience of being locked up. The stage of the studio production
showed a dark interior of brick walls, with a small window looking
at a narrow outside corridor with the same dark brick wall. The
characters came onto and left the stage through this corridor. The
concept of the production stressed the characters' struggle for life,
not in the Darwinian sense, but as a life strategy. They had to find
their means to be able to survive in the given inner and outer
conditions. The director included a certain sequence of motifs in
the production, for instance Maureen sitting on the window sill,
once waiting for the end of rain, then flirting with Pato from this
place, and after her mother's funeral unpacking her belongings
prepared for the journey to America she again escaped to this
window sill like a haunted animal. The sequence of motifs included
comic counterpoints as well, like the characters slipping outside
the window and entering the house in mud-caked clothes. The
production domesticated this drama of family violence into a
lyrical realistic conversation piece, extirpating brutality and stressing the elegiac emotions of pain and sorrow.

The third and most recent premiere of *The Beauty Queen of
Leenane* using a new translation under a different title (*Poker*) took
place in Madách Chamber Theatre on 28 February 2004. The
translation was made by Lajos Parti Nagy (b. 1953), a celebrated
poet and playwright, known for his innovative poetic language.

The production enhanced the development of the theatre becoming independent of her mother institution, a process which began a few years ago. Madách Theatre has become the citadel of commercial (although state subsidized) theatre since the late 1980s, producing mostly musicals, well-made-plays, farces, and other light pieces. The owner (the City Council of Budapest) decided to give a new profile to the Madách Chamber Theatre, which has become an independent institution from the 2004/5 season and got a new name, Örkény Theatre (after István Örkény, 1912-1979, writer and playwright). The change of its artistic image is largely due to managing director Pál Mácsai (b. 1961), actor and director. The production of McDonagh's play can be considered as an important contribution to reshaping the theatre's image and artistic policy.

The production was praised first of all for the language of the play's new translation and its strong connection or reference to Hungarian experiences. Although the performance did not transplant the Irish location to a Hungarian place, and both stage design and props stressed Irish features, the depicted human relations and issues evoked familiarity in the critics and the audience with their Hungarian experiences. This time brutality was not omitted from the action, physical torture appeared in clear and rather naturalistic ways, which was supplemented by emotional torture affected by strong atmospheric acting. Reduced, limited lives were represented by the reduced and limited language, the misuse of words and phrases, grotesque fracturing of sentences and words. The set design used brick walls like the previous production, but here the bedrooms could be reached by a very steep flight of steps going up right, as if into a tower on the second floor. The symbolic object pushed forward into the title of the production was lying on the top of the iron stove throughout the play, like a Checkovian gun to be used at the end of the plot. The living room/kitchen looked very poor, dismal, depressing. Director Sándor Guelmino (b. 1972) stressed the failure, and misery of the characters, the fact that they have no way out of their conditions, that their dreams and desires are rather like fantasies, and they cannot step out of the circle of social and psychological games. The performance focused on the mother-daughter relationship, presenting not only the differences between Mag and Maureen, but the similarities or even equalities showing in Maureen, a future Mag. The spinster included the withered old woman.

The first two productions of *The Cripple of Inishmaan* were achieved by the same director. The Szolnok premiere took place on 3 April 1998, the first night in the Budapest Chamber Theatre happened on 28 November of the same year. The latter production was based on the same directorial concept and can be considered as a move of the Szolnok premiere to Budapest, though with a different cast. While the production in the country received almost no critical attention, the premiere in the capital gave rise to some professional reviews; therefore I restrict the discussion of reception to the second occasion.

The production of Robert Sturm (German-Hungarian director) received contradictory reviews: some critics described his directing as grotesque, others as melodramatic, some underlined its Irish characteristics, others its being very much Hungarian, one of them even identifying the two cultures writing, 'Ireland depicted on the stage is our homeland, characters living the everyday life of the village are our doubles, their feelings are ours'.[8] Both premieres were described as having the features of an amateur production which in Hungary means being poor but enthusiastic, having mistakes but being dedicated. Sturm's production played with the expectations of the audience, depicting Cripple Billy's story once as a Greek tragedy, then as an American psychological drama, later stressing comic elements in the boy's fate, and by these means guiding the spectators through the twists and turns of the complex style and emotional world of the play. Although the characters have different sorts of handicaps, in the Budapest Chamber Theatre production by the end of the play they all seemed to become glorified, creating a sort of emotional happy ending. The set design depicted grocery shelves of raw wood, holding mostly tinned beans. The costumes were made of cheap wool and linen, colourless, out of shape, depicting the characters as poor, grotesque rural figures. The Irish local colour was primarily represented by Irish music. The translation of the play by Anna Szabó T. (b. 1972, poet and translator) was criticized for the lack of creativity, not being more than a merely literal interpretation.

The premiere in Radnóti Theatre Budapest took place on 19 October 2001, and turned out to be the most successful Hungarian McDonagh premiere so far. A new translation was made by Dániel Varró (b. 1977, poet and translator) which has been praised for its linguistic inventions, creativity and complexity. Critics have said the translation functioned as an independent part of the production's effect, and it seemed to sound from the stage like a contemporary Hungarian play. (Varró's previous translation, *Knives in Hens* by David Harrower had been a celebrated work already.) Péter Gothár (b.1947, film director, directing for the stage since the early 1980s) created a very strong atmosphere in the production of Radnóti Theatre, a small artistic stage and company with excellent actors in downtown Budapest. The possibility of several interpretations offered by the play was not reduced, but maintained and reinforced. Some reviewers criticized this by calling the performance eclectic, while others praised the simultaneity of naturalism and absurd, harsh realism, and high stylization in the performance. Among the several genres and stylistic characteristics recognized or envisioned by the reviewers have been ballad-like features, the qualities of the grotesque, farcical, poetic, surreal, melodramatic, etc. The director emphasized the deformed nature of the characters, both physically and mentally. The cripple, the catatonic, the alcoholic, the erotomaniac, etc., were all equal members of the community, which was as important in the production as the individual fate of the protagonist, Cripple Billy. The production did not tend to be illustrative, acting was limited to a minimal technique with a strong and characteristic presence of the cast. In the second part, which was cut significantly, the stage was flooded by water up to the ankle, the sound of water became a basic acoustic element of the performance. The final scene was taken from indoors to the seashore, a bleak, desolate sight, where the preparation for suicide was more authentic, and where Billy's dialogue with Helen seemed to forecast a tragic outcome. In the 2001/02 season this production was selected as part of the official program of the Pécs National Theatre Meeting (POSZT), which is a festival presenting the best productions of the season including some 12-16 of them. Although the play received no awards on the festival, in October 2002 Judit Schell got the best supporting female actress award for her Eileen, and the production got half a dozen of the votes (out of 21) for best directing/production.

In an interview before the RSC premiere of *The Lieutenant of Inishmore*, Martin McDonagh described himself as an anarchist in an anti-violent way. Regarding *The Lieutenant* he said:

> I have tried to be as vicious or as attacking as the groups on both sides have been over the last twenty-five years, but have no one get injured for it. To do something creatively that was almost as vicious or as explosive as what they have been doing in a non-creative way.[9]

Reviewing the same premiere at the RSC, David Nowlan wrote,

> Every caricature is dim-witted to the point of retardation, and violence seems endemic in all souls. It is, of course, a seriously surreal piece of theatre. But its surreality is such that any kind of suspension of disbelief becomes almost impossible, so that its considerable comedy and its angry gore become almost irrelevant to the actual situation at which he is farcically laughing.[10]

The play is soaking in blood and spilt brains; two cats and four people (half of the cast) are killed, one is tortured. This extent of direct, on-stage violence is a great challenge for the theatre, in terms of how these events and actions can be represented authentically on the stage. The play had two Hungarian productions so far, the first premiered in the studio of the Comedy Theatre in Budapest on 20 September 2002, the second in Kaposvár on 28 November 2003. The two productions handled the staging of natural and brutal scenes in a very different manner, giving alternative examples for how violence can be represented on stage.

The difference was already present in the two different Hungarian titles of the play and the names of the characters. Both translations were the work of Kornél Hamvai (b. 1969, writer, playwright, translator). In Kaposvár the title and the name of characters followed the original in the literal sense. While the production in the Comedy Theatre included a play with words in the title, translating it into 'Alhangya', which combined two features of the protagonist, being mad and being a lieutenant at the same time. ('Hangyás' is a person who is nuts, who has ants in his mind, and 'alhadnagy' means sub-lieutenant.) The names in this production were translated into nicknames, Padraic became 'Pitbull', Donny became 'Szenyor', Mairead became 'Vakond' (mole), Davey became 'Gida' (fawn), etc.

Tamás Ascher's (b.1949) direction in Kaposvár turned the play into a horrible farce. All brutal and naturalistic events were pretended to take place on the stage. When the three paramilitaries returned to the stage blinded, they had black spots under their eyes, indicating the effect of gunpowder. When they were shot to death blood was spreading all around their bodies. There were corpses on the table in Scene Nine cut and sawed into parts. Their arms, legs and heads seemed real, as if being parts of the people previously attacking Padraic.

In the Comedy Theatre's production a kind of stylized acting and theatrical representation was dominant. Péter Forgács (b.1968) excluded naturalism and physical brutality from the performance. When in Scene Two Padraic tortured a drug dealer and took off his toenails, in the production he tore off the sole of James' boots by a pliers. When the members of the group of para-militants were blinded, the three characters simply closed their eyes. In Kaposvár there was a real shooting between Padraic and the group, in Budapest the deaths were represented in a symbolic way. The three fighters sang a marching song, and stopped singing one by one, this way expressing their being shot to death.

The set design already demonstrated the different concept of the two productions. In the Comedy Theatre there was no stage, it was part of the studio's small black box hall that functioned as a space for acting. There were several square-shaped couches put together creating stage space. The arms and backs of the couches created a network of paths, while the seats between them functioned as locations. In Kaposvár the play was performed on the main stage (it was the only main stage production so far of McDonagh in Hungary). The house of Donny was represented only by an L-shape wall. The domestic scenes took place inside (and in front of) this wall, while during the open-air scenes the wall was drawn aside, and the stage became roughly empty.

The differences described above have to be specified though. In Kaposvár the scenes were separated (or linked) by live rock (or punk) music played in a backstage corner, one actor from the cast joining the band for each song. This was a non-realistic element in the performance. Similarly, the way of acting was different from a merely naturalistic, psychologically realistic performance. The style of acting was beyond realism with an ironic edge. In the Comedy Theatre the stylized directing determined the way of acting as well. The cast did not so much impersonate these Irish folks but they presented a collective stylized way of acting.

The next to last McDonagh premiere was *The Lonesome West* with the Hungarian title 'Vaknyugat' literally meaning *Blind West*, translated by Dániel Varró, directed by Péter Gothár in Pesti Színház (chamber theatre of the Comedy Theatre) on 21 May 2004. Being almost a fiasco, hardly reviewed in the theatrical press, taken off from the repertoire after a few performances, to discuss it here would give a false image of the significance of the performance. A possible explanation for the failure is that it had premiered before the production was really ready for the stage, as it was remarked by critics.[11]

The most recent McDonagh premiere was the first Hungarian production of *The Pillowman* on 21 October 2005. This was a production of Kretakör Színház (Chalk Circle Theatre), a leading artistic theatre group lead by artistic director Árpád Schilling (b. 1973). The production was directed by Tamás Ascher, and translated by Anna Merényi (dramaturg, translator, member of Kretakör Theatre). The theatre group is often on tour, beside other places they played in Belfast in 2004, in London in 2004 and 2005. In the rehearsed reading the actors were limited to basic gestures, the instructions were read by the director. *The Pillowman* which is based on a chain of short stories and structured as a mathematical exercise requires a strong and permanent concentration by the audience. The intensity and the elaboration of the production helped the spectators to put together the puzzles of the play and to receive a complete aesthetic experience. Sixteen years after the collapse of communism there was still an authentic insight into the mechanisms of a totalitarian political regime for the Hungarian audience, which experience was employed in the direction of Tamás Ascher. The production created a very strong influence which was described by some critics as an almost mysterious or religious experience, placing the theatre of cruelty and horror of *The Pillowman* into the mind and imagination of the spectators. Critics also praised the actors for their intense, multi-coloured, delicate way of expressing the characters through this restricted theatrical form of rehearsed reading.

The few Hungarian productions of the plays of Martin McDonagh so far represent a variety of interpretations, in terms of directorial concept, way of acting, set design, etc., but there is a clear tendency of domesticating these plays for the Hungarian stage in two senses. On the one hand, to stress those parts and motifs of the plays that can be linked to Hungarian experiences both social and individual, and on the other hand to respond to the challenge of the stage representation of cruelty, by taming violence to a bearable level. The first feature of McDonagh's Hungarian reception fits into the tendency of his international success, for even in the case of the same Druid Theatre productions on tour, 'audiences received the plays as local productions'.[12] The second characteristic has more to do with Hungarian theatre traditions, namely the predominance of the Stanislavski method based acting, and the view of theatre as belonging to entertainment primarily.

McDonagh's *oeuvre* has a metatheatrical feature, confronting theatre with the general problem of representation. Although in practice anything can be represented by anything else on stage there are some basic human activities which have always been a challenge for the theatre. Since film can show everything directly, e. g. any parts of the human body – both from inside and outside – and every kind of action, therefore theatre cannot compete with the film in naturalistic-realistic representation. Such basic human activities as eating, giving birth, having sex, dying, bleeding etc. are very difficult to be represented on stage. If the act is stylized it can become ridiculous; if it is rendered realistic the spectators will meditate on the technique of managing to make it seem real. McDonagh regards the issue of representation as something of a problem primarily for the theatre and not so much for the play-wright. In his plays he includes all sorts of theatrical impossibilities. Reading these plays as literature, the brutal, violent scenes have a full value. The problem of how this savagery is to be put on stage is to be managed by the theatre. Hungarian theatre has had a soft answer to this problem making McDonagh's theatre of cruelty into an easy world of familiarity, similar to the example of an American production described by Patrick Lonergan.[13] But perhaps this domestication tells more of the premises and preferences of Hungarian theatre than of the world of the plays of Martin McDonagh.

———————————

[1] I owe thanks to Dr Mária Kurdi for her comments on the first version of this essay.

[2] This phrase has leaped into the title of a Hungarian monograph on W.B. Yeats by poet, translator, essayist, Ágnes Gergely in her *Nyugat magyarja*, (*Hungarian of the West*) (Budapest Szépirodalmi, 1991).

[3] Patrick Lonergan, 'Druid Theatre's *Leenane Trilogy* on Tour: 1996-2001', *Irish Theatre on Tour. Irish Theatrical Diaspora Series: 1.* eds Nicholas Grene and Chris Morash Dublin: Carysfort Press, 2005), p.194.

[4] Sanja Nikčević, *Nova europska drama ili velika obmana*. Meandar, Croatia, 2005. (I have used the English translation of this work, entitled 'Stupid, old fashioned or backward, or how *in-yer-face* theatre, a violent British trend, became New European Drama'.)

[5] Malgorzata Sugiera, 'Beyond Drama: Writing for Postdramatic Theatre', *Theatre Research International* 29.1 (March 2004), pp.16-7.

[6] Fintan O'Toole, *The Irish Times* 6 February 1996. Reprinted in *Critical Moments. Fintan O'Toole on Modern Irish Theatre*, eds Julia Furray and Redmond O'Hanlon (Dublin: Carysfort Press, 2003), pp.160-1. Similar views have been expressed, beside others, in Mária Kurdi's *Codes and Mask: Aspects of Identity in Contemporary Irish Plays in an Intercultural Context* (Frankfurt/M: Peter Lang, 2000), pp.41-55, and in Ondřej Pilný's 'Martin McDonagh: Parody? Satire? Complacency?', *Irish Studies Review* 12.2, (2004), pp.225-231.

[7] On these playwrights see *Collision: Essays on Contemporary Hungarian Drama*, eds Péter P. Müller and Anna Lakos, (Budapest: Hungarian Theatre Museum and Institute, 2004). The volume was published as part of Magyar Magic – Hungary in Focus 2004 a year long celebration of Hungarian culture in the United Kingdom.

[8] Virág Farkas, 'Szép testben szép lélek' ('Beautiful Soul in Beautiful Body'), *Criticai Lapok* 3, 1999, p.15.

[9] Penelope Dening's interview with Martin McDonagh, *The Irish Times* 23 April 2001.

[10] *The Irish Times* 17 May 2001.

[11] György Karsai, 'Volt egyszer egy szezon. III' ('Once upon a Time in a Season III'), *Színház* 2005/7, 4.

[12] Patrick Lonergan, 'Druid Theatre's *Leenane Trilogy* on Tour: 1996-2001', *Irish Theatre on Tour. Irish Theatrical Diaspora Series: 1*, eds Nicholas Grene and Chris Morash (Dublin: Carysfort Press, 2005), p.194.

[13] Patrick Lonergan, '"The Laughter Will Come of Itself. The Tears Are Inevitable": Martin McDonagh, Globalization, and Irish Theatre Criticism', *Modern Drama* 47.4 (Winter 2004), pp.636-658.

22 | The Beauty Queen of Leenane in Australia

Frank Molloy

> Not a place you'll want to stay but I can recommend a visit.

'Irish plays have experienced somewhat of a renaissance in Sydney theatres lately', declared former Druid actor, Maeliosa Stafford, in September 1999.[1] By way of example he referred to Conor McPherson's *This Lime Tree Bower*, and the comment appeared in an article about a current production of Tom Murphy's *The Gigli Concert*. He possibly also had in mind Murphy's *Bailegangaire*, Marie Jones's *Stones in his Pockets*, Brian Friel's *Faith Healer* and *Dancing at Lughnasa*, all of which had enjoyed major productions in Sydney in the previous few years. And his comment could have been applied elsewhere in Australia. Mainstream companies in other capital cities were regularly featuring Irish plays in their annual seasons, and even regional and alternative companies were following this trend. Stafford would certainly have agreed that no Irish playwright had received more exposure in Australia in the late 1990s than Martin McDonagh, and few plays had been as successful as *The Beauty Queen of Leenane*. It first appeared on the Sydney stage as part of the touring Druid/Royal Court co-production of the *Leenane Trilogy* in the Sydney Festival in January 1998, a production promoted as 'so impressive that audiences are left gob-smacked',[2] and reviewed as 'classical theatre in the Irish tradition with design, direction and acting triumphant'.[3] Less than a year later, *The Cripple of Inishmaan* was a hit for the Sydney Theatre Company, the most commercially successful play in the company's program for 1998 according to one report,[4] and in July 1999, the STC produced *The Beauty Queen of Leenane*, albeit with Druid's Garry Hynes directing and Francis O'Connor designing the set. This production ran for nearly fifty performances, having been extended by a week, and in 2000 it had seasons at two Sydney suburban theatres as well as seasons in Melbourne, Brisbane, Adelaide, and Hobart, and short visits to numerous regional centres. In all, the play was on tour for six months. Touring in such a large country as Australia is not undertaken lightly or often – suitable venues can be hard to arrange and the whole venture financially risky – and yet this was happening not with a popular local success or an old favourite from the repertoire, but with a new play by a relatively unknown Irish playwright. This prompts such questions as what qualities in this play persuaded the company to take it on such a lengthy tour and why was this production so appealing to audiences in a country thousands of miles away from where the play is set.

Before discussing these questions, it is important to review the context in which the play was produced. After generations of taking productions from overseas, principally London, Australian theatre started to acquire its own voice in the late 1960s. Aided for the first time by Federal and State government subsidies, playwrights and companies were keen to experiment with forms to create an Australian identity audiences were not used to seeing. Telling our own stories in our own accents – all part of a newly resurgent nationalism – was in vogue. Suddenly, it seemed, the best theatre was not just local, it spoke in a contemporary voice. Playwrights were raising social and political issues that delighted and shocked audiences, and their work was in demand. 'There was a hunger for Australian works, a preference for them over the classics and new foreign works, not only with the theatre cognoscenti but also with the wider general public as well. The baby boomer generation, now thirty-five-up, educated, and reasonably affluent, was a major factor in this'.[5]

This so-called 'new wave' did not last, however. By the early 1990s a ceiling was placed on government funding for mainstream companies with ever reducing subsidies redirected to alternative theatres or companies that would accede to an artistic program in line with government social goals. In a public spat with the federal agency, the Performing Arts Board of the Australia Council, in 1991 the Sydney Theatre Company was forced to defend its right to artistic freedom when choosing plays: Australian works, yes, but not exclusively so, and especially not new plays if nothing worthwhile was available. The company insisted on choosing the best from what was available overseas and from the classical repertoire. As a result, its subsidy started to decline from 47.5 per cent of annual turnover in 1980 to 7.5 per cent two decades later. Programming was then geared towards the marketplace. Experimental plays or plays by unknown writers were seen as too risky; instead 'safe' plays, plays with small casts and plays that had been successful elsewhere were heavily featured. And audiences gradually accepted this. Rather than clamouring to see their own culture portrayed on stage, they settled back into a comfort zone of entertainment. Gone was the desire to constantly face images of contemporary Australia and be puzzled, shocked or excited by some experimental mode. The baby boomer generation was now middle-aged, and even more affluent, but largely content to be diverted from the pressures of daily life.

Enter Martin McDonagh and *The Beauty Queen of Leenane*. From the first report on the playwright in the press in 1996 it was his whirlwind rise to theatrical prominence that was frequently noted. He answered perfectly the public's insatiable demand for individual success stories in any field of endeavour. Here was a young man in his mid-twenties and already he had won the London *Evening Standard*'s Most Promising Playwright award, a point repeated more than once before the *Leenane Trilogy* visit. He was claimed to be London's 'hottest new playwright to emerge this decade,'[6] and in another flight of hyperbole, it was asserted that the trilogy 'was one of the most exciting theatre events in years'.[7] By the time of the STC production of the *Beauty Queen*, the play had won four Tony Awards on Broadway, including Best Director for Garry Hynes, and the playwright further awards in London, so phrases such as 'universal critical acclaim' and 'golden boy of play-writing'[8] flowed seductively into publicity material and reviews.

Theatre promoters and journalists were tapping into a colonial mindset not completely eliminated by the decades of the 'new wave'. If the flag of 'an overseas success' were raised, potential audiences would immediately take note and be keen not to miss the show, accepting the proposition that whatever was a popular triumph abroad must be worth seeing. This had long been a feature of theatre from the mid-nineteenth century until the 1960s. For generations theatre managers had been serving up to eager audiences a diet of overseas productions, and an expectation had grown that the best theatre was always from somewhere else. As early as 1892, critics were complaining that plays stamped with the 'London Hallmark' were exerting an undue influence on audiences and that theatrical managements were interested only in importing work and even companies, and not in taking any financial risks with local plays. The principal criterion in selection was likely commercial success. So when the Abbey Theatre, for example, toured Australia in 1922, Lennox Robinson's *The Whiteheaded Boy* was chosen by Australian producers not because it was re-presentative of the best plays staged by the company since its inception but because it ran for over three hundred performances in the West End.[9] By the mid-1990s with commercial imperatives again in the ascendant, the familiar catch-cry of 'the London Hallmark' had been re-established. *The Beauty Queen of Leenane* fitted the bill admirably.

However, a lingering influence of the 'new wave' surfaced in regard to one feature of this play: the Australian elements. Pride in nationalism awakened in the 1960s and 1970s did not entirely evaporate. As I shall indicate later, the success of the STC production was due in part to the well-regarded local actors playing the roles of Maureen and Mag. Considerable interest was also shown in references in the script to the television soap operas which Mag Folan and Ray Dooley consume so avidly. In an interview, Garry Hynes was quoted on the significance of these programs. 'Australian soaps have made a very big contribution to these plays, and to the writer generally'.[10] This was somewhat of an overstatement, but either Hynes, or more likely the interviewer, was aware that here was a drawcard for the trilogy, and reviews and commentaries on the 1999 *Beauty Queen* production and 2000 tour often drew attention to soaps as well. For Australians, McDonagh's inclusion of *The Sullivans* and *Sons and Daughters* in a play set in remotest Connemara was proof indeed of the international penetration of Australian popular culture. While many theatregoers would not admit to watching such programs, they are always fascinated to learn that many people overseas eagerly devour them. Curiosity about how they were woven into the plot would hopefully be reflected at the box office. Additional satisfaction would accrue from the belief that these populist melodramas influenced the playwright: 'he learnt his craft watching the same Australian soap operas as Mag watches', according to more than one report.[11] The inference was clear: McDonagh might be an Irish playwright (his English birth and upbringing were only fleetingly acknowledged), but without an infusion of Aussie soaps, the plays would never have happened.

Audiences would also have been responsive to the dissimilarity between their own world, portrayed in these soap operas, and the world of Leenane. The public is often reminded by television columnists how such programs present a positive image of their own country. 'There is a sense of freedom and the new world about Australia that the older world looks upon with some envy. They watch our soaps and think that everybody lives in a beautiful home, everybody is young and attractive, everybody goes to the beach, and that it's always sunny'.[12] In short, it seems utopian, and despite the irony in such comments readers are invited to congratulate themselves on living in such a fortunate land. Contrasts between 'sunny soaps' and 'rain-soaked Connemara'[13] could often be inferred from newspaper items, and occasionally, the bleakness of the play's location was spelt out:

> It portrays the West of Ireland as a place where it's always raining, the sun never shines, everyone has a perpetual cold, there's never enough heat and nobody has any money, everyone is unemployed and unhappy and looking for a ray of hope in their lives.[14]

In the play itself, audiences no doubt noted how in his humorous way, Ray Dooley pointed out the contrast between an exciting world elsewhere where 'a lot of the girls do have swimsuits' whereas Leenane, a 'bastarding town',[15] was decidedly boring and would never be a subject for television.

Some of these observations, especially those relating to lack of opportunity, could also be made about Australian isolated towns and villages, but even in regional centres, audiences were largely urban and so most removed from the lifestyle of the inhabitants of Leenane. In this regard, Australian audiences were little different from those elsewhere, and the gap between urban audiences and rural Irish setting has been noted by Nicholas Grene in a commentary about Conor McPherson's *The Weir*, equally applicable to this play:

> Its remoteness and difference from the reality inhabited by audiences in London, Brussels, Toronto, New York – or indeed Dublin – is part of what makes it funny and moving, what makes it creditworthy. Ireland in the Irish play is a world elsewhere.[16]

And not just in terms of quality of life but also of behaviour and values. In a society such as Australia *The Beauty Queen of Leenane* confirms a view of rural Ireland that has never entirely disappeared: a primitive, violent community where intense personal grudges predominate over reasonableness, and the rule of law does not prevail. This is a dystopian world very different to that enjoyed by audiences in Sydney, Melbourne, Hobart, or Wagga Wagga. Australians, moreover, would easily extrapolate conditions in Leenane to Ireland in general. Commentators, unlike those in Ireland itself, were unlikely to see the *mise-en-scène* as dated or limited in reach. Violence in a Connemara village readily became linked in the public mind with the Northern conflict, for example. Despite positive reports in recent years about the Celtic Tiger and the benign community portrayed in popular television series such as *Ballykissangel*, the notion of the Irish as irredeemably Other lingers on from earlier generations. Novelist David Malouf admitted he was drawn to Irish characters in his novel *Conversations at Curlow Creek* for just this reason: they were 'a symbol almost in our Anglo-Saxon world of disorderliness, of something which can't be included, something which we recognize as having an enormous force of life, but being not orderly'.[17] For audiences, such Anglo-Saxon notions were confirmed in the McDonagh play, and descendants of Irish immigrants might well have momentarily congratulated their forebears for leaving such a benighted land for the sun and civilization of the antipodes.

Conversely, the *Beauty Queen* featured a domestic situation that many in an Australian audience could relate to. McDonagh stated that one of the principal elements with which he started 'was a mother-daughter relationship that was hateful'.[18] This was picked up in posters advertising the production in Sydney and on tour. The actors playing the roles of Maureen and Mag were fore-grounded with Maggie Kirkpatrick as Mag dressed in drab cardigan and beanie, sitting arms folded with a scowl on her face, while Pamela Rabe as Maureen was standing behind her with a harried, exasperated look. Clearly, here was a play pitched at women, and such plays often do well in Australia since nowadays the majority of regular theatregoers are female, most men being enticed away by increasing media coverage of sport. In interviews Pamela Rabe referred to the domestic situation as 'recognizable. The germ of it is so true and it is something we recognize in our own relationships',[19] and Maggie Kirkpatrick said of Mag, 'she's an ageing woman terrified of being left alone and sent into a home; it's a universal concept'.[20] Given the demographic composition of theatre going audiences, this was an issue with particular re-sonance. Not only are most theatregoers female, many are middle-aged professional women or older retired women. Most could identify with Maureen; they too would have experience of looking after aged parents or knew someone who does, and the question of keeping aged relatives at home or placing them in a nursing home is a source of uneasy discussions in middle class households in the leafy suburbs. Older women might see in their own domestic circumstances something of Mag's plight, or at least a fore-shadowing of what might occur, with that fear of being abandoned never far away. While these urban women would recoil in horror from what Mag and especially Maureen resort to, they would not be oblivious to the emotions that give rise to devious or violent actions. And in moments they would admit that cruelty in such situations might not be restricted to faraway Connemara.

Maggie Kirkpatrick and Pamela Rabe (as well as Tracey Mann who later took over the role of Maureen during the tour) are well-known to audiences nationwide. Australian actors successfully taking on complex roles, especially in an overseas play, are always a cause of national satisfaction ('we may not write world-class plays but we produce world-class actors'). Reviews everywhere were most complimentary of the performances of Kirkpatrick and Rabe. The *Sydney Morning Herald*, for example, stated that 'Kirkpatrick is outstanding as the pathetically anchored Mag' while 'the play's heartache dwells in Rabe's intelligent, sensuous portrayal, and she makes the character's collapsing quest disconcerting and emotionally stirring'.[21] The [Brisbane] *Scene* said there 'are phenomenal performances by the two female leads: Maggie Kirkpatrick is utterly convincing in her portrayal of the hypochondriac mother. She manages to generate understanding rather than sympathy for the mother by just letting her fears show through. Pamela Rabe as Maureen breathes the resignation, the hope and the frailty of the trapped woman'.[22] Moreover, wherever the play was performed, journalists were keen to focus on the careers of the two actresses. Interviews with one or the other were prominent in city and regional newspapers. Kirkpatrick is best known for her role in a television soap opera, *Prisoner*, a happy coincidence given the presence of soaps here, and Rabe had recently won awards for roles in films. Their lives were a source of fascination and both made enticing comments about the play and the demands of their character. In passing, Kirkpatrick (and Mann particularly) raised a general issue of the lack of roles for older women. A plea for recognition from playwrights and producers was made, but they were also touching on a concern shared by many in the community. Job opportunities for older women is an issue that crops up frequently and the airing of it in connection with this production would have done no harm in engaging the attention of potential audiences.

Arguably, the main reason for the play's success was the comedy. In the popular mind, Irish theatre, and the Irish more generally, are associated with humour. Perhaps this is based on a belief that from colonial times an otherwise drab British society (at least until the 1950s) was enlivened by Irish wit and verbal dexterity. Perhaps it's a belief that Australians and the Irish share a similar sense of humour, a point made by Tracey Mann.[23] For generations certainly, it has been assumed that the most engaging Irish theatre will be funny, so, for instance, that Abbey production of *The Whiteheaded Boy* in 1922 was a success whereas the most recent Abbey production of *The Gigli Concert* (2004) was not. Pre-production publicity for the McDonagh play made sure that comic aspects were highlighted. On the poster, a quote from the [London] *Times*, 'a dark bubbling Irish comedy', pinpointed the central elements, and newspaper reports took up this theme. Darkness was never ignored with phrases such as 'blackly comic', 'bog-black Irish humour', 'precise black humour', and 'darkly comic tale' drawing attention to the mordant nature of the humour. Not that this was considered a deterrent. On the contrary, the events of Scenes Seven and Eight were seen as sending a *frisson* through audiences wanting more than a banal comic romp. However, few reviews or commentaries or interviews with actors failed to make the point that this play was funny. 'Bubbling' was never downplayed.

Audiences were not disappointed. The opening established a mood they immediately warmed to. The teeming rain cascading loudly down the windows at the rear of the set followed by an obviously drenched Maureen coming through the door and prompting Mag's droll question, 'Wet, Maureen?', (4) set up a humorous tension in the relationship that the audience was going to enjoy. The repartee continued through this opening scene reaching a climax in Maureen's fervently expressed view that the 'fella' that murdered 'the poor oul woman in Dublin' was 'exactly the type of fella I would *like* to meet'. (10) Ray's exasperated outbursts about the chickens in the second scene continued the mood, although here and later in Scene Six there was a sense that he was overacting for comic effect, especially with his exaggerated displays of boredom at waiting for Maureen's return. Garry Hynes had apparently sought to 'broaden the comedy' for this production, presumably on advice that this would increase the play's drawing power.[24] The broadening was most evident in these scenes and in Scene Four when Mag waddles in, empties the chamber pot into the kitchen sink, and wipes her hands on a dirty dressing-gown, followed a few moments later by Pato picking a porridge spoon out of the same sink and his obvious unease when he realizes what he's done. Audiences were in stitches. While the mood darkened from Scene Seven with the horror produced by the violence and the lack of resolution for the now adrift Maureen, there was still room for humour, in particular from Ray complaining about his lost tennis set, babbling on about Wagon Wheels and Kimberleys and displaying exasperation at Maureen's strange moods. Performance reports from the 1999 Sydney season stressed the responsiveness and enthusiasm from audiences, largely based, one can infer, from the humour.[25]

Garry Hynes told a Sydney newspaper that Martin McDonagh 'has an extraordinary ear, an extraordinary sense of character [and] a gift for telling stories',[26] skills much in evidence in *The Beauty Queen of Leenane*, and partly accounting for its 'incredible success' wherever it has played. Australia was no exception to this. Reviews of the STC production frequently praised these qualities, and audiences were equally impressed. They were not, however, sufficient to result in a sell-out season in 1999 and a successful national tour a year later. Other factors were at work. An award-winning overseas play featuring well-known local actors undertaking demanding roles was sure to arouse interest among potential audiences. In addition, there is a belief that an Irish play will be entertaining, largely through its humour, in this instance mingled with cruelty and violence that both attracted and repelled middle-class female urban dwellers who comprise the majority of the theatre-going public. Contrary reactions extended to feeling remote from Leenane and its earthy primitivism, while recognizing that the domestic circumstances of the Folan family for all its Irishness had universal application. For Australians, *The Beauty Queen* was a night out on the wild side. As one reviewer concluded, the world of the play is 'not a place you'll want to stay but I can recommend a visit'.[27] There was an enthralling plot, full of dark humour and multifaceted characters, and violence to shock. Certainly, plenty to reflect on over a cappuccino in a harbourside restaurant afterwards, before leaving for the suburbs determined to recommend this show to friends and acquaintances.

---

[1] *Daily Telegraph* [Sydney] 10 September, 1999, p.53.

[2] *Daily Telegraph* 3 January 1998, p.27.

[3] *Sydney Morning Herald* 12 January 1998, p.12.

[4] *Irish Echo* 1-14 June 1999, p.25.

[5] Peter Wherrett, *The Floor of Heaven: My Life in Theatre* (Sydney: Hodder Headline, 2000), p.153.

[6] *Australian* 20 December 1997, Review, p18.

[7] *Daily Telegraph* 3 January 1998, p.27.

[8] *Adelaide Advertiser* 16 November 1999, p.26.

[9] A point made by Peter Kuch in 'The Abbey Down Under in 1922', a paper delivered to the IASIL conference in Galway, July 2004.

[10] *Daily Telegraph* 5 December 1997, p.45.

[11] For example, *Australian* 23 July 1999, p.10.

[12] *Sydney Morning Herald* 'The Guide' 1-7 November 2004, p.4.

[13] *Sydney Morning Herald* 23 July 1999, p.13.

[14] *Daily Telegraph* 16 July 1999, p.41.

[15] *The Beauty Queen of Leenane* (New York: Vintage International, 1997), pp.52 and 76. Other references to the play, cited in brackets, are to this edition.

[16] *The Politics of Irish Drama: Plays in Context from Boucicault to Friel* (New York: CUP, 1999), p.262.

[17] Helen Daniel, 'Interview with David Malouf', *Australian Book Review* 184 September 1996, p.10.

[18] *Australian* 20 December 1997, p.17.

[19] *Daily Telegraph* 16 July 1999, p.41.

[20] *Sunday Tasmanian* 6 August 2000.

[21] 23 July 1999, p.13.

[22] 12 April 2000, p.47.

[23] See *Daily Telegraph* 10 September 1999, p.53.

[24] See *Newcastle Herald* 29 July 1999, p.25.

[25] I am indebted to the STC archives for permission to watch a video of the production and consult their files.

[26] *Daily Telegraph* 5 December 1997, p.45.

[27] *Sunday Telegraph* 25 July 1999, p.188.

23 | Martin McDonagh's Irishness: Icing on the Cake?

Karen Vandevelde

Since the premiere of *The Beauty Queen of Leenane* in 1996, the debate on the achievements of Martin McDonagh has been dominated by issues of Irishness in his repertoire. The locality as well as topicality of McDonagh's second and third plays, *A Skull in Connemara* and *The Lonesome West,* confirmed the relevance of 'Irishness' as the defining constituent of meaning, as did the plots of each of the three plays in McDonagh's second trilogy, set on the Aran Islands. Audiences in Ireland and in the English-speaking world interpreted these two trilogies within a horizon of expectations shaped by their familiarity with Irish culture and society. Whether this familiarity was based on memory or experience, or on tourist-brochure 'knowledge' of Ireland, arguments concerning the authenticity of McDonagh's representation of Irishness continued to fuel these discussions.

Patrick Lonergan, however, identified a sense of frustration in the debate on McDonagh's merits as a playwright, rooted in the 'apparently irreconcilable extremes' in opinions about his depiction of the Irish: supporters believe he is 'cleverly subverting stereotypes of the Irish', opponents are convinced he is 'exploiting those stereotypes, earning a great deal of money by making the Irish look like a nation of morons'.[1] The frustration persists as, according to Lonergan, there is strong evidence to support both sides of the argument.

Although the debate on McDonagh's treatment of Irish life and Irish culture is certainly relevant to an understanding of his work, it can also distract attention from many other interesting features of his work. Would it be possible – and indeed desirable – to discuss his work outside of an Irish context? An adaptation of the Leenane trilogy presented in the Netherlands and Flanders in fact offers an interesting opportunity to re-enter the Irishness debate from a different angle. In 2000-2001, a Dutch and a Flemish company co-produced *De Leenane Trilogie,* a four-hour-long adaptation of McDonagh's three plays into a single production. The trilogy's dramatic structure changed significantly, but also many of its typically 'Irish' features such as place names, cultural references and language, were reduced or omitted. Staging McDonagh's play either as an authentic or an ironic representation of Ireland was not an issue for the director, dramaturges, and actors of the adaptation. When comparing the Irish/English production with the Dutch/ Flemish adaptation, some challenging questions emerge: Is the Dutch/Flemish adaptation still the author's Leenane trilogy? Is *Irishness* an integral part to the trilogy, or is it merely the 'icing on the cake'? And, most importantly, what remains of McDonagh's play when most of the Irish features have been cut?

In order to facilitate a comparison between two different dramatic texts – on the one hand the author's text as staged by Druid/Royal Court and printed in the Methuen Drama series, and on the other the Dutch/Flemish adaptation – I refer to the schedule at the end of this article which gives an overview of how the three McDonagh plays are merged into one. References to McDonagh's text refer to the *Plays: 1* volume, including *The Beauty Queen of Leenane* (BQ), *A Skull in Connemara* (SC), and *The Lonesome West* (LW).[2] As no script is available for the Dutch/Flemish *De Leenane Trilogie* (DLT), I refer to the time sequence of the scenes.[3] By focusing on what is altered or left out in the Dutch/Flemish adaptation, I hope to identify the 'Irishness' in McDonagh's Leenane trilogy by means of different criteria, and to point out other significant features of the play which have been over-shadowed by the Irishness debate.

McDonagh's Leenane Trilogy was adapted for Het Toneelhuis and Zuidelijk Toneel Hollandia by two dramaturges, Kurt Melens and Paul Slangen. Johan Simons directed the play and a well-known Flemish poet, novelist and playwright, Peter Verhelst, was commissioned to translate the text following the structural changes suggested by the dramaturges. Like many other major theatre productions in the Dutch-speaking theatres of today, this was a co-production between a Flemish theatre company (Antwerp) and a Dutch one (Eindhoven). With a Flemish and a Dutch dramaturge, a Dutch director and a Flemish writer, and a mixed cast of Flemish and Dutch actors, the balance between two cultural entities was fairly even. The partnership was comparable to the production history of McDonagh's Leenane Trilogy (co-produced by an Irish theatre company, Druid Theatre, and a British one, Royal Court), but in terms of casting and language there was a significant difference: McDonagh's Leenane Trilogy was acted by an Irish cast, in a language that was recognizably Irish-English. The Dutch/Flemish dramaturges, working with actors from widely different dialect areas, chose not to use colloquialisms or a regionally coloured language. Instead, they commissioned the translation, *De Leenane Trilogie,* to be written and enacted in the more universally understood 'Standard Dutch'.[4]

All of McDonagh's speaking characters re-emerge in the adaptation, with the exception of Mary Rafferty, the woman who features in the first and last scene of *A Skull in Connemara.* Cutting Mary's character proved fairly easy: Her purpose in the play is to introduce Mick Dowd and his past, to facilitate the 'exposition', and to give substance to the stifling closeness of the villagers. Instead, the new trilogy introduces Mick Dowd throwing around sand and life-size rubbish bags during the ten minutes when the audience enters the auditorium; Dowd's shady past is not revealed by Mary, but in the gravedigger's first dialogue with Mairtin and Thomas Hanlon; and Scene Four of the play is rewritten partly as monologue – Mick Dowd talking to himself/to his dead wife – and partly as dialogue between the three remaining characters.

Removing the character of Mary and rewriting some of the scenes in which she featured was the most invasive reworking of McDonagh's text. Generally, the dialogues in the Dutch/Flemish

Leenane Trilogie echo the original text almost line-by-line, but the scenes are interwoven laterally rather than chronologically. In McDonagh's original trilogy, *A Skull in Connemara* is set about a month after Mag Folan was buried (SC 71); Thomas Hanlon and Father Welsh, alive in *A Skull in Connemara,* both drown themselves shortly after, during the events taking place in *The Lonesome West* (LW 147, 177). In the Dutch/Flemish version, the sense of chronology is dropped. Each of the trilogy components develop gradually and simultaneously, comparable to the multiple plots of, for example, Robert Altman's *Short Cuts* or P.T. Anderson's *Magnolia.* The scene changes, too, refer to film editing techniques: characters belonging to a new scene often interfere with the earlier scene by commencing their lines a few seconds before the previous scene has fully closed. Double-casting the male roles also leaves traces of one character onto another, and at once connects and juxtaposes different characters.[5]

Juggling the scenes from the three different plays into one production modifies their coherence. The shared set and props illustrate Leenane's lack of individual privacy; the 'pruning' of less relevant characters, jokes, and references allows for deeper psychological development of the remaining characters, and the lateral rather than chronological interweaving constructs a tight network of intertextual references. Scene Four of *A Skull in Connemara,* for example, in which Thomas Hanlon's incompetence as a policeman is painfully exposed (DLT 1.20'), is followed immediately by scene two of *The Lonesome West,* which brings the news of Thomas Hanlon's suicide (DLT, 1.34'). In the Dutch/-Flemish version, a causal relationship between the two events not only replaces the lack of order and understanding in the world McDonagh created, but as such also forewarns of Father Welsh's suicide, triggered by his own realization of failure. The parallel plot development, then, intensifies rather than repeats the dramatic tension. This gives the audience a slightly less depressing image of the village of Leenane: instead of experiencing the exposition, tension, denouement, and bleak return to the status quo three times over, spectators can choose to interpret the dark events in Leenane as a peculiar aberration which commenced and closed with the opening and the closing of the curtain.

Another interesting dramaturgical change concerns the letter reading monologues. In *The Beauty Queen of Leenane* Pato reads out his letter for Maureen while he is writing the piece (*BQ* Scene 5, 34-36). *The Lonesome West* contains a similar scene, in which Father Welsh begs Coleman and Valene to become 'true brothers' (*LW* Scene 5, 186-170). In the Dutch/Flemish adaptation, the recipients rather than the authors of the letters read them aloud. These recipients, however, are not the ones to whom the letters were addressed. Here, reading a letter becomes a dramatic act: Mag Folan reads out the letter intended for her daughter before she burns it in the stove (*DLT*, 2.49'), while Girleen reads Fr Welsh's letter in order to find out if it mentions anything about her (*DLT*, 2.52'). By giving these characters the opportunity to display the authors' information to the public, the villagers' prying into each others' lives becomes all the more oppressive.

The stronger sense of cohesion between the three parts of the trilogy has an impact, too, on the amount of cross-referencing between the plays. In Martin McDonagh's trilogy, various characters from the trilogy are referred to in other parts – particularly in the final play, *The Lonesome West* – and additional references to other villagers in Leenane demonstrate to what extent each person's life is gossiped about, spied on, and manipulated by the others. Dolores Hooley (Pato and Ray's cousin), and Alison O'Hoolihan (Coleman's school friend) are the only non-acting villagers named in the Dutch/Flemish trilogy, and when characters address each other or refer to one another, this is more often done anonymously or by description ('the priest') than by name ('Father Welsh'). Cross-referencing in the Dutch/Flemish *Leenane Trilogie* is visual, not textual: twice, Girleen appears on stage observing the other characters in action; for most scene changes, the new characters appear on stage a few seconds before the earlier scene is finished; or characters from one part of the trilogy change the setting and props for their neighbours in their respective roles as 'characters', not as 'actors'. Leenane's culture of gossiping is here translated into visual gossiping or *voyeurism*. In the adaptation, the social fabric of Leenane is ripped not by people who gossip, but instead by people who witness murder and abuse but do not talk.

When plays travel internationally, the 'abrogation of localizing references' is one of the key practices to make a dramatic work relevant to a diversity of spectators.[6] Having fewer references to people's names is only one of the ways in which *De Leenane Trilogie* aspires to a more universal appeal. Another, more obvious means to obtain this is to minimize references to placenames, and not to zoom in on one well-defined place in Ireland.[7] This is done so radically in the Dutch/Flemish version that Pato's noteworthy description of Maureen as 'the beauty queen of Leenane' becomes 'de schoonheidskoningin van het dorp' – *the beauty queen of the village*. Similarly vague, the Irish emigrate to 'het buitenland' – *abroad,* not to America or London*;* Yanks become simply 'buitenlanders' – *foreigners;* and Connemara is here 'de hele streek' – *the entire region.* A handful of references to Manchester, Boston Massachusets, Carraroe, the woman from Trinidad, and once, to Leenane, are sufficient to give the trilogy a true-to-life relevance, but they do not make Leenane into an idyllic country village, nor do they turn rural Ireland into a recognizable area of economic failure or moral emptiness.

Reflections on language, emblematic in language jokes such as the Father Walsh-Welsh pun and misunderstandings over the pronunciation of 'oul' ghoul' ('oul' whore'; SC, 116), become a more complex issue in translation. Language plays a significant role in McDonagh's trilogy: not only do Maureen and Mag argue over the language they should be speaking – English or Irish (*BQ*, 4-5), most of the characters in the trilogy are particularly conscious of their use of vocabulary and the register of language they draw on. Amongst many other examples, Maureen orders Mag not to 'go using big words' (*BQ*, 17); Mick and Thomas ponder over the use of 'convulse' and 'spasm' (*SC*, 117); and Coleman, Valene and Fr Welsh fuss over the word 'unbare' (*LW*, 133). Hypercorrection in language is a sign of linguistic insecurity. Had the dramaturges of the Dutch/ Flemish trilogy chosen not to replace the microscopic picture of Leenane by a more universal perspective, they would have found a very appropriate and locally recognizable equivalent in contemporary discussions on standard language, colloquialisms and dialects in Flanders.[8] Cutting all linguistic references and jokes was, however, a consequence of other decisions made by the director and dramaturges. Their Leenane trilogy was designed to be more anonymous, and could therefore be more universally understood as 'the epic of an unemployed rural village'[9] – which one Dutch newspaper critic immediately linked to the horrific hidden stories of incest and abuse in two remote Dutch villages, which had recently been made public.[10]

'Ireland', in *De Leenane Trilogie*, is not a place where people fight over language (Maureen and Mag's 'crux of the matter' discussion on the Irish language [*BQ*, 4-5] is cut); is not the island where tourists come to visit (*SC*, 67); nor is it a place where people eat Kimberley biscuits, drink Complan and poteen, or argue over Tayto, McCoys and Honey Nut Loops. These references mean either very little or something very different to Dutch and Flemish audiences. Localizing references, Kurt Melens argues, show merely the outside of a story. 'We wanted to approach Leenane from the inside and therefore had to get rid of placenames and specific objects'.[11] Melens also believes that McDonagh subverts cliché images of Ireland: Mag Folan is no helpless Cathleen Ní Houlihan, Pato's story of emigration trivializes the famine legacy, and Christian symbols are merely a sign, bearing no content or morality. In accordance with this interpretation, the dramaturges refused to stage a cliché Ireland. The advance publicity of the Dutch/Flemish *De Leenane Trilogie* still referred to McDonagh as an Irish playwright and to the trilogy as set on the West Coast of Ireland, but in the play's revivals in 2001-2002 and 2003-2004, Ireland was not mentioned at all in the company's programme or newsletter. 'Revival. The Disconcerting Portrayal of a Village. An isolated village where no one is anonymous, and perversion and abuse are rife.'[12] With such geographical indications, the audience's expectations of the adapted Leenane trilogy were very different from those of the Druid/Royal Court touring production. An Irish expatriate community or nostalgic tourists were not the kind of spectators the Dutch and Flemish theatre companies had in mind.

At this point, the authority of the author becomes a matter of discussion. Although theatre is by its very nature a collaborative medium, most contracts between a living playwright and a theatre company or director include certain provisions that a play be staged as it was written, without significant omissions, additions, or alterations to the text. A playwright is even *legally* entitled 'to a performance that he or she judges to be satisfactorily in accord with its script'.[13] Nevertheless actors and directors not only 'interpret' a play privately, they also shape the audience's interpretation. When a play is staged for the first time, it is crucial that the playwright supports the staging of his work. Martin McDonagh sent his script for the Leenane Trilogy to Druid Theatre under the direction of Garry Hynes, a director known for her naturalist style of production.[14] Judging by interviews with the author after the first production of the Leenane trilogy, the author supported Garry Hynes's naturalist/realist interpretation and staging of his dramatic debut. McDonagh's detailed stage directions, too, indicate that he viewed his trilogy as naturalist drama set in a particular place in Ireland, and performed in a realistic acting style. The level of naturalism in the original staging of the Leenane trilogy can be illustrated by a small anecdote. At the time when the Druid company was performing on Broadway, I was researching press reviews in Druid's cosy archive-cum-secretary space in Galway. There I was able to witness how a phone call from abroad that the packets of Kimberley biscuits were lost or destroyed in transport, led to major discussions amongst the staff on whether they would be able to send a new load of the *authentic* biscuits on time, or whether they could change them for similar looking packets on the set of *The Beauty Queen of Leenane.*.

The Dutch/Flemish adaptation *De Leenane Trilogie* was not authorized by McDonagh or by his agent, the London-based Rod Hall Agency. Nevertheless, the three-in-one *Leenane Trilogie* was given permission to be performed, but not to be published. Interesting, too, is the fact that the German Staatstheater Stuttgart recently contacted the agency asking for permission to translate this Dutch/Flemish adaptation into German and stage this adaptation, but, according to Melens, McDonagh's agent refused.[15] The tradition of the well-made play, of which McDonagh's trilogy is so much a part – fourth-wall illusion drama with the odd blink to the audience – is not a universally dominant stage tradition. In the Netherlands and Flanders, and in Germany, too, alternative styles of production, reworkings of dramatic texts and heightened theatricality are not confined to fringe theatres, as they tend to be in most English speaking countries (examining the historical forces which can explain this difference is matter for another lengthy article). It is no surprise, then, that the Stuttgart theatre was more interested in the adapted three-in-one trilogy than in McDonagh's originals.

Literary agents occupy a crucial strategic position for the international circulation of texts.[16] They safeguard the integrity of their clients' work, but they occupy a position of power which extends further than protecting a play's copyright and financial rights. While the decision not to let this adaptation of the *Leenane Trilogy* circulate beyond the Dutch language border probably had more to do with money than with aesthetics (agents and authors receive more copyright fees and production fees if three original plays are staged separately than if one adaptation circulates), literary agents do make indirect decisions on a play's aesthetics. Admittedly, there is ample ground to the argument that the Dutch/Flemish adaptation is no longer the trilogy McDonagh wrote, but McDonagh's or his agent's reluctance to support this reworking of the text must also be regarded as a missed opportunity. In a number of early interviews McDonagh stated that he did not see himself as part of an 'Irish' tradition of playwriting, even though he started his dramatic career as part of the Irish theatre scene.[17] Supporting this 'European' adaptation of the Leenane trilogy would have given him an excellent opportunity to prove that his drama is able to take part in the postmodern debate on social and cultural identity as a universal, not just as an Irish problem.

Adapting a play is not a case of improving the original or covering up certain flaws, on the contrary. The three-in-one *Leenane Trilogie* is a tribute to McDonagh's original work of drama, but it is reshaped to suit the conventions and expectations of a director-centred theatre tradition as it exists in Flanders and the Netherlands. Although much more could be argued to promote the creativity with which the Dutch/Flemish adaptation replaced English language puns by other jokes, swapped typically Irish concerns for universal human anxieties, and transformed the Leenane Trilogy from a realistic well-made play into a postmodernist, theatrical performance, I will return to the initial question of how a detour to an international production of McDonagh can offer new insights into the question of Irishness.

The apparent ease with which Irish topicality in McDonagh's Leenane trilogy was removed in the adaptation, does pose the question whether these Irish features are in fact an integral part of the original text. Placenames, cultural references, brand names as well as personal names were easily disposed of in the Dutch/-Flemish trilogy. The picture of Ireland as an exotic dystopia, recalled through the confrontation between the trivial and the sublime, disappeared with the purging of placenames, consumer products, and Christian names. Instead, the new trilogy voices the dreams and anxieties of any small community, cut off geographically or culturally from the rest of the world.

Irish literature has a strong tradition of giving voice to the flip side of the so-called Irish jovial temperament. The exploration of the inner darkness of the Irish psyche in, for example, three very different works such as Samuel Beckett's *Waiting for Godot,* J.M. Synge's *Playboy of the Western World,* and Patrick McCabe's *Butcher Boy* – is continued in McDonagh's Leenane trilogy. When McDonagh, however, sets his trilogy in a remote village in the West of Ireland, Irish audiences, expatriates abroad and foreigners can watch the play and distance themselves from the events because they are geographically and historically removed from the place. Despite the plays' naturalism, their contemporary setting, and level of 'self-recognition', audiences can maintain a safe distance from these warped characters because their fears and dark sides are contained within a different locality and within an earlier phase in the process of modernization. Modern Ireland can now look back on these events and laugh, because modern Irish society has moved away from all this horror. What the Dutch/Flemish adaptation of this trilogy however allows us to see is that these features, enacted in a non-Irish context, are not part of the fabric that makes up Ireland. On the contrary, they are part of the human condition. The horrific violence and abuse in the Leenane trilogy are not an exclusively Irish problem. Those who witnessed the Dutch/Flemish adaptation did not have the comforts of a cultural distance; this *Leenane Trilogie* brought the audience into the inside of the turmoil and of the characters' secrets, fears, and cruelty.

There is no catharsis in the new plot, but relief is instead provided through the more theatrical production style which constantly subverts the fourth-wall illusion so closely associated with the well-made play.

What this adaptation of the Leenane trilogy makes clear is that Irish society does not have a monopoly on problems of authority within the church, within family relationships or within state hierarchies. Confrontations between modern and postmodern systems of organization, between on the one hand authority, security and understanding, and on the other fragmentation, insecurity, and miscommunication, have inspired the greater part of international postmodernist writing. What does make McDonagh's Leenane trilogy uniquely Irish, and impossible to translate into a different locus, is that the author has complicated this confrontation by adding a 1960s plus 1990s setting to the trilogy, illustrating how rapidly, and how confusedly, Ireland has joined the rest of Europe in reshaping its fabric to suit that of a (post)modern society. To this confrontation McDonagh added the weight of Ireland's history, illustrated in the significance of emigration and in the attention to detail given to the characters' use of language. Typically postmodern in McDonagh's treatment of these 'Irish' features, then, is that Ireland's language issues, emigration history, and process of modernization are at once problematized and trivialized, and as such are not dealt with in-depth. McDonagh does not take a stance as a writer, possibly because as a first-generation emigrant he cannot have the perspective of complete insider nor that of absolute outsider. This he has in common with some of the most innovative and inspiring writers of today, growing up at the crossroads of two cultures, two societies, two nations.

Scene by scene overview of the adaptation by Toneelhuis / Zuidelijk Toneel Hollandia

Time sequence	McDonagh's play + scene reference	Description of scene & adaptation
0'		While audience enters, Mick Dowd throws sand and rubbish bags down from platform
9'	SC 2	Mick Dowd, Mairtin Hanlon and later also Thomas Hanlon, digging in the graveyard
29'	LW 1	Introduction Coleman, Valene, Father Welsh and Girleen
44'	BQ 1	Introduction Mag and Maureen
52'	BQ 2	Message Ray Dooley, Maureen discovers lies
1.09'	SC 3	Mick Dowd and Mairtin Hanlon batter skulls off-stage
1.20'	SC 4	Mick Dowd talks to himself (not to Mary Rafferty / Thomas & Mairtin Hanlon enter – mystery Oona's body resolved / Mick Dowd talks to Oona's skull (not to Mary)
1.34'	LW 2	Coleman & Valene fight, Welsh's message of Thomas Hanlon's death
1.50'	BQ 3	Maureen and Pato arrive home after party
2.00'		PAUSE
2.01'	BQ 4	Mag, Pato and Maureen, the following morning
2.18'	LW 3	Fight Coleman and Valene, priest is told about murder, scalds his hand
2.29'	LW 4	Father Welsh says goodbye to Girleen at the lake
2.40'	BQ 6	Ray gives letter for Maureen to Mag
2.49'	BQ 5	Mag reads Pato's letter out loud
2.52'	LW 5	Girleen reads Welsh's letter out loud
2.54'	BQ 7	Mag and Maureen talk about Pato; cross-examination & chip-pan burn
3.05'	BQ 8	Maureen's monologue while Mag crawls on floor in pain; Mag's death
3.10'	LW 6	Fight Coleman and Valene; Girleen brings message Welsh's suicide
3.20'	BQ 9	Maureen packing, Ray brings news from Pato
3.34' - 4.00'	LW 7	Coleman and Valene's confession competition Curtain

[1] Patrick Lonergan, '"The Laughter Will Come of Itself. The Tears are Inevitable": Martin McDonagh, Globalization, and Irish Theatre Criticism', *Modern Drama* 47:4 (Winter 2004), p.636.

[2] McDonagh, Martin. *Plays: 1. The Beauty Queen of Leenane, A Skull in Connemara, The Lonesome West* (London: Methuen Drama, 1999).

[3] *De Leenane Trilogie*. Prod. Zuidelijk Toneel Hollandia/Toneelhuis, 2001, Video courtesy of NTGent.

[4] The Netherlands and Flanders (the northern half of Belgium) share the same standard language, but show significant variation in their respective accents. In dialects and informal use of language, this variation may cause problems in cross-border communication, but at standard level the difference is minimal, and comparable to the difference between British English and, for example, Irish English, American English or Australian English. Most speakers of Dutch consider this standard language variant as the culturally superior one.

[5] There is one possible anachronism in McDonagh's trilogy: In *The Beauty Queen of Leenane* we hear that Fr Welsh has punched Mairtin Hanlon (*BQ*, 9; 59). Unless the priest has a habit of doing so, this confrontation must be the one described in *A Skull in Connemara*, when Mairtin tries to find out from the priest what happens to a man's genitals when he dies (*SC*, 91). Elsewhere in *A Skull in Connemara*, however, we read that this play is set a month after the ending of the first part of the trilogy (*SC*, 71). In the Dutch/Flemish adaptation, however, the logic is restored: Mairtin Hanlon gets hit by the priest a short while before this is referred to by Mairtin's friend Ray (respectively DLT 0.19' and DLT 0.54').

[6] Lonergan, p.643.

[7] Of the three parts in the *Leenane Trilogy*, only *The Lonesome West* is literally set 'in Leenane, Galway' (*LW*, 129). However, the title of the first play in the trilogy as well as Father Walsh's references to the villagers, give the audience plenty of suggestions that the entire trilogy is set in the same parish, Leenane.

[8] Interesting to note in this context is that in the 1990s, two Flemish authors were commissioned by a Dutch publishing house to provide a new translation of Joyce's Ulysses, with the explicit request to use Flemish colloquial language, not Standard Dutch, as an equivalent for Joyce's use of Irish English in the original. (James Joyce, *Ulysses*, trans. Paul Claes and Mon Nys. Amsterdam, Bezige Bij: 1994).

[9] '… een epos van een werkloos boerendorp', *De Toneelgazet* 3:8 (11). (newsletter of theatre company Het Toneelhuis)

[10] *Algemeen Dagblad* 7 May 2001, Newspaper Cuttings, Vlaams Theater

Instituut.

[11] Kurt Melens, interview with Karen Vandevelde, Ghent, 19 September 2005.

[12] 'Herneming. Het verbijsterende portret van een dorp. Een geïsoleerd dorp, waar geen anonimiteit bestaat, en perversie en misbruik welig tieren...' *De Toneelgazet* 5:5 (8 May 2003) p.7.

[13] Robert Hapgood, 'The Rights of Playwrights: Performance Theory and American Law', *Journal of Dramatic Theory and Criticism* 6:2 (1992). Reprinted in: Jeane Luere, *Playwright Versus Director. Authorial Intentions and Performance Interpretations* (London: Greenwood Press, 1994), p.141.

[14] See, for example, Dominic Dromgoogle's comments on Garry Hynes and the Druid Theatre company in *The Full Room, An A-Z of Contemporary Playwriting* (London, Methuen, 2000), p.212.

[15] Interview Kurt Melens.

[16] This is particularly so in English-speaking countries. In many respects, Belgium and Holland may be regarded as the opposite. Apart from a royalty agency SABAM which negotiates author's fees, no organisation promotes or protects the work of playwrights. Mainstream theatres tend to be 'director's theatres'. There is a culture of commissioning plays from authors; not of authors offering new creations to theatre companies.

[17] Take, for example, Fintan O'Toole, 'Nowhere Man' *The Irish Times* 26 April 1997.

Reports and Reviews

'The Real Ireland, Some Think'
New York Times 25 April 1999
Declan Kiberd

The West of Ireland really is wild. Its people are more roguish and its landscapes more windswept than those in the east. It is the place where pent-up instincts are released and where a young London playwright of Irish background named Martin McDonagh went for his holidays every year. His blackly comic Leenane Trilogy, in which J.M. Synge meets Sam Shepard, has offered theater audiences in Galway, Dublin, London, and Sydney, Australia, a somewhat surreal and postmodern account of a locality made famous by earlier playwrights.

The Beauty Queen of Leenane, the first part of the trilogy, opened on Broadway a year ago. The second, not yet seen in America, is entitled *A Skull in Connemara*. The third, *The Lonesome West*, opens in New York on Tuesday at the Lyceum Theater on Broadway. Like *Beauty Queen*, *The Lonesome West* focuses on a family – two warring brothers this time, rather than a mother and daughter – who live in the same house in the far western town of Leenane. Directing, as she did in the case of *Beauty Queen*, for which she won a Tony Award, is Garry Hynes, the artistic chief of the Druid Theater Company in Galway. Brian F. O'Byrne (who played the suitor in *Beauty Queen*) and Maeliosa Stafford portray the two brothers in the Druid Theater/Royal Court Theater production.

In Ireland, as in America, going west means many things: getting back to rural roots; seeking a final confrontation on the frontier between civilization and wilderness; perhaps even fixing to die. All those meanings are present, for instance, in James Joyce's great story 'The Dead' and in the movie *Into the West*, written by Jim Sheridan and seen in the United States in 1993. It tells of two Dublin boys fleeing west on a white horse in a variant on the old mythical search for a happy land beneath the Atlantic waves.

Yet for all their spontaneity, westerners are generally conservative people. In referendums on divorce and abortion in Ireland, they voted an emphatic no, and at election time most show scant sympathy for liberals. A paradox ensues: in the west, people are conservative but wild; in the east, liberal but buttoned down. It's the sort of paradox long familiar to many Americans.

The split between east and west runs far deeper through Ireland than the over-reported partition between north and south. A thousand years ago, a huge dike separated west from east, bisecting the island. If the current peace process holds, that deeper bifurcation may re-emerge. Even within Northern Ireland, a city like Derry, on its western edge, would be seen as traditional but artistic, while Belfast back east is considered to be industrialized and prosaic. Where do these stereotypes come from?

More than three centuries ago, the rampaging armies of Oliver Cromwell told natives to go 'to hell – or to Connaught'. The western province – including the wild, stony, mountainous region of Connemara in the county of Galway where the village of Leenane can be found – was so bleak and infertile that the planters willingly ceded most of its badlands to the Irish. Ever after it became a byword for all that was primitive and undeveloped. The word 'culchie' (pronounced KUL-chee and based on the Mayo town of Kiltimagh) is Dublin slang to denote what in America would be called a redneck.

There is, of course, another view. It was summed up at the start of this century by the poet W.B. Yeats, who said: 'Connaught for me is Ireland'. To him, it was the repository of an essential national identity embodied in folklore, poetry, the Irish tongue. It was the landscape of dreams and imagination.

Not all of his contemporaries shared this view. In *A Portrait of the Artist as a Young Man*, Joyce described an encounter between a romantic student from Dublin and a peasant in the west. After a few token phrases in Irish, their conversation lapses into English, either because the peasant's Irish-speaking act falls through or (more likely) because the student's phrase book is soon exhausted. Whatever the reason, Joyce was mocking the very idea of a Gaelic revival. At the end of the scene, the peasant smokes, spits and says, 'Ah, there must be terrible queer creatures at the latter end of the world.' For Joyce, the west is just another of those modern places that has no 'there' there anymore. It can no longer serve as an authentic elsewhere. The very construction of the 'west' as a zone of native primitivism is, in his view, an effect of colonialism rather than a real answer to it. So he indicts the British colonial authorities, but then goes on to indict Irish nationalists for making the peasant the embodiment of pious values that the peasant himself would never claim to uphold.

This is the tragic recognition that awaits Joyce's Gaelic revivalist. He comes to the native quarter in search of the exotic and finds instead a countryman whose culture is as broken as his own. Yeats's pastoral proved far more seductive than Joyce's bleak realism. On millions of postcards, rural Ireland was depicted as real Ireland, and cities were often discounted as fallen places, evidence of dire Anglicization. When the census of 1971 revealed that more people lived in towns than in the countryside, that rural myth, far from being exploded, took on new life. Now, more than ever, the Irish needed to look back in tenderness at the bucolic scenes of their childhood, before they all became (in the words of a character by the contemporary playwright John B. Keane) 'perverts from built-up areas'.

Such a pastoralism tended to sentimentalize backwardness, to find poverty saintly and primitivism heroic. Its exponents in drama were Yeats and Augusta Gregory. They had gone from cottage to cottage collecting stories of the Celtic hero Cuchulain as material for their plays, and marveling at the contrast between the material poverty of the tellers and the verbal splendor of their tales. Others were troubled by such discrepancies. Synge decided that such heroic tales were a myth of compensation, told by a people too timid to think of emulating heroic feats. His mockery of what he called 'Cuchulanoid' writing was based on the belief that hero cults were a sign of weakness rather than a spur to self-respect. Synge's *Playboy of the Western World'* provoked a largely male audience to riot in 1907 as a protest against its alleged slurs on Irish manhood. The play also sent up ideas of peasant holiness: 'Well, there's a sainted glory in the lonesome west.' Pious nationalists in Dublin had wanted to be shown a peasantry ready for the responsibilities of self-government; instead, Synge showed them a world filled with repression, violence and colorful speech. This was, in fact, closer to the country people's own self-image. One old Sligo shoemaker had complained bitterly to Yeats that he was sick of peasant heroes and wanted 'a work in which the people would be shown up in all their naked hideousness'.

Mr McDonagh draws on all these traditions, but especially Synge. He seems to have turned 'To hell – or to Connaught' and 'Connaught is Ireland' into a syllogism whose conclusion might possibly be 'Ireland is hell'. But his plays capture also the lyricism of Yeats and Gregory, as well as the bleakness picked up on by Synge and Joyce. Not all Irish audiences approve the ensuing blend. Some accuse the playwright of being a 'plastic Paddy' from London who traduces rather than represents western people, exploiting them for purposes of caricature rather than expressing the pressure of a felt communal experience. Synge, as a gentleman from Dublin, faced similar charges, and answered by claiming to depict 'the psychic state of the locality' rather than its actual sociology. He found the richness of the people's nature 'a thing priceless beyond words'. The west has changed a lot in the nine decades since the death of Synge. The full benefits of modern technology have reached its villages, but the old elaboration of personality through a good story or a finely turned phrase survives. So does the sophistication of a people who can combine seemingly opposed ideas in the conduct of everyday life. One old Galway woman, when asked by an American anthropologist whether she really believed in fairies, replied after some thought, 'I do not, sir, but I'm dead afraid of them.'

'Gained in Translation'

Irish Times 12 October 1999[1]
Declan Kiberd

The Italians used to say that all translators are traducers, and that the poetry of a language invariably gets lost in any such transaction. Yet the Irish have never shrunk from that challenge. Back in 1901, some of our greatest writers wondered how best to translate the ancient tale of Diarmuid and Grainne into the language of the modern world. Eventually, George Moore suggested he would compose a version in French, Augusta Gregory would next translate it into Hiberno-English, Tadhg Ó Donnchada would then convert it into Irish, and Gregory would finally put that back into English. Moore's point was that more would be gained than lost with every single version. The more 'translated' the work would be, the more fully would it achieve its destined form.

That theory will be put to the test next week when Micheál Ó Conghaile's version of *The Beauty Queen of Leenane* comes to the stage of the Town Hall Theatre under the title *Banríon Álainn an Líonáin*. The organizers of Feile 2000 – billed as 'the biggest Irish-language arts festival ever' – believe that in this flagship production the speeches of Mag and Maureen will be translated back into the Irish language and cultural codes, 'which were their true source'. They promise that this version of Martin McDonagh's Broadway hit will go close to the bone, and to the funnybone, of Connemara.

It's an intriguing prospect and all portents are encouraging. Ó Conghaile understands that a successful translation is always like a good lover: faithful without seeming to be so. And he isn't afraid to recognize the bits of Bearlachas and modern international slang which have crept into the language of the Gaeltacht, as well as into McDonagh's own script.

This won't, however, be the first time that plays in Hiberno-English have made the perilous voyage back to Irish. The ease with which many of the works of J.M. Synge have been staged in Irish was one way for that Anglo-Irish playwright's admirers to defend him against charges of caricaturing the people of the west. In recent years, productions of *Uaigneas an Ghleanna* (*The Shadow of the Glen*) and *Chun na Farraige Síos* (*Riders to the Sea*) have played to a full house on Inis Meain (a full house in this very special case meaning that everyone on the island went to the production). And it's many decades since Liam O Briain wrote his version of *Deirdre an Bhróin* (*Deirdre of the Sorrows*).

McDonagh, like his predecessor, has had detractors who accuse him of being a 'plastic Paddy'. He may not be Anglo-Irish by social class, as Synge was, but he is Anglo-Irish in the geographical sense of having grown up in London as the child of Irish parents. Some people contend that his plays exploit rather than express the western communities depicted, by providing a rather external and cruel rendition of character.

The communities of the west have for more than a century been seen as repositories of native tradition and of pure language. It has been an awesome burden to carry. In recent years, we've begun to recognize that, far from being an answer to colonialism, the Gaeltacht may be just another of its effects. The 'native quarter' in post-colonial literature and film is often a zone visited by touristic outsiders in search of a frisson.

Some critics see McDonagh as just another London-Irish lad 'home' on holidays, moving into Connemara in search of the exotic: but his plays also mock previous attempts by official Ireland to fetishize the western peasantry. In the use of language, however, he remains utterly faithful to the people's speech.

Synge, for his part, tried to depict the folk as he found them at the start of the century, still thinking in Irish syntax and idioms, while using English words. He discovered (according to George Moore) that if you translated Irish word-for-word into English, the result was poetry. The deviations from standard grammar in his dialect sounded lyrical to an ear pitched to the inner acoustic of Oxford English. By disrupting standard syntax and rewriting its rules, Irish people had been releasing hidden, forgotten potentials in English. An imperial language which seemed jaded by over-use and journalese was reinvigorated by contact with Gaelic codes.

The great final speech of Old Maurya in *Riders to the Sea*, for instance, was sourced not in the plays of Sophocles (as many early reviewers seemed to think), but in a letter written to Synge by an Inis Meain youth reporting a death in his family. 'Caithfidh muid a bheith sásta mar nach féidir le áon duine a bheith beo go deo' became 'no man at all can be living forever, and we must be satisfied'. More subtly still, Synge discovered that the key-word in a sentence in Hiberno-English, as in Irish, is brought forward. Emphasis is achieved by location rather than tonal underlining – 'Is it you that's going to town tomorrow?', 'Is it tomorrow that you're going to town?', 'Is it to town that you're going tomorrow?' etc.

Synge's lines went back beautifully into Irish with no trace of Bearlachas, a proof of the closeness with which he had rendered the people's own translation in the other direction. This was possible because the changeover of languages had occurred with such speed in the previous few decades: in some Galway families the parents spoke Irish while their children responded in English. When Douglas Hyde met a boy in the area he asked 'Nach labhrann tú an Ghaeilge?' (Don't you speak Irish?), only to be told 'Isn't it Irish I'm speaking, sir?' In a sense the boy, who didn't realize that they were communicating in two languages, was right. Some decades before that encounter, William Carleton had recorded a wedding where the bride spoke only Irish, the groom only English, and the very language of love cried out (he said) for an interpreter.

McDonagh's case is somewhat different from Synge's. He has not claimed any deep knowledge of Irish, and his distance from his source material is much greater: but then, it should be added, Galway today is itself rather distant from the county of 100 years ago through which Synge walked and talked. The English spoken in Spiddal or Leenane now is a lot less close to Irish than it would have been in the 1890s.

How well, then, does *The Beauty Queen of Leenane* translate? Is it really possible to use Irish to 'bring it all back home'? Only the production itself will answer those questions: but the script confirms the suspicion that modern translation, far from traducing the text, has merely given it some added value. There is far less likelihood now of the play seeming to be an exercise in stage-Irishry which encourages sophisticated audiences to patronize hopeless peasants: and a far greater chance of seeing it as an auto-critique of Irish culture offered from within. In that light its true forerunner may not be Synge at all, but rather Myles na gCopaleen, who in *An Béal Bocht* (The Poor Mouth) produced an anti-pastoral, deglamorized version of Gaeltacht life. Striking analogies may also be found between old Mag and Paidin Mhaire of Cré na Cille (Graveyard Clay), that other great work of debunkery in Irish which led to its author, Mairtin Ó Cadhain, being accused of a travesty.

In terms of pure language, Ó Conghaile's version works brilliantly. 'Is the radio a biteen loud?' becomes 'an bhfuil an raidio sin beagáinín ró-árd?' And the key words are indeed brought forward in the sentences: 'Isn't it you wanted it set for the oul station?' becomes 'agus nach tusa a bhí ag iarraidh an raidio a chur ar an seanstaisiún sin?' But the existence of Bearlachas is honestly rendered too, in a way which would seem strange in a work of Synge. 'Ta tú sean agus stupid agus níl cliu agat ceard atá tu fein a rá' is true enough to 'You're ould and you're stupid and you don't know what you're talking about.'

The scene from which these examples come reads like a brilliant commentary on this whole project. Mag complains of the Irish spoken on Céili House and calls it nonsense: but her daughter Maureen demurs:

> **Maire:** Ní seafóid é ar áon nós. Nach Gaeilge atá air?
> **Mag:** Mhuise, ta sé cosuil le seafóid do chuid mhaith daoine. Cén fath nach bhféadfadh siad Béarla a labhairt ar nós chuile dhuine?
> **Maire:** It isn't nonsense anyways. Isn't it Irish?
> **Mag:** It sounds like nonsense to me. Why can't they just speak English like everybody?

In an age when there are no monoglot Irish-speakers left, some might echo Mag and question the need for this translation. Yet the exercise is vitally important in making the text even more our own. Deepest of all is the question of language. When that earlier skit on western stereotypes, *An Beal Bocht*, was sent by its author to Sean O'Casey in England, the playwright congratulated Brian O'Nolan on his feat. In his letter of response, O'Casey suggested that the Irish language 'supplies that unknown quantity in us that enables us to transform the English language – and this seems to hold good for people who know little or no Irish, like Joyce'. Or, he might now add if he were with us, Martin McDonagh.

'Drama Sails to Seven Islands'

Irish Times 27 November 1996
Uinsionn Mac Dubhghaill

Druid Theatre's 21 years of pushing out the theatrical boat have been marked by many surprises, many rapturous reviews, many extraordinary tours to venues in which no professional company dreamed of playing before. This year's birthday tour with Martin McDonagh's *The Beauty Queen of Leenane* was more ambitious than ever, covering seven island venues and seven mainland ones from Oileán Chléire in West Cork to Rathlin Island off the Antrim coast. It came to a triumphant finale in Leenane in Connemara on Saturday, with a moment of unexpected theatre.

The play is the stark and unsettling story of Maureen Folan, a forty-year-old virgin trapped in a dysfunctional relationship with Mag, her ageing and manipulative mother. Leavened with comic moments which arise from the petty tyrannies the women inflict on each other, it sucks the audience into complacency before delivering a killer punch at the end. The final scene forces the audience to confront the truth that what seemed hilarious earlier on is, after all, not so funny.

As such, the play had a special resonance with many of the local audiences it played to during the tour. Again and again, in the feedback cast and crew were given on their way up the western seaboard, people identified the play with certain dysfunctional relationships in their own areas. Then it came to Leenane and sitting in the front row – on a specially-reserved seat was the person believed locally to be the real 'Queen' of Leenane, Bina McLoughlin.

Ms McLoughlin is one of those characters whose presence enriches many rural communities. She lives alone in a small cottage on the side of a hill near Leenane, with her flock of sheep and her other animals. She has had a hard life and is viewed with a certain amount of awe and respect in the local community. On Saturday night she dressed up for the play, putting on her long dress embroidered with Celtic designs and a bright red woollen hat, before making her way down to Leenane parish hall. When the performance ended the audience stood, almost in unison, and gave the actors a thunderous ovation – par for the course during this tour. After a slight pause, Ms McLoughlin opened her arms wide in benediction, before rising to her feet and joining in the applause.

Outside the hall, she sought out Martin McDonagh to congratulate him for writing such a play. She told *The Irish Times* it 'reminded me of nothing at all, but I thought it was one of the finest I ever saw'. Half the audience was there because they thought the play was going to tell her story, she said. Then she laughed loudly and added, enigmatically, 'mine is a lot harder'.

The Beauty Queen is transferring to the West End this week, where it opens for a short season next Monday at the Duke of York's, the temporary home of the Royal Court. The island venues have been particularly intense and intimate, with audiences up close and reactions in terms of laughter, exclamations or comments – freely given and immediate. On Arranmore island the locals were tickled pink that theirs was the only Donegal venue. On Inis Oirr they turned out in a howling gale, walking or travelling by tractor to pack the venue known simply as 'An Halla'.

The move to more restrained audiences for the play's second tour to London will be a big change: 'There is a kind of a feeling, funnily enough, that London is the anticlimax to what has happened. It has been such an amazing tour. Even though it's the West End and all that, and there will be the first night glitz and all that, we're all not going: 'Yeah – London!', says actor Tom Murphy, who is wonderful in his bored-to-tears role in the play. 'London will be a big culture shock after this', says Anna Manahan, who delivers a subtle and powerful performance as the manipulative Mag Folan. 'I think we'll all be longing for the islands.' The play sold out everywhere it went, with the exception of Bangor Erris, where the first night clashed with an important Manchester United match. When the seats were full, standing places were sold off at a £1 a throw. In most of the venues these too sold out.

While these unusual venues added to the play's power, the reason for its success lies in the play itself. Like in atomic physics, where the act of observing a particle may change its nature, *The Beauty Queen* becomes a different play in different places. Watching the play in Galway before the tour started, one is struck by the poignancy and starkness of the lives exposed on stage. The tone is serious, sombre. On Inis Mór, the audience laughs heartily at every misfortune, every minor cruelty – perhaps because the only other choice is to cry. The response comes from the gut, while in town it comes from the head. There is a point near the start of the play when Maureen turns up the radio. A song in Irish is playing, which Mag dismisses as 'oul' nonsense'. Viewed in Galway, the ensuing spat over the language seems laboured, as if the writer – born in London but whose father comes from Leitir Meallain – is trying to make some kind of didactic statement.

But in Halla Ronain on Inis Mór the perspective is different. At the back of the hall, a gaggle of teenagers chat in English during the first half of the play, pausing to giggle occasionally at the curses on stage. Half-way up the hall, an old man's face becomes animated with amusement as Mag voices a deeply-felt conviction, held in many Gaeltacht communities, that Irish is of no value. It is a feeling that is not often articulated openly in public, for fear of jeopardizing the community's chances of getting any grants that might be going. Now here is somebody on stage saying what many privately feel, and the audience is loving it. 'Oh, 'tis true, 'tis true,' chortles the old man, as Mag asks what use is Irish on a building site in London or Boston?

In Leenane, the audience is silent during the same scene. Perhaps it is an unwelcome reminder in an area where the decision to abandon Irish as a community language is still uncomfortably close. It is one of the many nuances in the response to the play that make touring such an enriching experience, not only for the people who get to see it but also for the company itself. Maybe this ability to make different meanings for different people is the secret of eternal youth, the reason that after 21 years Druid is still as fresh and as vital as ever. As artistic director Garry Hynes explains, the tour is both a continuation of a process which began in the early 1980s and an opportunity for renewal. 'In our 15 years of touring we have visited about 71 different venues,' she says. 'It's not just something we do after we do everything else. Touring has become central, not just to the strategic policy of the company but to the artistic policy as well.'

'It's not a one-way thing where the theatre company goes to the community and brings something with it. You also get something back.'

'The Beauty Queen of Leenane: 2000'

Irish Theatre Magazine Autumn 2000
Susan Conley

Martin McDonagh's *The Beauty Queen Of Leenane*, now in its fourth year of production, is making a victory lap of some of Ireland's major booking houses. Its reputation precedes it, via hit runs in London and on Broadway; kudos in the form of four Tony Awards are hard to ignore. Equally impossible to miss have been the queues waiting to collect their tickets on South King Street. The production's done such great box office at the Gaiety, in fact, that Druid have re-booked the venue for yet another run in July.

So much has already been written about this now-overexposed production; but at last the dissenting, questioning voices are starting to be heard, primarily in the non-mainstream press and specialist journals. Add my voice to their number: As a play that has been representing Irish theatre in the big leagues, *Beauty Queen* offers a simplistic, violent, and dated vision of life on this island. It is a deeply disturbing vision that, most disturbingly, leaves its audiences laughing themselves silly.

The plot, for the uniniatied: Maureen Folan is an unhappy 40-something woman charged with caring for her mother, Mag. Almost exclusively in each other's company, they torture one another relentlessly, Mag through child-like demands and sabotage, Maureen via verbal and physical abuse. The return of friend and neighbour Pato Dooley from America disrupts the (im)balance of the Folans' relationship. When it appears that Maureen may actually escape Leenane, Mag ensures that her daughter will remain by destroying a letter containing Pato's marriage proposal. A poker, much admired throughout the play, gets its 15 minutes of fame when Maureen realizes what her mother has done. But murdering Mag only serves to trap Maureen completely.

Of the several themes at work in the play – emigration, sexuality, the romanticization of the West of Ireland, Kimberley biscuits – the most problematic is this mother/daughter relationship. Mag and Maureen are trapped not only on a boreen in the desolate wilds of the West, but also in a hateful yet symbiotic bond. Their interdependence is apparent in Maureen's inability to leave Leenane. This is pathos – it is played as panto. Every insult is greeted with gales of laughter. The threats, the curses, the sheer unadulterated nastiness is delivered and accepted as a joke. Even the instances of physical abuse inspire nervous titters. These flashes of violence are meant to be provocative; instead they merely provoke, leaving one to feel cheapened by the event rather than lifted into catharsis.

Laughter is a form of catharsis, but *Beauty Queen*'s humour is as low as a bucket of wee dumped down the sink. The audience's wholesale enjoyment shocks on yet another level: Under the cosmopolitan circumstances (Dublin's city centre) it becomes smug, superior chuckling at those ignorant culchies who haven't got the spunk to get out and make it in the big city. As the history of Irish theatre was built on the country plays of Synge, Yeats, and Lady Gregory, this is tantamount to cultural insult. As part of that history largely figures Ireland as a woman (i.e. Cathleen Ní Houlihan), the vengeful, immature, stunted women presented by McDonagh are even more disturbing.

Yet the audience laughs and laughs. Is Irish theatre so devoid of representation of the collective? The product references alone swept the audience along on waves of glee. The Complan, Dettol, and Zip Firelighters dotted the set as cannily as cans of Coke in a Hollywood blockbuster. The easy vulgarity suffices as indigenous language for the punters who embrace it. The whole endeavour smacks of elitism and smugness. It is clear that this play fills some void: The Irish wants to see themselves onstage, and this fact guarantees a place in the canon for this highly-lauded but mean-spirited piece of theatre.

'Ireland feels power of Beauty'.

Variety 21-27 August 2000
Karen Fricker

The Martin McDonagh phenomenon may be on the fade in the US, but in this country his much-lauded plays are still doing the business – and generating controversy. The original Druid Theatre Company/Royal Court Theatre production of McDonagh's *The Beauty Queen of Leenane* is currently enjoying a well-subscribed eight week run (ending Sept. 9) at the Gaiety Theatre, a 1,160-seat commercial venue in Dublin. This follows on from an 11-venue UK and Ireland tour earlier this year, which included three weeks of performances at the Gaiety, all of which were sold out.

'That initial run in March caught us by surprise,' says Ciaran Walsh, Druid's managing director. 'The demand was staggering, and that's why we decided to bring it back this summer. It's great to be able to put on a show that audiences want to see.'

The production's March dates were actually the first sustained opportunity that Dublin audiences had to see *Beauty Queen*; its only other showing here was a very limited run, as part of McDonagh's complete Leenane Trilogy, during the Dublin Theatre Festival in October 1997. If it seems strange, to an outside eye, that Dublin didn't figure until now in the extraordinary trajectory of McDonagh's play (which included two runs in London, a tour of seven remote island communities in the West of Ireland, and, most famously, stints off and on Broadway), it is clearly something of a point of pride for Druid, which is based in the western city of Galway and has long toiled to counteract the prevailing wisdom that the only culture in Ireland happens in its capital. 'I don't think it's any coincidence that it took *Beauty Queen* four years to get to Dublin', says Walsh, with more than a whiff of second-city scorn.

The feeling is evidently mutual, at least among the chattering classes: it is only in its Dublin runs that *Beauty Queen*'s until-now virtually spotless critical record has started to tarnish. While international and mainstream Irish critics, by and large, have gone mad for McDonagh's tightly plotted tragicomedies, the Dublin intelligentsia has been considerably less impressed.

'[McDonagh presents] a simplistic, violent, and dated vision of life on this island,' argues Susan Conley in *Irish Theatre Magazine*. The work is characterized by 'nostalgic viciousness', Kevin Barry told *Magill Magazine*'s Ian Kilroy, in an article titled 'The One-Trick Pony of Connemara?' To Vic Merriman in *The Irish University Review*, McDonagh's plays offer 'a sustained dystopic vision of a land of gratuitous violence, craven money-grubbing, and crass amorality … gross caricatures with no purchase on the experience of today's audiences'.

Clearly the crux of the critics' problems with McDonagh's work is what they see as the extremity and datedness of his portrayal of rural Ireland. The Leenane of his trilogy is peopled with murderous, desperate, lonely individuals locked into outdated societal roles and family relationships which they can only break out of through violence – to others and to themselves. While ostensibly set in contemporary times, the plays look and feel as if they were depicting an Ireland of fifty years ago.

To McDonagh's advocates, his use of these 'stage Irish' images is actually proof of the country's growing maturity, the indication of an emerging postmodern Irish sensibility that is newly able to send itself up. The highest-profile of these voices is Fintan O'Toole, columnist for *The Irish Times* and theatre critic for the New York *Daily News*. 'Of course he's dealing with stereotypes, of course he's dealing in a stage Irish mode,' O'Toole told *Magill*, 'but it seems to me that he's the first writer of his generation where these stereotypes can be played with in an almost innocent way.'

While most who dislike McDonagh's work take particular offence in the fact that McDonagh is not actually from the culture he so gleefully sends up – he is the London-bred son of Irish parents – O'Toole sees McDonagh's distance from Irish culture as something essential to his voice: his is an 'emigrant vision', free to toy with images and ideas in a way that people actually raised in Ireland still may be unable to.

For some of McDonagh's critics, his depiction of the Irish is particularly problematic when it's exported, because, in Barry's words 'It feeds the whole *Angela's Ashes* view of Ireland. When it travels it's taken at face value.' But the emergence of the McDonagh backlash at this particular juncture in his career clearly indicates that his work raises the most issues when viewed in an urban Irish, rather than an international, context.

The problem, in short, is who's laughing at whom. McDonagh's plays are all pitch-black comedies, and indeed he is a skilled creator of comic situations and writes fantastically idiosyncratic, barbed dialogue. But observers find something particularly insidious in the spectacle of the urban Irish bourgeoisie (who are, in the current boom economy, a heady and powerful constituency) taking in the spectacle of rough country folk eating each other alive for a night's entertainment.

While many would argue that what those audiences are laughing at is themselves – the 'scratch any Irish person and you'll find a bumpkin' logic – others say this argument ignores the diversity of Irish culture, the fact that huge disparities now exist between the cosmopolitan city centers and the rural, depressed countryside. The laughter of those Dublin audiences, the argument goes, is that of combined relief and derision: we're not like that anymore, so we're going to laugh at those who are.

There is certainly something quite jarring in seeing the production in its current Gaiety incarnation, as opposed to its Dublin Theatre Festival outing in the smaller Olympia Theatre three years ago. In that context, when international interest in McDonagh's work was starting to accelerate, there was a respectful, art-house atmosphere – lots of laughter, to be sure, but overall the sense that one was attending a work of significance and weight.

Three years on, the production is playing like Christmas pantomime: the guffaws when the loathsome mother Mag, played by Anna Manahan (the only cast member to have stuck with the show throughout), pours her pot of pee down the sink stop the action for a solid minute; the second-act hijinks involving a stolen letter and a murderous poker have the audience shouting at the stage.

One of *Beauty Queen*'s biggest selling points throughout its life has been the strength and integrity of Garry Hynes's production; while the production values and the performances here are as strong as ever (Marie Mullen is reprising her role as the down-trodden Maureen, while Peter Gowen and Ruaidhri Conroy have taken over the male roles), there is the sense that the show has been both slowed down and broadened out for the larger venue – some of Mullen's gestures are so exaggerated that they seem like they're happening in slo-mo.

This can't help but feed into the feeling that the play is staging a cartoon version of Irishness. Some people think that's dangerous. Other people think it's all just for the laugh. The debate is surely evidence of this country's still-uncertain sense of itself, but it's also proof of the power that theatre still has here to both inform and inflame the Irish public.

'The Beauty Queen of Leenane'

Irish Times 6 February 1996
Fintan O'Toole

As well as being one of the most auspicious debuts by an Irish playwright in the past 25 years, Martin McDonagh's *The Beauty Queen of Leenane*, which opened last week at the new Town Hall Theatre in Galway, is also the most intriguing Anglo-Irish fusion since Jack Charlton first pulled on a green tracksuit.

In it, Harold Pinter and Joe Orton blend seamlessly with Tom Murphy and John B. Keane to create a vibrantly original mixture of absurd comedy and cruel melodrama. McDonagh's London-Irish background allows him to hold in perfect tension an extraordinary range of elements from both sides of the Irish Sea.

As in Pinter, everyday banality acquires sinister undertones. As in Orton, mundane speech is bent into outrageous shapes without ever losing its demotic feel. But there is also a dark comedy of yearning and despair reminiscent of Murphy, and a situation – a 40-year-old spinster trapped with a monstrous old woman in a remote house in the West – that echoes his great play *Bailegangaire*.

There is a wildly melodramatic plot of which the early John B. Keane might have been proud. And all of this is held together with an utterly 1990s sensibility, in which knowing and playful pastiche becomes indistinguishable from serious and sober intent.

The mixture of elements makes sense because the country in which McDonagh's play is set is pre-modern and postmodern at the same time. The 1950s is laid over the 1990s, giving the play's apparent realism the ghostly, dizzying feel of a superimposed photograph. All the elements that make up the picture are real, but their combined effect is one that questions the very idea of reality.

One of the superimposed pictures is a black-and-white still from an Abbey play of the 1950s: West of Ireland virgins and London building sites, tyrannical mothers and returned Yanks. In it, Marie Mullen's Maureen lives with her terrible mother (Anna Manahan) in a house up a Connemara hill. A meeting with Pato, a local man back on holiday from the building sites (Brian F. O'Byrne holds out the promise of happiness that you know from the start will be destroyed by the mother.)

But the other picture is a lurid Polaroid of a postmodern landscape, a disintegrating place somewhere between London and Boston, saturated in Irish rain and Australian soaps, a place in which it is hard to remember anyone's name, in which news of murders floats in through the television screen, in which the blurring of personal identities makes the line between the real and the unreal dangerously thin. And behind these garish colours, there are shadows in which madness and violence lurk, waiting to emerge.

Looking at both pictures at the same time, you experience a series of double takes. You are drawn into the comfortable, melodramatic rush of the plot, knowing all the time that it is taking you to places you don't want to go, wondering why conversations keep throwing up images of violence and death, wondering why Maureen's party dress looks as if it could be for a funeral as well as a hooley. You find yourself in two minds most of the time.

And as the real and the unreal become for Maureen increasingly hard to tell apart, the whole idea of theatrical realism becomes itself the biggest double take of all. The conventions of domestic drama are at once followed and parodied. The kitchen sink is present and prominent, but only to provide a pungent running gag. The domestic details – Kimberley biscuits, lumpy Complan – that are meant to provide a 'realistic' backdrop to the action are instead pushed relentlessly into the foreground by McDonagh's brilliant dialogue. And the domestic appliances that dominate Francis O'Connor's subtle set become gradually less cosy and more sinister, as objects like the cooker, the cooking oil, and the poker become portents of violence and cruelty.

All of this is accomplished with an assurance astonishing in a first play. There is just one scene, dictated by the need to tell the audience the contents of a crucial letter from Pato to Maureen, where the stylistic integrity of the piece is broken. But what is really important is that McDonagh is more than just a very clever theatrical stylist. His tricks and turns have a purpose. They are bridges over a deep pit of sympathy and sorrow, illuminated by a tragic vision of stunted and frustrated lives, that make any comparison with Quentin Tarantino, prompted by outward similarities of violence and language, merely superficial.

And in Garry Hynes's superb production, perfectly pitched between the comic and the grotesque, it is Marie Mullen who embodies that vision. In one of her finest performances, Mullen combines a minute sense of detail in her movements and expressions with the ability to suggest all the time that those details don't ever add up to a stable whole. Her Maureen is now girlish, now old, now vulnerable, now cruel, now warm, now cold – a bundle of tentative possibilities in search of a personality. With the disciplined, assured work of Manahan, O'Byrne, and Tom Murphy as Pato's brother Ray around her, she forms the broken heart of the play's clever games of form and meaning.

In his stunning final scene, McDonagh brings together the trivial and the tragic, an ascent into the heights of loopiness and a descent into the depths of despair. The effect is hysterical in both senses – wildly funny in its incongruity, crushingly bleak in its madness – and deeply unsettling. And as it starts to sink in, you realize that a new force has hit Irish theatre.

'Murderous Laughter' – 'The Leenane Trilogy'

Irish Times 24 June 1997
Fintan O'Toole

At a key point near the end of Martin McDonagh's great Gothic soap opera, *The Leenane Trilogy*, one of the characters looks guiltily at another and says: 'We shouldn't laugh'. It is a simple line, but, for the audience, a devastating one. We have, at that point, spent nearly six hours laughing ourselves sick at some of the blackest, bleakest stories that have ever been told in the Irish theatre. We have laughed at the Famine, at murders and suicides, at children drowning in slurry pits, and old men choking on vomit. And the question that McDonagh asks us is: when does the laughing stop and the thinking begin? For at its core, the trilogy is a comedy about the need to take some things seriously.

It is often said, with a great deal of truth, that the characteristic mode of Irish theatre is tragicomedy. And in that sense, McDonagh, for all the complexity of his background and influences, is clearly an Irish playwright. The difference though is that whereas in the classic Irish repertoire, comedy and tragedy tend to alternate in the same play, here they become indistinguishable. These plays are so brilliantly entertaining that we are still laughing halfway down the street. But because we know we shouldn't laugh, they are also deeply disturbing.

The disturbance comes from the sense of being in a world where the kind of responses implied by words like comedy and tragedy just don't work anymore. It is not accidental that the Ireland of these plays is one in which all authority has collapsed. The family, from *The Beauty Queen of Leenane* onwards, is a site for psychological and even biological warfare. The law, in the shape of Garda Tom Hanlon (Brian F. O'Byrne) in *A Skull in Connemara*, is a joke, and everyone is literally getting away with murder. The Church, embodied by David Ganly's Father Welsh in *The Lonesome West*, is a lost, despairing young alcoholic, whose flock console him with the thought that at least he is not a paedophile. The Catholic Church's great point, says Maeliosa Stafford's Coleman Connor in the same play, is the ability to supply good *vol-au-vents* at funerals.

This is a world where the difference between the real and the unreal is increasingly hard to grasp. On the one hand, there is a sense of isolated people clinging to a remote and inhospitable landscape. But on the other, this isolation is also suspended in the airwaves. From the start, through television and emigration, bits of other places – Australia, America, England, Trinidad – float into consciousness. And the plays themselves are plugged into the television screen – with its continual references to Australian domestic dramas, American detective series and, in *The Lonesome West*, to *The Odd Couple*. The trilogy is a giant soap opera, but one that makes *Twin Peaks* look like *The Riordans*.

At one level, then, the trilogy maps a very real and immediate Ireland. However grotesque the exaggerations, they inflate a recognizable truth so that it can be seen more clearly. But at another level, the world that is imagined in this way is also a version of one of the great mythic landscapes – the world before morality. It is the ancient Greece of *The Oresteia* – a cycle of death and revenge before the invention of justice. It is, perhaps more to the point, the Wild West of John Ford's westerns or Cormac McCarthy's novels, a raw frontier beyond civilization.

McDonagh's brilliance, though, lies in the way he drains the heroics out of the myth. He suggests that what happens when order collapses is not just the big, epic horrors, but a hysterical riot of incongruities. What makes his characters so like old, mad children is that everyone has forgotten what adults are supposed to learn – the difference between what matters and what doesn't.

Much of the best of his comedy comes from the contrast between the savage intensity that the characters invest in un-important objects – Kimberley biscuits, Tayto crisps, plastic figurines of saints – and the carelessness with which they treat each other's lives. The appalling hilarity of this contrast reaches its logical conclusion in *The Lonesome West* when Coleman, about to be knifed by his brother Valene, realizes that the best way of defending himself is to point his shotgun, not at Valene, but at the latter's beloved new gas cooker. In this demented pre-moral world, things matter much more than lives.

If Martin McDonagh had not existed, Garry Hynes would have had to invent him, for all of this is uncannily in line with what she and Druid have been about over the last 21 years. For one thing the trilogy is the culmination of a long demythologization of the West that she and the company have conducted through such great productions as *The Playboy of the Western World*, M.J. Molloy's *The Wood of the Whispering*, and Tom Murphy's *Bailegangaire* and *Conversations on a Homecoming*. At a profound level, McDonagh's plays represent a final reversal of Romanticism. To the Romantics, the West was proof of the Utopian belief that life was better and purer before the imposition of modern society. Here, the West, without a functioning society, proves the opposite.

The plays fit in with Garry Hynes's work at Druid in another way, too. The company's veterans – Marie Mullen, Maeliosa Stafford, Mick Lally – have often been at their very best when exploding naturalism from within, starting with the apparently familiar and making it very strange.

This is precisely the way McDonagh's writing operates. It takes the conventions of kitchen sink drama and exaggerates them into a kind of dirty naturalism. As Hynes has done so often, it takes the elements of literary Western speech and writes them out with the kind of fluorescent pens that Maryjohnny Rafferty in *A Skull in Connemara* uses for doing bingo. For these people not only talk – they talk about talk, discussing curses, insinuations, aspersions, insults, and coinages: 'There's no such word as un-bare'. They have a theatrical self-consciousness that has been the hallmark of so much of Druid's work.

This confluence of Druid's history with McDonagh's intentions makes for a magnificently seamless production in which play and players are inseparable. There are great technical achievements – the simplicity which designer Francis O'Connor distils from a very complex use of space, the odd grandeur of Ben Ormerod's lighting, the flawless pacing, and relentless physicality of Hynes's direction.

But this is above all a triumph in the direction of actors. The sheer facility of McDonagh's writing for the stage is such that it would be difficult to imagine an entirely bad production. But an entirely good one is a ferocious challenge for it requires an ability to maintain a highly distinctive tone over three plays.

McDonagh's style is not quite like anything else on earth. The characters are cartoon creatures who really die when someone fires a shotgun at their heads. They are sitcom people in desperate situations and horrific comedies. They are puppets who continue to move around long after the strings of logical control have been cut. To inhabit them, the actors have to both believe in them utterly and yet maintain the kind of cool distance they would bring to a farce or a knockabout silent movie.

They do it – collectively and almost perfectly. Brian F. O'Byrne's achievement in creating three different characters with the same accent and the same age who are yet utterly different is the most remarkable. But there are brilliant performances, too, from Anna Manahan, Marie Mullen and Maeliosa Stafford, and all the acting is extraordinarily intelligent.

The result is undoubtedly one of the great events of the contemporary Irish theatre. It would be greater if Martin McDonagh had managed to find, in his exploration of a world that has imploded, some basis for the new morality he seems to be seeking, some ground for reconciliation. But given that he has not yet found it, there is something deeply admirable in the way he refuses to concoct it merely for the sake of completeness. The openness of his ending suggests that he is still on a journey and the exhilaration of this strange stretch of the road suggests that anyone who travels it will want to go all the way with him.

'*The Pillowman* Program Note'

Cottesloe, Royal National Theatre, London, November 2003
Fintan O'Toole

In the search for life beyond Earth, most scientific interest is focussed on one of the moons of Jupiter, Europa. It is named after the beautiful Phoenician princess who, according to Greek mythology, was pursued by the mad love of Zeus and carried away into exile forever. In particular, the astrophysicists are interested in a region of Europa where the Galileo probe spotted an icy crust, suggesting the presence of water. In their informed imaginations, they can picture what might lie beneath the surface: a possible biosphere of suspended animation where putative organisms, trapped in the ice, wait for the next warm tide, generated by the moon's chemistry, to flow through and release them again into vivid existence.

And the name of this strange territory where the scepticism of science and the stirrings of hope and fantasy come together? The area is described in geological terms as a 'chaotic region'. Looking at the images sent back by Galileo, the wife of the NASA team leader was reminded somehow of a place she had recently visited on holidays. At her prompting, the chaotic but haunting region of Jupiter's moon has been named Conamara, the Irish-language spelling of the Connemara area of the West of Ireland. Together with its geological extension, the Aran Islands, it has been the setting of six of Martin McDonagh's seven plays. The connection seems appropriate to his work. McDonagh's habitual landscape has the name of a real, terrestrial place: Leenane, Inishmaan, Inishmore. But that place is also way out there in the planetary space of the imagination, in a chaotic region shaped by myth and exile where trapped lives wait for the warm tide to release them. Like NASA's Conamara, it is a place that can be observed with rational scientific detachment but that is imbued with irrational hopes and desires. We scrutinize it, not just as an exercise in observation, but because of the vague but potent possibility of what might lie beneath the surface. Some trace of what was once there draws us to believe, perhaps in complete delusion, that it has not vanished completely and might somehow return.

Some Irish critics have accused Martin McDonagh of being inauthentic, in the sense that his Ireland is, to them, unreal. Leaving aside the fact that comedy, however dark, does not aspire to realism, this seems to miss the point that he is in fact entirely true to his own place – that strange territory, half real and half dreamworld, known as exile. Pato Dooley in *The Beauty Queen of Leenane* sums up the convoluted ambivalence of a hyphenated identity: 'when it's there I am, it's here I wish I was, of course. Who wouldn't? But when it's here I am ... it isn't there I want to be, of course not. But I know it isn't here I want to be either.' Perhaps the easiest way to place McDonagh is to think of Shane McGowan, the great London-Irish songwriter who, in the heyday of The Pogues, gave voice to a jagged lyricism that caught the imagination of both Ireland and England. Both men grew up in the big bad world of London, and were force-fed Irish cultural forms as part of the staple diet of the diaspora. Yet while previous generations of London-Irish felt they had to choose between wallowing in Irish nostalgia on the one hand or in English amnesia on the other, both McGowan and McDonagh belonged to a generation that had the confidence to shrug off these false alternatives. They saw another way to express their own situation: to take the outer shells of the forms they had been told were theirs and fill them with their own sensibilities. McGowan took the Irish ballad and rammed the pungent energies of punk down its throat.

McDonagh, for his part, grabbed the Irish rural melodrama and infused it with the punkish energy, the sardonic comedy and the menacing strut of the London council estates. As a child of the Irish diaspora in England, he has both a native place (London) and an imaginary homeland (the West of Ireland). As a dramatist, his habitation is both of these places and neither of them. It is everywhere and nowhere, beyond the beyonds, a chaotic region where the banal and the grotesque, the terrible and the terribly funny, violence and yearning, continually morph into each other. For the Irish exile in England, home thoughts from abroad are supposed to carry a familiar resonance.

Over a century ago, W.B. Yeats popularized the mode in *The Lake Isle of Inishfree* when he stood in London 'on the roadway or on the pavements grey' and heard 'lake water lapping with low sounds by the shore' of an idyllic island in the West of Ireland. Later, the commercial songwriters and folk balladeers churned out songs about exiles writing to the sweethearts they left behind where the Mountains of Mourne sweep down to the sea or promising to take the sweethearts they brought with them home again, Cathleen. The melancholy allure of a lost paradise, where the sweet sorrow of parting will one day be transformed into the joy of homecoming, hung over everything, making London a bleak nowhere and Ireland a primeval fantasy.

Martin McDonagh, the son of a Sligo mother and a Galway father, grew up in this kind of London. He had Irish aunts and uncles all around. His family lived on a block in Elephant and Castle where half the houses were occupied by Irish families. It was a similar story when they moved down the road to Camberwell. He spent his summer holidays in Easkey, County Sligo, and in Connemara. He became a choir boy in the Catholic parish church and grew up steeped in the emotive stories of Irish nationalism. Later, his parents moved back to Lettermullan in Connemara, and although he and his older brother stayed behind in London, they continued to spend their summers in Ireland. He was, and is, a citizen of an indefinite land that is neither Ireland nor England, but that shares borders with both. His style is, in a completely new sense, Anglo-Irish. *The Pillowman* reminds us that he has an English ear as well as an Irish one. In his dialogue,

Harold Pinter and Joe Orton blend seamlessly with Tom Murphy and John B. Keane to create a vibrantly original mixture of absurd comedy and cruel melodrama. As in Pinter, everyday banality acquires sinister undertones.

As in Orton, mundane speech is bent into outrageous shapes without ever losing its demotic feel. But there is also a dark comedy of longing and despair reminiscent of Murphy, and a taste for wildly melodramatic plots of which the early John B. Keane might have been proud. This sense that McDonagh inhabits a no-man's-land between two worlds is also relevant to the violence of his work. The savagery of the plays may not be literal but neither is it pure invention. It comes from a vividly imagined sense of cultural confusion, from a world in which meanings and values have been shattered into odd-shaped fragments. And this sense of confusion is also innately comic.

McDonagh reveals the common roots of comedy and violence. Both come from a distortion of perspective, the loss of a sense of proportion. The exaggeration that makes an action comic is also the hyperbole that is implicit in the way violence functions as a wildly disproportionate response to circumstances. From his apprehension of a world in which things are out of place McDonagh makes a kind of dark comic that is created, not by simply putting horror beside humour, but by exposing the common origins of both. But what's important is that the plays themselves try to put those odd-shaped fragments of meaning back together again.

McDonagh weaves an extraordinary range of images into the assured stage-craft of the well-made play. There are touches of Shakespeare and soap opera, Grand Guignol and the Bible, melodrama and the Brothers Grimm. Dirty realism is continually shading into heightened epic. While his characters often struggle to articulate themselves in terms that transcend the cliches of have forgotten movies or shards of gossip from old magazines, McDonagh's own use of language has the rich texture that comes from being pitched perfectly between the sublime and the ridiculous, the farcical and the tragic, the mundane and the mythic. And what matters in the end is that McDonagh is more than just a very clever theatrical stylist. His tricks and turns have a purpose. They are bridges over a deep pit of sympathy and sorrow, illuminated by a tragic vision of stunted and frustrated lives. Moments of love and loss, of yearning, and even of faith catch the light now and then. That they cannot abide long in such a blighted world seems somehow less remarkable than the fact that they arise at all.

'New themes in Synge-song land: *The Beauty Queen of Leenane*'

Royal Court Theatre Upstairs
The Guardian 8 March 1996
Michael Billington

Hardly a week goes by without the emergence of a 25-year-old dramatist. The latest, in a rich period for new writing, is Martin McDonagh, whose *The Beauty Queen of Leenane* – co-produced by Galway's Druid Theatre and the Royal Court – is an astonishingly assured debut. It exploits Irish theatrical tradition and, at the same time, subtly undermines it.

McDonagh's setting is familiar, a rural cottage in the Connemara mountains. And when one is confronted by the 40-year-old Maureen tethered to a vindictive, repressive mother, the nagging Mag, one suspects one is in for one of those plaintive dramas about the denial of life. The impression is confirmed when Maureen has a brief, one-night fling with Pato Dooley, who navvies in London and who is about to leave for Boston and whose invitation to her to join him, we know, is foredoomed.

This is Synge country, a study of solitude and desertion in western Ireland. But McDonagh takes a stock form and reanimates it in several ways. In the first place, by showing that Maureen, far from being a self-pitying spinster, is every bit as ruthless as her exploitative mother. As excellently played by Marie Mullen, Maureen is full of ancient grudges and gets a savage delight out of serving her mum lumpy Complan or even pouring boiling fat over her. Maureen, we gradually realize, is not so much wistful as severely damaged.

McDonagh also brings a postmodern irony to his Synge-song fable. The Galway village has become a global village as the characters moodily stare at Australian soaps on the box. And there is one tremendous scene in which Pato's brother, Ray, delivers a crucial love-letter to the absent Maureen. As the mother greedily eyes the all-important letter, it becomes a plot-device straight out of Boucicault. At the same time, as Ray beats his head against the wall in frustration, the scene wittily catches the poleaxing boredom of Irish rural life.

McDonagh, who has Galway forebears but lives in London, where he is attached to the National Theatre Studio, is both exploiting and exposing Celtic myth. This is a world where the radio still spews out Delia Murphy singing The Spinning Wheel, while the young, like Ray, yearn for Mancunian drug culture and regard the passing by of a calf as an event.

Garry Hynes's production expertly catches the play's tension between ancient and modern. Francis O'Connor's cottage set, down to the illuminated crucifix, is a model of rustic realism, and Anna Manahan as the slyly oppressive mother and Tom Murphy as the message-bearing Ray lend their big scene the tension of high comedy. Only Brian F. O'Byrne seems slightly miscast as Pato since he looks a generation younger than Mullen's magnificently entrapped Maureen. But it's an outstanding first play that makes you impatient for more from McDonagh.

'The Pillowman'

Cottesloe, Royal National Theatre
The Guardian November 14, 2003
Michael Billington

Martin McDonagh has built up an enviable reputation as a writer of postmodern melodramas and black comedies. But where previous work, such as *The Lieutenant of Inishmore*, fed off existing Irish forms, in his new play he is shooting in the European dark. The result, while clever, has a feeling of hollowness.

McDonagh's subject is clear: the dangerous power of literature. The hero, Katurian, is a writer who has been arrested by the police in a totalitarian state. His crime is not, as we initially assume, political subversiveness: it is that his short stories, dwelling on persecuted children, bear a resemblance to some child murders. Although Katurian protests his innocence, it transpires that his retarded brother committed the crimes. The question facing Katurian is whether he should sacrifice his own life and that of his brother in order to ensure the preservation of his stories.

As a moral dilemma, it never acquires dramatic momentum for two reasons. One is that Katurian is so convinced of the sanctity of literature that he will do anything, even confess to crimes he has not committed, to save his stories: no internal doubt means no drama. But McDonagh never convinces you of the reality of the totalitarian background: it is a strange, secular tyranny where New Testament iconography is part of common myth and where the interrogating cops owe as much to Z-Cars as to Kafka.

Admittedly the police-cell scenes, largely because of the presence of Jim Broadbent, have a louche vitality; and, in one inspired touch, McDonagh shows that literary vanity is not confined to writers. Broadbent, as one of the two cops, at one point tells his own allegorical story which he thinks outshines anything related by his prisoner. It is wonderful to watch Broadbent's face light up with pride and his Lincolnshire vowels acquire a swelling authority: writing, you feel, is what defines him more than detection.

There is also good work from David Tennant as the imprisoned writer, Adam Godley as his literature-imitating brother, and Nigel Lindsay as the hard cop who cannot wait to brandish the electrodes. John Crowley's Cottesloe production also creates a genuine Gothic frisson in a series of scenes illustrating the parental persecution that has warped Katurian's imagination. But, in the end, you sense that McDonagh is playing with big issues to do with literature's power to outlast tyranny rather than writing from any kind of experience.

'Pack up your Troubles ...'

The Observer 30 November 2003 [2]
Susannah Clapp

The young Turkish director who was staging a play about Irish terrorism in Istanbul when the bombs exploded is also the force behind one of Britain's most innovative fringe theatres. The theatre director Mehmet Ergen was at home in Istanbul writing a press release when suddenly 'everything went black': outside his window, the street filled up with yellow dust. The play he was describing is set in a bomb-torn, beleaguered country; it opens with a small corpse being found on a lonely road. Was this, Ergen wrote, 'a terrorist attack'?

Not exactly. The corpse in question is that of a cat, a creature with a starring role in *The Lieutenant of Inishmore*. This is a satire by Martin McDonagh set off the West coast of Ireland. It's a play about terrorism, nevertheless, which mocks terror in the shape of a torturer besotted with his pet moggie. And not just 'about' terrorism as an abstraction. It's the goriest play of the last 10 years: the stage is awash with blood. It shows people having their toenails gouged out; limbs being blown off bodies and cats coming in for terrible times. And it unceasingly ridicules its assassins and their justifications. The worst killer remembers his kind-eyed cat 'egging me on, saying, 'This is for me and for Ireland, Padraic. Remember that, as I'd lob a bomb at a pub, or be shooting a builder.'

The drama proved too much for some people in Britain – 'too grisly and too full of jokes about grisliness' – and was turned down by both the Royal Court and the National before being put on two years ago by the RSC. How will it play when it opens on 12 December in Istanbul, itself swimming in blood, less than a month after bombs have ripped open the city centre?

The Turkish company assembled by Ergen (his day job is actually as the artistic director of London's Arcola theatre in Dalston) had 'a bit of a panic' about going ahead: some of the cast thought they should cancel. They had all heard about people picking up body parts in the streets; the play ends with body parts strewn over the stage. And the most recent bombs had come very close to them: the theatre district of Istanbul – 'a little West End' with twenty or thirty theatres and cinemas – is in the same area as the British consulate. One of the actors from the country's National Theatre was killed as he was making his way to do a voice-over at a TV studio.

The company (mostly young and local) considered testing opinion by staging the play in front of an invited audience. They decided against it: their own enthusiasm for the play had been strong from the beginning and wasn't (with some exceptions) diminished. After the synagogue bombings in the city, they did stop a newspaper advertising campaign which was to have run teasing trails on the lines of 'Terror in the Theatre: Two Cats Blown Up': this, they thought, looked like cashing in. But in some respects, the new violence reinforced the case for their play.

Istanbul is a city with a big appetite for theatre. The day after the most recent bombings, audiences were down at the Turkish National Theatre, but the next evening, after the Prime Minister had appeared on stage appealing to people to return, shows played to capacity. It is, Ergen points out, a city used to bloodshed: 'every decade there's a new wave'. But Turkish theatre has no tradition of looking straight at the world outside, of tackling current issues. Influenced by Ionesco and Beckett, its history is of obliqueness and indirection. This was a chance to change that indirection. And to cause 'a revolution in Turkish theatre'.

The Kenterler Theatre, in which Ergen is directing *The Lieutenant of Inishmore*, has never seen anything like it. One of the oldest theatres in Istanbul, it is run by a brother and sister who were both stars in the old star-system of Turkish theatre. It has never shown a play containing so much swearing, and never one which even touched on terrorism.

The play they'll be staging will be both Turkish and Irish. Ergen, who first saw McDonagh's play in London, has translated it himself, creating for the terrorists a mixture of rural idiom and street slang. Like the RSC production, the Kenterler version will feature a live cat, Deniz (whose name means 'ocean'). Some props – 'the dead cats and the hacked-off limbs' – came from the original production, which has just finished touring in Manchester: one of the actors ferried them across Europe in a Jeep. The setting is still an out-of-the-way cottage; people refer to the IRA and the INLA, but in Turkish. Ergen thinks it'll be like seeing 'Fuenteovejuna with a Newcastle accent'.

Everyone is expecting strong reactions. At the start of rehearsals, when Ergen raised the question of causing offence, the cast, 'reacting much as many did in Britain', thought there were more likely to be protests against the mistreatment of cats than about poking fun at terrorists. That's changed since the bombings. Some actors had qualms about going ahead. Outside the theatre, people have said they're anxious about revisiting violence, but they seem curious rather than antagonistic.

But Turks are 'very sensitive' says Ergen: 'there's always a union of taxi drivers or caretakers ready to rise up and say they've been misrepresented'. So far, the Istanbul media have been supportive, but there could be difficulties when the play goes on tour, when local mayors often object to productions: *Accidental Death of An Anarchist*, though performed at the National, was turned away in the regions. With so much at stake, Ergen claims that he's likely to end up 'either dead or with a sold out show'. The signs are looking promising. Last week the daily newspaper Sabah ran a story – nothing to do with McDonagh's play – about a 'Nazi syndrome', describing terrorists who kill thousands but cry about their cats.

Either way, he's likely to make theatrical history. Has this transporting of a play from one active war zone to another happened before? Ergen's own aim has simply been to make theatrical history in Turkey: the production of McDonagh's play (cheered on by McDonagh himself) is part of a larger plan. Though Istanbul is full of Western plays, there's a tendency to go for 'second-rate comedies', or easy West End fodder. Anything that gets a Tony has a chance. *Proof* did well; *Master Class* was a big success. But Pinter's Turkish plays – *Mountain Language* and *One for the Road* – have never had professional performances. Caryl Churchill and Edward Bond aren't produced.

Ergen would like to put on Brian Friel's *Translations*, which deals with the appropriation of Irish culture by the English, using Kurdish parallels. He has put to the British Council a proposal for a social-realist programme of theatre in Turkey. He wants to see young dramatists writing about homosexuality or terrorism or the army or relations with Israel.

At the moment, while Turkish intellectuals look inward, no one puts on stage the ordinary life of the capital 'the lives of the caretakers and chestnut sellers'. If anyone can pull it off, Ergen can. He is the theatrical dynamo of Dalston: in fact, the person who has managed to put Dalston and theatre into the same sentence. Born in Istanbul, he was twenty-two when he came to London in 1988: he had only a smidgen of English picked up from songs he'd played as a DJ. He expanded his vocabulary by listening to audiobooks of Shakespeare, and on the basis of a nine-month acting course he'd completed in Turkey, declared himself a director: he put an ad in the Stage inviting applications to join a new theatre company, and began to put on plays in pub theatres. His life history may sound a bit Shakespearean, and there's more of that to come.

He was in at the beginning of Southwark's rebirth as a theatre district when he became artistic director of Southwark Playhouse, established not far from the Globe, in what had been a tea and coffee warehouse. He persuaded West End theatres to lend him lighting and sound equipment, and lived in the playhouse itself.

Later, while teaching in Dalston, he discovered the building that was to become the Arcola Theatre, an old clothing factory down a small dark street off the very unthespy Stoke Newington Road. Other Turkish entrepreneurs had their eyes on the property for a snooker hall or a cash'n'carry, but Ergen got together £5,000 and sent invitations to all the actors and directors he knew to join him in a paint party. They decorated, tidied up sewing machines and cleared up thousands of coat hangers. Cutting tables were made into benches for the audience.

The Arcola has the provisional, on-its-toes appearance of all good fringe theatres: it looks as if could change into something else in a wink. The entrance hall and booking office house a bar and cafe. The auditorium has an industrial echo, with iron pillars punctuating a performance area which can be reconfigured from show to show; the space is low-ceilinged but with great depths: characters can go from being within spitting distance of an audience into distances that look infinite. It's a theatre that has drawn on its immediate surroundings ever since it opened three years ago.

The first play it commissioned was David Farr's *Crime and Punishment in Dalston*, which transposed Dostoevsky's thriller to Hackney, making the hero a young black who belongs to the Nation of Islam, and the murder victim a Turkish landlord; a fizzing soundtrack was composed by local students. The play later made its way on to Radio 3. In 2002, drawing on the help of the textile workers who remembered the building as a factory, the Arcola was restored to its former condition to stage *I Can Get It For You Wholesale*, the show set in a clothing factory that made Barbra Streisand's name. And this last year has been the most impressive yet. They've staged a hard-hitting production of *Americans*, Eric Schlosser's study of American imperialism, and a breakthrough documentary about the Hackney siege last Christmas, called *Come Out Eli*.

Despite the sell-out success of *Come Out Eli*, the theatre is still strapped for cash. It has had some Arts Council grants, but no consistent funding; it relies heavily on volunteer labour. It's now making a drive to secure finance, and looking both for a development director and a front-of-house manager. It's also, of course, looking for money-making shows.

The Arcola's next production will bring Istanbul to Hackney. Ergen's idea, though he won't be back in time to direct it, is to put on an Arabian tale: *Kismet*, the big 1953 musical based on melodies by Borodin and set in Baghdad, has 'some of the campest songs ever'. It tells of a poet who on one magical day, becomes an emir; it opens with the muezzin calling the faithful to prayer; it's got *Stranger in Paradise* and the less well-known, *Was I Wazir?* Ergen is clear about his favourite line: 'Don't underestimate Baghdad'.

'Beauty Queen of Leenane'

'A Gasp for Breath Inside an Airless Life'
Atlantic Theater Company
New York Times 27 February 1998
Ben Brantley[3]

Sometimes you don't even know what you've been craving until the real thing comes along. Watching the Druid Theater Company's production of *The Beauty Queen of Leenane,* the stunning new play from the young Anglo-Irish dramatist Martin McDonagh, is like sitting down to a square meal after a long diet of salads and hors d'oeuvres. Before you know it, your appetite has come alive again, and you begin to feel nourished in ways you had forgotten were possible.

For what Mr McDonagh has provided is something exotic in today's world of self-conscious, style-obsessed theater: a proper, perfectly plotted drama that sets out, above all, to tell a story as convincingly and disarmingly as possible. *The Beauty Queen of Leenane,* which opened last night at the Atlantic Theater Company with the sterling team that first performed it two years ago in Galway, Ireland, is on many levels an old-fashioned, well-made play. Yet it feels more immediate and vital than any new drama in many seasons.

Simply saying what the play is about, at least on the surface, is to invite yawns. A plain middle-aged woman, trapped in a life as a caretaker to her infirm but iron-willed mother in rural Ireland, is offered a last chance at love. Haven't we all been this way before? Doesn't this sound like an eye-glazing variation on the themes so reliably manipulated in the revival of *The Heiress,* the stalwart stage adaptation of Henry James's *Washington Square,* several seasons ago?

But wait. If *Beauty Queen* is a bucolic cousin to *The Heiress,* it also has the more toxic elements found in Grand Guignol films like *Whatever Happened to Baby Jane?* And Mr McDonagh, who is only 27 years old, has a master's hand at building up and subverting expectations in a cat-and-mouse game with the audience, of seeming to follow a conventional formula and then standing it on its head. The play offers the satisfactions of a tautly drawn mystery, yet it is by no means airless. There's plenty of room for ambiguity and for the intricacy of character that actors live for.

Under the finely modulated direction of Garry Hynes, a founder of the Druid Theater Company, the splendid four-member ensemble gives full due to the play's cunning twists and reversals while creating the sense that character is indeed fate. It's the thorough integration of every element that astonishes here, the meshing of psychology and action. There's not a single hole in the play's structural or emotional logic, and yet it constantly surprises. Even as the plot grips and holds you, the performances engage you on a darker, deeper level.

Mr McDonagh's reputation is already so firmly established in Britain that it has undergone a full cycle of star-making praise and skeptical backlash. Since the debut of *Beauty Queen* in London at the Royal Court Theater (a co-producer of the New York incarnation), the city has seen the two other plays in his *Leenane Trilogy,* as well as the popular National Theater production of his *Cripple of Inishman,* to be staged here later this month with a largely American cast at the New York Shakespeare Festival.

The excitement is justified, at least on the basis of *Beauty Queen*. The work isn't revolutionary; it doesn't open a window onto new experimental vistas. It's intelligent but not intellectual. And while it uses language with wit and precision, it is not, as so many contemporary plays are, about language and its limitations.

Instead, *Beauty Queen* confirms the viability of the well-made play, reminding us at the same time of how difficult the genre is to execute. Compare it to such current examples of the form as *The Last Night of Ballyhoo* or even the compelling revival of Arthur Miller's *View From the Bridge.* There's always at least a slight feeling of something imposed from without, of plot as a pegboard for theme.

With *Beauty Queen,* on the other hand, nearly everything feels organic, an inevitable outgrowth of character and environment. The play never leaves its single setting, realized with merciless detail by Francis O'Connor, a shabby room in the hilltop country cottage inhabited by old Mag Folan (Anna Manahan) and her embittered daughter, Maureen (Marie Mullen). And though we are told the women do in fact step out of their house from time to time, you feel they never really leave it.

They come to seem as imprisoned as the characters in Sartre's *No Exit*. The evening's opening image finds Mag seated, stock-still, before a television set, and she looks as if she has been there for centuries. Ms Manahan is a large woman, her girth enhanced by Mr O'Connor's scruffy layers of clothing, and Mag seems to fill and anchor the room. It is obvious that if Maureen is ever to escape into a life of her own, she will have to dislodge a mother who appears as immovable as a mountain.

The symbiosis between Ms Manahan and Ms Mullen is extraordinary as Mag and Maureen swap insults, demands and re-criminations in a circular game of one-upmanship. It is a game that has obviously been going on for many years, and while the resentment behind it is real, so is the devious pleasure each takes from it. Mr McDonagh's spare, brutal dialogue is measured out by these actresses with a refined timing that is both comic and ineffably sinister.

For as the talk continues, spanning topics from Mag's peevish demands for tea and biscuits to local gossip to a murder in Dublin, the subtle shifts in power become dizzying. Who really has the upper hand? Why do references to banal subjects seem so menacing? Who is the victim of whom? Mr McDonagh is too smart to provide hard and fast answers. When two visitors from the outside world, the Dooley brothers, Ray (Tom Murphy) and Pato (Brian F. O'Byrne), are used as pawns by Mag and Maureen in their continuing war, the rules that govern the women's relationship become more and more complicated. With small flicks of the eyes and resettings of their mouths, both actresses trans-form, at different moments, from torturer to hostage and back again.

Ms Mullen, a pale, red-haired woman who can look terminally worn out one instant and electrically vibrant the next, undergoes another metamorphosis. That's when Maureen brings Pato, a local man working in England, home from a party. In the awkward, exquisitely rendered courtship scene between them, Maureen acquires a melting gentleness and openness that is infinitely sad. Neither actress nor playwright, however, allows you to bathe for very long in the sentiments called forth here.

As performers, the men are a match for the women, which is high praise. Mr O'Byrne's Pato is a delicate study in self-consciousness, a shy man pulling himself into postures of virile dignity before he makes sexual overtures or a pretty speech. When he gallantly calls Maureen by the epithet of the play's title, it jolts both lovers in unexpected ways. The silence that follows echoes with the sense that a perilous frontier has been crossed.

As Pato's much younger brother, who serves a plot function out of *Romeo and Juliet,* Mr Murphy offers comic relief without ever presenting it as such. His, more than any other character, must embody the provincial society beyond the women's home, and Ray's irritable restlessness is eloquent on the subject. In all of Mr McDonagh's plays, there's a sense that life is cheap and a piquant awareness of the skull beneath the skin. (His second play in the Leenane trilogy is called *A Skull in Connemara* for literal reasons.) Ms Hynes accordingly brings a haunting physical dimension to her production, an aura of mortal decay.

It's evident not only in the presentation of the sheer bulk of Mag, but also in the arresting moment when Maureen takes off her coat to reveal a sleeveless dress that is too young for her. Seen later in a pearlescent slip after her night with Pato, Ms Mullen's Maureen brings to mind the anatomical portraits of Philip Pearlstein, with their sobering suggestions of the way of all flesh.

Correspondingly, seemingly prosaic objects acquire resonant weight in Mr McDonagh's plays, much as they do in the movies of Alfred Hitchcock. Even in reading *Beauty Queen,* you can gather how carefully Mr McDonagh sets up and develops the use of such things as a frying pan, a pair of rubber gloves and, most classically, an unopened letter.

It's all the more pleasurable to see how Ms Hynes, with the invaluable assistance of the lighting designer, Ben Ormerod, summons those objects into our consciousness at different times, miraculously achieving on stage what Hitchcock did with cinematic close-ups. And you may find images from *Beauty Queen* creeping unbidden into your imagination long after you've seen it.

Toward the end of the play, Ray talks about his affection for foreign shows on television. 'Who wants to see Ireland on telly?' he asks. 'All you have to do is look out your window and see Ireland. And it's bored you'd be.' He adds, pantomiming a slow, sweeping gaze, 'There goes a calf.' In Mr Murphy's interpretation, it's a pricelessly funny moment. Fortunately, though, Ray's creator understands that the most static picture is often teeming with hidden life, that frustration and boredom create dangerous diversions and that simple lives are often filled with contradiction.

Beauty Queen finds the tragic pattern in these things, while acknowledging that the forces beneath it can never be fully explained. In the telling, this play seems as clear as day. When you look back on it, it's the shadows that you can't stop thinking about.

'The Cripple of Inishmaan'

'Twisted Lives in a Provincial Irish Setting'
Newman Theatre
New York Times 8 April 1998
Ben Brantley

His body a study in conflicting angles, as if contorted by unseen winds, Cripple Billy moves athwart through a world where most people are either ramrod vertical or flat on their backs. The other villagers on the island off western Ireland where Billy lives are fond of pointing out how his twisted form sets him apart from them, and his name is seldom pronounced without the distancing epithet of *Cripple*.

But as played by a 19-year-old from Dublin named Ruaidhri Conroy, the title character of Martin McDonagh's *The Cripple of Inishmaan*, which opened last night at the Joseph Papp Public Theater, comes to seem less like the outcast of the island than its very essence.

There's a resonant emotional poetry in Billy's misshapen body: it registers in the struggle that seems to accompany every step he takes, in the yearning forward slope of his shoulders. It is the form of frustration made flesh, and of longings that can never be assuaged. Little wonder that his fellow townspeople, themselves shaped by discontent and a nagging sense of social inferiority to the world at large, keep insisting on the boy's otherness.

Mr Conroy (his first name is pronounced ROAR-ree) created his part in *Cripple* in the widely praised production at the Royal National Theater in London last year, and his affecting presence is invaluable in the New York incarnation of the play, which has been directed by Jerry Zaks with a largely American cast. Otherwise, it would be almost impossible to fathom the appeal of this portrait of souring provincial lives or to understand why the 27-year-old Mr McDonagh has become one of the great, glowing hopes of the English-speaking theater.

Cripple has the misfortune to arrive in the wake of another drama by Mr McDonagh, *The Beauty Queen of Leenane,* which opened in March at the Atlantic Theater Company and transfers to Broadway later this month. Although darker and more intensely focused than *Cripple, Beauty Queen* shares many of its themes, notably the warping effects of small-town claustrophobia, as well as the playwright's startling gift for subverting audience expectations.

But the New York production of *Beauty Queen* is blessed with the original Irish cast and director that first presented the play in Galway two years ago, and its four performers have developed a profound intimacy and ease with their characters. Most of the actors in *Cripple* still seem to be only on nodding terms with their roles, as though they might like to know them better but still find them strange and intimidating.

Unfortunately, this is a play that, even more than *Beauty Queen,* requires a natural sense of flow and a fine hand for shading. Mr McDonagh flirts dangerously here with the sort of grotesquerie and stereotypes that have led some English critics to describe his work as a synthetic and even cartoonish portrayal of Irish eccentricity. Mr Zaks, a director most at home with the stylized zip of a musical like *Guys and Dolls,* introduces a quality of comic exaggeration to *Cripple* that is the opposite of what it needs.

Even on the page, *Cripple* verges on the unbearably quaint. Set in 1934, it chronicles the disruption of Inishmaan when the filmmaker Robert Flaherty comes to the Aran Islands to work on his movie *The Man of Aran* and to scout for local talent. For Billy, the film represents a possible escape route from the stultifying, eventless life he shares with his protective elderly guardians, Kate (Elizabeth Franz) and Eileen (Roberta Maxwell). To everyone's surprise, it is the cripple who gets a part in the movie and who journeys to America.

The story of Billy's departure and return is the framework for exploring the secrets, lies and limited diversions of the people of Inishmaan. These characters have been given outsize tics of personality as conspicuous as Billy's hunched, hobbled gait. The fretful Kate talks to stones in times of stress, while her sister, the prim-seeming Eileen, steadily consumes the supplies of candy from the small store they run together.

Johnnypatteenmike (Donal Donnelly), the self-appointed disseminator of local gossip, keeps pumping his ancient mother (Eileen Brennan) with liquor in hopes of speeding her demise. Helen (Aisling O'Neill), the vital young woman whom Billy adores, likes nothing more than to smash raw eggs on people, while her younger brother, Bartley (Christopher Fitzgerald, who seems to have stepped directly out of a Fox sitcom), is obsessed with telescopes.

All this calculated local color comes close to turning Inishmaan into an Irish Dogpatch. You expect Ms Brennan's cuddly, twinkling alcoholic, who brings to mind a Cabbage Patch doll, to pull a corncob pipe out of her bedclothes. Much of the dialogue is correspondingly picturesque, with gossip that touches on such subjects as the town trollop's predilection for torturing worms and a feud involving a goose and a cat, and is often couched in the form of needling insults.

Beneath the volley of barbs and loopy postures lies the same bedrock of wistfulness and exasperation that makes *Beauty Queen* so poignant. Mr McDonagh has again created characters for whom the line between cruelty and kindness is slender. This confusion of impulses keeps you guessing about the motives and responses of the people of Inishmaan: there's no score card of good guys and bad guys. And the script features some unsettlingly surprising demonstrations of both affection and aggression.

For the most part, however, Mr Zaks and his cast don't highlight these moments or let them reverberate as they should. The play's central mystery, surrounding the death of Billy's parents, nearly gets lost. The scene in which the middle-aged widower Babbybobby (Michael Gaston) greets the returning Billy should shock; here it is perversely muffled.

The performers, seen against Tony Walton's atypically un-inspired sets, proceed stiffly: they consistently get laughs for their characters' oddities, but they seem not so much to possess those traits as to present them. Of the supporting cast, Ms O'Neill comes off best, finding a spirited continuity in Helen's volcanic mixture of friendliness and hostility.

It is Mr Conroy, however, who gives the production its only moments of visceral life. This young actor uncannily uses Billy's infirmities, from his gnarled physique to his labored breathing, to convey a deeply felt sense of entrapment that pervades the rest of the play. He avoids blatant bids for compassion. Cripple Billy, Mr Conroy makes clear, is no angelic Tiny Tim but as manipulative and selfish as anyone onstage. This radiant performance illumi-nates the raw pain and the foolish, daring hope behind such behavior.

'The Lonesome West: Another Tempestuous Night in Leenane'

('Sure, It's Not a Morn in Spring')
Lyceum Theatre
New York Times 28 April 1999
Ben Brantley

Ah, the sounds of the Irish countryside: the patter of rain, the lowing of cattle, the gentle hiss of scalding human flesh. Welcome back to Leenane, that quaint rural town where the skies are always gray, the people are always angry, and domestic homicide and mutilation are the No. 1 recreational activities.

It is a place where, according to the local priest, he would 'have to have killed half me … relatives' to fit in. This being Leenane, or at least Leenane as envisioned by the young playwright Martin McDonagh in his formulaic comic drama *The Lonesome West*, the good father modifies 'relatives' with an adjective that, even in western Irish dialect, is unprintable here. Leenane inspires people to strong and surly language.

Broadway audiences were first introduced to this gleefully macabre landscape only last season, when Mr McDonagh's gripping *Beauty Queen of Leenane*, with its original Irish cast, director and production team, came to the Walter Kerr Theater to reap Tony Awards for three of its actors and for its director, Garry Hynes.

That production shut down last month (to make way for another Irish play, Conor McPherson's *The Weir*). And now, before we've had a chance to mourn it properly, here is *The Lonesome West*, which opened last night at the Lyceum Theater, with Ms Hynes again directing, and which suggests *Beauty Queen* as reinterpreted by Beavis and Butt-head.

Bringing in *West* with such haste was not a great idea. Part of a trilogy of Leenane plays by Mr McDonagh (*A Skull in Connemara* is the third), the work offers many of the contempt-making aspects of familiarity and few of the comforts. Seen in repertory with its sibling plays, as it was at the Druid Theater in Galway, where it originated, and at the Royal Court in London, *West* might register as part of an enriching marathon experience.

On its own, however, with the memory of *Beauty Queen* still warm, comparisons are not in its favor. It is directed and acted with comic precision and flair, and it is occasionally quite funny. But it lacks the narrative intricacy of *Beauty Queen* and the attendant suspense and psychological mystery. What you see at the start is what you get for the rest of the evening, and it all starts to seem as repetitive as a *Tom and Jerry* cartoon.

A feeling of *déjà vu* descends as soon as you set eyes on Francis O'Connor's set, which looks a lot like the shabby, claustrophobic living room-kitchen in which *Beauty Queen* took place. Whereas *Beauty Queen* was a four-character work that portrayed a mother and her middle-aged daughter locked in hostile interdependence, *West* is a four-character work that portrays two middle-aged brothers locked in hostile interdependence.

Those are the O'Connors, Coleman (Maeliosa Stafford) and Valene (Brian F. O'Byrne), who have just buried their father when the play begins. Dad, it seems, was blasted with a shotgun by Coleman, an occurrence officially described as an accident, although no one seems to believe that except for Father Welsh

(David Ganly), the naive young parish priest who has under-standably developed a powerful thirst for alcohol.

The violent deaths that are central to *Beauty Queen* and *Skull* are alluded to here, just as references to some mayhem around the O'Connor brothers, involving the fatal severing of a dog's ears, worked their way into *Beauty Queen*. But for body count *West* handily tops the trilogy, with two deaths by drowning in addition to the plot-propelling patricide. There is also a rather grisly mortification of the flesh that concludes the first act and brings to mind a similar scene in *Beauty Queen*.

The small-town despair, restlessness and plain old boredom that inspire such behavior are again conjured by Mr McDonagh, though in such broad terms that it rarely arouses emotions other than mild laughter. It seems clear that the dramatist was aspiring, as in *Beauty Queen*, to a more nebulous mixture of elements. The scene-setting music by Paddy Cunneen is like a Gaelic instrumental answer to *Gloomy Sunday*.

The play features several lovely tragicomic speeches for Welsh, played with an affecting blend of ingenuousness and bleakness by the strapping Mr Ganly, that suggest vernacular variations on Hamlet's suicide soliloquy. And there's a wryly bittersweet discussion of ghosts by Welsh and Girleen Kelleher (Dawn Bradfield), a comely, foul-mouthed local lass with a crush on the priest.

Mostly, however, the show is devoted to the ways in which Coleman and Valene, who exist in a moldy state of suspended adolescence, needle each other with endless insults and re-criminations, which every so often degenerate into fisticuffs, with the occasional appearance of a knife or firearm. Mr O'Byrne, who was wonderful as the awkward suitor in *Beauty Queen*, and the excellent Mr Stafford have created a mutually dependent, festering yin and yang relationship not unlike that of Laurel and Hardy or Oscar and Felix in *The Odd Couple*.

Mr O'Byrne's Valene, who controls the family purse strings for reasons that quickly become apparent, is all goony, exaggerated primness as he struts through the house marking his possessions with giant V's and arranging his collection of figures of saints. Dressed by Mr O'Connor in undersize clothes that bring out the ungainliness of his height and leanness, he ingeniously folds and unfolds his limbs as though they were collapsible telescopes.

Mr Stafford, who is the doughy circle to Mr O'Byrne's ruler-straight line, is gruffer and more self-contained and makes efficient use of a more deliberately limited body language. Ms Hynes exploits these geometric differences with some astute physical comedy. And the actors do generate a sense of siblings to whom animosity and affection are the same thing.

The problem is that this is implicit from the first sight of the brothers, and there is minimal room for development and none for real revelation. By the time Valene and Coleman engage in a competitive round of confessions of past sins, the whole thing has started to feel like an old *I Love Lucy* episode in Irish Gothic drag. One can't help thinking of Sam Shepard's slyer, more engagingly sustained take on battling brothers in a play with a similar title, *True West*.

The fey, barbaric charm of the O'Connors' eccentricities, as well as those of Leenane itself, cumulatively reach a level of self-parody that evokes the satiric skit in the revue *Forbidden Broadway*, which presents *Beauty Queen* as a lugubrious Punch and Judy show. *How are things in Irish drama?* is the musical question (set to the tune of *How Are Things in Gloccamora?*) asked in that sketch.

Along with Mr McPherson, Mr McDonagh has already made a convincing argument that Irish drama is quite healthy, thank you. Even in *The Lonesome West* there is evidence of an exhilaratingly original voice. It has just gone hoarse in this outing. Repetition and strain can do that.

'A Skull in Connemara'

Leenane III, Bones Flying
The Gramercy Theatre 23 February 2001
Ben Brantley

Excuse me, but is that a piece of tibia that's just landed in my lap? Be prepared to ask yourself such questions if you sit anywhere near the stage of the Gramercy Theater, home to the gleeful, bone-crushing antics of *A Skull in Connemara,* the final play in Martin McDonagh's Leenane trilogy to arrive in New York.

When you give a couple of strong, drunken Irishmen a pair of mallets and a set of skeletons to demolish, as only Mr McDonagh would, it's only natural that some of those soiled white fragments would fly beyond the proscenium arch. Audience members should be prepared to duck. On the other hand, who could possibly take his eyes off such a mordant, morbid and oddly ecstatic spectacle?

And you thought that Mr 'Alas Poor Yorick' Hamlet had the last word on how to pose with human skulls. In *A Skull in Connemara,* which opened last night in a Roundabout Theater Company production directed by Gordon Edelstein, the title object is central to the snarled and squalid plot.

But it and the other crania on view here (there are several) serve the equally important roles of playthings for the annihilatingly bored – though never boring – inhabitants of the grim, gray village that is Mr McDonagh's Leenane. As one young fellow, earlier seen making two skulls kiss like Dutch dolls, announces happily: 'Oh, jeebies, this has turned into a great oul night. Drinking and driving and skull battering ... '

O, Leenane, Leenane: that inbred, claustrophobic world in which existence has become so tedious that nothing is held sacred – including matricide, patricide, fratricide, and suicide – if it livens things up a bit. Portraying such a place has shot the young Mr McDonagh to international fame as a playwright with an anarchic streak as wide and twisting as the River Liffey. And in no work to date has he given that streak such exhilarating license.

That's what the robustly acted Roundabout production picks up on most successfully: the pure infantile joy of crashing against taboos, giggling all the way. As a dark lark, it's as choice (and literal) a piece of graveyard humor as the city has ever seen.

What the evening doesn't get is the tension beneath the carousing, generated by profoundly lonely people who would seem to know one another all too well yet still keep their unsettling secrets. As was demonstrated by the superb Druid Theater production of *The Beauty Queen of Leenane,* which won four Tony Awards in 1998, there's more than gallows merriment to Mr McDonagh. Mr Edelstein's lively staging of *Skull* draws astonished laughter, but not the more heartfelt shudders that the play could elicit.

As a piece of writing, it falls between the taut *Beauty Queen,* which portrayed a mortal mother-daughter struggle limned in desperate isolation, and the looser, loopier *Lonesome West*, in which two middle-aged brothers whacked away at each other like a liquored-up Punch and Judy.

Skull has the physical rowdiness of *West*, but it also has the quieter, brooding elements of *Beauty Queen*. Its story isn't as satisfyingly shaped as that of *Beauty Queen*; there are plot holes you could drive a lorry through. But when you read it, it haunts you in a way that the entertaining Roundabout version doesn't allow.

That a classy warped cartoonishness is the aim here is signaled by the first glimpse of David Gallo's set. Granted, the scene on the stage itself is what we have by now come to identify as standard-issue Leenane: a simple, shabby room with desolate-looking furniture and the requisite central crucifix.

But look up and you'll see, mounted upside down on the ceiling, rows of turfy grave plots with classic spookhouse tombstones. It's hard not to grin, like a child anticipating Halloween, at this inversion of the sacrosanct.

Graves loom large for the play's central figure, Mick Dowd (Kevin Tighe). He earns the odd quid from the local priest by digging up coffins from the overcrowded churchyard (to make room for new arrivals) and disposing of the bones. Now, he learns, it is time to take on the south side of the yard.

There lies Mick's wife, killed in a car crash when he was drunkenly at the wheel. Local gossip has it that she may have been dead before. Tormenting one's friends being a prime recreational activity in Leenane, the subject is often brought up by the play's three other characters: the poteen-slugging bingo queen Mary-johnny Rafferty (Zoaunne LeRoy) and her grandsons, Thomas Hanlon (Christopher Evan Welch), a police officer, and his younger brother, Mairtin (Christopher Carley), a professional dimwit.

Though the question of Mick's guilt is at the center of *Skull*, it doesn't seem a matter of much urgency here. Mr Edelstein, who directed an earlier version of the play at A Contemporary Theater in Seattle, has adopted an easygoing approach that keeps truly disturbing elements at bay.

This has its advantages. The self-conscious, labored effect often evident in American stagings of Irish plays is absent here. The four ensemble members are appealingly relaxed as they swap insults in dialect, even if Mr Welch's accent tends to travel. Mr McDonagh's appetizingly bizarre lines, which could be killed by overemphasis, are delivered with welcome matter-of-factness.

'You can't go digging up Oona,' says Ms LeRoy's Maryjohnny to Mick, as if the subject were a minor point of etiquette. Thomas laments the uneventfulness of a policeman's lot by wistfully saying, 'I would like there to be dead bodies flying about everywhere, but there never is.' A drunken debate between Mick and Mairtin on choking to death on urine as opposed to vomit is conducted with scientific seriousness.

Not coming across are the festering rancor and sadism born of frustration, which are needed to give *Skull* emotional clout. Mr Tighe, who here brings to mind a sleepwalking Lee Marvin, is right to choose understatement over old-codger caricature, and he is all the more effective when he lets rip in the bone-smashing scene. But you only rarely catch the suggestion of danger within Mick, the passing shadows that make others keep their distance.

As the eager, inept policeman – so hapless that his brother says he would charge a shoplifting child with the Kennedy assassinations – Mr Welch is often very funny. He brings to mind Kevin Kline stylishly playing stupid. But as with Mr Tighe, you don't feel the threat of Thomas's poorly concealed hostility. He's too much the Keystone Kop.

What the production lacks is never clearer than in the first-act scene in which Mick and Thomas stare penetratingly at each other across an open grave. It's a crucial moment, anticipating the show's denouement, yet it has so little intensity that you scarcely notice it.

Ms LeRoy, on the other hand, is nigh perfect. Her Maryjohnny seems a pure, unconscious product of Leenane, as substantial, earthy, and moldy as a sprouting potato. Clucking into her shot glass over the wicked ways of the young folk, she has the placid conviction of her hypocrisies.

She also has a controlled gleam of nastiness when she interrogates Mick about his wife. She knows just how far she can push the taunting without losing access to Mick's liquor. And it is Maryjohnny who gives wonderfully casual utterance to what might be the motto of Mr McDonagh's Leenane: 'When I see them burned in hell,' she says of some schoolchildren who called her names 27 years earlier, 'that's when I let bygones be bygones.'

The find of the production, however, is Mr Carley. At first, I thought he was going to be too perky by half as the play's resident know-nothing. But his performance slowly acquires depth, turning mere loutishness into a radiant, highly affecting innocence. Mairtin's final scene becomes the play's epiphany, a transfiguration that blurs the lines between drunkenness and saintliness.

Both unexpected and inevitable, a moment like that is a rare gift to theatergoers. It says much about Mr McDonagh's talent that *Skull* has room for such occurrences. It's what makes him more than an impudent satirist with a Gothic flair. This interpretation only partly realizes the play's fertile potential. But it's still a zesty testament to Mr McDonagh's uncommon sensibility. Besides, who can resist the nerve of a production that shatters a new set of skulls every night?

'The Pillowman'

A Storytelling Instinct Revels in Horror's Fun
Booth Theater
New York Times 11 April 2005
Ben Brantley

Comedies don't come any blacker than *The Pillowman,* the spellbinding stunner of a play by Martin McDonagh that opened last night at the Booth Theater, starring Billy Crudup and Jeff Goldblum. Even those familiar with this British dramatist's blithe way with murder, mutilation and dismemberment, from works like *The Beauty Queen of Leenane* and *A Skull in Connemara,* may be jolted by the events described and simulated so picturesquely in his latest offering. (Advisory note: severed fingers and heads, electric drills, barbed wire, and premature burial all figure prominently.)

The laughs elicited by *The Pillowman* are the kind that trail into gulps and gasps, appropriate to a show that concerns a man under suspicion of torturing and killing children with no mercy and lots of imagination. The exquisitely lurid look of the show, directed by John Crowley and designed by Scott Pask, speaks to fears people mistakenly think they leave behind when they outgrow night-lights. And one electric shock of a moment in the first act jolts comfort-food-fed Broadway audiences the way the shower scene in *Psycho* must have slapped moviegoers four decades ago.

Yet for all its darkness of plot and imagery, *The Pillowman* – which won the Olivier Award in London for best new play last year and arrives in New York in a shrewdly recast version – dazzles with a brightness now largely absent from Broadway. Mr McDonagh's true subject is not gruesome crime and unjust punishment, although that's what a synopsis of the play, set largely in an interrogation room in an unnamed totalitarian state, might lead you to believe.

No, what *The Pillowman* is about, above all, is storytelling and the thrilling narrative potential of theater itself. Let's make one thing clear: Mr McDonagh is not preaching the power of stories to redeem or cleanse or to find a core of solid truth hidden among life's illusions.

And he is certainly not exalting the teller of stories as a morally superior being. The play's protagonist, Katurian (Mr Crudup, in a first-class performance), is a touchy, arrogant fellow, whose 400 short pieces of fiction (all but one unpublished) might be read, to borrow from the play, as a how-to guide of '101 ways to skewer a 5-year-old.'

The stories' existence are what have landed Katurian and his mentally defective brother Michal (Michael Stuhlbarg) in prison, since the killings described in his simply told fables have been replicated in the town where they live. The team of policemen who interrogate Katurian – the sardonic Tupolski (Mr Goldblum) and his explosive associate, Ariel (Zeljko Ivanek) – aren't entirely off base in their disdain for what their prisoner has written.

Artistic merit, however, is irrelevant here. So, for that matter, is fiction's significance as social commentary, autobiographical revelation or metaphysical map. As Katurian exclaims in exasperation, 'I'm not trying to say anything at all.'

For what *The Pillowman* is celebrating is the raw, vital human instinct to invent fantasies, to lie for the sport of it, to bait with red herrings, to play Scheherazade to an audience real or imagined. For Mr McDonagh, that instinct is as primal and energizing as the appetites for sex and food. Life is short and brutal, but stories are fun. Plus, they have the chance of living forever.

Every character in *The Pillowman* is some kind of storyteller. The narrative styles range from Katurian's gruesome fairy tales (which, in successive coups de théâtre, assume wondrous storybook life before our eyes) to the deceptions practiced by the policemen; from the official, torture-punctuated interrogation that is the play's motor to Ariel's unexpected, maudlin fantasy of what his old age might be like.

These forms of fiction are infused with the same dynamic, wherein information is parceled out in teasing increments and the line between fact and falsehood keeps shifting. The relationship between narrator and listener has its sadomasochistic aspects. And on one level *The Pillowman* recalls what the French director Henri-Georges Clouzot said about his 1955 cinematic chiller, *Diabolique*: 'I sought only to amuse myself and the little child who sleeps in all our hearts – the child who hides her head under the bedcovers and begs, "Daddy, Daddy, frighten me."'

Under the carefully measured direction of Mr Crowley – with brilliant production work by a team that includes, in addition to Mr Pask, Brian MacDevitt (lighting), Paul Arditti (sound) and Paddy Cunneen (music) – the cast members act out different degrees of that relationship, as the characters tantalize one another in ways friendly, consoling, manipulative and vicious.

Mr Goldblum and Mr Ivanek turn the classic good cop/bad cop formula into a coruscating vaudeville routine. Mr Goldblum's trademark deadpan wryness has rarely been put to better use, as his Tupolski toys with Katurian like a jaded latter-day version of the police inspector in Dostoyevsky's 'Crime and Punishment.' Mr Ivanek, in turn, comes up with delicious variations on the cliché of the combustible, torture-happy cop with a secret past. Their dialogue is appallingly funny, and endlessly quotable, but never out of sync with their characters.

The relationship between Katurian and his brother, the childlike Michal, is mostly rooted in a more amiable storytelling, as befits a fraternal relationship in which one sibling assumes the parental role. (What happened to Katurian's and Michal's Mom and Dad is, well, another story, and it is divulged in several versions.) Mr Stuhlbarg boldly and expertly captures both the innocence and ugliness of Michal.

Mr Crudup's finely chiseled features turn out to be ideal for registering the seductiveness, defensiveness and pure vanity of an artist for whom writing means even more than the brother he has protected for many years. Katurian's self-enchanted satisfaction when he tells a story is that of a young magician, pulling off a tricky sleight of hand. And Mr Crudup makes it clear that the flame of anger burns brightest in Katurian when his stories are criticized or threatened with extinction.

An academic could make endless hay out of this play's narrative complexities and literary evocations (they notably include Kafka as well as Dostoyesvky), just as a sociologist or psychologist could go on about the sources and effects of fiction and its moral responsibility. You could even make a pretty thorough case for *The Pillowman* as an artistic apologia of sorts, directed at those who have dismissed Mr McDonagh's previous works, set in a mayhem-prone rural Ireland, as pointlessly sensational and whimsical.

But to pursue these lines of thought is to fall into the very traps Mr McDonagh has set to mock such analysis. Asked by Tupolski to explain symbols and subtext in one of his stories, Katurian answers, 'It's a puzzle without a solution.' Which is pretty much Mr McDonagh's credo. But, oh, how he enjoys his puzzles. In this season's most exciting and original new play, he makes sure that we do, too.

---

[1] http://www.ireland.com/newspaper/features/1999/1012/archive.99101200072.html

[2] http://observer.guardian.co.uk/review/story/0,,1096030,00.html

[3] Copyright © 2006 by *The New York* Times Co. This and following reviews reprinted with permission.

Biographical Notes

Aidan Arrowsmith is Senior Lecturer in English at Manchester Metropolitan University. He has published various articles on Irish diaspora culture and is currently completing a book entitled *Fantasy Ireland: Cultural Memory and the Literature of Diaspora.*

Michael Billington joined *The Guardian* as theatre critic in October 1971. He has written a biography of Peggy Ashcroft and critical studies on the work of Tom Stoppard, Alan Ayckbourn, and Harold Pinter. His book *One Night Stands: A Critic's View of British Theatre from 1971 – 1991* was published in 1993. He has extensive broadcast experience, both radio and TV, since the 1960s.

Ben Brantley became chief theatre critic of *The New York Times* in September 1996 after having served as its drama critic since joining the newspaper in August 1993. Prior to joining *The Times*, Mr Brantley was a staff writer at *The New Yorker* magazine from August 1992 to July 1993. Before that, he was a writer at *Vanity Fair* magazine from January 1987 to August 1992 and he reviewed films for *Elle* magazine from September 1988 to March 1993. He is the editor of *The New York Times Book of Broadway: On the Aisle for the Unforgettable Plays of the Last Century.* He received the George Jean Nathan Award for Dramatic Criticism for 1996-1997.

Patrick Burke lectures in the Dept. of English at St Patrick's College, Dublin City University. He has published extensively on Irish drama and theatre, in particular on Brian Friel, Tom Murphy, J.M. Synge and T.C Murray, as well as on Shakespeare on film. He is a regular lecturer at conferences and summer schools, especially those of the International Association for the Study of Irish Literatures. A well-known play director and adjudicator, in 1996 he was awarded a scholarship to an International Theatre Seminar at Salzburg, where he worked with Arthur Miller, Ariel Dorfman, and André Brink.

Lilian Chambers has an MA in Modern Drama Studies from UCD, is an award winning director and actor, is one of the founding Directors of Carysfort Press and, with Eamonn Jordan and Ger FitzGibbon, a co-editor of *Theatre Talk: Voices of Irish Theatre Practitioners* (2001).

Susannah Clapp is the theatre critic of the *Observer* and a regular contributor to Radio 3 Nightwaves. She is the author of *With Chatwin*, a portrait of Bruce Chatwin, and helped to found the London Review of Books. She has worked as the theatre critic of the *New Statesman*, as the radio critic of the *Sunday Times*, and as a publisher reader and editor at Jonathan Cape.

Susan Conley is a filmmaker, holds an MPhil. in Irish Theatre Studies from Trinity College, Dublin, and is art director of *irish theatre magazine*.

Laura G. Eldred is a Senior Fellow at the University of North Carolina at Chapel Hill, where she will receive her PhD this year. She wrote her dissertation on '"A Brutalized Culture": The Horror Genre in Contemporary Irish Literature'. She has an article, 'Francie Pig Versus the Fat Green Blob from Outer Space: Monsters and Horror Films in McCabe's *The Butcher Boy*', forthcoming at the *New Hibernia Review*. She has also published an essay on incest in the works of Arundhati Roy and Salman Rushdie in the volume *Transgression and Taboo*, and her essay 'Martin McDonagh and the Gothic' is forthcoming in Routledge's *Martin McDonagh: A Casebook*. As an avid horror film fan, Laura regularly contributes film reviews to RevolutionSF.com.

Lisa Fitzpatrick lectures in drama at the University of Ulster at Magee. She was awarded her PhD from the Graduate Drama Centre at the University of Toronto. Her main research interests are contemporary Irish theatre, women's writing, Canadian theatre, and post-colonial theatre.

Karen Fricker recently completed a PhD on the original stage works of the québécois theatre director Robert Lepage at the School of Drama, Trinity College, Dublin, and in 2005-2006 will be a postdoctoral research fellow at the International Institute of Integration Studies, also at Trinity. She reviews theatre in Ireland and Northern Ireland for *The Guardian* and *Variety*. From 1998 to 2005 she was editor in chief of *irish theatre magazine*.

Nicholas Grene is Professor of English Literature at Trinity College Dublin. He has written widely on Irish drama and on Shakespeare: his books include *The Politics of Irish Drama* (1999) and *Shakespeare's Serial History Plays* (2002), both published by Cambridge University Press. With Chris Morash, he co-edited *Irish Theatre on Tour*, the first volume in the Irish Theatrical Diaspora series, published by Carysfort Press in 2005.

Werner Huber holds the chair of English Literature at Chemnitz University of Technology in Saxony, Germany. His research interests are in the fields of Irish Studies, British Romanticism (esp. the Romantic-era novel), Samuel Beckett, and contemporary drama. He is the author of a study of James Stephens's early novels (1982) and of *'I was Ireland': Studien zur irischen Autobiographie im 20. Jahrhundert* (forthcoming). He is a co-author of *Critique of Beckett Criticism: A Guide to Research in English, French and German* (1994), the co-editor of *Contemporary Drama in English: Anthropological Perspectives* (1998) and *Biofictions: The Rewriting of Romantic Lives in Contemporary Fiction and Drama* (1999), and the editor of *The Corvey Library and Anglo-German Cultural Exchanges, 1770-1837* (2004). He is also the acting President of the German Society for Theatre and Drama in English (CDE).

Eamonn Jordan is Lecturer in Performing Arts at the Institute of Technology Sligo. He has written extensively on Irish Theatre. His book *The Feast of Famine: The Plays of Frank McGuinness* (1997) is the first full-length study on McGuinness's work. In 2000 he edited *Theatre Stuff: Critical Essays on Contemporary Irish Theatre* and Fallons Educational Publishers issued *Death of a Salesman: A Critical*

Commentary and *Someone Who'll Watch Over Me: A Critical Commentary*, both of which were written to cater for second level students. In 2001 he co-edited *Theatre Talk: Voices of Irish Theatre Practitioners* with Lilian Chambers and Ger FitzGibbon.

Sara Keating is completing her PhD on The Irish Catholic Family in twentieth century drama at the School of Drama, Trinity College, Dublin. Her research interests include theoretical developments in Irish Studies, and twentieth century Irish and American theatre. Sara is also Theatre and Visual Arts Editor with *In Dublin Magazine* and has written about theatre for *irish theatre magazine* and *Village Magazine* among other publications.

Declan Kiberd is Professor of Anglo-Irish Literature and Drama at UCD School of English and Drama, has been recently appointed to the new board of the Abbey Theatre. His publications include, *Synge and the Irish Language* (1979), *Idir Dhá Chultúr* (Essays on Interaction of Gaelic and English-language culture) (1993), *Inventing Ireland: The Literature of the Modern Nation*, (1995) and *Irish Classics* (2000).

Mária Kurdi is professor in the Department of English Literatures and Cultures at the University of Pécs, Hungary. Her publications include three books: a survey of contemporary Irish drama in Hungarian (1999), a volume of essays entitled *Codes and Masks: Aspects of Identity in Contemporary Irish Plays in an Intercultural Context* (2000); and a collection of interviews with Irish play-wrights, which came out in her Hungarian translation in 2004. She guest-edited the Brian Friel special issue of the *Hungarian Journal of English and American Studies* (1999), several essays from which form the core of the book *Brian Friel's Dramatic Artistry: "The Work Has Value"*, edited by Donald E. Morse, Csilla Bertha, and Mária Kurdi, published by Carysfort Press in 2006. Currently she is guest-editing the special issue of the *Hungarian Journal of English and American Studies* in memory of Arthur Miller. She is also author of scholarly articles and editor of an anthology of critical excerpts of modern Irish literature in Hungary.

Patrick Lonergan teaches at the English Department, NUI Galway. He is books editor of *irish theatre magazine*, and reviews theatre in the West of Ireland for *The Irish Times*. He is currently working on a book on Irish Theatre and Globalization.

Mary Luckhurst is Senior Lecturer in Modern Drama at the University of York. She is author of *Dramaturgy: A Revolution in Theatre* and of many articles on contemporary theatre. She has edited *Theatre and Celebrity 1660-2000*, is currently editing two companions on modern drama for Blackwells, and writing a book on Caryl Churchill.

Uinsionn Mac Dubhghaill began his career in journalism in the late 1980s with *The Irish Skipper*, a fishing industry journal. In 1992 he was staffed by the *Irish Times* in a dual role as general reporter and Irish Language Editor. He was later appointed Western Correspondent and moved to Galway, while retaining his beat as Irish Language Editor. In the late 1990s he left the newspaper to become founding editor of *Cuisle*, a monthly current affairs and arts magazine in Irish, and later joined the staff of IntraFish, an internet-based global news agency. During 2003 he worked as a television news reporter with TG4. He lives in Connemara with his wife and family, and teaches journalism with Acadamh na hOllscolaíochta Gaeilge, a subsidiary of the National University of Ireland, Galway.

John Mc Donagh is a lecturer in the Department of English Language and Literature at Mary Immaculate College, Limerick. He is the author of *Brendan Kennelly – A Host of Ghosts* (2004) and editor, with Stephen Newman, of *Michael Hartnett Remembered* (2006). He is the 2005/6 MIC Research Fellow and his biography of Brendan Kennelly will be published by Bloodaxe Books in 2007. He is also an Associate Editor of the Irish Review of Books.

Victor Merriman is Head of Department of Creative Arts at Waterford Institute of Technology. He wrote his doctoral thesis on 'Dramas of Post-colonial Desire: Nation, Representation and Subjectivity in Contemporary Irish Theatre' (2004). In 2004-2005, he convened a series of interdisciplinary colloquia, funded by Dundalk I.T.: 'Generating Radical Perspectives on Globalisation, Civil Society and Cultural Work' He publishes regularly on contemporary Irish theatre, pedagogy and public policy. He was a member of An Chomhairle Ealaion/The Arts Council (1993-1998), and chaired the Council's Review of Theatre in Ireland (1995-1996).

Frank Molloy teaches English at Charles Sturt University in New South Wales. He has recently published a biography on the Irish Australian poet, Victor Daley, and regularly presents papers at Irish Literature and Irish Australian Studies conferences. He currently chairs the Bibliography Committee of IASIL.

Péter P. Müller is Professor and Chair at the University of Pécs in the Department of Modern Literature and Literary Theory where he has taught since 1982. From 1999 to 2004 he was director of the Hungarian Theatre Museum and Institute in Budapest. In 1990/91 he was Visiting Professor at the Indiana University of Pennsylvania, USA, in 1993/94 he was Fulbright Professor at Duquesne University, Pittsburgh, USA. In 1996 and 1999 he was Research Fellow at the University of Cambridge, Darwin College, UK. His books are, *The Dramaturgy of the Grotesque, On Sopianae's Stages, Central European Playwrights Within and Without the Absurd* (in English), *Dramatic Form and Publicity*.

Paul Murphy lectures in Drama at Queen's University Belfast. He has recently published articles on a number of Irish playwrights including W.B. Yeats, Padraic Pearse, J.M. Synge, George Shiels and Tom Murphy. Paul is currently working on two monographs engaging with the cultural politics of representation in Irish theatre in the first half of the Twentieth Century, a critical biography of George Shiels, and a documentary history of Irish Theatre 1925-1951.

Christopher Murray is Associate Professor of Drama and Theatre History in the School of English and Drama, UCD Dublin. A former editor of *Irish University Review* (1986-1997) and chair (2000-03) of the International Association for the Study of Irish Literatures (IASIL), he is author of *Twentieth-Century Irish Drama: Mirror Up to Nation* (1997) and *Sean O'Casey Writer at Work: A Biography* (2004), and has edited *Brian Friel: Essays, Diaries, Interviews 1964-1999* (1999). He is currently editing *Selected Plays of George Shiels* for Colin Smythe's series and editing a collection of

Thomas Davis lectures on Beckett for the centenary in 2006 (New Island Press).

Fintan O'Toole is an award-winning columnist and drama critic with *The Irish Times*. He is the author of many acclaimed books and has broadcast extensively. His work has appeared in many international newspapers and magazines, including the *New Yorker*, the *New York Review of Books*, *Granta*, *The Guardian*, the *New York Times*, and the *Washington Post*.

Ondřej Pilný is Director of the Centre for Irish Studies, Charles University Prague. He is editor of *From Brooke to Black Pastoral: Six Studies in Irish Literature and Culture* (2000) and co-editor of *Petr Skrabanek: Night Joyce of a Thousand Tiers – Studies in Finnegans Wake* (2002). He has also edited an anthology of modern Irish short stories in Czech translation and co-edited a dual-language anthology of contemporary Irish poetry. His translations include McDonagh's *The Cripple of Inishmaan*, Synge's *The Well of the Saints*, Friel's *Translations* and *The Third Policeman* by Flann O'Brien. He is currently finishing a book on *Irony and Modern Irish Drama*, to be published by Litteraria Pragensia in 2006.

Shaun Richards is Professor of Irish Studies at Staffordshire University. He has published widely on Irish drama and was the co-author of *Writing Ireland: Colonialism, Nationalism and Culture* (1988). His most recent project was *The Cambridge Companion to Twentieth-Century Irish Drama* (2004).

Catherine Rees is currently working on a PhD at the University of Wales, Aberystwyth, which seeks to provide an appropriate contextualization for the plays of Martin McDonagh. She has presented papers on his work at an Irish Literature conference at the University of Central Lancaster in 2003 and at a joint American Conference for Irish Studies and British Association of Irish Studies conference in 2004. She has published on-line encyclopaedia entries for McDonagh and also for Marina Carr. This article was originally given as a conference paper at the 'Contemporary Irish Literature: Diverse Voices' conference at University of Central Lancaster in April 2003 and was subsequently published by *New Theatre Quarterly* in February 2005.

Ashley Taggart is Director of the Institute for the International Education of Students (Dublin). He holds a PhD in Theatre from York University.

Rebecca Wilson was a professional actress and dancer in England and founded a small-scale, London Arts Council-funded dance-drama company (Rafe Earth). She taught dance and drama in London under the aegis of ILEA (Inner London Educational Authority). She holds an MA. (Dist) in Dance Studies from the University of Surrey and an MA in Modern Drama Studies from UCD and is currently pursuing a PhD in Melodrama and the Irish Dramatic Tradition at the National University of Ireland, Galway.

Karen Vandevelde received her PhD from NUI Galway, taught at the University of Limerick and at NUI Galway, and spent two years carrying out postdoctoral research at NUI Galway and at the University of Ghent (Belgium). She is now a lecturer at a teacher training college in Ghent. Articles on Irish revival drama have appeared in Études Irlandaises, Eire-Ireland and New Hibernia Review. Academica Press/ Maunsel published her book *The Alternative Dramatic Revival in Ireland, 1897-1913* (2005.

Select Bibliography

Clarke, Brenna Katz, *The Emergence of the Irish Peasant Play at the Abbey Theatre* (Ann Arbor: UMI, 1982).

Dean, Joan FitzPatrick, 'Tales Told by Martin McDonagh', *Nua: Studies in Contemporary Irish Writing* Vol. 3 No. 1 & 2 (2002): 57-68.

Dening, Penelope, 'The Wordsmith of Camberwell', *The Irish Times* 8 July 1997.

Diehl, Heath A. 'Classic Realism, Irish Nationalism, and a New Breed of Angry Young Man in Martin McDonagh's *The Beauty Queen of Leenane*', *JMMLA* 34.2 (2001): 98-117.

Dromgoole, Dominic, *The Full Room: An A-Z of Contemporary Playwriting* (London: Methuen, 2000).

Feeney, Joseph, 'Martin McDonagh: Dramatist of the West', *Studies* 87.345 (1998): 24-32.

Furay, Julia and Redmond O'Hanlon, eds, *Critical Moments: Fintan O'Toole on Modern Irish Theatre* (Dublin: Carysfort Press, 2003).

Fynn, Joyce, 'Stage, Screen, and Another Ireland', *American Repertory Theatre News* 20 January 1999.

Gibbons, Luke, *Transformations in Irish Culture* (Cork: Cork University Press, 1996).

Graham, Colin, *Deconstructing Ireland: Identity, Theory, Culture* (Edinburgh: Edinburgh University Press, 2001).

Grene, Nicholas, *The Politics of Irish Drama: Plays in Context from Boucicault to Friel* (Cambridge: Cambridge University Press, 1999).

--- 'Black Pastoral: 1990s Images of Ireland', *Litteraria Pragensia* 20.10. 23 October 2004. <http://komparatistika.ff.cuni.cz/litteraria/no20-10/grene.htm>

Harris, Peter James, 'Sex and Violence: The Shift from Synge to McDonagh', *HungarianJournal of English and American Studies* Vol. 10, Nos 1 & 2 (2004): 51-59.

Harris, Susan Cannon, *Gender and Modern Irish Drama* (Bloomington and Indianapolis: Indiana University Press, 2002).

Herr, Cheryl, 'The Erotics of Irishness', *Critical Inquiry* (Autumn 1990): 1-34.

James, Caryn, 'Critic's Notebook: A Haunting Play Resounds Far Beyond the Stage', *New York Times* 15 April 2005.

Kiberd, Declan, *Inventing Ireland* (London: Vintage, 1996).

Kurdi, Mária, *Codes and Masks: Aspects of Identity in Contemporary Irish Plays in an Intercultural Context* (Frankfurt/M: Peter Lang, 2000), 41-55.

--- 'American and Other International Impulses on the Contemporary Irish Stage: A Talk with Playwright Declan Hughes',*Hungarian Journal of English and American Studies* Vol. 8 No. 2 (2002): 223-41.

Lachman, Michal, ' "From Both Sides of the Irish Sea": The Grotesque, Parody, and Satire in Martin McDonagh's *The Leenane Trilogy* ', *Hungarian Journal of English and American Studies* 10:1-2 (2004): 61-73.

Lanters, José, 'Playwrights of the Western World: Synge, Murphy, McDonagh', *A Century of Irish Drama: Widening the Stage*, eds Stephen Watt, Eileen Morgan, and Shakir Mustafa (Bloomington: Indiana University Press, 2000), 204-22.

Lawson, Mark, 'Sick-Buckets Needed in the Stalls', *The Guardian* 28 April 2001.

Lenz, Peter. ' " Anything new in the feckin' west?" Martin McDonagh's *Leenane Trilogy* and the Juggling with Irish Literary Stereotypes', *(Dis)Continuities: Trends and Tradition in Contemporary Theatre and Drama in English*, eds Margarete Rubik and Elke Mettinger-Schartmann (Trier: Wissenschaftlicher Verlag, 2002), 25-37.

Llewellyn-Jones, Margaret, *Contemporary Irish Drama and Cultural Identity* (Bristol, UK: Intellect, 2002).

Lonergan, Patrick, 'Druid Theatre's *Leenane Trilogy* on Tour: 1996-2001', in *Irish Theatre on Tour*, eds Nicholas Grene and Chris Morash (Dublin: Carysfort Press, 2005).

Morash, Christopher, *A History of Irish Theatre 1601-2000* (Cambridge: Cambridge University Press, 2002).

Murray, Christopher, *Twentieth-Century Irish Drama* (Manchester: Manchester University Press, 1997).

O'Hagan, Sean, 'The Wild West', *The Guardian* 24 March 2001.

O'Toole, Fintan, 'A Mind in Connemara: The Savage World of Martin McDonagh', *New Yorker* 6 March 2006, 40-7.

Pilný, Ondřej, 'Martin McDonagh: Parody? Satire? Complacency?', *Irish Studies Review* 12.2 (2004): 225-31.

Ravenhill, Mark, 'Tforum: A Tear in the Fabric', *Theatre Forum* 26 (Winter/Spring 2005): 85-92.

Rego, Paula, *The Pillowman* Triptych. http://www.tate.org.uk/britain/exhibitions/rego/theme3.shtm

Roche, Anthony, 'Re-Working *The Workhouse Ward:* McDonagh, Beckett, and Gregory', *Irish University Review: Special Issue: Lady Gregory*, 34 (2004): 171-84

Sierz, Aleks, *In-Yer-Face Theatre: British Drama Today* (London: Faber & Faber, 2000).

Smyth, Gerry, *Decolonisation and Irish Criticism: The Construction of Irish Literature* (London: Pluto Press, 1998).

Vandevelde, Karen, 'The Gothic Soap of Martin McDonagh' in *Theatre Stuff*, ed. Eamonn Jordan (Dublin: Carysfort Press, 2000), 292-302.

Waters, John, 'The Irish Mummy: The Plays and Purpose of Martin McDonagh' in *Druids, Dudes and Beauty Queens: The Changing Face of Irish Theatre*, ed. Dermot Bolger (Dublin: New Island, 2001).

Wolf, Matt, 'Martin McDonagh on a Tear', in *American Theater* 15:1 (2000): 48-50.

List of Plays

Stage Plays

The Beauty Queen of Leenane
A Skull in Connemara
The Lonesome West
The Lieutenant of Inishmore
The Cripple of Inishmaan
The Pillowman
The Banshees of Inisheer
The Retard is Out in the Cold
Dead Day at Coney

Radio Play

The Wolf and the Woodcutter (chosen as one of the five winners of the London Radio Playwrights's Festival during late 1994/early 1995)

Screenplays

Barney Nenagh's Shotgun Circus
Suicide on Sixth Street
In Bruges
Seven Psychopaths

As Writer/Director:

Six Shooter (short film)

First Performances

Beauty Queen of Leenane

First Performance	1 February 1996
Venue	Town Hall Theatre, Galway
Produced	Druid/Royal Court Theatre co-production

Cast

Mag Folan	Anna Manahan
Maureen Folan	Marie Mullen
Ray Dooley	Tom Murphy
Pato Dooley	Brían F. O'Byrne

Director	Garry Hynes
Designer	Francis O'Connor
Lighting	Ben Ormerod
Sound	David Murphy
Music	Paddy Cunneen

A Skull in Connemara

First Performance	4 June 1997
Venue	Town Hall Theatre, Galway
Produced	Druid/Royal Court Theatre co-production

Cast

Mick Dowd	Mick Lally
Maryjohnny Rafferty	Anna Manahany
Tom Hanlon	Brían F. O'Byrne
Mairtín Hanlon	David Wilmot

Director	Garry Hynes
Designer	Francis O'Connor
Lighting	Ben Ormerod
Sound	Bell Helicopter
Music	Paddy Cunneen

The Lonesome West

First Performance	11 June 1997
Venue	Town Hall Theatre, Galway
Produced	Druid/Royal Court Theatre co-production

Cast

Girleen	Dawn Bradfield
Fr Welsh	David Ganly
Valene Connor	Brían F. O'Byrne
Coleman Connor	Maeliosa Stafford

Director	Garry Hynes
Designer	Francis O 'Connor
Lighting	Ben Ormerod
Sound	Bell Helicopter
Music	Paddy Cunneen

The Cripple of Inishmaan

First Performance	Previewed 12 December 1996/ Opened 5 January 1997
Venue	Royal National Theatre, London Cottesloe
Produced	Royal National Theatreproduction

Cast

Billy	Rúaidhrí Conroy
Mammy	Doreen Hepburn
Babybobby	Gary Lydon
Jonnypateenmike	Ray McBride
Eileen	Dearbhla Molloy
Helen	Aisling O'Sullivan
Kate	Anita Reeves
Doctor	John Rogan
Bartley	Owen Sharpe

Director	Nicholas Hytner
Designer	Bob Crowley
Lighting	Mark Henderson
Sound	Simon Baker
Music	Paddy Cunneen

The Lieutenant of Inishmore

First Performance	11 May 2001
Venue	The Other Place, Stratford-upon-Avon
Produced	Royal Shakespeare Company

Cast

Joey	Glenn Chapman
Mairead	Kerry Condon
Donny	Trevor Cooper
Brendan	Stuart Goodwin
Christy	Colin Mace
James	Conor Moloney
Davey	Owen Sharpe
Padraic	David Wilmot

Director	Wilson Milam
Designer	Francis O'Connor
Lighting	Tim Mitchell
Sound	Matt McKenzie
Movement	Jonathan Buttereil
Fight Directo	Terry King

The Pillowman

First Performance	13 November 2003
Venue	Royal National Theatre, London - Cottesloe
Produced	Royal National Theatre

Cast

Tupolski	Jim Broadbent
Boy	James Daley
Michal	Adam Godley
Girl	Jennifer Higham
Ariel	Nigel Lindsay
Mother	Victoria Pembroke
Father	Mike Sherman
Katurian	David Tennant

Director	John Crowley
Designer	Scott Pask
Lighting	Hugh Vanstone
Sound	Paul Arditti
Music	Paddy Cunneen

Six Shooter
First Broadcast   **2005**

Irish Film Board/Film Four/
A Missing in Action Films and Funny Farm Films

Running Time	27 minutes
Written and Directed	Martin McDonagh
Produced	Kenton Allen, Mia Bays, Mary `
	McCarthy, John McDonnell
Cinematography	Baz Irvine

Cast

Donnelly	Brendan Gleeson
Kid	Rúaidhrí Conroy
Man	David Wilmot
Woman	Aisling O'Sullivan
Cashier	Domhnall Gleeson
Policeman	Gary Lydon

Production Photos

The Beauty Queen of Leenane
http://www.royalcourttheatre.com/archive_reviews.asp?play=197
(Accessed 20/04/2006)

Steppenwolf 1999 production
http://www.steppenwolf.org/backstage/history/productions/gall
ery.aspx?id=204
(Accessed 20/04/2006)

A Skull in Connemara
http://www.druidtheatre.com

The Lonesome West
The Lyric Theatre in association with An Grianán Theatre, 2005
production photos
http://www.angrianan.com/lw.html (Accessed 20/04/2006)

The Lieutenant 2003
http://dublintheatrefestival.com/festival_programme/2003/The_
Lieutenant_of_Inishmore/2.htm (Accessed 20/04/2006)

The Lieutenant/Atlantic Theater, New York 2006
http://www.broadway.com/gen/Buzz_Story.aspx?ci=525767
(Accessed 20/04/2006)

The Pillowman
http://www.nationaltheatre.org.uk/?lid=6096&dspl=images
(Accessed 20/04/2006)

Index

George Devine Award, 13, 42, 246
Gergely, Ágnes, 336
Gibbons, Luke, 128, 268, 279, 293, 322
Gifford, Terry, 12
Gilbert, Helen, 292
Ging, Debbie, 322
Giroux Henry Armand, 279
global culture, 18, 104
global factors, 301, 303
globalization, 6, 82, 177, 193, 271, 277, 301-308, 315, 318f.
Godley, Adam, 391
Goldblum, Jeff, 175, 411
Gothic, 8, 15, 29, 34, 39, 41, 114, 207f., 261, 381, 391, 407, 411, 424
Gowen, Peter, 225, 378
Graham, Brian, 121,128
Graham, Colin, 285, 293, 322
Grand Guignol, 29, 36, 38, 180, 192, 257, 388, 397
Green, Blake, 293
Greenslade, Liam, 236, 243
Gregory, Lady Augusta
 Hyacinth Halvey, 80
 Image, The, 80, 85, 90, 92, 93
 Spreading the News, 80-2, 86, 90-4, 201
 Workhouse Ward, The, 89f., 94, 424
Grene, Nicholas, 12, 42, 123, 128, 131, 136, 139, 141, 153f., 199, 211, 249, 262, 287, 293, 302, 321, 336f., 343, 416, 423
grotesque, 15, 20f., 38, 46, 52, 57, 71, 101, 104, 106, 109, 112f., 148, 162, 181, 185, 192, 207, 215, 220f., 251, 273, 328-31, 381, 383, 387

Hall, Stuart, 242, 245
Hanrahan, Johnny, 272, 279
Hansen, Miriam Bratu, 305, 311, 321f.
Hapgood, Robert, 362
Harasym, Sarah, 292
Hardt, Michael, 301, 321
Hare, David, 137, 321
Harmon, Maurice, 94
Harrington, John P., 263
Harris, Mary N., 146
Harris, Peter James, 103, 115, 423
Harrison, Alan, 94
Harvey, David, 321
Healy, Gerald, 156, 161
hegemony, 92, 242, 270, 282f., 289
Herr, Cheryl, 113, 115
Hewison, Robert, 124, 129
Hiberno-English, 7, 53, 86f., 91, 94, 141, 145f., 367, 369
Hickman, Mary, 244f.
Higgins, F.R., 67, 77
history, 17, 20, 40, 43, 46, 52, 56, 92, 100, 102, 109, 121, 128, 135-37, 143, 145, 159, 161, 196, 209, 238-48, 254, 260, 283, 287, 289, 291, 300f., 351, 359, 375, 384, 393, 394f., 419
Hodge, Bob, 293
Hoffmann, E.T.A., 217f., 222
Hogan, Robert, 77
Hoggard, Liz, 118, 129
Hollywood, 18, 23, 83, 90f., 160, 175-78, 242f., 256, 305, 313, 321, 375
homophobia, 7
horror genre, 198, 202, 207
Howes, Marjorie, 114
Hughes, Eamonn, 238, 244
Hughes, Declan, 97, 114, 423
Hutcheon, Linda, 258, 263, 294
hybridity, 239, 243, 270, 283, 287
Hynes, Garry, 2, 10-13, 25, 66, 224, 246, 275f., 316, 339-47,

CARYSFORT PRESS

Carysfort Press was formed in the summer of 1998. It receives annual funding from the Arts Council.

The directors believe that drama is playing an ever-increasing role in today's society and that enjoyment of the theatre, both professional and amateur, currently plays a central part in Irish culture.

The Press aims to produce high quality publications which, though written and/or edited by academics, will be made accessible to a general readership. The organisation would also like to provide a forum for critical thinking in the Arts in Ireland, again keeping the needs and interests of the general public in view.

The company publishes contemporary Irish writing for and about the theatre.

Editorial and publishing inquiries to:

CARYSFORT PRESS Ltd

58 Woodfield, Scholarstown Road, Rathfarnham, Dublin 16, Republic of Ireland

T (353 1) 493 7383 F (353 1) 406 9815
e: info@carysfortpress.com
www.carysfortpress.com

NEW TITLES

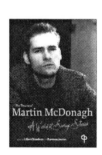

**THE THEATRE OF MARTIN MCDONAGH
'A WORLD OF SAVAGE STORIES'**

EDITED BY LILIAN CHAMBERS AND
EAMONN JORDAN

The book is a vital response to the many challenges set by McDonagh for those involved in the production and reception of his work. Critics and commentators from around the world offer a diverse range of often provocative approaches. What is not surprising is the focus and commitment of the engagement, given the controversial and stimulating nature of the work.

ISBN 1-904505-19-8
€30

**EDNA O'BRIEN
'NEW CRITICAL PERSPECTIVES'**

EDITED BY KATHRYN LAING
SINÉAD MOONEY AND MAUREEN O'CONNOR

The essays collected here illustrate some of the range, complexity, and interest of Edna O'Brien as a fiction writer and dramatist…They will contribute to a broader appreciation of her work and to an evolution of new critical approaches, as well as igniting more interest in the many unexplored areas of her considerable oeuvre.

ISBN 1-904505-20-1
€20

OUT OF HISTORY
'ESSAYS ON THE WRITINGS OF SEBASTIAN BARRY'
EDITED WITH AN INTRODUCTION BY CHRISTINA HUNT MAHONY

The essays address Barry's engagement with the contemporary cultural debate in Ireland and also with issues that inform postcolonial critical theory.The range and selection of contributors has ensured a high level of critical expression and an insightful assessment of Barry and his works.

ISBN 1-904505-18-X
€20

BRIAN FRIEL'S DRAMATIC ARTISTRY
'THE WORK HAS VALUE'
EDITED BY DONALD E. MORSE, CSILLA BERTHA, AND MÁRIA KURDI

Brian Friel's Dramatic Artistry presents a refreshingly broad range of voices: new work from some of the leading English-speaking authorities on Friel, and fascinating essays from scholars in Germany, Italy, Portugal, and Hungary. This book will deepen our knowledge and enjoyment of Friel's work.

ISBN 1-904505-17-1
€25

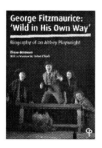

GEORGE FITZMAURICE:
'WILD IN HIS OWN WAY'
BIOGRAPHY OF AN ABBEY PLAYWRIGHT
BY FIONA BRENNAN
WITH A FOREWORD BY FINTAN O'TOOLE

Fiona Brennan's...introduction to his considerable output allows us a much greater appreciation and understanding of Fitzmaurice, the one remaining under-celebrated genius of twentieth-century Irish drama.
Conall Morrison

ISBN 1-904505-16-3
€20

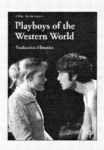

PLAYBOYS OF THE WESTERN WORLD

PRODUCTION HISTORIES
EDITED BY ADRIAN FRAZIER

'Playboys of the Western World is a model of contemporary performance studies.'

'The book is remarkably well-focused: half is a series of production histories of Playboy performances through the twentieth century in the UK, Northern Ireland, the USA, and Ireland. The remainder focuses on one contemporary performance, that of Druid Theatre, as directed by Garry Hynes.The various contemporary social issues that are addressed in relation to Synge's play and this performance of it give the volume an additional interest: it shows how the arts matter.' *Kevin Barry*

ISBN 1-904505-06-6
€20

EAST OF EDEN

NEW ROMANIAN PLAYS
EDITED BY ANDREI MARINESCU

Four of the most promising Romanian playwrights, young and very young, are in this collection, each one with a specific way of seeing the Romanian reality, each one with a style of communicating an articulated artistic vision of the society we are living in.
Ion Caramitru, General Director Romanian National Theatre Bucharest

ISBN 1-904505-15-5
€10

IRISH THEATRE ON TOUR

EDITED BY NICHOLAS GRENE AND
CHRIS MORASH

'Touring has been at the strategic heart of Druid's artistic policy since the early eighties. Everyone has the right to see professional theatre in their own communities. Irish theatre on tour is a crucial part of Irish theatre as a whole'. *Garry Hynes*

ISBN 1-904505-13-9
€20

CRITICAL MOMENTS

FINTAN O'TOOLE ON MODERN IRISH THEATRE
EDITED BY JULIA FURAY & REDMOND
O'HANLON

This new book on the work of Fintan O'Toole, the internationally acclaimed theatre critic and cultural commentator, offers percussive analyses and assessments of the major plays and playwrights in the canon of modern Irish theatre. Fearless and provocative in his judgements, O'Toole is essential reading for anyone interested in criticism or in the current state of Irish theatre.

ISBN 1-904505-03-1
€20

THE POWER OF LAUGHTER

EDITED BY ERIC WEITZ

The collection draws on a wide range of perspectives and voices including critics, playwrights, directors and performers. The result is a series of fascinating and provocative debates about the myriad functions of comedy in contemporary Irish theatre. *Anna McMullan*

As Stan Laurel said, it takes only an onion to cry. Peel it and weep. Comedy is harder. These essays listen to the power of laughter. They hear the tough heart of Irish theatre – hard and wicked and funny. *Frank McGuinness*

ISBN 1-904505-05-8
€20

POEMS 2000–2005

BY HUGH MAXTON

Poems 2000-2005 is a transitional collection written while the author – also known to be W. J. Mc Cormack, literary historian – was in the process of moving back from London to settle in rural Ireland.

ISBN 1-904505-12-0
€10

SYNGE: A CELEBRATION

EDITED BY COLM TÓIBÍN

Sebastian Barry , Marina Carr, Anthony Cronin, Roddy Doyle, Anne Enright, Hugo Hamilton, Joseph O'Connor, Mary O'Malley, Fintan O'Toole, Colm Toibin, Vincent Woods.

ISBN 1-904505-14-7
€15 Paperback

THEATRE OF SOUND

RADIO AND THE DRAMATIC IMAGINATION
BY DERMOT RATTIGAN

An innovative study of the challenges that radio drama poses to the creative imagination of the writer, the production team, and the listener.

"A remarkably fine study of radio drama – everywhere informed by the writer's professional experience of such drama in the making…A new theoretical and analytical approach – informative, illuminating and at all times readable." *Richard Allen Cave*

ISBN 0-9534-2575-4
€20

HAMLET

THE SHAKESPEAREAN DIRECTOR
BY MIKE WILCOCK

"This study of the Shakespearean director as viewed through various interpretations of HAMLET is a welcome addition to our understanding of how essential it is for a director to have a clear vision of a great play. It is an important study from which all of us who love Shakespeare and who understand the importance of continuing contemporary exploration may gain new insights."

From the Foreword, by Joe Dowling, Artistic Director, The Guthrie Theater, Minneapolis, MN

ISBN 1-904505-00-7
€20

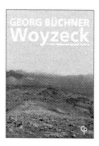

GEORG BÜCHNER: WOYZECK
A NEW TRANSLATION BY DAN FARRELLY

The most up-to-date German scholarship of
Thomas Michael Mayer and Burghard
Dedner has finally made it possible to establish
an authentic sequence of scenes. The widespread view that this play is a prime example of
loose, open theatre is no longer sustainable.
Directors and teachers are challenged to "read
it again".

ISBN 1-904505-02-3
€10

THE THEATRE OF FRANK MCGUINNESS
STAGES OF MUTABILITY
EDITED BY HELEN LOJEK

The first edited collection of essays about
internationally renowned Irish playwright Frank
McGuinness focuses on both performance and
text. Interpreters come to diverse conclusions,
creating a vigorous dialogue that enriches
understanding and reflects a strong consensus
about the value of McGuinness's complex work.

ISBN 1-904505-01-5
€20

GOETHE AND SCHUBERT
ACROSS THE DIVIDE
EDITED BY LORRAINE BYRNE & DAN FARRELLY

Proceedings of the International Conference,
'Goethe and Schubert in Perspective and
Performance', Trinity College Dublin, 2003. This
volume includes essays by leading scholars –
Barkhoff, Boyle, Byrne, Canisius, Dürr, Fischer, Hill,
Kramer, Lamport, Lund, Meikle, Newbould, Norman
McKay, White, Whitton, Wright, Youens – on Goethe's
musicality and his relationship to Schubert;
Schubert's contribution to sacred music and the
Lied and his setting of Goethe's Singspiel, Claudine.
A companion volume of this Singspiel (with piano
reduction and English translation) is also available.

ISBN 1-904505-04-X
Goethe and Schubert: Across the Divide. €25

ISBN 0-9544290-0-1
Goethe and Schubert: 'Claudine von Villa Bella'. €14

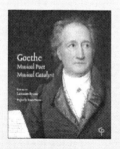

GOETHE: MUSICAL POET, MUSICAL CATALYST
EDITED BY LORRAINE BYRNE

'Goethe was interested in, and acutely aware of, the
place of music in human experience generally - and of
its particular role in modern culture. Moreover, his own
literary work - especially the poetry and Faust -
inspired some of the major composers of the
European tradition to produce some of their finest
works.' *Martin Swales*

ISBN 1-904505-10-4
€30

THEATRE TALK

VOICES OF IRISH THEATRE PRACTITIONERS
EDITED BY LILIAN CHAMBERS &
GER FITZGIBBON

"This book is the right approach - asking
practitioners what they feel."
Sebastian Barry, Playwright

"... an invaluable and informative collection of
interviews with those who make and shape the
landscape of Irish Theatre."
Ben Barnes, Artistic Director of the Abbey Theatre

ISBN 0-9534-2576-2
€20

THE THEATRE OF MARINA CARR

"BEFORE RULES WAS MADE" - EDITED BY
ANNA McMULLAN & CATHY LEENEY

As the first published collection of articles on
the theatre of Marina Carr, this volume explores
the world of Carr's theatrical imagination, the
place of her plays in contemporary theatre in
Ireland and abroad and the significance of her
highly individual voice.

ISBN 0-9534-2577-0
€20

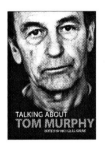

TALKING ABOUT TOM MURPHY

EDITED BY NICHOLAS GRENE

Talking About Tom Murphy is shaped around the
six plays in the landmark Abbey Theatre Murphy
Season of 2001, assembling some of the best-
known commentators on his work: Fintan
O'Toole, Chris Morash, Lionel Pilkington,
Alexandra Poulain, Shaun Richards, Nicholas
Grene and Declan Kiberd.

ISBN 0-9534-2579-7
€15

THE DRUNKARD

TOM MURPHY

'The Drunkard is a wonderfully eloquent play.
Murphy's ear is finely attuned to the glories and
absurdities of melodramatic exclamation, and
even while he is wringing out its ludicrous
overstatement, he is also making it sing.'
The Irish Times

ISBN 1-904505-09-0
€10

SACRED PLAY

SOUL JOURNEYS IN CONTEMPORARY IRISH THEATRE BY ANNE F. O'REILLY

'Theatre as a space or container for sacred play allows audiences to glimpse mystery and to experience transformation. This book charts how Irish playwrights negotiate the labyrinth of the Irish soul and shows how their plays contribute to a poetics of Irish culture that enables a new imagining. Playwrights discussed are: McGuinness, Murphy, Friel, Le Marquand Hartigan, Burke Brogan, Harding, Meehan, Carr, Parker, Devlin, and Barry.'

ISBN 1-904505-07-4
€25

THE IRISH HARP BOOK

BY SHEILA LARCHET CUTHBERT

This is a facsimile of the edition originally published by Mercier Press in 1993. There is a new preface by Sheila Larchet Cuthbert, and the biographical material has been updated. It is a collection of studies and exercises for the use of teachers and pupils of the Irish harp.

ISBN 1-904505-08-2
€35

THREE CONGREGATIONAL MASSES

BY SEÓIRSE BODLEY, EDITED BY LORRAINE BYRNE

'From the simpler congregational settings in the Mass of Peace and the Mass of Joy to the richer textures of the Mass of Glory, they are immediately attractive and accessible, and with a distinctively Irish melodic quality.' *Barra Boydell*

ISBN 1-904505-11-2
€15

SEEN AND HEARD (REPRINT)

SIX NEW PLAYS BY IRISH WOMEN
EDITED WITH AN INTRODUCTION
BY CATHY LEENEY

A rich and funny, moving and theatrically
exciting collection of plays by Mary Elizabeth
Burke-Kennedy, Síofra Campbell, Emma
Donoghue, Anne Le Marquand Hartigan,
Michelle Read and Dolores Walshe.

ISBN 0-9534-2573-8
€20

UNDER THE CURSE

GOETHE'S "IPHIGENIE AUF TAURIS",
IN A NEW VERSION BY DAN FARRELLY

The Greek myth of Iphigenie grappling with the
curse on the house of Atreus is brought vividly
to life. This version is currently being used in
Johannesburg to explore problems of ancestry,
religion, and Black African women's spirituality.

ISBN 0-9534-2572-X
€10

IN SEARCH OF THE
SOUTH AFRICAN IPHIGENIE

BY ERIKA VON WIETERSHEIM
AND DAN FARRELLY

Discussions of Goethe's "Iphigenie auf Tauris"
(Under the Curse) as relevant to women's issues
in modern South Africa: women in family and
public life; the force of women's spirituality;
experience of personal relationships; attitudes to
parents and ancestors; involvement with religion.

ISBN 0-9534-2578-9
€10

THE STARVING
AND OCTOBER SONG

TWO CONTEMPORARY IRISH PLAYS
BY ANDREW HINDS

The Starving, set during and after the siege of
Derry in 1689, is a moving and engrossing
drama of the emotional journey of two men.

October Song, a superbly written family drama
set in real time in pre-ceasefire Derry.

ISBN 0-9534-2574-6
€10

THEATRE STUFF (REPRINT)

CRITICAL ESSAYS ON
CONTEMPORARY IRISH THEATRE
EDITED BY EAMONN JORDAN

Best selling essays on the successes and
debates of contemporary Irish theatre at home
and abroad.

Contributors include: Thomas Kilroy, Declan
Hughes, Anna McMullan, Declan Kiberd, Deirdre
Mulrooney, Fintan O'Toole, Christopher Murray,
Caoimhe McAvinchey and Terry Eagleton.

ISBN 0-9534-2571-1
€20

URFAUST

A NEW VERSION OF GOETHE'S
EARLY "FAUST" IN BRECHTIAN MODE
BY DAN FARRELLY

This version is based on Brecht's irreverent and
daring re-interpretation of the German classic.

"Urfaust is a kind of well-spring for German
theatre… The love-story is the most daring and
the most profound in German dramatic
literature." *Brecht*

ISBN 0-9534257-0-3
€10

HOW TO ORDER
TRADE ORDERS DIRECTLY TO

Gill & Macmillan
Unit 10
Hume Avenue
Park West
Dublin 12

T: (353 1) 500 9500
F: (353 1) 500 9599
E: sales@gillmacmillan.ie

www.gillmacmillan.ie

FOR SALES IN NORTH AMERICA AND CANADA

Dufour Editions Inc.,
124 Byers Road,
PO Box 7,
Chester Springs, PA 19425,
USA

T: 1-610-458-5005
F: 1-610-458-7103